An OPUS book

A History of Western Philosophy: 3

RENAISSANCE PHILOSOPHY

Brian Copenhaver is Professor of History and Philosophy and Provost of the College of Letters and Science at UCLA. His recent publications include *Hermetica* (1992).

Charles Schmitt, who died in Padua in 1986, was lecturer in the History of Science and Philosophy at the Warburg Institute of the University of London. His publications include *Cambridge History of Western Philosophy* (ed.); *Aristotelian Tradition and Renaissance Universities*; *Reappraisals in Renaissance Thought* (ed., with C. Webster).

From the reviews:

'For those, philosophers and historians of ideas alike, who wish to enlarge their understanding of these complex patterns of influence, *Renaissance Philosophy* provides a comprehensive and richly documented guide.'
Times Literary Supplement

'a brilliantly successful piece of work. . . . The presentation of material is clear; the writing lively with welcome touches of wit.'
Renaissance Quarterly

'The wealth of information in this book is amazing'
Times Higher Educational Supplement

'informative and entertaining, combining copious research with intellectual verve . . . it is one of the finest and most delightful scholarly works I have read in years'
Seventeenth-Century News

D1225656

OPUS General Editors

Christopher Butler
Robert Evans
John Skorupski

OPUS books provide concise, original, and authoritative introductions to a wide range of subjects in the humanities and sciences. They are written by experts for the general reader as well as for students.

A History of Western Philosophy

This series of OPUS books offers a comprehensive and up-to-date survey of the history of philosophical ideas from earliest times. Its aim is not only to set those ideas in their immediate cultural context, but also to focus on their value and relevance to twentieth-century thinking.

Classical Thought
Terence Irwin

Medieval Philosophy
David Luscombe

Renaissance Philosophy
C. B. Schmitt and
Brian Copenhaver

The Rationalists
John Cottingham

The Empiricists
R. S. Woolhouse

English-Language Philosophy 1750–1945
John Skorupski

Continental Philosophy since 1750
Robert C. Solomon

English-Language Philosophy since 1945
Thomas Baldwin   (forthcoming)

A History of Western Philosophy: 3

Renaissance Philosophy

BRIAN P. COPENHAVER

AND

CHARLES B. SCHMITT

Oxford   New York

OXFORD UNIVERSITY PRESS

Oxford University Press, Great Clarendon Street, Oxford OX2 6DP

Oxford New York

*Athens Auckland Bangkok Bogotá Buenos Aires Calcutta
Cape Town Chennai Dar es Salaam Delhi Florence Hong Kong Istanbul
Karachi Kuala Lumpur Madrid Melbourne Mexico City Mumbai
Nairobi Paris São Paulo Singapore Taipei Tokyo Toronto Warsaw*

*and associated companies in
Berlin Ibadan*

Oxford is a registered trade mark of Oxford University Press

*British Library Cataloguing in Publication Data
Data available*

*Library of Congress Cataloging in Publication Data
Copenhaver, Brian P.*

*Renaissance philosophy | Brian P. Copenhaver, Charles B. Schmitt.
p. cm.—(A History of Western philosophy; 3).
"An OPUS book"—Ser. t.p.
Includes bibliographical references and index.
1. Philosophy, Renaissance. I. Schmitt, Charles B., 1933-1986.
II. Title. III. Series.
190'.9'031—dc20 B775.C67 1992 91-39554*
*ISBN 0-19-219203-5
ISBN 0-19-289184-7 (pbk.)*

5 7 9 10 8 6 4

*Printed in Great Britain by
Cox & Wyman Ltd.
Reading, Berkshire*

P. O. Kristeller

indagatori terrae renatae indefesso

Foreword

by Paul Oskar Kristeller

The philosophy of the Renaissance—that is, of the fifteenth and sixteenth centuries—unlike the political and religious developments, the literature, and the art of the same period, and unlike the philosophy of classical antiquity, of the modern period after Bacon and Descartes, and even of the Middle Ages, has been the subject of serious historical study only for the last hundred years or so, and most of the detailed monographs and text editions have been published only since the end of the First World War. Recent contributions have been so numerous and so widely scattered that bibliographical control of the relevant monographs and editions, and especially of the comprehensive or marginal studies pertinent to the subject, has become increasingly difficult. The recent publication of comprehensive handbooks in English is especially welcome, therefore, since they will serve as introductions and reference works for scholars and non-specialists, for teachers and students alike, keep the interest in the field alive, make the available information easily accessible, and also stimulate the further investigation of authors, problems, and their connections that have remained unexplored so far.

The books I have in mind are Arthur Rabil's *Renaissance Humanism*, *The Cambridge History of Renaissance Philosophy*, edited by the late Charles B. Schmitt, Quentin Skinner, Eckhard Kessler, and Jill Kraye (Cambridge University Press, 1988), and the present volume—begun by Charles B. Schmitt and completed by Brian P. Copenhaver. These three works are all different in scope and content, and hence do not compete with but supplement each other. Rabil limits himself to Renaissance humanism, a movement which made important direct and indirect contributions to Renaissance thought, and especially to its moral philosophy, but which constitutes only one sector of Renaissance philosophy and which, on the other hand, comprises many subjects that fall outside the area of philosophy, even when broadly understood, such as rhetoric and historiography, poetry, and grammatical as well as classical studies. The *Cambridge History*, on the other hand, covers all areas of Renaissance philosophy, but is divided into chapters, contributed by a number of scholars, that cover separately the main philosophical disciplines such as logic and natural philosophy, and includes a substantial introduction and a comprehensive bibliography. The present volume is conceived differently and serves a different purpose. It will be useful for those familiar with the *Cambridge History* but will also attract additional readers. It is much shorter, and therefore more suitable for continuous reading, although it may be used as a reference book. It is written by just two authors and hence is more uniform in its conception and content, and it is arranged according to the major schools of Renaissance philosophy, such as Aristotelianism, Platonism, Stoicism, Epicureanism, Scepticism, and the Philosophy of Nature, and gives a concise monographic treatment of all major thinkers of the period, including Pomponazzi and Zabarella, Cusanus, Ficino, Pico and Patrizi, Valla, Ramus, Montaigne and Lipsius, Cardano, Telesio, Bruno and Campanella, More and Machiavelli. A substantial introduction provides the ancient, medieval, and Renaissance context and deals with humanism and also with the political and religious background. The last chapter relates Renaissance philosophy to modern and contemporary thought and will be of special interest to students of philosophy, many of whom ignore the history of philosophy or dismiss it as irrelevant.

I have found the volume most interesting, informative, and reliable; I greatly appreciate it as a balanced, concise, and well-written treatment of a difficult and complex subject; and I hope that most readers will agree with me. I also wish to congratulate Brian Copenhaver, who has carefully and successfully carried out Charles Schmitt's intentions and also added many valuable insights of his own.

Columbia University, New York
November 1990

Preface

Anyone who had the good fortune to know Charles Schmitt, to study with him, or to read his many books and articles will know how much better this history would have been had so learned and creative a scholar lived to finish it. The present volume (not counting notes and bibliography) runs to about 117,000 words. Charles left a draft of about 40,000 words, of which perhaps a fifth dropped out in rewriting. The book's framework was his conception—six chapters corresponding more or less to those that follow. The first two chapters contain more of his writing, down to the sentence level, than the last four, where his voice can be heard more in the larger structure of the chapters than in their sentences. The whole of the present text represents a considerable expansion of what he left. The first chapter of his draft had no section on church and state. In Chapter 2 the sections on Trapezuntius, Lefèvre, Mair, and Vitoria are additions. Chapters 3, 4, and 5 are much larger than the corresponding parts of the draft: Charles's 22,000 words in those three chapters grew to 66,000. Charles left only a title, slightly different than the present wording, for chapter six.

Charles's views on larger issues pertinent to this volume will be well known to many readers, and I have tried to preserve his opinions even in some cases where mine are different. Aristotelian and sceptical thought are prominent because Charles rightly believed that early modern philosophy owed more to them than past interpretations have allowed. A number of topics and figures on which he was expert stand out in this history: the importance of natural philosophy; the role of university education; the development of the textbook tradition; the revival of the ancient Peripatetic commentators and the continuation of Averroist influence; the place of Cicero among ancient authorities or of the younger Pico among Renaissance thinkers. These and many other points of fact and interpretation were his special contributions to the history of philosophy, and they are visible in what follows. However, because he was prevented by his untimely death in April 1986 from completing this volume, it doubtless includes some things that he would have excluded and may omit others that he would have added. Few mistakes that remain would have survived his scrutiny. Given my own interests, the book probably contains more about language, logic, Platonism, and occultism than it might have, perhaps less about natural philosophy.

Charles's draft included little about contemporary historiography; he may have left it for the last chapter, for which he supplied only a title.[1] The current text says a good deal about early modern history of philosophy as the foundation of the contemporary canonical picture, but beyond mentioning a few founders of Renaissance studies—Burckhardt, Cassirer, Warburg, Kristeller—it contains little about twentieth-century scholarship. Twentieth-century philosophy comes up in the concluding chapter, which offers a few suggestions about links with the early modern period that may interest contemporary students of philosophy. The bibliography is not a comprehensive or even a representative collection of literature on Renaissance philosophy; it lists works that were crucial to the writing of the book, but it also provides a general bibliographical orientation on the more important thinkers and issues. No effort has been made to catalogue the multitude of specialist studies on Renaissance philosophy. Although much of the best writing about the period continues to appear in Continental languages, the bibliography emphasizes English works accessible to a broad readership when these are available. A relatively recent bibliography for more specialized use appears in *The Cambridge History of Renaissance Philosophy*, published in 1988 under the general editorship of Charles Schmitt with Quentin Skinner, Eckhard Kessler, and Jill Kraye. Notes provide references for direct citations of primary sources and a few quotations from secondary studies; they also refer more broadly not only to secondary literature upon which the text is

---

[1] Schmitt (1989: ch. 15).

based but also to a wider range of sources that the reader may find useful: i.e., the combination of notes and bibliography may serve as a starting-point for the reader who wishes to learn more about the major figures and movements discussed in the text. Obviously, the scope of the book and the format of the series preclude extensive and systematic annotation of the huge secondary literature that stands behind any such effort. Some sections digest interpretations of individual contemporary scholars—Monfasani on Trapezuntius, Watts on Cusanus, Noreña and Pagden on Vives and Vitoria, and so forth—but most debts are more diffuse, obligations to a larger republic of letters of which Charles was so eminent a citizen. In the first two chapters that follow Charles's draft most closely, apologies to scholars whose work may go unrecognized are especially in order. Charles left no notes with his draft, and he doubtless intended acknowledgements that I have missed.

Renaissance philosophers wrote mainly in Latin; Greek texts that they translated into Latin were major sources of philosophical inspiration. The role of Latin and Greek became especially complex and problematic when early modern thinkers philosophized about language and logic, so that ancient languages, Latin especially, became prime objects of philosophical analysis, often inseparable from grammatical and rhetorical investigations. In two or three cases where the original wording is critical, I have reproduced as well as translated Latin texts. Otherwise, passages originally written in foreign languages appear in translations, which are mine except as indicated in the notes. Greek words are transliterated, with *u* standing for *upsilon*, *ê* for *eta*, and *ô* for *omega*. Assuming a broad readership, I have not used the standard abbreviations for classical texts, whose full titles appear translated in the notes. Because important Renaissance works are often known by their Latin titles, I have usually provided the original within a few lines of its translation or some other indication of meaning. When technical issues arise—in dealing with syllogisms and other logical issues, for example—I have tried to provide the minimal background as close as possible to the passage in question, but where reference to another part of the book is particularly important, the words 'see below' in the text will lead to the required material by way of the subsequent note. Dates of historical persons will be found in the index. Most of the book is arranged by subject rather than chronology; however, each chapter except the first and last moves roughly in historical order, although the reader will notice some inversions (Cusanus and Pico, Valla and Vives, More and Machiavelli) and interruptions (Bruno) where theme rather than personality becomes the dominant organizational principle.

A number of people have read or heard the typescript in whole or in part at one stage or another of its gestation, and I owe them a large debt of thanks: Michael Allen, Rebecca Copenhaver, Carl Cranor, David Glidden, Edward Gosselin, Russell Jacoby, Pierre Keller, Jill Kraye, Paul Kristeller, John Monfasani, Richard Popkin, Alex Rosenberg, Nancy Siraisi. Catherine Clarke handled the book for Oxford with great expertise. My children, Gregory and Rebecca, and especially my wife, Kathleen, have always supported my research and writing with great patience and understanding, and I can only hope that they may find the result in some way an adequate outcome of their indispensable participation in the work.

B.P.C.

University of California, Riverside
25 August 1990

Contents

The Historical Context of Renaissance Philosophy

The philosophical heritage of antiquity and the Middle Ages

During the Renaissance, people taught and learned philosophy with a reverence for authority that the modern reader may find misplaced or alien, but not because philosophers simply aped their predecessors or put no premium at all on original thought or novel solutions to old problems. Ancient authority sometimes bestowed a paradoxical licence for innovation on thinkers accustomed to hide their creativity behind antiquity and precedent. A new thought reflecting a pattern hallowed by custom might seem safer, even if its deference to the past was superficial. A distinctive trait of philosophical discussion in the Renaissance, in any event, was that it usually began with reference to some distant authority, some sage of ancient Athens or master of medieval Paris—a Plato or an Aristotle, a Thomas Aquinas or a Duns Scotus. Moreover, many people assumed not only that God had given a single unified truth to humanity in the distant past but also that the remains of Greek philosophy, especially the works of Plato and Aristotle, had preserved part of this original deposit of divine wisdom. Hence it was no surprise and no scandal if an ancient answer to some questions was the right one. In the beginning of his *Lives of the Philosophers*—the closest thing to a comprehensive history of philosophy to have survived from antiquity and an important find of fifteenth-century humanism—Diogenes Laertius provided historical evidence for the ultimate unity of dogma, implying that truth is one because many peoples found different paths to the same wisdom in a primeval past. This ancient idea was also widespread among Renaissance philosophers, whether Platonist or Aristotelian.[1]

Diogenes also taught that philosophy—both the word and the concept—was a Greek invention. Renaissance thinkers agreed, and so did their medieval predecessors. Even medieval philosophers whose faith convinced them that philosophy was Queen Theology's handmaiden acknowledged philosophy's Greek pedigree, despite doubts among the Church Fathers about the propriety of philosophy and about claims for Hellenic priority. In the thirteenth century the sainted Aquinas gave due credit to the heathen Greeks, for example, and the worldlier Jacopo Zabarella did the same three centuries later. It goes without saying that the coming of Christ, the founding of the Christian church and the accumulation of a vast Christian literature profoundly influenced Western religion and culture. Yet it was in the literary remains of pre-Christian Greece that one looked for the first evidences of philosophy, conceived as a quest for the special kind of truth wherein reason and the interests of this world might be distinguished from faith and hopes for the next. Christian philosophers of all ages took the Greeks as their starting-point because the Greeks had forged the tools of reason and analysis that shaped those parts of knowledge not fixed in God's revelation.

After the fall of Rome, Western Europe's intellectual fabric unravelled. By the tenth century the brilliant tapestry of the ancient arts and sciences lay tattered and threadbare. Whole fields of inquiry such as mathematics, astronomy, and medicine declined catastrophically from the levels attained by the Greeks and their Roman imitators. As the Latin empire of Western Europe decayed, a more durable Greek culture thrived in Byzantium and passed eventually to the new world of Islam, which spread over much of the Mediterranean basin. Later, beginning in the eleventh century, the forgotten learning of antiquity re-entered Western Christendom. Thereafter, and for many reasons in addition to this intellectual awakening, the for-

---

[1] Diogenes Laertius, *Lives and Opinions of Famous Philosophers* 1.prologue.1–6; Kristeller (1972*b*: 43–63).

tunes of European civilization so much improved that the same historians who apply Petrarch's term 'Dark Ages' to the medieval period also speak of a Twelfth-Century Renaissance.[2] Scholars of that century reconnected the Judaeo-Christian West with its Graeco-Roman heritage, effecting a reintegration that still shapes the major contours of European civilization — the civilization to which Renaissance philosophers made such important contributions. Their Renaissance, the one that began in the fourteenth century, was only a later stage of a process started in the twelfth century, a rebirth that continued. Though it is conventional and useful to distinguish medieval from Renaissance philosophy, history cut the two from the same cloth which, if not seamless, was whole enough to make a unity of the four centuries or so between Dante's birth and the death of Descartes. This book focuses on the latter part of that period, the fifteenth and sixteenth centuries.

The customary divide between the Middle Ages and the Renaissance is particularly artificial for intellectual history, including the history of those ideas and thinkers called 'philosophy' and 'philosophers'. Much of the most admired, most discussed, and most characteristic philosophy of the Renaissance was indeed 'medieval' philosophy, which flourished in the sixteenth century and whose weaker effects were felt still later. One of the high points of medieval philosophy, for example, was surely the progress made by logicians of the fourteenth century, but this technical success lasted the course of the fifteenth century, in Italy as elsewhere, just at the time when the humanists were in their prime. The works of Thomas Bradwardine and William of Heytesbury and the logical writings of Paul of Venice were all printed, read, and discussed well into the sixteenth century. On a broader front, the writings of Averroes (Ibn Rushd), whom medieval philosophers called *the* commentator on Aristotle, remained central to many different areas of philosophy until the end of the sixteenth century. Editions of Aristotle running to many volumes and

<hr>

[2] Mommsen (1942); Ferguson (1948: 8, 26–8); Haskins (1957); Ker (1958); Hay (1977: 90–1); Cochrane (1981: 15–17).

accompanied by the commentaries of this twelfth-century Moorish author were printed repeatedly in sixteenth-century Italy, to be widely read and studied throughout Europe. Ramon Lull, a Catalan whose highly original thought took shape at the junction of Islam and Christianity in medieval Spain, suffered no loss of authority in the Renaissance. When humanism prospered in Florence and Paris, some French and Italian thinkers of the first rank found Lull's works absorbing.

If there were nothing distinctive about the Renaissance, one could not talk about it, and without important distinctions the talk would be insignificant. But the differences that separated the humanists from their forerunners of the twelfth century should not obscure the continuities and transitions that linked the Renaissance to the Middle Ages.[3] With this caution, and recognizing the indispensable medieval contribution to sustaining and enriching the learning 'rediscovered' by Petrarch and his humanist heirs, one may identify the hallmark of Renaissance philosophy as an accelerated and enlarged interest, stimulated by newly available texts, in primary sources of Greek and Roman thought that were previously unknown or partially known or little read. This great intellectual renewal began dimly in the eleventh century as one of many transformations whereby life became more urban, more secure, and more secular, producing many of the new institutions—including universities—now characteristic of Western Europe. In this context philosophy also blossomed, beginning a season of growth uninterrupted through our own time. Philosophy was not unknown in the central Middle Ages, but it was a thin remnant of what had been available to Augustine or Boethius. Then, when new works from old Greece emerged in Latin versions, the writings of Euclid, Galen, and especially Aristotle became accessible, rendered either directly from Greek or indirectly from Arabic and Hebrew translations. The translators did their crucial work chiefly in two places: in Sicily and Southern Italy, where ancient Greek culture had never entirely

---

[3] On the relation between the Renaissance and the Middle Ages, see Kristeller (1956: 553–83; 1961a: 92–119; 1972b: 110–55; 1974: 3–25); see also Di Napoli (1973: 279–309).

vanished; and in Spain, where Muslim civilization had brought with it an intellectual splendour reflecting Greek sources and shining more brightly than indigenous Latin learning. This critical initiative in the transmission of culture established the foundations upon which medieval and Renaissance philosophy rested.

Aristotle became the primary authority for philosophy — *ille philosophus*, he was called, *'the* philosopher'. Although a number of philosophical schools competed for primacy in antiquity, the range and internal coherence of his system put Aristotle in a commanding position when ancient learning passed to the Christian world east of Greece, then to the new empire established by Mohammed's followers, and finally to the West in the twelfth and thirteenth centuries.[4] In the fourth and fifth centuries CE, Nestorian Christians of Edessa in Syria had put Aristotle and other Greek authors into Syriac, their native language. When monophysite Syrians later moved to Persia, they took these texts with them to form the basis for more systematic Arabic translation of Greek literature after the seventh century; in ninth-century Muslim Baghdad, Arabic renderings of Aristotle, Plato, Peripatetic commentators, and Neoplatonists rose to impressive levels. Muslim scholars wanted Greek science as much as or more than philosophy, and in the eleventh century at Monte Cassino Constantine the African made seminal Latin translations of Arabic medical works. In fact, secular uses of Muslim medicine and astronomy were more attractive than speculative philosophy to early Western students of Arab learning. Adelard of Bath, Peter the Venerable, and other Christian scholars took notice of Muslim authors in the first half of the twelfth century, and after 1150 Latin translation of Arabic texts gathered speed, initially out of scientific interest. In the south of Italy by the middle of the

[4] For the transmission of Aristotle and other Greek, Muslim, and Jewish authors to the Latin West, see: Copleston (1960–6: ii. 186–200, 205–11); Kristeller (1956: 495–551; 1957; 1976*b*; 1977; 1980*b*; 1986*b*); Düring (1968); Birkenmajer (1970); Minio-Paluello (1972); Weiss (1977: 3–133); Lindberg (1978*b*); Dod (1982); Lohr (1982); Grant (1978; 1982; 1984); Sirat (1985: 205–344); Siraisi (1987; 1990: 12–14, 57–8); Jolivet (1988); Jacquart (1988); Maccagnolo (1988).

tenth century, a famous centre of medical practice had emerged in Salerno, and by the mid-twelfth century Salernitan physicians were using Aristotle's logic and natural philosophy, making a marriage between medicine and Peripatetic naturalism fateful for European and especially Italian philosophy. Until just before the year 1200, the school of Salerno increased its fame in anatomy, in pharmacy, in a new genre of medical 'questions', but chiefly for the celebrated *Articella*, a Latin collection of Hippocratic, Galenic, and other Greek medical works with Muslim commentary that formed a syllabus of set texts for notes and lectures by medical professors. A major piece of the *Articella* was the *Introduction to Galen's Art* by Johannitius, derived from an Arabic original and attracting Latin commentary that referred to Aristotle's physics and logic.

By the time Aristotle's *libri naturales* (books on natural philosophy) found a following in Salerno and in northern France, the work of Latinizing the Stagirite and his commentators was well under way. Only two Aristotelian translations by Boethius, called the 'old logic', could be read at the start of the twelfth century, but after 1120 the other three Boethian versions joined new translations of parts of the *Organon* by James of Venice and Gerard of Cremona to form the syllabus of the 'new logic'. James, a North Italian Greek who travelled to Constantinople in 1136, was one of three major and five minor Latin translators who worked from Greek in the twelfth century. Another was Henry Aristippus of Catania, who also went to the Greek East in 1158; the third, probably a Sicilian as well, was an obscure scholar named John. Translators from Greek in the next century were Robert Grosseteste of Oxford, Nicholas of Sicily, Bartholemew of Messina, Durandus of Alvernia, and, most important, William of Moerbeke. Strange to say, translations of a given text from Arabic sometimes followed its rendering from Greek, but many of the versions based on Arabic quickly fell out of use. In the twelfth century, John of Seville and Alfred of Sarashel worked from Arabic, but they produced less than Gerard of Cremona, who made Toledo his base. Michael Scot moved through Toledo, Bologna, and Sicily in the next century, finishing much of the enormous body of Averroes' writings by 1230 or so. Averroes of Cordoba died in 1198 and thus outlived Dominicus Gundissalinus; the latter used Spanish drafts by Avendauth (Ibn Daud, alias John the Spaniard) to turn parts of the encyclopedic *As-Sifa* by Avicenna (Ibn Sina), a Persian of the early eleventh century, into the Latin *Sufficientiae*, a Neoplatonized *summa* of Peripatetic metaphysics, physics, logic, and other subjects available to Western students by the latter half of the twelfth century. Avicenna's *Canon of Medicine*, influential in philosophy as well as medicine, was also Latinized shortly afterward by Gerard of Cremona. Algazel (al-Ghazali), Alfarabi (al-Farabi), Alkindi (al-Kindi), Avicebron (Ibn Gabirol, Avencebrol), Maimonides, and other Muslim and Jewish philosophical authors were translated into Latin as well.

All these new versions of Aristotle, his commentators, and other Greek, Arabic and Hebrew sources put extraordinary strains on the slim lexicon of philosophical Latin. One estimate suggests that medieval translators covered more than thirty different Arabic terms with the Latin *esse* ('to be'), and Greek brought its own set of challenges.[5] Translators responded early, often, and ingeniously, devising a new philosophical dialect of Latin unknown to Cicero or Virgil. For Renaissance humanists who strove to purify Latin, these inventions were a constant irritant, as one illustration will show. When Aristotle needed to distinguish the singular from the universal, he used an artificial expression, *tode ti* (literally, 'this particular what'), possible in Greek, if not beautiful. In similar contexts, Scotus and other medieval thinkers wrote *haecceitas*, a less elegant Latin neologism composed of the feminine singular (*haec*) of a demonstrative pronominal adjective, plus an emphatic particle (*-ce*), plus an ending (*-itas*) suggesting abstract quality. Unclassical coinages of this type enraged Lorenzo Valla and other humanists, who shamed later users of Latin into dropping some, but not all, of them. The cumbersome Scotist *haecceitas* died off, but in the same context *identitas* (*idem*, 'same', + *-itas*, '-ness') went on to a lively philosophical career. Cicero

---

[5] Jolivet (1988: 118–23).

himself had approved earlier neologisms such as *qualitas*, answering to the Greek *poiotês*, and all but the most recalcitrant antiquarians had to permit some new terminology.[6] The need for lexical growth became clearer as more and more of the central Aristotelian texts filled the reading-lists.

James of Venice prepared the first Latin *Metaphysics* from Greek in the second quarter of the twelfth century, soon revised and followed by two more from Greek and one from Arabic. William of Moerbeke finished the last medieval *Metaphysics* based on Greek before 1272, in time for Aquinas to use it. Late in the twelfth century and early in the thirteenth, parts of the *Nicomachean Ethics* went through two translations before Grosseteste's complete rendering of 1246–7. Grosseteste, William of Moerbeke, Gerard of Cremona, and James of Venice also made commentaries by Simplicius, Ammonius, Themistius, Alexander, Philoponus, and Eustratius partially accessible to a Western readership during the century-and-a-half that saw almost all of Aristotle Latinized. By the end of the thirteenth century, of all the Aristotelian works now usually counted as genuine, only several books of the *Eudemian Ethics* were still missing from the Corpus, though the *Poetics* in William of Moerbeke's version seems to have found few readers. Book 7 of the *Eudemian Ethics* joined a piece of the *Magna Moralia* between 1258 and 1266 in a compilation called *De bona fortuna*. With the arrival of this treatise *On Good Fortune*, Europe had almost as much of Aristotle as it has now, but Peripatetic fortunes were not all good.

Having amassed a huge primary and secondary literature, scholastic philosophers soon found conflicts and contradictions *within* the Aristotelian tradition, not to speak of the dissent that lay beyond. Tracts by Albert the Great *On Fifteen Problems*, by Aquinas *On the Unity of the Intellect against Averroes*, and by Giles of Rome *On the Errors of Philosophers* showed in their titles how a great deal of learning could be a dangerous thing. The University of Paris declared its allegiance to Aristotle in 1255, but in 1270 and again in 1277 the Bishop of

[6] Cicero, *Academica* 1. 25; Copleston (1960–6: ii. 272–3, 491–4, 511–17).

Paris condemned naturalist teachings of Averroist Aristotelians that seemed to put irreverent limits on God's power. Anxieties about Aristotle had surfaced even before. In 1210 a committee of Parisian clergy condemned the *Notebooks* of David of Dinant, a translator who studied in Greece and wrote books that threatened to spread the disease of natural philosophy. The synod ruled that David's *Notebooks* were to be burned and that 'no lectures are to be held in Paris either publicly or privately using Aristotle's books on natural philosophy or the commentaries. . . . Anyone . . . in possession of Master David's *Quaternuli* . . . shall . . . be considered a heretic.' A papal legate to Paris added Aristotle's metaphysics to the ban on natural philosophy a few years later, decreeing also that no parish priest

may learn the secular sciences. . . . And if anyone obtains . . . permission to attend the schools, let him not learn anything that is not the true letter of the law or holy writ. . . . If from his schools he brings . . . the dregs of the secular sciences . . . , he shall be rejected like one besotted and trampled underfoot by all people.

Within a decade or two, this first gush of ecclesiastical panic proved too weak to quench the flames of curiosity lit by the new Aristotle, whose influence survived the condemnations of the 1270s and remained vigorous for the next three centuries and more.[7] Although many of Aristotle's works perished in antiquity, those that survived had re-entered a Western Europe ready to greet them enthusiastically. Most readers of the Corpus and its outliers still missed two works that were to become quite important, however. The *Poetics*, extant only in a few manuscripts and a paraphrase until revived around 1500, was to surpass even the *Ars poetica* of Horace in its influence on literary criticism. The pseudo-Aristotelian *Mechanics*, the only work of applied science remaining from the Lyceum, attracted great attention through the fifteenth and sixteenth centuries

[7] Translations from the condemnations by Jonathan Hunt in Maccagnolo (1988: 429–34); see also Copleston (1960–6: ii. 183–5, 435–41); Lohr (1982: 88–92); Grant (1982: 537–9); Mahoney (1982c); Kuksewicz (1982b); Schmitt (1984: ch. 7). The word 'oeconomics' is used throughout to distinguish the content of Aristotle's work from the modern discipline of economics.

and interested even Galileo. When Galileo first saw the moons of Jupiter in 1610, Aristotle was still the starting-point for philosophical and scientific discourse in Western Europe, although new humanist discoveries beginning in the fifteenth century had supplemented and challenged the Peripatetic system with Platonic and other Greek philosophies.

'System' is perhaps the key word in appreciating the scope and structure of Aristotle's heritage. To enter that system, a medieval or Renaissance student would begin with Aristotle's logical works (the *organon* or 'tool') to find rules and techniques for clear thinking, advice on constructing valid and persuasive arguments, and a method for reaching what we would call 'scientific' conclusions demonstratively or deductively. Next came the works known in Latin as the *libri naturales* and including treatises with such titles as *Physics*, *On the Heavens*, *On Generation and Corruption*, *Meteorology*, and *On the Soul*. Less frequently would a student encounter the large group of works on zoological subjects full of data from Aristotle's scrupulous observations of the animal life of the Eastern Mediterranean, but, if he took philosophy more seriously than most, he might spend time with the *Metaphysics*, a text that created its own category and became the fountain-head of medieval and Renaissance speculation on the subject that it names. Aristotle dealt with moral philosophy in a series of works on politics, ethics, and 'oeconomics' (household management), and the Corpus also includes a number of treatises on other topics. These writings were the most influential texts read by philosophers during the Middle Ages and Renaissance. Their rate of survival in manuscript before the invention of printing and their multiplication in printed editions after 1470 attests to their great popularity and wide distribution. Throughout Europe and into the seventeenth century the Aristotelian Corpus was the basis of learning in general and of philosophy in particular. Aristotle's influence was pervasive in the university curriculum, paramount in those parts of it closest to philosophy, in which subject he long remained the focus of instruction.[8]

[8] Kristeller (1961a: 24–47; 1990a: 111–18); Lohr (1967–74; 1974; 1975–80); Flodr (1973); Schmitt (1981: ch. 6); Kenny and Pinborg (1982); Cranz and Schmitt (1984).

If Aristotle's dominance of literate discourse unified the medieval and Renaissance West, it was not his native Greek but the Latin of his translators that gave Europe another kind of coherence. A decisive factor in the intellectual explosion sparked in the twelfth century was the Latinizing of Aristotle. Especially in the sixteenth century, some Greek authors— including a few philosophers—attracted vernacular translators, but Latin remained the functional language of learning throughout the whole period. Italian, French, Spanish, German, English, and other modern languages became the ordinary vehicles of serious philosophy only after the mid-sixteenth century. Even Kant wrote most of his pre-critical works in Latin, only later helping to fashion the modern German philosophical vocabulary. Before Bruno, Montaigne, Descartes, Hobbes, and Kant, philosophers wrote, read, and often spoke Latin. The humanist movement of the fifteenth century and later equipped more and more philosophers to cope with Plato or Aristotle in Greek, but even the most skilful Hellenists continued to express their own thoughts in Latin. This common language of learning connected not only Paris and Rome but also Aberdeen and Cracow, Stockholm and Prague. Duns Scotus in Oxford, Marsilio Ficino in Florence, and Francisco Suárez in Salamanca could rely on this linguistic bond with colleagues in distant and alien lands, a useful convention that broke down only after the Renaissance of philosophical learning had done its work.

Another of Europe's unities was the educational system of the medieval and early modern periods. Students and masters had organized universities in Paris and Bologna by the end of the twelfth century. In the thirteenth century, though not without resistance, Aristotle became well-entrenched in the universities and philosophy prospered, thus establishing the institutional and curricular structures that dominated the discipline until well into the seventeenth century and beyond. The new universities grew and spread on two models, the Parisian in northern Europe and the Bolognese in Italy. Of the many structural and organizational differences between the two plans, it was of special importance for the history of philosophy that Paris gave a preliminary arts degree before students progressed to higher faculties of law, medicine, or theology, while at Bologna arts and medicine were part of the same degree course, leading to a qualification usually described as a degree 'in arts and medicine'. In this context 'arts' meant mostly philosophy, not painting or poetry or even the 'liberal arts' of modern usage. The term embraced geometry, mathematics, music, astronomy, grammar, and other subjects, but in the main the arts course consisted of philosophical subjects as defined by the works of Aristotle. At Paris and most northern universities, philosophy and allied arts subjects were seen as preliminaries to theology; this was the curriculum in which the greatest medieval theologians learned and taught philosophy — Bonaventura, Aquinas, Scotus, and Ockham. Italian practice was quite different. Philosophical studies in Italy were preparatory to the study of medicine or law. The logic and natural philosophy in the Aristotelian Corpus served as a 'pre-medical' curriculum meant to introduce the aspiring physician to those technical subjects thought to support his profession. Because of this focus on natural philosophy, there was little formal study of theology in Italian universities until after the Council of Trent.[9]

Thus, in medieval and Renaissance universities, both north and south, philosophy was part of a programme of 'general education' meant in principle to prepare students for more advanced subjects, medicine, law, and theology — though many stopped with the arts curriculum and spent no time in these higher faculties. It was not just professors and their students who cared about philosophy, however. Whether in private or in the developing academies or as part of the court culture, philosophy also prospered in less scholastic surroundings, especially in the late fifteenth century, although the universities remained responsible for systematic philosophical education and most of the original philosophizing. Intellectual life in the Renaissance continued to revolve around this central medieval institution, in philosophy as in other fields. Universities and professors altered their approaches to philosophy, but in the texts they studied, in their methods of teaching, and in their basic motivations they kept many of their medieval habits.

Almost as soon as Aristotle became widely known in Western Europe, there followed a large body of interpretation and commentary on the core Aristotelian texts read in universities. Commentaries, compendia, disputed questions, and discussions of difficult passages—some original, others translated from Greek, Arabic, and Hebrew works—multiplied with the decades. By the fourteenth century a vast Latin literature had grown up which came to be called 'Peripatetic' by analogy with Aristotle's ancient successors in the Lyceum. Particularly numerous were commentaries on one or more of the set university texts by such medieval masters as Robert Grosseteste, Albert the Great, Thomas Aquinas, Giles of Rome, and William of Ockham, authors still consulted and widely quoted through early modern times. Even more important and just as durable were the extensive and provocative commentaries and expositions prepared by Averroes for nearly the whole Aristotelian Corpus—another instance of a strong medieval current in the philosophical waters of the Renaissance. Although the ancient commentators on Aristotle left a much larger literature than that surviving from Aristotle himself, only a few of their commentaries were known to the medieval West. In the four decades after 1490, the interpretations of Alexander, Themistius, Ammonius, Philoponus, Simplicius, and other Greek commentators were added to the familiar views of Averroes, Albert, and Thomas, thus stimulating new solutions to Aristotelian problems.

The chief novelty in Renaissance philosophy was hugely improved access to a great deal of previously unknown literature from ancient Greece and Rome. Though Greek, Arabic, and Hebrew materials continued to enter the West after the twelfth century, appearances of new classical philosophical texts were fewer during the following two hundred years. Then, with the turn of the fifteenth century, Greek texts previously unknown in Western Europe poured in at an unprecedented rate, largely through the efforts of Italian scholars who returned to Italy from their Greek journeys laden with precious manuscripts. Most of their work of 'rediscovery' was done before the Turks overran Constantinople in 1453 to destroy whatever remained there of living Byzantine culture.[10] Even earlier, the generation of Petrarch had promoted a renewed interest in classical studies that stimulated the search for unread Latin texts, some of them philosophical, and brought them into wider circulation. Nearly all of Aristotle had been available to medieval readers, but other ancient philosophers were less well represented in the great monastic and academic libraries. Pre-Socratics, Platonists, Stoics, Epicureans, Sceptics, and Neoplatonists were known mainly through indirect channels. Ancient Scepticism, for example, could be studied in Augustine's critique, *Against the Academics*, and Neoplatonism was prominent in a number of Christian authors; but direct and broad access to original Greek texts of non-Aristotelian philosophers was an achievement of the Renaissance.

Since the Renaissance, Plato has been considered at least Aristotle's equal, often his better, as one of the patriarchs of Western philosophy. Since the Romantic period, in fact, important philosophers and leading thinkers in other fields have looked more often to Plato and his followers than to Aristotle for inspiration. The thin state of direct knowledge of Plato during the Middle Ages and early Renaissance may surprise modern observers accustomed to Plato's celebrity. Of the surviving dialogues and letters, only the *Meno*, the *Phaedo*, some of the *Timaeus*, and a piece of the *Parmenides* were anywhere available in Latin translation.[11] With the exception of the *Timaeus*, a part of which at least could be read in most important libraries, even these few of Plato's works that were Latinized were rarely seen, although Roger Bacon, Thomas

---

[10] Voigt (1893); Nolhac (1907); Sandys (1908); Clark (1909); Sabbadini (1885; 1922; 1967); Cammelli (1941–54); Billanovich (1951; 1953; 1981); Bolgar (1954); Ullman (1960; 1963); Ullman and Stadter (1972); Geanakoplos (1962; 1966; 1974; 1976; 1988; 1989); Pfeiffer (1968; 1976); Weiss (1969; 1977); Kristeller (1972b: 64–85); Rizzo (1973); Gordon (1974); Kenney (1974); Buck (1976; 1981b); Buck and Heitmann (1983); Grafton (1983; 1988a; 1988b; 1990; 1991); Wilamowitz-Moellendorf (1982); Monfasani (1983b); Garin (1983b); Witt (1983); Reynolds (1986); Reynolds and Wilson (1991).

[11] Below, Ch. 3, n. 7.

Aquinas, and a few others made use of them. Dialogues as important and (eventually) influential as the *Republic*, *Theaetetus*, and *Symposium* were wholly unavailable until the fifteenth century, when all of the extant Platonic Corpus became a common property of the Latin-reading republic of letters. Leonardo Bruni and others Latinized a few dialogues early in the century, but the great accomplishment was Marsilio Ficino's, who by 1469 had translated or retranslated all of Plato's works and saw them printed for the first time in 1484. Through such efforts as Ficino's, it gradually became possible to take a broader view of philosophy than the traditional Peripatetic framework permitted. In 1400 almost no one in the West could have direct experience of Plato's dialogues, but within a century all of Plato was in print, along with most of the extant ancient literature interpreting him, all of which naturally led to original speculation in the Platonic or Neoplatonic style.

After many centuries of analytical, historical, and philological work, modern scholars have learned to discriminate among the varieties of Platonic philosophy and to try to distinguish Plato's views from those of his master Socrates and also from the teachings of his followers — Academics, Middle Platonists, and Neoplatonists.[12] Disagreements on the interpretation of so rich a tradition as Platonism still run hot and frequent, but some distinctions have become generalized, as, for example, that several centuries and much dogma stood between Plato and Plotinus. The Renaissance, however, recognized no deep divide between Plato's teachings and those of the Neoplatonists. This blurring of categories was particularly momentous for the fifteenth century when an immense Neoplatonic literature — several times the size of the Platonic Corpus — also became known. A primary task of translation for Ficino was the *Enneads* of Plotinus, one of the subtlest and most penetrating philosophical works of late antiquity and one that played a major role in the destiny of Renaissance Platonism. Ficino also translated treatises and commentaries by Porphyry, Iamblichus,

[12] Merlan (1970: 14–15, 53); Lloyd (1970: 272–82); Wallis (1972: 1–36); Dillon (1977: 1–11, 22–3, 43–62); Long (1986: 75–6, 88–106); below, Ch. 3, nn. 6–7.

Proclus, Synesius, and other Neoplatonists scarcely or not at all known to the Middle Ages in the direct tradition. He and other Renaissance thinkers associated these important texts with a body of semi-philosophical religious material called the Hermetic Corpus because of its false attribution to Hermes Trismegistus, a Greek avatar of the Egyptian god Thoth. Because this Hermes was thought to have lived around the time of Moses, his teachings were taken to be a source of ancient theology, a *prisca theologia* supplementing the holier revelation that Moses had received on Sinai and sanctifying the gentile wisdom that culminated in Plato and Plotinus. This misbegotten genealogy, certified by Lactantius, Augustine, and other Church Fathers, was to have a profound effect on the historiography of philosophical and other fields of learning even after Isaac Casaubon proved it mistaken in the early seventeenth century. Hymns thought to come from Orpheus, various writings attributed to Pythagoras, the *Chaldaean Oracles* associated with Zoroaster and the Magi, the Jewish and Christian prophecies called the *Sibylline Oracles*, and other pseudepigraphal literature spoke as forcefully to Renaissance readers as texts now regarded as genuine works of Plato or the Neoplatonists.

Much more fragmentary, in the Renaissance as now, was knowledge of other schools of ancient philosophy with intellectual or institutional identities independent of the Platonic and Peripatetic traditions. Even today, much of what we know about Stoics, Epicureans, and Sceptics is second-hand information transmitted by opponents or by careless compilers. None the less, the humanists were naturally impressed that Cicero had taken these schools seriously as rivals of the Academy and Lyceum, and even the incomplete information bequeathed us by the Renaissance is a rich philosophical legacy. However partial our knowledge, it was crucial to the later evolution of Western philosophy that the Renaissance not only assimilated these disparate and independent traditions but also transformed them into new currents of speculation as powerful as the Epicureanism that stimulated the scientific revolution or the Stoicism that so deeply affected early modern moral philosophy. A key event in this process was the recovery of Diogenes Laertius' *Lives of the Philosophers*, a late ancient compilation poor in critical insight but, compared to anything else available, packed with information and misinformation about a number of ancient philosophies of interest to early modern scholars. Diogenes' detailed account of ancient atomism from Democritus and Leucippus to Epicurus enabled sixteenth- and seventeenth-century thinkers dissatisfied with Aristotle's physics to reshape this material into a coherent philosophy of nature, advocated by such scientific revolutionaries as Pierre Gassendi and Robert Boyle.[13] Diogenes' description of other philosophies, including the various pre-Socratic formulations, supplemented and sometimes contradicted the other chief sources of such information, from Plato and Aristotle through Simplicius. Likewise, Cicero and Seneca and other Latin writers had given the Middle Ages some knowledge of the ancient Stoics, but because these Romans had little to say about certain aspects of Stoicism, especially physics and logic, a more comprehensive approach to Stoic thought awaited the recovery of Diogenes, Sextus Empiricus, and other Greek texts of historical as well as philosophical value.[14]

The revival of ancient philosophy was particularly dramatic in the case of Scepticism. This critical and anti-dogmatic way of thinking was quite important in antiquity, but in the Middle Ages its influence faded. What little was known about Scepticism attracted scant attention from medieval thinkers, most of whom regarded philosophy as a medium of belief, not as its solvent. In the fifteenth century, however, the two most prominent Greek authorities on Scepticism to survive antiquity disturbed Europe's conscience again. Neither was a thinker of philosophical depth, but both provided new data, enabling Renaissance thinkers to assemble fresh ideas into a useful and novel way of philosophizing. Diogenes Laertius furnished doxographic material on the Sceptical schools and left a sketch of one of their founders in his life of Pyrrho. Sextus Empiricus,

---

[13] Below, Ch. 4, n. 2.
[14] Below, Ch. 4, n. 89.

who compiled information in late antiquity on the various schools of ancient Scepticism, provided a much fuller account. When the works of Sextus and Diogenes were recovered and read alongside texts as familiar as Cicero's *Academica*, a new energy stirred in philosophy; by Montaigne's time, Scepticism was powerful enough to become a major force in the Renaissance heritage prepared for Descartes and his successors.[15]

The Renaissance resurrected not only whole texts but also fragmentary material from a wide variety of sources which allowed scholars of the time to sketch—albeit very incompletely—outlines of philosophical opinion otherwise not well delineated. Because no original Greek Stoic survived on a Platonic or Aristotelian scale, for example, one had to go to Diogenes, Galen, or Sextus to learn the logic of Chrysippus, or to Cicero, Plutarch, and Seneca to discover the ethical teachings of Zeno. For some of the most innovative and influential ancient philosophers, not only Stoics but also pre-Socratics, Epicureans, Sceptics, Neoplatonists and others, the process was the same. Since the Renaissance had to discover or rediscover the tools of philology and history needed for such detective work, the pioneering labours of obscure humanist scholars—Gentian Hervet, who translated Sextus, or Willem Canter, who first published a Greek text of the *Eclogae* of Stobaeus—certainly deserve our memory and admiration. It was they who first edited, organized, translated, printed, and disseminated the philosophical remains of antiquity that succeeding centuries have come to take for granted. If Thales and his successors were the fathers of Western philosophy, the humanist scholars of the Renaissance were the midwives of its rebirth in a classical form.

Philosophy in a Renaissance context

What should the Renaissance mean to us? The French word means rebirth, and when the Swiss art historian Jacob Burck-

---

[15] Below, Ch. 4, nn. 56–9.

hardt applied it more than a century ago to the period of our inquiry, he meant to suggest that the warm sun of Italian culture had revived learning, statecraft, and the arts after a dormant millennium in Europe's cold Gothic tomb. The geographical and chronological reference of the term has expanded since Burckhardt's day, until now it extends to most of Europe from the early fourteenth to the early seventeenth century, but its use is still strongly coloured by Burckhardt's original interests, which today we would call art history, intellectual history, and cultural history. Even Burckhardt's memorable conception of the Renaissance city-state as 'a work of art' implies a different sense of the political order from what is conveyed in the great categories—mainly political categories—that distinguish ancient, medieval, and modern times. If the common image of Western history is a panorama of states and wars, the usual tableau of the Renaissance looks somewhat different: the props include paintings, buildings, books, and, suffusing the whole, the bright light of a less concrete mentality expressed in terms like "individualism" or 'the dignity of man'. Machiavelli and Cesare Borgia fascinated Burckhardt as political agents of solitary genius, but he was also dazzled by the romances of Boccaccio, the paintings of Leonardo, and the polymath brilliance of Leon Battista Alberti. It was in painters and poets as much as in princes and diplomats that Burckhardt detected the values that created the modern world and marked the end of the Middle Ages. His Renaissance brought with it not only secularism and individualism but also new expressions of style and original patterns of thought, including philosophical thought. Though he admitted some continuity between medieval and modern times, he stressed what seemed to him most discontinuous with the proximate past, looking ahead to the innovations of modernity rather than backward to what endured from the Middle Ages. Thus, he treated the individualist morality of the Renaissance as a great novelty, a defining feature of modernity, and undervalued the debt of Renaissance thinkers to their ancient, early Christian, and medieval predecessors. Burckhardt's conception of the Renaissance has been controversial but enormously influential, leading other historians to replay his themes in an amazing array of variations.[16]

Philosophy as such had little to do with Burckhardt's conception of the period. That he paid small attention to the common practice of philosophers in the Renaissance is unsurprising, since what remained central for them was part of the very thing against which he defined his new cultural ideal—the lively tradition of philosophy invented in the medieval universities and sustained in early modern Europe in forms more congenial to Abelard or Albertus than to Hobbes or Hume. Inasmuch as Burckhardt set out to write a broad 'essay' on intellectual and cultural history, what he says about so technical a subject as philosophy is meagre. Moreover, both in his day and in the Renaissance, 'philosophy' meant something different from what it does now. In the medieval and early modern periods, philosophers were expected to master not just logic, moral philosophy, and metaphysics but also a range of subjects now considered disciplines of the natural sciences. Close institutional and intellectual ties also kept the philosopher in touch with medicine, theology, history, rhetoric, grammar, and other fields. The compass of twentieth-century philosophy, especially in the Anglo-American tradition, has narrowed; even within the university, most people who read philosophy in any depth are practitioners, and the broader educational influence of the discipline is confined to a corner of the curriculum. Philosophy no longer plays a large part in the pedagogic formation of an educated public in the English-speaking world, but things were very different in the Renaissance. To have a university education meant encountering philosophy as a prominent part of the curriculum, which in turn required reading a variety of ancient and medieval texts. Even people without a systematic university education could be well versed in philosophical subjects, sometimes as a matter

[16] Garin (1938); Ferguson (1948: 179–204); Keller (1957); Kristeller (1972*b*: 24; 1981; 1982; 1985*d*; 1985*e*: 3–23; 1990*a*: 2–3, 20–4; 1990*b*); Trinkaus (1970; 1983: 343–403); Di Napoli (1973: 31–84); Burke (1974: 14, 20–6, 239, 275–6); Sozzi (1982); Burckhardt (1990).

of amateur acquaintance, sometimes as a mark of real expertise. If the term 'Renaissance philosophy' is to have any historical meaning, one must admit such differences. It will not do simply to extract issues from the past that may bear on twentieth-century problems and then to treat a collection of such topics as history. Presentism can only distort our sense of the past, just as antiquarianism deprives the past of a living voice. The point is to learn how philosophy worked in the Renaissance as a period with a distinct historical identity, and then, having met Renaissance philosophers on their own terms, to appreciate their work as valuable in its own right before trying to trace its influence or weigh its utility in our time.

Since Burckhardt published his great book, debate about the meaning and value of the term 'Renaissance' has been continuous and copious. Without rehearsing these controversies, we will apply the word to European history from the early fourteenth to the early seventeenth century, avoiding any prior commitment to a stronger sense of the term than this chronological use. At the start, we will try to carry little of the usual baggage about 'the discovery of the world and of man' and other broad conceptions familiar from textbook accounts of the Renaissance—even though some of them may be well justified in the end. Our task, in other words, is to describe and evaluate philosophy as practised and read in early modern Europe, recognizing that the colourless phrase 'early modern' refers roughly to the same period imbued with much brighter tones by the word 'Renaissance'. Whatever words we choose, we must insist at all points on the historicity of the philosophy of the period, its development in a particular context of intellectual, social, economic, political, and other forces that shaped its distinct historical identity.

Among the major events and movements of the early modern period, a few stand out for their special relevance to the history of philosophy, and some—the religious and political changes that shook church and state in Europe during the same centuries when humanism transformed her culture—are important enough to require extensive treatment below. Here, we may begin by noting the enormous impact of the invention of printing in movable type.[17] The first book produced by this revolutionary technology appeared about the middle of the fifteenth century, and the first philosophical text was published around 1470. From that time until our own day, the printing press became Europe's chief instrument of learned communication. Within thirty years of 1470, for example, about seven hundred books relating to Aristotle were printed, and during the same period Marsilio Ficino brought a complete Latin Plato into circulation, evidence of a quickening pace of publication that accelerated throughout the next century, when thousands of editions of philosophical books saw the light. Manuscript production did not cease entirely; handwritten texts of some philosophical books considered dangerous or suspect continued to circulate, while dedication copies and lecture notes remained in manuscript for different reasons. In general, however, print became the dominant medium, making books cheaper for all and speeding the circulation of new and old ideas alike. Publishers were an industry of subversives when they disseminated the tracts of Luther or the treatises of Machiavelli, but they also increased the weight of ancient and medieval tradition when they printed Aristotle or Aquinas in a form more accessible, more convenient, and more accurate than anything that literate people had ever before enjoyed.

As the world of learning expanded with the growing reach of the printed word, the world of experience widened in broader and bolder voyages of exploration, whose repercussions in the philosopher's study were unexpectedly great.[18] Discoveries of new lands and peoples shattered the space in which Plato and Aristotle had lived and thought, breaking the narrower boundaries that they naturally took as a framework for natural and moral philosophy. An especially urgent question was whether the people of the New World were as human as Europeans or

[17] Butler (1940); Goldschmidt (1943); Bühler (1960; 1973); Febvre and Martin (1971); Ullman and Stadter (1972); Hirsch (1974; 1978; 1980); Gerulaitis (1976); Lowry (1979); Eisenstein (1980); Grendler (1984); Chartier (1987).
[18] Parry (1966); below, pp. 112–16, 253–60, 274–8, 299–300.

perhaps some strange and lower kind. This question screamed through sixteenth-century Spain, and it still echoed in philosophical discussions of human equality and slavery after the founders of the United States drafted their Constitution. The new discoveries also raised questions about the scope of man's ingenuity in exploring and then exploiting the human condition as part of this novel experience of nature, another Renaissance discovery whose effects are still with us, for better or for worse.

Historians give the name 'Scientific Revolution' to another series of discoveries on a different frontier; they occurred mostly in the seventeenth century and hence largely outside the scope of a book about the Renaissance. But some of the new science had its roots in our earlier period.[19] The year 1543 saw the publication not only of the epochal work of Nicolaus Copernicus *On the Revolutions of the Heavenly Spheres* but also of Vesalius' magnificent volume *On the Structure of the Human Body*, texts that transformed the sciences of astronomy and anatomy. Less spectacular efforts of physicians, natural historians, mathematicians, and others led to progress in zoology, botany, mechanics, mathematics, and various applications of what we now call 'science', and what the Renaissance called 'natural philosophy'. The very terminology implies that these new scientific achievements would have caught the attention of philosophers, when Vesalius, Copernicus and others held the ancient macrocosms and microcosms of Plato and Aristotle up to the mirror of contemporary speculation and experience. Even though many Peripatetics wished to dismiss or ignore such novelties as irrelevant and impertinent, proponents of Aristotelian physical science had eventually to confront the new claims, if only to refute them. Not many were as fixed in their recalcitrance as Cesare Cremonini, remembered as the man who refused to look through Galileo's telescope. When he observed a new star in 1572, the more inquisitive Tycho Brahe saw trouble in the changeless heavens of the *De*

---

[19] For a review of current opinion on the Scientific Revolution, see Lindberg and Westman (1990); see also Trinkaus (1983: 140–68).

caelo (*On the Heavens*) and set a strenuous empirical test for Aristotelian physics and cosmology. At the same time, discoveries in biology and medicine penetrated the standard treatments of life, perception, and cognition which had accumulated for centuries under the rubric of Aristotle's *De anima* (*On the Soul*). By the end of the sixteenth century, major battles had been fought in the war between Aristotelians and innovators— *Peripatetici* against *novatores*—and they continued through the next hundred years. Galileo brought the conflict to a head in 1632 with his *Dialogue on the Two Great World Systems, Ptolemaic and Copernican*, but his ecclesiastical defeat and moral victory by no means settled the struggle.

Humanism

In his most provocative book even the adventurous Galileo took an ancient text, Ptolemy's *Almagest*, as his point of departure; at least to this extent, the Florentine rebel showed himself loyal to the humanist habits of Renaissance intellectuals. So far as philosophy is concerned, humanism was the key cultural phenomenon of early modern Europe. The word 'humanism' has been the subject of much learned controversy in our time, both because it was a coinage of the nineteenth century, not a term used by Renaissance people, and also because in some contexts it connotes an aggressive anthropocentric secularism quite foreign to the Christian world of early modern Europe. None the less, the word has proved useful, perhaps indispensable, in describing central and distinctive features of early modern culture.[20] No neat definition of

[20] Current conceptions of Renaissance humanism derive mainly from the work of P. O. Kristeller; see Kristeller (1956: 11–15, 261–78, 553–83; 1961*a*: 3–23, 92–119; 1964*a*: 147–65; 1972*a*; 1974: 3–25; 1985*e*: 111–27; 1988*b*; 1988*c*); 1990*a*: 1–88); see also Sabbadini (1922); Toffanin (1929; 1964); Campana (1946); Weiss (1947; 1949; 1964; 1967); Garin (1965*a*; 1967*a*); Bouwsma (1973); Ullmann (1977); Witt (1982; 1988); Trinkaus (1983: 3–31, 52–139; 1988*a*); Perreiah (1982); Overfield (1984); Grafton and Jardine (1986). Rabil (1988) is a 3-volume collection of current scholarship on humanism; especially relevant to this volume are the contributions by D'Amico, Geanakoplos, Grafton, Kristeller, Monfasani, Percival, Ruderman, Santoro, Trinkaus, and Witt. See also above, n. 10.

humanism will be meaningful, especially as applied over several centuries of intellectual development, but its ancestry can be traced to classical times. Cicero and other ancient authors used such expressions as *studia humanitatis* and *litterae humaniores* to describe a liberal education centred on authoritative texts in Greek and Latin that taught grammar, rhetoric, poetry, history, and moral philosophy. In Italy of the fourteenth and fifteenth centuries, when the urge quickened to revive ancient culture as a model for contemporary life, the first people to be called 'humanists' studied and taught Latin and eventually Greek texts in those subjects. Cicero, Horace, Livy, Ovid, Priscian, Quintilian, Seneca, and Virgil were prominent among the ancient authors who first interested the humanists. As knowledge of Greek became more common, they turned their attention to Homer, Pindar, Sophocles, Thucydides, Demosthenes, Isocrates, and other Greek authorities. A curriculum grounded in such writers naturally had more to do with linguistic, literary, and historical issues than with philosophical problems, least of all with those questions that fell outside the province of moral philosophy.[21]

As a distinctive feature of medieval Latin culture, humanism first emerged in the (by medieval standards) increasingly secular world of Northern Italy; in particular, lay notaries who rose in the ranks of town and chancery and law teachers who organized new universities were important advocates of early humanism. In eleventh-century Pavia and twelfth-century Bologna, new interest in Roman law stimulated curiosity about the ancient world, and the rise of an urban economy helped liberate the classics from the old grammar curriculum of the cathedral schools and the sole dominion of the church. The *ars dictaminis*, which crafted letters by applying Cicero's rhetoric to written rather than spoken language, began in the great Benedictine monastery of Monte Cassino in the late eleventh

[21] Cicero, *For Archias the Poet* 1. 1–4; *On the Orator* 1. 4. 13; *Familiar Letters* 11. 27. 6; *On the Republic* 1. 17. 28; Aulus Gellius, *Attic Nights* 13. 17, 19. 14. 1–5; Marrou (1956: 98–9, 217–26); Kristeller (1961a: 8–11; 1990a: 3–5). On humanism and history, see Garin (1954: 192–210); Buck (1957); Burke (1970); Huppert (1970); Kelley (1970a; 1970b; 1984; 1988); Struever (1970); Hay (1977); Cochrane (1981); Fryde (1983).

century. By the early twelfth century, this new type of prose had narrowed its educational scope as its centre moved to the more practical precincts of Bologna, whence it spread to other parts of Europe. Another medieval form, the *ars arengandi*, imitated the pseudo-Ciceronian *Rhetorica ad Herennium*. It developed in Italy as a guide for secular oratory, while the *ars praedicandi* first arose in northern Europe as a genre of manuals for the preparation of sermons. From the mid-twelfth century, Italy sent her scholars to France for theology, dialectic, and grammar, but French students who wanted Roman or canon law travelled to Italy, where the pragmatic needs of notaries and lawyers discouraged the cruder classicism of the medieval grammar curriculum. But after the mid-thirteenth century, Italian *dictatores* began to read manuals of poetry and grammar written in France and to decorate the previously spare style of their *dictamen* with classical allusion. Meanwhile, Bolognese professors who had been deaf to Ciceronian oratory were lecturing on the *Ad Herennium*, thus planting the rhetorical temptations that would eventually seduce humanists from their earliest loyalties to grammar and poetry.[22]

One of the most effective heralds of the new classicism was Lovato Lovati, a judge in Padua who lived until 1309. Lovati searched the abbey library of Pomposa for forgotten classical authors, poets especially, whom he advertised to his circle of legal friends. Foreshadowing the Renaissance obsession with the physical remains of antiquity, he thought he had identified the bones of Antenor, a Homeric hero, unearthed in a construction project. Lovati's most important associate was Albertino Mussato, a Paduan notary, who made himself an expert on Senecan tragedy and even wrote his own Latin play, the *Ecerinis*, a work of dramatic propaganda on the tyrant Ezzelino da Romano that showed how ancient literary forms could address current affairs. Mussato's play won him the laurel crown in Padua in 1315, the first such poetic coronation recorded in more than a millennium.[23] From the beginning,

[22] Witt (1982; 1988); Murphy (1974: 135–6, 191–212, 253–9, 266–8, 300–18, 343–55); Grendler (1989: 111–17); Kristeller (1990a: 228–46).
[23] Weiss (1947; 1949; 1964: 14–22; 1969: 16–29).

the movement inaugurated by Lovati, Mussato, and their friends attracted people who for professional or personal reasons were more interested in grammar, rhetoric, and poetry as literary studies than in dialectic or in the technical disciplines of the medieval quadrivium (arithmetic, geometry, astronomy, and music). As their ambitions reached from poetry into prose, humanists invaded the territory of logicians and natural philosophers who controlled the arts faculties of the universities. By the turn of the fourteenth century, this contest was already under way in Padua, which was a centre for the philosophy and medicine taught by Pietro d'Abano as well as the humanistic studies pursued by Mussato and Lovati.

Thus, Francesco Petrarca—or Petrarch, as he is usually called in English—was not the first restorer of antiquity, but he was the earliest figure of European eminence to cultivate the *litterae humaniores* as the Renaissance conceived them.[24] While remaining a devout Christian, Petrarch wished to revive certain values that had died with antiquity because he disliked some features of the medieval world in which he was born, and other early humanists agreed with him that the Middle Ages were barbarous and uncultivated. Petrarch was particularly hostile to medieval philosophy as he came to know it in the Italy of the mid-fourteenth century. He found its language ugly, contrived, and cumbersome, falling far short of the classical norms that he esteemed in Cicero; the content was also distasteful, too dependent on infidel sources followed blindly by medieval imitators. Averroes, Islam's most esteemed scientific and philosophical thinker, was his *bête noire*; Petrarch called him a 'mad dog' (*canis rabidus*) at one point.[25] If religious and racial prejudice of this sort was one of Petrarch's instincts—a common failing of his time that survives in our

---

[24] For an English life and works, see Wilkins (1961); Mann (1984) provides an even briefer treatment. See also Nolhac (1907); Mommsen (1942); Billanovich (1947; 1951; 1953; 1981); Kristeller (1955*b*; 1964*a*: 1–18; 1983*c*); Wilkins (1955; 1958; 1959; 1960; 1978); Baron (1968*b*: 6–50; 1985); Bosco (1968); Kessler (1978); Trinkaus (1979); Foster (1984). The Latin works are in Petrarch (1965) and (1975) with English translations of selected pieces in (1971) and in Cassirer, Kristeller, and Randall (1948).

[25] Petrarch (1965: ii. 812); Cassirer, Kristeller, and Randall (1948: 143).

own—we may also credit him and other humanists with establishing trends in philosophy that continued for centuries. Because medieval logic and natural philosophy seemed so unlike the admired classics, ugly in their technical language and remote from human concerns, the humanists despised just those parts of fourteenth-century philosophy that seem most 'progressive' from some twentieth-century perspectives. Petrarch, like many of the humanists who came after him, thought that moral philosophy was useful to people as a guide for right living, but that logic and natural philosophy, the parts of philosophy most prominent in university curricula, were of little value. While knowing little about the Greek context, he took a position like the one expressed long before by Socrates and the Sophists. Until the end of the sixteenth century, humanists stressed moral philosophy as the branch of philosophical studies that best met their needs. They subordinated philosophy as a whole to moral interests because only through moral inquiry could they discover how all the various uses of reason ought to be integrated within some larger scheme of value and action.[26]

Humanists were not professors of philosophy; they were neither producers nor even large consumers of philosophy as that discipline was practised in late medieval and early modern universities. They cared most about poetry, rhetoric, grammar, and history, but also about ethics, politics, and oeconomics. Their model was Cicero, the ancient Latin master of the philosophical as well as the literary *studia humanitatis*. Cicero wrote in a forceful, elegant style that the humanists preferred to the living but unlovely Latin of the scholastics, and his writings covered many of the topics that they found most necessary for an active life in the contemporary world. Besides stylish letters to friends and relatives, finely crafted revisions of his speeches in the courts, and theoretical dialogues on the rhetoric of Roman lawyers, Cicero also left treatises on moral philosophy such as *On Duties* and the *Tusculan Disputations*. The curri-

---

[26] Kristeller (1990a: 20–68); on the term 'dialectic' below, see Michaud-Quantin (1969).

culum sanctified by Cicero's example stirred the hearts of humanists unmoved by the logic and natural philosophy that dominated the Italian universities of the period.

From Petrarch's time onward, when professional humanists took any interest at all in philosophy, they nearly always concerned themselves with ethical questions.[27] If they worried about logic, it was usually to demand reform of scholastic techniques taught in universities. In the arts faculties, especially in Italy, the primary role of logical instruction was to equip the student with tools of thought needed for natural philosophy and medicine, but the humanists wanted a logic more closely allied to rhetoric and better suited to practical persuasion than to scientific demonstration. In the middle of the fifteenth century, this was the core of Lorenzo Valla's critique of the scholastic logic fathered by Boethius and still paramount in the classrooms of later medieval Europe. Like many other humanists, Valla had studied law, and he saw logic—dialectic, in his terminology—as an adjunct to pleading in the law courts, arguing in the political arena, or preaching and persuading in daily moral and religious life. Throughout the fifteenth and early sixteenth centuries, condemnation of scholastic university education was the ceaseless hue and cry of the humanists. In this regard, although he encouraged Aristotelian studies within certain limits, Leonardo Bruni was a true disciple of Petrarch, scornful of the late medieval logic developed primarily at Oxford and Paris but imported into Italy in its full vigour during Petrarch's lifetime. After the humanist movement had become international in scope, three of the most eminent humanists of the early sixteenth century echoed the same themes: Thomas More, a pious Englishman, Desiderius Erasmus, a cosmopolitan Netherlander, and Juan Luis Vives, a widely travelled Spaniard of Converso descent, were unanimous in their contempt for university logic. They saw logic as barbaric, inelegant, hypertechnical, and ultimately devoid of any truly human purpose. When they saw logicians using

[27] Garin (1961a: 60–72); Schmitt (1984: ch. 7); Kristeller (1988b); Kraye (1988).

words, phrases, and constructions not certified in classical usage, they became hostile to the precise technical language found in the widely read works of Peter of Spain and his followers.

Whether as critics or contributors, the professional humanists who took a lively interest in philosophy—Petrarch, Bruni, Valla, Vives, and others—were the exceptions. Most of their colleagues were educators or classical scholars. Their ideological goal was to revive standards and values of classical antiquity for which the evidence was more philological than philosophical, even though the humanist ideology had great implications for philosophy. Humanists often earned their keep as teachers or tutors, charged with educating the young in growing cities or in rich princely households. In the first quarter of the fifteenth century, Gasparino Barzizza, Vittorino da Feltre, and Guarino Guarini founded schools in Padua, Mantua, Venice, Verona, and Ferrara that preached the new classicizing ideal and eventually drew students from all over Europe. Meanwhile, around 1402, Pier Paolo Vergerio issued the first humanist educational manifesto, *On Gentle Behaviour and Liberal Studies for Youth*, followed by many other proclamations of the *studia humanitatis* from Leonardo Bruni, Eneo Silvio Piccolomini, Maffeo Vegio, Battista Guarini, and their imitators in the sixteenth and later centuries. Humanists taught their charges to master the best Latin and to acquire some Greek along with the literary trappings of the two languages. Rhetoric and prose, including history and moral philosophy, became more fashionable than poetry and grammar. Grammar and style were to be learned not through logical prescription but by imitating the ancients, most of all Cicero— not so much his philosophical writings as his letters and speeches. Humanists abandoned most textbooks commonly used in medieval classrooms, and they prepared simple teaching editions of the classics. Their aims were vocational inasmuch as they prepared students for civil and ecclesiastical careers that depended on the new oratorical literacy. Similar schools grew up outside Italy, and by 1500 or so humanist education had become fashionable for the wealthier families of Europe, initiating a tradition that still survives, as in St Paul's School in London, founded by John Colet in 1509. Even in the distant north, the wealthy and powerful found humanism prestigious: Thomas Linacre, an English humanist and physician who died in 1524, was given the task of educating Prince Arthur, the son and heir of Henry VII who died in 1502. Colet, Linacre, and their predecessors taught not only the elements of Latin and Greek but also the values of the Roman and Hellenic literature from which they drew their examples and made their assignments. Like the French governess of more recent times, the humanist pedagogue was proof of status as well as a channel of culture. The education that he purveyed was a class and gender privilege, but in strictly academic terms it was a rich curriculum. As scholars, diplomats, politicians, professors, clergy, lawyers, physicians, or managers, some beneficiaries of humanist education went on to make cultural contributions of their own—like Angelo Poliziano, who translated Homer while still a teenager, entered the Medici household in Florence as tutor to the children of Lorenzo the Magnificent, and became the greatest philologist of the later fifteenth century and a major poet in Latin and Italian.[28]

After the religious split provoked by Luther, Catholic and Protestant education diverged somewhat, though both remained heavily committed to their common heritage of scholasticism and humanism. Humanist pedagogy served philosophical and theological interests in all the major confessions. The Lutheran curriculum established by Philip Melanchthon and Johann Sturm stressed classical languages and literature while propagating the Peripatetic tradition, but now students were expected to read Greek well enough to cope with Aristotle's *Nicomachean Ethics* and the New Testament in the original. Education in the new Jesuit schools of the sixteenth century

---

[28] On humanist education, see esp. Grendler (1989: 117–271); also Woodward (1906; 1963); Bush (1939: 63–77); Garin (1957a); McConica (1965: 24–5, 42–54); Weiss (1967: 84–127); Caspari (1968: 28–40); Grafton and Jardine (1986: 1–28); Grafton (1988a); Gleason (1989). On Poliziano, see also Micheli (1917); Scaglione (1961); Maier (1965; 1966); Bigi (1967); Garin (1967a: 131–62); Tateo (1972); Branca (1983); Kraye (1983); Grafton (1991: 47–75). Poliziano (1971) is a reprint of the 1553 *Opera*.

was likewise exacting and efficient. Codified in the famous *Ratio studiorum* (plan of studies) of 1586, the Jesuit curriculum shaped the education of powerful Catholic populations in Europe until Clement XIV suppressed the Society of Jesus in 1773. The Jesuits promoted a sound humanist curriculum based on Cicero, Vergil, and other classical texts as the foundation for a rigorous introduction to the philosophy of late scholasticism. When Descartes went to La Flèche in the early seventeenth century, scholastic manuals summarized the philosophy that he eventually rejected and humanist Jesuits taught the classical erudition that he finally abandoned.

Even though humanism often clashed with the philosophical culture of the arts faculties, the universities, especially in Italy, felt its influence from early on. Since students and professors read, wrote, and spoke a late form of Latin, it was inevitable that new standards for the classical languages would cause profound transformations in the intellectual life of the universities—not least in philosophy, which had long depended on its own Latin patois not only as a medium of technical discourse but also, in some applications, as a kind of metalanguage. In Paris around the turn of the sixteenth century, for example, Jacques Lefèvre d'Étaples transformed habits of learned communication in northern Europe by reissuing and revising humanist translations of Aristotle and other authors meant to replace medieval vulgate versions that were often philosophically unreliable and always, in the eyes of the humanists, philologically and aesthetically inadequate. Since Paris was the Athens of medieval thought, it was fitting that by the middle of the sixteenth century students and professors of her university could read Aristotle in Greek, thanks to the promotion of Greek in humanist education as well as the propagation of the humanist principle that an ancient text could be read properly only in its own language. Paris was relatively advanced, though not unique, in raising philosophy's philological and historical consciousness. Inasmuch as the medieval vulgate texts that the humanists wished to eradicate had been deeply embedded for centuries in the practice of philosophy—the best-known commentaries, for example, being keyed to old Latin translations—it is difficult to exaggerate the impact of the new philology on the development of early modern philosophy.

Prerequisite to the reform of philology was the recovery of ancient texts, including the ancient philosophical works that humanists made newly available to Europe. Without the labours of the humanists, we and our Renaissance ancestors would know much less of such towering figures as Homer, Pindar, Aeschylus, Sophocles, Plato, Ptolemy, Archimedes, Galen, Quintilian, Cicero, and Lucretius; in other words, much of classical literature as we came to have it was a humanist re-creation, hard won in searches of monastic libraries that had lain fallow for centuries or in risky voyages to the lands of the Greek East. But rediscovery was only part of the story. From the time of Petrarch's pioneering studies of Livy and Cicero, humanists worked hard to refine their understanding of what they found: comparing, correcting, editing, translating, anno-tating, interpreting, and, in an excess of enthusiasm for their new storehouse of wisdom, sometimes even forging the texts that they venerated.[29] They modernized the study of classical manuscripts by improving their knowledge not only of ancient languages but also of the history and institutions of the people who had spoken them. Renaissance philology, in other words, was a historical enterprise, a point worth bearing in mind when one examines the philologized philosophy of that age. Philology and philosophy were married most creatively in the person of Lorenzo Valla, who made himself notorious in 1440 by showing that the so called 'Donation of Constantine' (a priceless document that traced papal power and property in the West to an imperial gift) was a forgery.[30] Valla also applied his awesome critical powers to the terminology and taxonomy of school philosophy, but his challenge to prevailing modes of discourse was too radical to be effective in the pre-Cartesian period, though other critics followed his philological example by questioning the authenticity of works attributed to Dionysius the Areopagite or Hermes Trismegistus. The Middle Ages attributed nearly a hundred titles now regarded as spurious

[29] Grafton (1990; 1991: 76–103).
[30] Below, Ch. 4, n. 18.

even to the staid Aristotle, but Renaissance scholars helped pare the Corpus down to the forty or so works in which one can hope to discern a genuine Aristotelian position.[31] Since a number of ancient philosophers were familiar to the Middle Ages through false attributions or distorted secondary accounts, the work of the humanist critics was cut out for them. Some questions of attribution could be answered satisfactorily neither by the humanists nor even by modern philology, with all its advanced armament of critical judgement, so that scholars still dispute the authenticity of a work as central as Aristotle's *Categories*.

From the time when Plato first wrote his dialogues until the invention of printing in the middle of the fifteenth century, the transmission and survival of written works of philosophy depended entirely upon their being copied and recopied again and again by hand. Without the technology of print, philosophical literacy could be disseminated only as far as the laborious process of manuscript production could reach; books of any length remained scarce goods as long as each copy consumed many hours of tedious effort. The accurate and complete preservation of texts was as problematic as their distribution, which is why whole periods and schools of ancient philosophy are represented only by fragments. Even in texts that survived in complete copies, scribal errors piled up over the centuries, leaving the humanists with more work than they could handle as they pioneered the field of textual criticism. Poliziano and others collated copies of the same work to locate the differences that make errors conspicuous; they dated manuscripts in order to decide which was the more authoritative; and they analysed the language, style, and cultural milieu of ancient authors as aids to establishing their texts. The result was a more precise and a more profound understanding of philosophy through philology, so that by the time printing became a common medium, new scholarly techniques were at hand to produce more accurate texts which, once in print, would enjoy

---

[31] Schmitt and Ryan (1983); Schmitt and Knox (1985); Kraye, Ryan, and Schmitt (1986); Schmitt (1989: ch. 1).

much improved conditions of stability and dissemination. Thus, the invention of printing greatly amplified the impact of humanist scholarship, whose textual products would otherwise have been subject to the same chronic degradation that plagued the medieval scriptoria. Aldo Manuzio printed the first Greek Aristotle in Venice between 1495 and 1498, the first Greek Plato in 1514, inaugurating a unique age in the history of high culture during which the humanists edited the first philosophical texts—ancient, medieval, and contemporary—to be widely distributed and reproduced in a relatively precise manner. Aristotle's collected works were often printed in Greek during the sixteenth century, individual works even more frequently, in a process that encouraged improvement of the text through cumulative editorial experience and increased philological expertise. A Greek Diogenes Laertius first appeared in 1533, Plotinus in 1580, Sextus Empiricus only in 1621; during the same period many other works of antiquity saw the light.[32]

Greek became increasingly widespread in Europe from the early fifteenth century, but even for those who studied Greek philosophers, mastery of the language was never a universal attainment. For every sixteenth-century Greek printing of an Aristotelian work there were five or ten in Latin. Latin translations of Greek texts remained the chief medium of ancient philosophy, and it was Leonardo Bruni and his many humanist successors who prepared the first Latin versions or revisions of Greek works answering to the new philological and aesthetic norms. Better understanding of ancient language and culture made the humanist renderings more accurate and, from a classicist point of view, more readable; in fact, because the humanists meant to educate and persuade their readers, a pleasurable text was normally their conscious aim, creating a concern for eloquence and elegance seldom evident in the philosophical books read in the medieval schools. But because professional philosophers, especially as students of Aristotle, had depended for so long on translations of an altogether different kind and had constructed their lessons and commen-

[32] Grafton (1988*b*).

taries to fit these earlier versions, some professors of the discipline felt uncomfortable with the modish classicism and
wished to keep their Aristotle in scholastic Latin. After Rome
fell and Byzantium lost touch with the West, where the
Romance and Germanic vernaculars were developing, Latin
had also evolved away from Cicero's usage. The language of
philosophers in particular acquired a syntax and a lexicon that
fell heavy on the humanist ear, but by the fifteenth century
much of this novelty had become indispensable to philosophical
discourse, though critics like Valla and Vives would never
admit the necessity. Erasmus, like Cicero, was more flexible
and pragmatic, admitting that 'there is no human art to which
we do not grant the right of using its own terminology'.[33]

As time went on and co-operation grew, humanism and philosophy interacted more closely. Many philosophical authorities of the period were well trained by humanist standards:
Marsilio Ficino, Giovanni Pico, and Francesco Patrizi among
the Platonists, for example, or Leonardo Bruni, Ermolao
Barbaro, Lefèvre d'Étaples, and Giulio Pace among the
Aristotelians. By the same token, Valla was a philologist of
great philosophical gifts. Humanism was not a field of learning
in its own right but a method, a style, and a curriculum that
various disciplines found useful. There were medical, legal,
and mathematical humanists as well as philosophical humanists.
At the same time, the anti-philosophical impulse that had
motivated the movement since Petrarch's time continued to
operate, especially in the ancient contest between the orator's
wish to charm and persuade and the philosopher's need to
speak clearly and say the truth.[34] Some humanists pursued
philology of a quite narrow kind, poring over the old texts in

---

[33] Erasmus (1965b: 148); Weiss (1977); Grafton and Jardine (1986: 99–
121); Copenhaver (1988b).

[34] On rhetoric, grammar, and poetics, see Spingarn (1908); Cantimori
(1937); Garin (1954: 124–49); Marrou (1956: 48–59, 79–91, 211, 220); Weinberg (1961); Seigel (1968); Sonnino (1968); Vickers (1968; 1970; 1988a; 1988b);
Patterson (1970); Jardine (1974a; 1981); Percival (1975; 1982; 1983; 1988);
Padley (1976); Grassi (1980); G. A. Kennedy (1980); Murphy (1974; 1978;
1983); Trinkaus (1983: 437–49); Vasoli (1968a; 1984b); Monfasani (1983b;
1987a; 1988).

an incessant hunt for the odd word or the strange turn of syntax; scholars of this type, who were disinclined to treat the classical tongues as means to an end, had little sympathy for the technical requirements of the philosopher. Such conflicts were never resolved, but when all is said and done, one must conclude that humanism's influence on philosophy was profound and beneficial.

Church and state

In their various spheres the scholar Erasmus, the astronomer Copernicus, the explorer Columbus, and contemporaries of like genius worked immense alterations on Europe, but the most turbulent upheaval of the period was the Reformation sparked by Martin Luther, a brilliant theologian and disquieted monk whose defiance of Rome after 1517 changed the world, transforming not only its religious but also its political order.[35] Luther, Calvin, Zwingli, and their followers split a Europe previously united by a single faith into credal fragments, each with its own educational practice and intellectual vision. Naturally, the impact on philosophy of so vast a change was considerable, though perhaps not so cataclysmic as one might think. Especially within the framework of higher education, all the major churches of post-Reformation Europe, Protestant and Catholic alike, drew on the same philosophical traditions that had been institutionalized in the Middle Ages and reintegrated with their ancient origins in the Renaissance. Catholic, Lutheran, and Reformed philosophers gradually acquired their separate identities, but by and large they all depended on Latin versions or interpretations of Greek materials adapted to a pedagogical context that remained scholastic, while making some concessions to the classicizing fashions of the age and yielding on other points to confessional needs. Like the word 'Renaissance', the term 'Reformation' is a convention meant to set certain events and processes within a more or less distinct framework of time; however, if we note the chrono-

[35] Kristeller (1961a: 70–91); Rupp (1964); Dickens (1976); Ozment (1980); Oberman (1981; 1983; 1989); McGrath (1987; 1990).

logical overlap between Renaissance and Reformation, recognition of their coincidence may dissuade us from assuming that a philosopher who lived in the century after 1517 would have felt himself, on any given occasion, bound more to the one movement than to the other—or bound to either of them, for that matter. Without the Reformation, the philosophical careers of Bacon, Bodin, Bruno, Campanella, Charron, Justus Lipsius, Montaigne, Patrizi, Sanches, Suárez, and many others would have been very different, but for all of them the debt to the Renaissance was just as great. A simpler way to put it is to say that they all took part in the great movements that reformed the European spirit, reordered its polity, and restructured its culture in the early modern period.

Philosophy was part of the Reformation both as cause and as consequence.[36] Theological quarrels about the action of grace in the soul and philosophical arguments about the formation of ideas in the mind stoked the furnaces of religious dissent that blazed forth all over Europe two years after Luther and other Wittenberg theologians started their local academic dispute in 1517. The philosopher who supplied most fuel for these fires was William of Ockham, although other scholastics of the later medieval period—especially Gregory of Rimini and Gabriel Biel—also played major parts in these controversies, many of which had troubled Christians since the time of Augustine. Defining a doctrine of justification required the Christian church to settle the relative roles of human effort and divine power in the drama of salvation; this task was one of Augustine's great accomplishments, recorded at length in his works against the Pelagians. Augustine, who saw fallen humanity as powerless to save itself, argued that the grace needed for salvation was God's free and unearned gift, but Aquinas, influenced by Aristotelian notions of acquired virtue and other considerations, believed that God would save those people whose moral effort co-operated with an original infu-

---

[36] Ozment (1980: 290–317); McGrath (1987: 1–8, 32–68, 175–203); Skinner (1988: 442–52); Lohr (1988: 621–38); D'Amico (1983; 1988a); Trinkaus (1983: 195–339; 1988a). On Renaissance and Reformation, see also Burdach (1963); Headley (1963; 1987); Spitz (1963); Dickens and Tonkin (1985).

sion of divine grace. Because the major variations on the scholastic theology of grace left some place for human effort, Luther rejected them all in his doctrine of justification, declaring in his *Appeal to the Nobility of the German Nation* of 1520 that 'any potter has more knowledge of nature than . . . these books [of Aristotle, which] . . . I can only believe . . . the devil has introduced. . . . His book on *Ethics* is the worst of all books. It flatly opposes divine grace and all Christian virtues.' Earlier, in his 1517 *Disputation against Scholastic Philosophy*, he had spoken just as boldly against Ockham, Scotus, and Biel.[37] Worse than the Thomists, the followers of the *via moderna* associated with Biel and Pierre d'Ailly introduced human effort into the soteriological equation at two points: the person who wants to be saved first earns an original injection of grace, then works to sustain the co-operation with grace whose reward is heaven. Luther's best known attacks on the efficacy of works (i.e. human moral effort) appeared in polemics that he exchanged with Erasmus, and these Renaissance extensions of medieval controversy reached into the seventeenth century and beyond, in Socinian and Arminian critiques of Reformed theology and Jesuit rebuttals of Jansenism.

Luther objected to Ockham's theology in so far as it preserved a false moral freedom, but Ockham and his followers insisted even more strongly that *God's will* is free, thus imparting a voluntarist cast to late medieval theology. In principle, only the logical limit of non-contradiction constrains God's 'absolute power', so that any physical or metaphysical disposition apart from God must be contingent upon his having willed it. At the same time, God can be trusted not to undo the particulars of creation actually established by his 'ordained power', the *potentia ordinata* that chose this world from the numberless possibilities available to his *potentia absoluta*. But if God's will is absolute, though only in principle, the human condition and, indeed, all creation rest uneasy in some degree. Various consequences of man's utter dependency on God's pleasure emerged in the epistemology and metaphysics

[37] Luther (1958– : xliv. 200–2 [Jacobs and Atkinson trans.], xxxi. 9–16); Ozment (1980: 231–9); McGrath (1987: 118–21); Oberman (1989: 113–23).

of the *via moderna*, whose roots also reached back to the early Christian centuries and beyond. Influenced by Plato and the Neoplatonists, Augustine had taught that the forms reside in God's mind, but that when Christ lights up the darkness of the human intellect, humans can know the universal forms of which individual things are shadows. For ordinary knowledge Aquinas saw no need of this divine illumination, ruling in a well-known phrase that 'there is nothing in the intellect which was not previously in the senses'.[38] Like Muslim students of Aristotle, Thomas posited an active intellect to abstract universals from particulars apprehended by the senses; God's mind contains the universals in their perfection, but the human sensory apparatus can also discover them from individuals without divine enlightenment. Although Aristotelian Thomists trusted the senses more than Augustinian Platonists, Aquinas agreed with Augustine in denying the mind any direct knowledge of sense objects. Thomists required an elaborate psychological apparatus to process sense data and produce an entity intermediate between the sensory and the ideal, called a *species* in Latin, which required further processing before the highest mental faculties could derive from it their knowledge of the universal. Ockham dispensed with such *species*, and the *via moderna* taught direct knowledge of individuals as such or of statements about individuals, wielding Ockham's razor to trim away the need for real universals. Knowledge arises in experience of particulars, and universals have no reality outside mind and language. They exist only as we think of them or talk about them in words, in names or *nomina*—hence the opposition between the Thomist and Augustinian *realism* of the early and high Middle Ages and the *nominalism* that was widespread in later medieval scholasticism, not only in the *via moderna* but also in the *schola Augustiniana moderna*, a distinct tradition propagated by the Augustinian friars.

The 'modern way' and the 'modern school of Augustine' agreed in rejecting the epistemological realism of the *via antiqua*, the 'old way' whose greatest days were in the thirteenth

[38] Aquinas, *De veritate* 2. 3. 19; Copleston (1960–6: ii. 388–97); Cranefield (1970); Mahoney (1982c: 605–11).

century. The two newer movements differed from one another not in their theories of knowledge but in certain aspects of their soteriologies, or theories of salvation. The new Augustinians preached a pessimist anthropology and a determinist, theocentric scheme of justification that derived, via Gregory of Rimini, from the anti-Pelagian crusade of their patron. But even the soteriology of the Augustinian 'school' followed Gabriel Biel and the *via moderna* in some respects. Most important, both groups used the distinction between God's absolute and ordained powers to eliminate grace as a created entity within the soul and separate from God's saving choice; grace is simply an aspect of God's will toward the person saved. Theologians and philosophers were still disputing these points when Luther came to teach moral philosophy at Wittenberg in 1508, perhaps as part of a shift toward the *via moderna* in that small, new outpost of learning. Through the year 1515, Luther continued to follow the gentler soteriology of Gabriel Biel, profiting especially from its non-Augustinian emphasis on the *pactum* or divine covenant in justification. By 1517 he had turned against his own exposition of the widespread theology of the *via moderna*, but he seems not to have reacted to the new *schola Augustiniana* before 1519.

In sustaining any dialogue at all with these late scholastic sects, Luther and his Wittenberg colleagues behaved like good professors, intent on academic taxonomies of small interest outside the universities. When Phillip Melanchthon defended Luther against the doctors of the Sorbonne in 1521, that learned Parisian company named no fewer than eight theological positions relevant to their complaints against the German reformers, not only Thomists, Scotists, and Albertists but also *Gregoriistae*, the disciples of Gregory of Rimini, and *Egidistae*, admirers of Giles of Rome, and other groups as well. The Swiss and French reformers led by Ulrich Zwingli and John Calvin yielded nothing to the Lutherans in their dislike of scholasticism; in fact, their contempt for the schools was greater, in that they rejected scholasticism globally without bothering to dignify its latest products with refutation. Soteriology was a key issue for Luther, and he owed its prominence to the robust theologizing and doctrinal pluralism of the later Middle Ages, but Zwingli and Calvin launched their movements with no special concern for medieval theologies of justification, whether of the *via moderna* or of the *schola Augustiniana*. Scholasticism interested the Reformed churches only in the last half of the sixteenth century, around the time when the post-Tridentine Roman church reaffirmed its own commitment to Aristotle. Theodore Beza codified Calvin's thought in a deductive system of speculative theology that put the doctrine of predestination at the head of its logical structure and took its methodological bearings from the Aristotelian tradition. Beza signalled his accommodation with Aristotle when he forbade the teaching of anti-Aristotelian Ramist logic in the Genevan Academy, where Aristotle's syllogisms were to rule despite Protestant acclaim for Ramus. French and English Protestants welcomed Ramism, however, while Arminius rejected Beza's whole project of a Reformed rational theology along scholastic lines. Ironically, the efflorescent scholasticism ignored by the first Reformed theologians became useful to their successors only when reshaped by the fusion with humanism apparent in the works of Jacopo Zabarella and his contemporaries.[39]

Before the church permitted or had to permit the theological diversity and uncertainty of the later medieval period, Thomas Aquinas had triumphed by proposing a synthesis of theology and metaphysics. Thomas asserted a rich complex of clearly known relations between uncreated and created being, secure relations that William of Ockham reduced to contingencies dependent on a divine will unhindered by inviolable metaphysical arrangements. God evidently willed the state of affairs that we call the world and obliged himself to preserve it, but the world is none the less *conventional* in the literal sense, the bottom line of a contract which it pleased God to make but which he might not have made. Thus, Ockham's universe was less a rational than a volitional construct; God made a covenant and *will* not break it, yet this promise leaves the world a more

[39] McGrath (1987: 69–85, 94–104, 191–6).

anxious and ambiguous place than Thomas had known. When the faculty of arts at Paris tried to repress the theological exuberance of the 'modern way' in the middle of the fourteenth century, admirers of the 'old way' faced challengers who loved to speculate on such puzzles of future contingency as God's ability to unravel the past and to spin out such ludicrous extrapolations of the theory of divine persons as God's freedom to have embodied himself as an insect, a vegetable, or a chunk of wood. The *via moderna* tightened the reins on theology as an assured product of logic, but by stressing the frailty of human knowing it also loosened the church's grip on speculation. Every conclusion of theology, even if correct, is an artefact of the divine covenant, a worrisome thought for the church as steward of divine science. Ecclesiastical structures themselves are contingent; Christ said that his church was built upon a rock, but later medieval theology seemed to expose it as a scaffold of possibilities, a shakier edifice than the metaphysically secure monument anchored in the timeless celestial hierarchies described by Dionysius the Areopagite. Naturally, many bishops and abbots who ruled the ecclesiastical establishment preferred the firmer foundations of realism and the *via antiqua*, while in some respects the *via moderna* better suited the mystical theologies that subverted priestly office and ambitious theologizing. Jean Gerson was a critic of Ockham, a chancellor of the University of Paris, and author of a work *On Mystical Theology* that turned the force of scholastic argument against scholasticism itself. He and his student, Nicolas de Clémanges, wanted to replace the subtleties of Scotus and Ockham with a simpler belief, less fixed on understanding an abstract deity than on loving the saviour who instituted the sacraments and died on the cross. By Gerson's time, scholasticism had lost the confidence of its thirteenth-century Aristotelian masters in reason's fitness to plumb the depths of faith. Later medieval Aristotelians unwittingly prepared the way for Luther's declaration that 'the whole of Aristotle is to theology as darkness to light'.[40]

[40] Luther (1958– : xxxi. 60 [Grimm trans.]); Ozment (1980: 73–80, 164–72, 236–9); McGrath (1987: 19–28).

One view of the Aristotelian Aquinas praises him for forging the grand scholastic synthesis of faith and reason, but a different analysis points out the Thomist basis of the bull *Unam sanctam*, issued by Pope Boniface VIII in 1302. Two years after the Jubilee of 1300 and only seven years before the papacy began its sojourn in Avignon, Boniface declared all lay and temporal authority subordinate to his own, but this restatement of the church's desire for a submissive laity only provoked anti-clerical and anti-ecclesiastical hatreds that still smouldered when Luther rekindled them more than two hundred years later. For more than a century after Philip IV of France humbled the theocratic Boniface, the popes lived some of their darkest and most clamorous days. While the papacy prospered in its worldly fortunes for seven decades in Avignon, Petrarch and other Italians viewed the period as ruinous exile, and nearly forty years of multiple claims to the throne of Peter followed this captivity in the French Babylon. The great council convened at Constance in 1414–17 to end these troubles had three aims: to heal the schism; to exterminate heresy; and to address complaints of corruption in a programme of reform. Dissidents were executed; rival popes yielded their claims; but, in the half-century of revived papal power that followed the bull *Execrabilis* issued against conciliar power by Pius II in 1460, the greatest and most infamous popes of the Renaissance were unable or unwilling to achieve much in the way of reform. The pope elected four years before Luther began his revolt was a Medici cardinal who took the name Leo X and—if we believe the story—greeted the news of his accession with a cynical and untimely remark: 'God has given us the papacy; now let us enjoy it.'[41]

The Council of Constance renewed debates on church government that had begun a century earlier in the contest between papal propagandists and supporters of secular power; especially important were Giles of Rome and James of Viterbo, speaking for the papacy, and Marsilio of Padua, John of Paris, and John of Jandun, arguing for temporal authority and popular sover-

---

[41] Schevill (1949: 185).

eignty. William of Ockham also sided with Louis of Bavaria against Pope John XXII, but the ideas most dangerous to papal power were those of the *Defender of the Peace*, written in Paris by Marsilio in 1324 and condemned as heretical three years later by Pope John, who also excommunicated William of Ockham in 1326. Most threatening to John was Marsilio's claim that 'Christ left no head of the church', but the deeper and more broadly subversive element in the *Defender of the Peace* was the principle that political authority comes *from* God *through* the people and only then to pope or king. Popular sovereignty, according to Marsilio, is inalienable; subjects who can always dismiss their ruler only delegate sovereignty, contrary to the view of Aquinas that the consent required of the governed causes them to lose sovereignty. Marsilio moved closer than Thomas both to the political theories that were to accompany vast changes in practical politics during the Renaissance and also to Aristotle's older conception of the *polis* as a human artefact, unprotected by the divine mandate that Augustine saw hovering over the city of man. Jean Gerson and other conciliarists who advocated the solutions worked out at Constance were less radical than Marsilio, whose ideas remained to incite not only the transformations of church government that came with the Reformation but also the greater novelties of political philosophy that emerged from new Renaissance statecraft. By the middle of the fifteenth century, however, in the narrower arena of church government, the conciliar movement had petered out. Nicholas of Cusa, one of the most original minds of his day, signalled its failure in the 1440s by abandoning earlier concessions to conciliar power expressed in his work of 1432–3 *On Universal Concord*.[42]

In the meantime, other traditions had emerged to engender ideals of liberty, both communal and individual, in the secular order. The medieval epistolary and oratorical techniques of

---

[42] Marsilio of Padua (1967: 267–73); Ozment (1980: 144–81, esp. 154 for the quotation from John's condemnation of Marsilius); Skinner (1978: i. 12–22, 49–65; 1988: 395–403). Most of what follows on political theory is based on Skinner's *Foundations*; for older works, see Cassirer (1946: 78–175); Figgis (1960; 1965); Allen (1960); Ullmann (1977).

the *ars dictaminis* and *ars arengandi* had taught Europeans to apply their growing literary skills and their increased appreciation of antiquity to moral and political tasks, and precursors of humanism in Northern Italy in the late thirteenth and early fourteenth centuries used new knowledge of ancient Rome to champion civic liberties against the overlords, the *signori*, who came to power in the faction-ridden Italian communes of the day. In the late fourteenth century, when a more settled internal politics eased worries in Florence about the good order of the city and shifted concern to the good life of the citizenry, another generation of humanists wrote chronicles, educational manifestos, and advice-books for rulers that shared certain fundamentals with scholastic political philosophy, especially the Aristotelian view of the commonwealth as a human product and of political conduct as a contest of virtue and vice. At the same time, these quattrocento humanists began translating Aristotle's moral and political philosophy into better Latin; following Petrarch's example, they also took up the Ciceronian style of politics as heroic oratory, using the tools of classical rhetoric and the examples of ancient history to create an activist and erudite vocabulary of civic life. A constant point of reference in their speeches and treatises was the eternal tension between virtue and fortune, increasingly interpreted in a way that led to hope for the triumph of individual and communal effort.[43]

But the promise of civic humanism faded in the second half of the fifteenth century when political conditions in Italian cities concentrated power in the hands of princes and dynasties. In Florence, for example, the might of the Medici family grew from the 1430s through the next century and beyond, interrupted by episodes of republican rule. One of the abler servants of any Florentine republic was Niccolò Machiavelli, who none the less dedicated his best-known work, *The Prince*, to a Medici duke when he found himself out of work after the restoration of their dynasty in 1512. In its theorizing on *virtù* and *fortuna*, this startling little book propagated a familiar

[43] Baron (1966); Ullmann (1977: 5–6); Skinner (1978: i. 1–12, 23–48, 69–112; 1988: 408–23); below, Ch. 2, nn. 17, 18, 20; Ch. 4, n. 100.

theme, but in divorcing the prince's *virtù* from the conventional catalogue of Christian and classical virtues and in constraining the ruler's behaviour solely by reasons of state, Machiavelli nullified Christendom's basic political principles. The counsels of *virtù* offered in *The Prince* respond mainly to threats against the security of the ruler's *stato*, a word that no longer referred just to the personal *status* of an individual prince but had not yet come to mean the *state* of a polity as expressed in its current institutions; this slippage of meaning occurred as the city-states of the peninsula and the younger nation-states of the continent were acquiring the trappings of modern national governments. The *Discourses on the First Ten Books of Livy*, Machiavelli's other great work of political philosophy, is a better reflection of the personal sentiments of the republican diplomat who wrote it. Machiavelli took examples from Livy's history of the early Roman republic to warn the Florentines against political passivity, individual greed, mercenary armies, and other dangers to the health of their city. Because the *Discourses* aimed to protect the city's liberty rather than the prince's security, critics have been friendlier to this longish treatise than to the brief but incendiary *Prince*. But even in the *Discourses* Machiavelli treats Christianity itself—especially its sanctification of the withdrawn, ascetic contemplative—as a source of political contagion.[44]

Luther, Machiavelli's contemporary, preached a contrary doctrine of righteous political quietism. The earliest heroes of the Reformation admired and revived the subversive theories of medieval conciliarism, but they directed these dangerous ideas mainly at the temporal claims of the Roman church. Insisting that the church was a purely spiritual gathering of the faithful, a *congregatio fidelium* without coercive authority, the first reformers taught that if an unjust ruler was entitled to no obedience, neither were his subjects allowed any right or duty

[44] Skinner (1978: i. 113–89; 1988: 423–42); for a selection from the enormous literature on Machiavelli, see, in addition to Skinner (1981): Meinecke (1965: 25–116); Sasso (1958); Baron (1961); Hale (1963); Ridolfi (1963); Chabod (1965); Gilbert (1965); Procacci (1965); Hexter (1973: 150–203); Pocock (1975: 156–218); Berlin (1982: 25–79); de Grazia (1989); below, pp. 278–84.

of active resistance. God's providence ordains the powers that be, even tyrannical powers divinely established to punish a sinful people. As political and military conditions evolved through the sixteenth century, Lutheran and then Reformed thinkers compromised their original docility, yet it remains true that the genealogy of absolutist government in early modern and modern Europe can be traced through early Protestant interpretations of such texts as the thirteenth chapter of Paul's letter to the Romans.

Supporters of Rome and the papacy also recalled the conciliarist controversies of the later Middle Ages; and although most of them wished to protect ecclesiastical hierarchy, their hostility to the Protestants led them to adopt constitutional theories of secular government that challenged the absolutist tendencies of the early reformers. This process began in the early sixteenth century with the revival of the Thomist *via antiqua* in Paris, where the enormously influential Francesco de Vitoria studied from 1509 to 1522. Vitoria spent most of his later life in Salamanca as a teacher, directly or indirectly shaping the careers of several generations of Dominican and Jesuit philosophers and theologians, of whom the greatest were Robert Bellarmine and Francisco Suárez. Whether they favoured passive or active resistance to tyranny, Protestant theorists connected the ruler's political authority with godliness or some other divine disposition, but in response their Counter-Reformation opponents emphasized the Thomist Aristotelian view of the state as a purely human construct whose legitimacy depended not on a divine mandate but on contractual arrangements among mortal creatures. Unlike Protestants, who denied mankind any innate capacity to improve its moral condition, Catholic thinkers trusted human reason to discover a better moral order and allowed that the individual moral agent, of whatever religious condition, can search within for the primary precepts of a natural morality. Thus it was the scholastics of Spain and Italy rather than the pastors of Geneva and Germany who resurrected medieval natural law theories and, *avant la lettre*, elaborated ideas of the social contract and state of nature that were to inform the more aggressively secularist and popularist political philosophies of the seventeenth and eighteenth centuries. Even the arguments for natural liberty advanced by Huguenot pamphleteers in the 1570s and after were derived from scholastic sources. After the Anabaptists, whose active following was much smaller than their fearsome reputation, disciples of John Calvin formulated the most radical political philosophies of the Renaissance and Reformation era, but the elements of these theories were not 'Calvinist' in any distinctive sense.[45]

After 1529, Martin Luther and his followers moved more quickly than their Reformed brethren toward permitting or advocating active resistance, developing positions not adopted by the Reformed churches until the 1550s and 1560s. Because John Knox and other leaders in Scotland and England were not surrounded by a hostile Catholic majority, they were able to advance more radical proposals than those condoned by Huguenots on the Continent. Before 1572, when the massacre of St Bartholemew's Day destroyed two decades of gradualist policy on both sides of the confessional divide, Reformed theorists derived a restricted religious duty — not a moral right — of resistance from violations of the godly purpose of government. The less timid English and Scots claimed that any subject had this duty, while the Huguenots confined it to legitimate magistrates; but both groups moved a long way from the Pauline doctrine of submission to ordained powers as Luther had originally taught it. After 1572, the Huguenots finally transformed the religious duty to resist into a moral right, thus adding a key ingredient to a secularized politics and public morality for Europe. The horror of St Bartholemew's Day provoked a variety of reactions. Montaigne, who despised the Huguenots as anarchists, wrote between 1572 and 1574 that he was 'disgusted with innovation in whatever guise, . . . for I have seen very harmful effects of it. The one that has been oppressing us for so many years . . . has itself to blame.' He accommodated his scepticism to the principle that subjects owed obedience to any established order, whatever its real

---

[45] Skinner (1978: i. 144–52; ii. 3–224).

claims to legitimacy, and the versatile Justus Lipsius was even less tolerant than Montaigne, who at least disapproved of outright persecution. Jean Bodin, who barely escaped the massacre himself, thought that princes should restrict themselves to affairs of state and not meddle in religious controversy, but he recommended toleration only *if* coerced uniformity was impossible, not *because* it was undesirable.[46]

François Hotman's *Francogallia* of 1573 was the single most important Huguenot response to St Bartholemew's Day in the realm of political philosophy. Finding themselves so ruthlessly abandoned by the Valois monarchy, Hotman and other Huguenot polemicists announced a robust theory of popular sovereignty based on the claim that people create rulers contractually to preserve the common welfare. If a ruler breaks the contract by endangering the public good, the people have a moral right of self-defence to resist the ruler actively, even though this right can be exercised only by legitimate magistrates, never by individuals or even by the people as a whole. The notions of natural right and contractual obligation used by the Huguenots were scholastic inventions, recognized as such when Beza and other Reformed leaders installed a clearly scholastic programme of education in Geneva and elsewhere. And it was the Spanish Jesuit Juan de Mariana as much as the Scots humanist George Buchanan who pushed the idea of active resistance to its limits in the last decades of the sixteenth century. Buchanan replaced earlier biblical descriptions of a divine covenant with a naturalistic version of the social contract based on Stoic accounts of primitive humanity. In this de-theologized framework Buchanan asserted that the whole commonwealth or any of its members could rightly use force to remove an unjust ruler. When the Protestant Henry of Navarre succeeded to the French throne in 1584, Catholic theorists began to make equally firm claims for the right to rebel and to kill a tyrant, and the most provocative call to tyrannicide came from the first book of Mariana's work *On the King* (1598), whose conclusions were no less naturalist and

[46] Montaigne (1965: 86 [Frame trans.]); Skinner (1978: ii. 225–301); see also Kelley (1973; 1981).

secularist than Buchanan's. Given Mariana's odious reputation among Protestants, it is worth noting that he was one of several Jesuits who criticized Machiavelli's *ragione di stato* on prudential and moral grounds alike. Machiavelli's status as a political philosopher suffered most of all from Huguenot critics in the 1570s who finally turned against Catherine de' Medici, holding her responsible for St Bartholemew's Day and knowing her to be the daughter of the Lorenzo de' Medici to whom Machiavelli had dedicated *The Prince*.[47]

The Renaissance transformation of philosophy

Politicians, reformers and humanists did not eliminate older approaches to philosophy but changed them in important ways, even though medieval styles of thought persisted into the seventeenth century and remained an effective force in philosophical discourse. In the eighteenth century, after Descartes and Locke had pushed the frontiers of philosophy beyond the limits explored in the Renaissance, scholastic manuals were still being read by Oxford undergraduates while Hume wrote philosophy in a neo-classical prose that echoed the linguistic innovations of the humanists. Examined year by year, the gradual transformation of philosophy may be hard to correlate with discrete events, but when viewed on a larger scale the major moments of modification become visible. In 1400, for example, Platonism was a rare commodity, scholasticism ruled the universities, and outside university walls there was little that deserved the name 'philosophy' beyond some conventional moral argumentation. Within a century, after university philosophers had greeted the first legions of humanism and scholars had learned again to read Greek, conditions altered remarkably: Plato, along with other newly exhumed Greeks, became a stylish alternative to Aristotle; discussions of philosophy unblessed by the universities became respectable and fashionable; and the proud masters of the schools faced the hot blast of humanist invective. By the end of the sixteenth century,

[47] Skinner (1978: ii. 302–58); Allen (1960: 360–6).

university philosophy was the resultant of the two forces of scholasticism and humanism, and philosophy outside the university moved beyond the confines of medieval custom. Even though Montaigne's longest work was an 'apology' for a scholastic theologian, it is hard to imagine him composing his sceptical essays in the environment of medieval Paris or Bologna, and impossible to contemplate his achievement in the absence of its humanist precedents.

As a layperson working without university support or protection, Montaigne found it possible to write influential philosophy only because the conditions of intellectual life had changed so much over the two hundred years before he died in 1592. The printing press, for example, gave him access as reader to a range of literature that would have dazzled Petrarch, who died in 1374, and the same technology enabled him to speak quickly and precisely as author to a public unimaginably large and diffuse by Petrarch's standards. Although he managed quite well without it, the university was still the common site of philosophical debate throughout Montaigne's lifetime; but he helped establish a new intellectual framework wherein most of his important successors—Bacon, Mersenne, Gassendi, Descartes, Hobbes, Spinoza, Locke, Leibniz—worked entirely or largely outside the university.

Montaigne also felt the effects of the Reformation and the ensuing wars of religion, calamities that nourished his fideist scepticism. But in other thinkers, both Catholic and Protestant, the Reformation inspired a renewed zeal for philosophy as a rational bulwark of belief. The Roman Catholic establishment emerged from the Council of Trent with a stronger dogmatic commitment to Aristotle (more and more a Thomist Aristotle) than the medieval church had ever enforced. And although Luther had raged against scholastic theology, his Protestant followers soon learned that they needed the philosophical equipment of the schoolmen to justify the theological distinctions that divided them from Rome and from each other. The partitions of philosophy familiar to the Middle Ages—logic, natural philosophy, moral philosophy, and metaphysics—proved indispensable to the Renaissance as well, so the traditional taxonomy persisted in the professorial appointments of universities, whether new or old, papist or Protestant. In Italy philosophy maintained its alliance with medicine and science and continued to favour logic and natural philosophy, except at the Collegio Romano, founded by the Jesuits in 1553 to advance the cause of the Counter-Reformation. The most famous philosophers in other Italian universities—Paul of Venice, Pietro Pomponazzi, Jacopo Zabarella—were hired to teach logic and natural philosophy in the usual preparatory programme for medical students. Elsewhere, whether in the Protestant and Catholic institutions of northern Europe or in the Catholic universities of the Iberian peninsula and the New World, philosophy remained a part of the arts course with strong ties to theology as well as science, allowing for local variations.

Since the university was the only large and powerful institution that promoted philosophy in the later Middle Ages, the humanist critique of the discipline provoked outrage mainly from professional practitioners whom the universities paid to teach. New approaches to philosophy met less resistance in courts, academies, and studies of private scholars. Intellectuals working in such freer circumstances, which had been scarce in the Middle Ages, could show less concern for the protocol, traditions, and academic requirements that make universities so conservative. The court philosopher had to honour no curriculum but his prince's whim, and the competitors he faced in winning his bread were rarely his peers in learning. His freedom of inquiry might be shallow, of course, if it stopped at the bottom of a capricious patron's purse, but, within such limits, heterodoxy was safer outside the university than inside. Unsurprisingly, some philosophers sought royal or aristocratic patronage, like poets, painters, or architects. Petrarch enjoyed papal and princely support. Nicole Oresme served Charles V of France for more than two decades. Ficino made his translations and studies of Plato at the behest of the Medici. Toward the end of our period, a whole constellation of intellectual stars, including Giordano Bruno, John Dee, Tycho Brahe, and Johannes Kepler, brightened the court of the Emperor Rudolf II, displaying not only the force of that sovereign's favour but also a new, if still dim, aura of enlightenment in Europe, a glimmer of tolerance, and, at times, even encouragement for independence of mind. Still, the prevailing outlook in the late sixteenth and early seventeenth centuries was gloomier, as Europe slouched toward thirty more years of religious slaughter. Cardano, Della Porta, and Patrizi were harassed by the Inquisition; Ramus fell in 1572 in the butchery of St Bartholemew's Day; Dee died in 1608 with the reputation of a wizard; and Bruno went to the stake in 1600, condemned for heresy. Giulio Cesare Vanini was burned in 1619, by which time Tommaso Campanella's daring had earned him his seventeenth continuous year in prison, with nine more to come. When Galileo's confinement in 1633 moved Descartes to suppress his *Principes*, he had good reason to fear that the stakes in the game of philosophy were more than metaphysical.

Repression was nothing new, of course.[48] Ockham was excommunicated in 1326. John Wyclif died a natural death in 1384, but only after having been condemned for heresy, the charge that sent John Hus to the stake at Constance in 1415. Wyclif and Hus defied the church on central issues of religious belief and practice, but Lorenzo Valla learned in 1444 that lesser offences could put a thinker at risk. Giovanni Pico's provocations of the late 1480s caused the most celebrated incident of philosophical suppression of the later fifteenth century. Philosophers helped persecute Johann Reuchlin a few decades later, in 1512. In the next year the Fifth Lateran Council commanded Christian professors to refute those who taught that the human soul is mortal, and by 1514 Pietro Pomponazzi had already been accused of heresy for holding suspect opinions about the soul. Soon afterward, when Leo X warned Pomponazzi to respect the Council's teaching, only a cardinal's intervention saved his career and permitted him to end it teaching in a university on papal territory. Meanwhile, Luther had caused graver problems for Rome. He last tried to conciliate the papacy in 1520, when he prefaced his pamphlet

[48] For what follows on censorship and printing, see esp. Grendler (1988); also Grendler (1977; 1981; 1984); above, n. 17.

on the *Freedom of a Christian* with an open letter to Pope Leo. Luther recommended 'a spiritual and true freedom [that] ... makes our hearts free from all sins, laws and commands', but the success of his Pauline preaching made the sixteenth century even more fearful of intellectual liberty than the fifteenth had been.[49] Pope and emperor both condemned Luther's writings in 1521, and Reformers followed suit by urging civil authorities to silence competing Protestant voices while they quashed the dogmas of the papist enemy. On neither side, however, was censorship systematic or effective. France was exceptional: the 'broadsheet incident' of 1534 — when Protestant posters denouncing the mass appeared not only in Paris but even on the door of the king's bedchamber in Amboise — occasioned stern measures of control and created the panic that culminated in the burning of Etienne Dolet, the humanist printer, in 1546. In 1559 Pope Paul IV inaugurated broad institutional censorship by approving a papal *Index of Prohibited Books*, a harsh and unpopular innovation enforced for less than a year. Pius IV's *Index* of 1564 was more moderate than Paul's, and neither this Tridentine version nor the Clementine *Index* of 1596 went especially hard on philosophy, though Valla, Pomponazzi, Bodin, Telesio, Patrizi, Bruno, and other thinkers all suffered one degree of restriction or another. (The church finally abandoned the *Index* in 1966, long after secular governments had invented more efficient machineries of silence.) Protestants, including Genevans who wanted no reading of Aquinas, were as quick as Catholics to ban books, but fragmented jurisdiction made Protestant censorship less effective and more dependent on local civil government.

It was the printing press, paradoxically, that gave the new and ineffective systems of censorship their technological basis. Besides the power to keep books from being printed and to restrict their distribution once published, censors who wished to manipulate opinion in large populations had to disseminate and control their own *lists* of banned works. They needed

[49] Luther (1961: 80 [Dillenberger trans.]); Pine (1986: 59–61, 127).

printed catalogues or anti-catalogues because once printed they were easier to stabilize and distribute. To appreciate the fear that printing inspired in the authorities, one need only recall a few numbers. By 1500, less than half a century after Gutenberg's discovery, presses were running in more than two hundred and fifty sites in Europe. By the end of the incunabular period (up to 1500), some 30,000 editions known to us (more were lost and unknown) had appeared in press runs that commonly produced a thousand copies by the start of the new century. Petrarch and Salutati were proud to have gathered libraries of a few hundred titles, but private collectors of the early sixteenth century acquired many thousands of volumes. Philosophy's fortunes rose on this flood of new information: print stabilized and broadcast the resurrected classics; the despised scholastics found a place in the new medium alongside the ancients; contemporary philosophers like Ficino saw their fame magnified in their own lifetimes; and forgotten thinkers like Sextus Empiricus enjoyed revivals quicker and broader than anything that could have happened in the age of manuscripts. Scholars looked more widely and deeply into the world of learning. The eclectic curiosity so characteristic of the sixteenth century fed on growing libraries. But eclecticism threatened orthodoxy; information bred contradiction; print nourished philology, and (with apologies to a great French playwright) philology led to crime. Books spread confusion as they enlarged communication, and print was a wonderful vehicle of controversy. By modern standards, early modern polemic was scarcely instantaneous, but it had grown wings since the era of pen and paper—as witness the broadsheets and pamphlets of the early Reformation. Philosophers also spoke louder through the new instruments of the press, but the same tools of discourse amplified the ancient risks of their trade.

One philosopher who suffered official censure was Giambattista Della Porta, whose Academy of the Secrets of Nature, established in Naples around 1560, failed when the Inquisition accused him of sorcery. Later he joined Galileo in the more successful Lincean Academy, founded in 1603.[50] These aca-

---

[50] Paparelli (1955); Badaloni (1959–60); Clubb (1965); Muraro (1978).

demies were the forerunners of the Royal Society in Britain, the Académie des Sciences in France, and the American Philosophical Society, all dedicated to the advancement and diffusion of knowledge. When the ancestors of the early learned societies first appeared in France and Italy, mainly in the sixteenth century, their objectives were sometimes narrower but their constituencies were usually diverse. Philosophy in the larger sense was one subject cultivated among others in the academies, whose members were often fond of the practical side of astrology and alchemy; but some important philosophers also used the new organizations to their benefit. Giovanni Pontano, vigorous as a patron of letters in Naples until his death in 1503, founded the Accademia Pontaniana, where he pursued his own philosophical studies and also assisted Agostino Nifo, a celebrated university philosopher of his day. One of the most venturesome minds of the later sixteenth century, Bernardino Telesio, supported another academy in southern Italy, the Accademia Consentina. By the middle years of that century, such institutional alternatives to the university were available as broader platforms for philosophy than the Middle Ages had known.

A few remarkably independent spirits worked with even less formal support. If the medieval centuries had their wandering scholars, the sixteenth had Giordano Bruno, a peripatetic only in the etymological sense of the term. In the course of his stormy life, Bruno talked philosophy with professors, princes, and academicians, and he also worked independently, roaming all over Europe until disaster overtook him. Bruno's philosophical influence was great, especially on the demise of Aristotelianism, yet his fame as a victim of repression became even greater. Bruno was one of audacity's noblemen, a rash artist of the idiosyncratic; but of all the autonomous voices of Renaissance philosophy, the clearest were Machiavelli's and Montaigne's. Employed as a diplomat in republican Florence, Machiavelli theorized about his trade in several volumes of history and political theory, but it was *The Prince*, written in 1513, that outraged Christendom by setting reasons of state above other reasons, including the religious, that should guide the conduct of a statesman endowed with *virtù*. Montaigne's was a softer voice than Machiavelli's but no less threatening to the orthodoxies of his day. In the countryside near Bordeaux, this learned and provocative genius withdrew to his tower to write some of the most original and readable philosophy of any age, a charming dose of sceptical introspection that helped corrode the convictions of readers seduced by his prose, experience, and erudition. Campanella produced equally original work in the less idyllic ambience of his several prisons. Coming to intellectual maturity as the grip of the Roman Inquisition grew to its tightest, he imprudently revealed a subversive, messianic vision for Christendom that terrified the authorities and kept him jailed for more than thirty years; but he put his miseries to good use, passing the days constructing a massive and intricate system that challenged Aristotelian orthodoxy ingeniously.

During the Renaissance, philosophy spoke to a broader public than it had known in the Middle Ages, not only by reaching beyond the walls of the university but also by expanding its role as the key element in a global structure of knowledge descending from the *enkuklios paideia* (general education) of ancient Greece and culminating in the great encyclopedic schemes of Comenius and Alsted in the seventeenth century and of Diderot's *Encyclopédie* in the eighteenth century.[51] Compared with the late twentieth-century discipline, Renaissance philosophy was less isolated as an academic specialty; it had more live channels connecting it in both directions to other disciplines; it was a functional basis and an active concomitant of all fields of learning. In the development of theory, in the regulation of practice, and in the education of professionals and laypersons, philosophers sustained lively conversations affecting physical science, medicine, law, magic, astrology, poetry, theology, history, and other areas as well. Ficino justified his astrological medicine by connecting it with the cosmology and matter theory that he found in prominent ancient and medieval philosophers. The competing theologies of Francisco Suárez and Richard Hooker both looked back to the metaphy-

[51] Marrou (1956: 176–7, 211, 220, 223, 281); Vasoli (1978); below, Ch. 6, nn. 6, 20.

sical heritage of the Middle Ages. Galileo's mechanics and Harvey's biology were daring novelties that owed something to the Peripatetic tradition, which generally met a less happy fate in the Scientific Revolution. The elder Scaliger found Aristotelian categories to suit his linguistic and poetic innovations, while Patrizi tried to formulate an alternative poetics in Platonic terms. Thus, long before the powerful Anglo-American tradition of the twentieth century clipped philosophy's ties with other fields, the Renaissance had tried to multiply and fortify the links among disciplines established in still earlier periods. Its eclectic curiosity makes Renaissance philosophy an unwieldy object of study, but a fascinating one, attractive enough—one hopes—to sustain the reader's interest despite the atomizing instincts of our more compartmentalized culture.

We might organize our inquiry into Renaissance philosophy in any of a number of ways; we might find a pattern, for example, in the divisions of philosophy or the rhythms of early modern politics or the differences among major personalities or the changing map of European geography and culture. But in the central part of this volume our principle of organization will be the ancient philosophical traditions that the Renaissance revived, broad categories that will expose continuities and modifications over a period of several hundred years. Any approach must have its defects, and this one will say more about larger issues—such as the differences between Aristotelianism and Platonism—than about smaller questions addressed by individual philosophers. Since eclecticism and creativity were such prominent items in the philosophical repertory of the period, the reader should keep this shortcoming in mind and remember that our treatment will not do justice to the contributions of many important and original thinkers.

Aristotelianism

Renaissance Aristotelianisms

For many students of pre-Cartesian thought, the words 'scho-lasticism' and 'Aristotelianism' have evoked visions of a sterile, derivative, and monolithic system obsessed with logic-chopping and leading its abstracted victims on a bookish hunt for the irrelevant.[1] Erasmus, Rabelais, and other humanist critics im-mortalized the depression, enervation, and terror that they suffered in interminable bouts of indoctrination into a subject-matter that they found impoverished and insipid, thus moving Descartes and his contemporaries to turn their backs on school philosophy and to revile Peripateticism as false, ridiculous, and redundant. Descartes thanked his teachers for 'the fact that everything they taught me was quite doubtful; . . . [other-wise] I might have been content with the smattering of reason which I found in it.'[2] To confirm such sour memories, we have more than enough evidence of bad, dull, doctrinaire perform-ance in early modern classrooms. Allowing for a natural urge in students of any period to resist the formal requirements of systems to which they are introduced, one none the less hears an insistent note in the chorus of complaint about the lifeless-ness of the late scholastic curriculum, its stony deafness to the prospect that philosophy might answer pragmatic human ques-tions. For those who despised scholasticism as a labyrinth of dreary trivialities, the contrast with humanist engagement in moral and political debate lowered the reputation of the

---

[1] For a recent analysis of Aristotelianism in the Renaissance, see Schmitt (1983a); see also the pioneering works of Kristeller, esp. (1961a: 24–47, 92–119; 1965c); and Garin (1947–50); Randall (1961); Düring (1968); Poppi (1970a); Grant (1978); above, Ch. 1, nn. 4, 7.

[2] Descartes (1985: ii. 411 [Murdoch and Stoothoff trans.]).

schools all the more, even though humanism left its own miasma of mind-numbing pedantry.

Humanist rhetoric spoke more persuasively than scholastic dialectic to Europe's bustling commonwealth of letters, so the mockery of an Erasmus or a Rabelais weighed deeper in modern memory than the achievements of scores of Aristotelians from Alessandro Achillini to Marcantonio Zimara, leading philosophers of the Renaissance who rated no entries when the *Encyclopedia of Philosophy* appeared in 1967. Although the humanist burlesque of the Peripatetics had a basis in fact, the picture they painted was by no means fair or complete; like all caricature it obscured the complexity and diversity of its victims. Possession of a common set of texts and deference to a single system enabled Peripatetic philosophers to talk coherently to one another, but their doctrinal unity was sometimes weak and their mutual allegiances superficial. No list of leading Renaissance Aristotelians longer than four or five names will guarantee a harmony much deeper than the habit of beginning philosophical investigation with Peripatetic texts or principles or problems. Consider these eminent names: Paul of Venice, Leonardo Bruni, George of Trebizond, Lefèvre d'Étaples, John Mair, Pietro Pomponazzi, Francisco de Vitoria, Joachim Périon, Jacopo Zabarella, John Case, Giulio Pace, and William Harvey. All were major actors in the development of Aristotelian thought, but their Aristotelianisms were, at the least, different from one another and, in some cases, antagonistic. Some disparities among disciples of the Stagirite reflected strong commitments by contemporaries or near contemporaries to incompatible methods — Pomponazzi and Périon, for example, who were only a generation apart; Périon meant his Ciceronian translations of Aristotle to displace the crabbed Latin that Pomponazzi found indispensable. Other differences emerged over longer spans of time. Paul of Venice, born around 1369, anchors one end of the list above to the great scholastic syntheses of the high Middle Ages; at the other end, William Harvey, who lived until 1657, connects the Aristotelian tradition with the birth of modern science.

Some Aristotelians were deeply immersed in natural philosophy as a demonstrative science, while others avoided scientific problems and followed the humanists toward ethics and politics as openings to the *vita activa*. Some saw their job as helping students understand precisely what Aristotle had discovered and codified; others took a broader view, finding useful signposts in Aristotle's works but admitting the Philosopher's deficiencies and supplementing his teachings with more reliable and more recent information. Of hundreds of thinkers who taught and wrote as Aristotelians between 1400 and 1600, few left any trace of real individual genius, and most marched on like good soldiers in an army battling for the one great truth; but the results of their struggles were far from homogeneous. The emergence of a wide variety of Renaissance Aristotelianisms can be explained from various perspectives.[3] Looking at the Peripatetic system from the inside, for example, it was inevitable that ambiguities or even contradictions in doctrine and interpretation would surface after centuries of scrutinizing the same range of texts. From an external point of view, it was natural that new cultural conditions in early modern times would raise questions not treated in the extant Aristotelian Corpus or its commentary tradition, thus stimulating new attitudes and interpretations even among philosophers who remained Aristotelian in some strong sense of the term. In the latter part of this chapter, the reader will meet eight Renaissance philosophers—Bruni, Trapezuntius, Lefèvre, Mair, Pomponazzi, Vitoria, Zabarella, and Case—who expressed their esteem for Aristotle in quite different ways; but first it may be useful to take a broader look at the rich tradition that such thinkers represented.

Unity and diversity in the Aristotelian tradition

The Aristotelian philosophy that passed from the Middle Ages to the Renaissance was a well-defined and clearly organized

[3] Petersen (1921); Ritter (1921–2); Garin (1937*b*; 1939; 1947–50); Kristeller (1961*a*: 24–47; 1965*c*; 1985*e*: 209–16; 1990*a*: 102–18); Rokita (1971); Margolin (1974); Schmitt (1981: ch. 6; 1983*a*; 1983*b*; 1984; 1987). For Achillini, see Münster (1953); Matsen (1968; 1974; 1975); Zambelli (1978); for Zimara, see Nardi (1958: 321–63); Poppi (1966: 237–56); Antonaci (1971–8).

system forged in the universities at a time when intellectual confidence ran strong. When critics spotted weakness or inconsistency, the schoolmen responded vigorously with new solutions and ingenious arguments, so that by the second half of the fourteenth century many internal problems had found answers more convincing to medieval thinkers than those provided by the Philosopher himself. From a twentieth-century perspective, logic is surely the leading case of a major division of philosophy in which medieval Aristotelians made great advances on the original Corpus. Peter of Spain's *Summulae logicales*, a thirteenth-century beginner's text that still dominated the introductory arts curriculum in the first decades of the sixteenth century, was meant to teach logic to boys, but it handled the problem of quantification better than any part of the *Organon*. Technical progress of this sort has endeared medieval logicians to their counterparts of the post-Frege period, but from an internal point of view the crowning triumph of scholasticism was, of course, the Christianization of the Peripatetic tradition.[4] Aquinas, the greatest scholastic, was no great logician, but his philosophical theology put the pagan Aristotle at the service of the church, an inestimable boon to a culture that badly needed to recover and purify the wisdom of its heathen past. Medieval Aristotelians also improved the state of natural philosophy. To cite but one example, Aristotle's implausible treatment of projectile motion gave way to a new analysis whose clarity and conformity to common experience improved greatly on the position of the *Physics* and pointed toward later progress in mechanics in the seventeenth century. Paris and Oxford masters of the fourteenth century also proposed new ways of handling those problems of physical

[4] For medieval and post-medieval logic and method, see Prantl (1855–70); Crombie (1953); Howell (1956); Vasoli (1958b; 1959; 1968a; 1983a; 1984a); Gilbert (1960); Kneale and Kneale (1962: 189–320); Risse (1964); Wightman (1964; 1973); Crescini (1965; 1972); Ashworth (1974; 1982; 1985; 1986; 1988); Michaud-Quantin (1969); Schüling (1969); Bochenski (1970); Wallace (1972–4; 1981b); Edwards (1976); Dumutriu (1977: vol. ii); Nuchelmans (1980); *CHLMP*: 101–381, 787–822); Schmitt (1983a: 21–2); Broadie (1985; 1987); Giard (1985); Jardine (1974b; 1977; 1981; 1982; 1983; 1988); Stump (1989).

quantity to which Aristotle's aversion was notorious.[5] Thus, as Aristotelianism reigned supreme in the universities and spread to the furthest corners of Europe in the years after the Black Death, it was still a growing organism whose coherence permitted change. The system remained flexible in the early fifteenth century, when the novelties of Renaissance culture required Peripatetics to let their beliefs and practices evolve even further.

A particularly lively source of new energies and troubling challenges was humanism, whose influence (despite the common view that all humanists abandoned Aristotle in favour of Plato) on the character of Aristotelianism in our period was enormous. On the assumption that the age of an idea was an index of its value, the humanists elevated antiquity itself—all of it—to a position of cultural superiority. Thus, although Plato was new and hence fashionable in many quarters, there was no exclusive commitment in humanist methodology or ideology to him or to any other ancient philosopher. Humanists with philosophical interests took Sceptical and Stoic as well as Platonist and Aristotelian positions. And since Aristotle's works were so numerous and influential, humanists from the early fifteenth century onward devoted considerable time and energy to making Aristotelian texts clearer, more precise, and more readable. Especially important were their efforts to produce better Latin translations of Aristotle and his ancient commentators. Leonardo Bruni began to classicize Aristotle in the fifteenth century, and the labour continued as a central task of humanism until after the time of Giulio Pace, who revised Isaac Casaubon's complete edition of Aristotle in 1597. During the two intervening centuries, scholars spilled much ink in debating how or whether Aristotle should be made to speak better Latin. Some wanted a Latin Aristotle who closely mimicked Cicero, widely regarded as the supreme exemplar of Roman eloquence. Others, valuing medieval terms and concepts as philosophical advances over the remains of antiquity, saw more utility in the language of scholasticism. By the end

[5] Weisheipl (1971); Grant (1971: 36–59); Wallace (1972–4: 27–139; 1978); M. Mahoney (1978); Brown (1978); Murdoch and Sylla (1978); *CHLMP*: 521–91.

of the sixteenth century, a compromise had evolved, applying new philological resources to traditional philosophical needs in an attempt to render the text of Aristotle in a Latin faithful to the Greek original, mindful of its own ancient usage but still attentive to philosophical requirements. Many translations meant for philosophical use were not written as free-standing texts to be read independently; they were designed to accompany a facing page of Greek, as in a modern Loeb volume. The publication of parallel texts, in the context of broader improvements in the study of Greek, made it easier to penetrate the meaning of Aristotle's sometimes enigmatic language and to place obscure passages more meaningfully in their larger textual surroundings. What one means by 'the genuine thought of Aristotle' remains evasive and always disputable, but the humanists helped philosophy get nearer this blessed state in the Renaissance.[6]

In the course of the sixteenth century, the humanist approach to Aristotle gradually merged with traditional scholastic methods, though fusion never removed all stresses between the two. Tensions had been stronger in the fifteenth century, however, when the few humanists who had any role in universities rarely worked as professors of philosophy. But humanists eventually gained firmer footholds in the universities. In 1497 the University of Padua established a chair for the teaching of Aristotle in Greek, though only a handful of students could take advantage of the opportunity at this early date. Fifty years later, philosophical instruction in Greek became more effective in several places, most notably the Collège Royal of Paris. Publishers in the scholastic citadel of Paris printed many Greek editions of Aristotle at low cost for use by students, whose notes often fill the margins and flyleaves of surviving copies of these Renaissance versions of the academic paperback. More advanced Aristotelian studies published in Paris in the early decades of printing also show the mark of humanism and its new Greek expertise; as the new fashion spread, even

[6] Garin (1947–50); Schmitt (1983*a*: 64–88); Hankins in Bruni (1987: 197–212); Copenhaver (1988*b*).

conventional commentators in Italy of the later sixteenth century sprinkled their treatises with Greek phrases and philological notes, though some of their colleagues insisted on philosophizing in a thoroughly medieval style. Some lectured on nothing written after the fourteenth century and used no humanist text or technique. Humanism did not win all its fights with scholasticism in the Renaissance, and among philosophers there was no complete and systematic resolution of the continuing contest between the two movements.

Almost all that we now have of the Aristotelian Corpus was available by the close of the thirteenth century, but by the early fifteenth century the humanist search for ancient texts had turned up two important and previously little-known works bearing the Philosopher's name—the *Mechanics* and the *Poetics*. Both these short treatises were copied in 1457 for Cardinal Bessarion in an important Greek manuscript that was to help shape the printed tradition of Aristotle's non-logical works. Most modern critics believe that the *Mechanics* (or *Mechanical Questions*) is spurious, composed in all probability by one of the master's disciples soon after his death. It is unique among works attributed to Aristotle because it focuses on simple machines, thus providing a rare look at ancient thinking about pulleys, gears, levers, and other devices that produce mechanical advantage. In fact, the *Mechanics* is one of the most advanced treatments of technology to have survived antiquity, but there is no good evidence of its being known in the West before a Greek manuscript appeared in Italy in the early fifteenth century. For nearly a hundred years thereafter, its main readers were humanist scribes and scholars who had little interest in its contents, but at the turn of the sixteenth century, around the time of its first Greek printing in the Aldine edition of Aristotle (1495–8), researchers began to look at the *Mechanics* more closely, creating demand for improved editions, Latin translations, vernacular versions, and commentaries that made the work more widely available; Niccolò Leonico Tomeo's Latin version of 1525 was especially influential, though it came eight years after the first Latin *Mechanics* by Vittore Fausto. Inside and outside the universities, mathematicians and engineers began to study it and apply it to various theoretical and practical problems. At the University of Padua from 1548 to 1610, professors of mathematics lectured on the *Mechanics*. The last in this line was Galileo Galilei, who taught at Padua from 1592 to 1610. His commentary on the *Mechanics* has been lost, but the imprint of this ancient treatise is visible in the great scientist's work during one of his most productive periods. Galileo's new physics far surpassed the state of the field expressed in the *Mechanics*, but, despite his scorn for things Aristotelian, he found this ancient work useful, referred to it frequently, and drew fruitful ideas from it. Galileo was not alone in admiring the *Mechanics*; many other authorities on mechanics and applied mathematics used it as well.[7]

No work of Aristotle's is more unlike the *Mechanics* than the *Poetics*, which entered Europe's consciousness at about the same time and with even more dramatic effect. Little known in the Middle Ages, when only a paraphrase by Averroes supplemented the few manuscripts of a translation by William of Moerbeke, this genuine fragment of Aristotle's original began to excite interest by the middle of the fifteenth century, even though it was not published until 1508 in the Aldine edition of the *Greek Rhetoricians*. Lorenzo Valla (possibly), Angelo Poliziano, and Ermolao Barbaro knew the *Poetics* before Giorgio Valla made his defective Latin translation in 1498, superseded in 1536 by the version of Alessandro Pazzi. Once accessible, its impact was extraordinary. Even in its partial state, the *Poetics* was the most comprehensive work on literary theory and criticism surviving from the classical period, and it soon came to dominate literary discussion. Since the *Poetics* bears the stamp of Aristotle's authority, it is unsurprising that modern critics regard its reappearance as a key event in the development of literary theory during the Renaissance and no wonder that it eventually surpassed the *Ars poetica* of Horace and ruled the field until Coleridge and the Romantics. Early modern scholars commented on the *Poetics* frequently and at

[7] Rose and Drake (1971); De Bellis (1975; 1980); Geanakoplos (1989: 114–29); Schmitt (1981: chs. 5, 12). For Galileo, see Gilbert (1963); Koyré (1966a); Drake (1976; 1981); Jardine (1976); Wallace (1981a; 1981b; 1984).

length, but only in the second half of the sixteenth century did they gradually dislodge it from the critical framework constructed by Horace, and they continued to read both works on poetics as if their aims were rhetorical. Although its subject-matter has not been a favourite of philosophers, the *Poetics* approaches issues of literary structure, genre, and quality with the standard tools of Aristotle's logic, metaphysics, and psychology. Along with the *Rhetoric*, with which publishers and interpreters often linked it, the *Poetics* naturally enjoyed great influence among thinkers of a humanist disposition, and it also attracted attention in the universities.[8]

The recovery of the *Mechanics* and the *Poetics* shows the range and vitality of Aristotelian thought in the Renaissance, when natural philosophers who prepared the way for the Scientific Revolution and humanists who reshaped Europe's habits of expression both felt the effects of new material from the ancient Stagirite, who had long towered over the medieval schools. Equally important for the continued growth of the Peripatetic synthesis was the recovery and diffusion of the Greek commentaries on Aristotle.[9] These treatises, about ten times longer than the works they discuss, were written by pagans and Christians, Platonists and Peripatetics in late antiquity, between the second and seventh centuries in the Greek world of the Eastern Mediterranean, and then again in twelfth-century Byzantium. The most important of the two dozen commentators were Alexander of Aphrodisias, Ammonius, Simplicius, Themistius, and John Philoponus. Of these five, only Alexander and Themistius were Aristotelians; the others, like most of the larger group of commentators, were Neoplatonists, and whether they were pagan or Christian, they saw Aristotle's philosophy as preliminary to a higher spiritual wisdom. Thus, long before James of Venice could visit the last of

[8] Weinberg (1961: 349–423, 474–7, 559–63, 632–4); Tigerstedt (1968); Boggess (1970); Garin (1983b: 16–19); Monfasani (1983b: 184–5); Vickers (1988b: 715–24).

[9] For the texts of the commentators, see Diels (1981); see also Cranz (1958; 1987); Nardi, (1958: 365–442); Lohr (1974; 1975–80); Buck and Herding (1975); Mahoney (1982b: 169–73); Schmitt (1983a: 23–5, 49–52, 92–3; 1984: ch. 6); Grafton (1988b: 776, 785–6, 790–1); Sorabji (1990: 1–30).

the commentators, Michael of Ephesus, in twelfth-century Byzantium, Neoplatonic students of Aristotle had already adapted his philosophy to religious purposes. Philoponus, the first Christian commentator, developed a creationist cosmology and wrote a tract *Against Proclus on the Eternity of the World* in 529; the last pagan commentator was Olympiodorus, who died in the last third of the sixth century. Earlier in the same century, Boethius had begun to transmit the commentary literature to the Latin West. Medieval scholars knew some commentaries, a few in Latin translation, but more from allusions, fragments, and summaries in the writings of Averroes and other Muslim philosophers. The ancient commentators enjoyed a fuller knowledge of classical Greek thought than any medieval writer could command, including access to lost works that could be reintegrated into philosophical discourse once the commentaries were recovered in the Renaissance. It was particularly significant that the commentators knew the objections raised in antiquity to Aristotle's positions on a number of topics. Their recovery, publication, and translation took some time, but almost all circulated in Greek and Latin by the 1530s. They do not cover all of Aristotle, but several treat such key texts as the *Organon*, the *Physics*, and *De anima*, thus making them useful ammunition in such controversies as the immortality dispute provoked by Pietro Pomponazzi and his colleagues.

Through the first two-thirds of the fifteenth century, Pomponazzi's predecessors at Padua seem not to have used the ancient commentators, but philosophers of the next generations—most notably Nicoletto Vernia and Agostino Nifo— began to consult them in new translations by Ermolao Barbaro and others. Barbaro's charge that Averroes had lifted his doctrines on the soul from the commentators surely helped excite interest in them. Vernia and Nifo both called on the commentators along with Neoplatonic and medieval sources when they joined the great debate on personal immortality and the unity of the intellect that had been under way since the Latin Averroes had first become available in the West. Until 1492 Vernia took Averroist positions on the human soul's relation

to the body, its individuality, and its immortality, but in that
year he composed an attack on Averroes, not printed until
1504, which was influenced not only by Albertus and by Plato
and Plotinus in Ficino's translations but also by Alexander,
Themistius, and Simplicius. Themistius helped persuade Vernia
that each person has an illuminated intellect that lives on after
the body dies, and Vernia maintained that Simplicius agreed
with Themistius in rejecting the unity of the intellect. Nifo,
who was Vernia's student, also used Plotinus in Ficino's version as well as the latter's commentary on the *Enneads*, but he
reached a conclusion at odds with his teacher's understanding
of Simplicius and Themistius, insisting that they had regarded
all humans as sharing a single intellect, but allowing that
Ammonius, Plotinus, Proclus, and other Platonists upheld
Christian doctrine on the plurality of souls. Sixteenth-century
philosophers in Zabarella's time and beyond also referred to
Themistius, Simplicius, and other commentators on these and
related points.[10]

Philoponus, a monophysite Christian in religion but a Neoplatonist in philosophy who lived in sixth-century Alexandria,
was another major commentator of great influence in the Renaissance. Like others of the Neoplatonic school, he looked to
Aristotle's works on logic and natural philosophy to compen-
sate for thin treatment of these subjects in Plato's dialogues.
Although he took his lead from Aristotle on these topics, he
felt free, as a Christian Neoplatonist, to register his firm disagreement with Aristotelian dogma on particular issues, such
as the eternity of the world. In Book IV of his *Physics*, Aristotle had argued forcefully against the possibility of a void or
empty space in nature. He maintained, for example, that objects falling in a void would all move at the same infinite
velocity if they met no resistance. Drawing upon earlier critics,
Philoponus saw defects in Aristotle's view, and he made good
use of experience and common sense to reach the conclusion
that the identical velocity at which all bodies would move in a
void must be finite, not infinite. After Philoponus' commentary

[10] Branca (1973; 1980); Mahoney (1982*b*: 169–73; 1986: 511–24).

on the *Physics* was published in 1535, his clever criticisms added fuel to the fire that eventually consumed Peripatetic natural philosophy. From medieval times onward, even loyal Aristotelians had questioned the master's judgement on one issue or another, and the accumulation of doubts and differences helped prepare the eventual downfall of the system. When the Renaissance recovered Philoponus, it created new access to a work of Aristotelian explication which hastened Aristotle's demise. Between 1504 and 1583, Latin and (in most cases) Greek texts of his commentaries on the *Posterior Analytics*, *Categories*, *Metaphysics*, *Physics*, *On the Soul*, *Meteorology*, *On Generation and Corruption*, and *Generation of Animals* appeared in print. Gianfrancesco Pico della Mirandola was the first to take full cognizance of Philoponus against Aristotle on place and the void in his *Examen vanitatis doctrinae* of 1520. By the last decade of the sixteenth century, Galileo had raised even more searching questions about Aristotelian physics, and a few years later he exposed fatal weaknesses in traditional natural philosophy, which he proposed to replace with his own new science. The criticisms of Aristotle in Galileo's early treatise *On Motion* include reference to the commentary of Philoponus.[11]

From Philoponus, Simplicius, Themistius, and the other ancient commentators it is evident that the Renaissance did not need to invent variation and disagreement among expositors of Aristotle. Indeed, such differences emerged with his earliest successors, Theophrastus and Strato, before wider cleavages in the structure of Peripatetic thought appeared in the Middle Ages. Peter Abelard and other masters of the *logica vetus* (old logic) debated nominalism and realism in the twelfth century. A later phase of the same controversy occupied scholastics of the fourteenth century, by which time followers of such influential doctors as Albertus Magnus, Thomas Aquinas, and Duns Scotus had taken well-defined and contrary positions that made them Albertist or Thomist or Scotist on various topics. In Paris, Cologne, Prague, and other centres, battles

---

[11] Schmitt (1983*a*: 25, 41, 49, 92–3, 162, 171; 1981: chs. 7, 8, 12; 1989: ch. 8); Mahoney (1982*b*); Sorabji (1987: 1–40). For Galileo, see above, n. 7.

over points of logic and metaphysics were particularly strenuous, and contending forces almost always deployed themselves
along institutional lines. If Dominicans were loyal to Thomas,
Franciscans backed the Scotist cause. The University of Padua
established separate Thomist and Scotist chairs in metaphysics
and theology, both of them occupied by prominent philosophers and theologians who involved themselves in wider struggles, including the religious rivalries of the Reformation. And
Padua was not the only place where the same university gave
official sanction to rival versions of Aristotle. Similar intellectual and organizational conflicts continued throughout our
period and beyond, so that seventeenth-century publishers still
found a good market for philosophical textbooks *ad mentem
Thomae* (according to Thomas) or *ad mentem Scoti* (according
to Scotus).

Another medieval distinction that made a difference in early
modern times was the contrast between the theological leanings
of philosophers in Northern Europe and the scientific bent of
Italian professors, a divergence traceable to famous disputes in
the thirteenth century between naturalist Aristotelians of the
Paris arts faculty and their conservative opponents in the theology faculty, culminating in the contest between Siger of
Brabant and Thomas Aquinas that led to the condemnation of
1277. As early as 1210, many works of Aristotle himself had
been forbidden, yet their suppression stimulated even more
troublesome analyses of physical problems unrestrained by the
usual Aristotelian conventions of inquiry.[12] Man's competing
obligations to God and nature excited the academic imagination throughout the early modern period and beyond, as new
social and intellectual conditions enriched the mix of philosophical motivations. Continuing friction in Renaissance Aristotelianism between theological and scientific interests does not
prove that Italy harboured a sect of atheist Aristotelians. It is
true, however, that some philosophers read Aristotle for scientific or secular reasons, with no direct interest in religious or
theological questions. While it is hard to make windows into

[12] Above, Ch. 1, n. 7.

souls, cultural circumstances prevailing in Italy before and after the Reformation suggest that most secular Aristotelians were pious Christians who simply had no reason to connect their piety with philosophy. They were paid to teach logic and natural philosophy as gateways to medicine, so they saw no strong bond between professional duty and personal spirituality. The very fact that professional life could distance private devotion from profane duty was, of course, a further inducement to secularization.[13] In philosophy, one of the consequences is that we know little of what Italian secular Aristotelians thought about theology, which is not true of our information on Peripatetic philosophy in Catholic Spain or Protestant Germany.

Consider three close contemporaries: an Italian, Cesare Cremonini (1550–1631), a Spaniard, Francisco Suárez (1548–1617), and a German, Bartholomew Keckermann (1571–1609).[14] All wrote copiously on many subjects, and all were professors of Aristotelian philosophy. Only Cremonini treated philosophy as a purely secular calling, making it clear that his task in the university began and ended with the explication of Aristotle. His large philosophical output (accompanied by a good deal of poetry and many ceremonial speeches) included commentaries, lectures, and other works meant to interpret Aristotle on a purely natural level. His naturalism attracted the attention of the Inquisition in the latter part of his career, all of which he spent at Ferrara and Padua. Cremonini applied philosophy to the natural cosmos in which humans live and left it at that, but the famous Jesuit Suárez went on to lead philosophy through the portals of theology to higher inquiries about the world of divinity. Thus, like many medieval doctors, Suárez

[13] Renan (1882); Charbonnel (1919); Nardi (1945; 1958); Kristeller (1961a: 24–47; 1968a; 1979a; 1985e: 135–46, 209–16; 1990a: 111–18); *Aristotelismo padovano* (1960); Randall (1961; 1968; 1976); Gilbert (1963); Di Napoli (1963); Poppi (1964; 1966; 1970a; 1983); Edwards (1967); Mahoney (1974); *Convegno . . . l'Averroismo* (1979); Schmitt (1983a: 25–33).
[14] Mabilleau (1881); Werner (1889); Van Zuylen (1934); Copleston (1960–6: iii. 353–405); Dibon (1954–); Gilbert (1960: 213–20); Seigfried (1967); Del Torre (1968); Andrés (1976–7); L. Kennedy (1979; 1980); *Simposio F. Suárez* (1980); Olivieri (1983: 637–59); Vasoli (1983a; 1984a); Muller (1984); Schmitt (1984: ch. 11); Lohr (1988: 609–18, 632–8).

kept philosophy subservient to theology in his many volumes, one of which was an extremely influential treatise on metaphysics. Although he lived a few years in Rome, mainly at the Collegio Romano, he spent most of his life in universities of Spain or Portugal. Like Suárez, the Lutheran Keckermann also used philosophy as a means to theological ends, but in a Protestant context. His confessional commitment made him a very popular interpreter of Aristotle in the Protestant countries of Northern Europe, where he taught at Heidelberg and Gdansk for many years. Neither the tension between religious and secular aims nor the hostility between Catholic and Protestant factions prevented Keckermann, Suárez, Cremonini, and their many colleagues from using Aristotle, along with other pagan thinkers, for a multitude of philosophical ends, and each religious party or ideological disposition produced its share of prominent Peripatetics.

In 1517, the year that started his epochal break with Rome, Martin Luther exulted that 'our theology and St. Augustine are progressing well, and . . . rule at our university. Aristotle is gradually falling from his throne, and his final doom is only a matter of time.'[15] Yet Melanchthon and other followers of Luther soon found that they could not see far without the Stagirite as they worked to fashion a reliable programme of education for the new faithful. After the Reformation, the Aristotelianism that survived and then prospered in Protestant lands was as strong or perhaps stronger than the Peripatetic tradition sustained in some Catholic regions. All the reformed universities, whether new foundations or renovations of previously popish institutions, looked steadfastly to Aristotle to show them the way in philosophy. In the course of the sixteenth century, Germany saw Freiburg and Cologne remain loyal to the old religion, as Tübingen and Wittenberg turned to the new faith, while Würzburg founded a Catholic university and Jena established a Protestant institution. Old or new, Romish or reformed, all kept Aristotle at the centre of philosophical studies, which is not to say that these universities were totally

---

[15] Luther (1958– : xlviii. 42); Rupp (1964: 46).

Aristotelian. At Tübingen in the 1570s and 1580s, for example, Platonizing members of the arts faculty may have inspired the young Kepler, but Protestant scholars in sixteenth-century universities rarely had to face temptations that might cause them to stray from the Peripatetic way, and the same was true for Catholic students. From the Collegio Romano, their headquarters in the ancient capital of Christendom, the Jesuits marshalled a stunningly effective campaign of educational reform whose philosophical armoury was aggressively Aristotelian. In the struggle against heresy another Peripatetic headquarters was the School of Salamanca, which nurtured Suárez and other heroes of the Counter-Reformation. Distant as they were from Paris, both Salamanca and the Collegio Romano grew in the long shadow of its ancient university, which had been the great bulwark of Aristotelianism since the age of Abelard and whose enduring intellectual might in the century of Calvin and Bruno continued to bolster the Peripatetic tradition.

Both Protestants and Catholics admired that tradition because its scope and coherence flattered their conviction that truth was one and theirs alone; but the eclectic reality of Renaissance Aristotelianism stymied the wish for a single, exclusive route to doctrinal conviction. As applied to early modern philosophy, the adjectives 'Peripatetic' and 'Aristotelian' cover a multitude of sins against dogmatic consensus. If an Aristotelian is someone who accepts the Stagirite's teaching at each and every point, there were no Aristotelians in the Renaissance—or in the Middle Ages, for that matter. Even Aristotle's most avid disciples differed with him on some issues. Those less devoted to him naturally took even more liberties when they found his views convincingly challenged by other philosophers—classical or contemporary—by personal experience or by the dictates of reason. Given the enormous impact on early modern Europe of broader access to the full range of ancient philosophical opinion, one must take special note of the variety of efforts to amalgamate Aristotle with the other philosophical riches newly mined from antiquity. When Renaissance thinkers blended Aristotelian ideas with these other materials, they produced alloys of as many kinds as there were philosophers newly equipped with the tools of humanism to prospect for inspiration, matter, or method among the ancient ruins. What they fashioned was a spectrum of eclectic Aristotelianisms. Some Renaissance philosophers who admired Aristotle also took up Platonic or Stoic positions at crucial points, as Philoponus had done a millennium before, and few of their peers regarded such eclecticism as anything but normal. On many issues Aristotle seemed the best guide, but for other questions the wiser answer might be found in Plato, Cicero, Albertus, Aquinas, Scotus, or Averroes. Even beliefs as disreputable to modern eyes as magic and astrology attracted Renaissance philosophers such as Nifo, Achillini, and Pomponazzi whose orientation was predominantly Aristotelian, despite the fact that the textual basis in the Aristotelian Corpus for such ideas is slim. The fifteenth and sixteenth centuries abounded in unorthodox thinkers, some of whom can be called Aristotelians only in the loosest sense. None was as influential as Thomas or Scotus, none as daring as Descartes or Bacon, few as gifted as Machiavelli or Montaigne, but some contributed new ideas on a humbler scale that echo some of the dominant themes of the Renaissance and anticipate the bolder novelties of the seventeenth century.

Eight Renaissance Aristotelians

Leonardo Bruni was born in Arezzo in 1370, when Petrarch was still alive, but while still a young man he came to Florence, the great city that shaped his destiny and in whose church of Santa Croce he has lain since 1444, in a fine marble tomb that expressed the life of its occupant by becoming a model of its kind.[16] His early education followed the standard medieval

[16] Bruni (1969) is a reprint of Baron's 1928 edn. of the 'humanistic-philosophical' works; Bruni (1987) contains introductions to translations of many of the most important texts and a full bibliography; the letters are in Bruni (1741). For secondary literature, see Troilo (1931–2); Soudek (1958; 1968; 1976); Garin (1961*a*: 3–37; 1965*a*: 33–43; 1972: 1–29); Baron (1966; 1968*a*; 1968*b*); Goldbrunner (1968); Harth (1968); Seigel (1968: 89–169); Cochrane (1981: 3–9, 15–33); Gerl (1981); Fryde (1983: 3–53); Schmitt (1983*a*: 16–17,

pattern, but after moving to Florence he came under the influence of Coluccio Salutati, the city's humanist chancellor, and of Manuel Chrysoloras, the Byzantine scholar from whom Renaissance Italy's first generation of Hellenists learned their Greek. Encouraged by Salutati's circle, he applied himself to translating a number of Greek works, including Plato's *Phaedo* in 1405, the *Apology* and *Crito* by 1409, and the *Gorgias* in 1409, after which time he produced no fresh version of any complete dialogue, though in 1426 he collected the dialogues translated earlier, adding selections from the *Phaedrus* and revising his *Apology* and *Crito*. He also translated the *Letters* in 1426 and a piece of the *Symposium* in 1435. Various features of these works interested Bruni: he saw them as historical sources for the life of Socrates, as educational examples of rhetoric in the service of ethics, and as a philosophical armoury for the Christian soldier. This last motive, amplified by Bruni's political and social attitudes, tempted him—especially in the later translations—to suppress or transform Plato's views when they offended him.

Having finished his most important Plato translations, and after a decade of service as papal secretary in Rome and elsewhere, Bruni returned to Florence in 1415, to start his *History of the Florentine People* and also to write a life of Cicero. Soon afterward, in 1416, he finished his first translation of Aristotle, the *Nicomachean Ethics*, though he may have turned toward Aristotle three years earlier. A classically Latinate Aristotle had begun to appear in 1406 with Roberto Rossi's *Posterior Analytics*; it was complete in its first phase by the first quarter of the next century. After the *Nicomachean Ethics*, Bruni contributed the *Oeconomics* in 1420 and the *Politics* in 1437–8. Around 1425 Bruni wrote an unoriginal but influential *Introduction to Moral Philosophy* that ignored Plato and Socrates and preferred Peripatetic to rival ethical systems outlined by Cicero; a more interesting *Life of Aristotle* appeared in 1429, two years after he rose to the chancellorship of

67–74); Copenhaver (1988*b*); Hankins (1990*a*: i. 29–81; ii. 367–400); Kristeller (1990*a*: 39–56, 78–89).

Florence. Thus, Bruni reached his apex as 'civic humanist' after his philosophical tastes had shifted from Plato to Aristotle; his mature thought owes no major debt to Plato.[17] Bruni's *Life of Aristotle* depicts the Stagirite as a man of wealth and property immersed in the political and social whirl that Petrarch had shunned in his later years. A worldly and engaged Aristotle answered Bruni's needs better than the ascetic Plato, whose *Republic* disturbed him by proposing the sharing of women and goods, whose *Gorgias* reviled the rhetoric that Bruni found essential to republican politics, and whose philosophical style seemed incoherent and badly suited to teaching. In his last recorded statement on moral philosophy, a letter to Lauro Quirini of 1441, Bruni went so far as to write that 'the contemplative life is not the proper life of man', thus distorting Aristotle's view in order to elevate the standing of the active life as lived by his Florentine compatriots.[18]

It was also in Bruni's interest to misapply Cicero's praise of Aristotle's prose by linking the great orator's commendation of the lost 'exoteric' writings with the surviving 'esoteric' works. When Bruni claimed in his preface to the *Nicomachean Ethics* that the Philosopher 'was ever studious of eloquence and connected wisdom with the art of speaking', his command of Greek made his judgement all the more credible to a humanist readership unlikely to heed those who feared philosophy's subjugation to rhetoric and denied that Aristotle cared about eloquence.[19] By propagating these views and others, Bruni inaugurated a tradition of humanist Aristotelianism that endured long after him. The other great Aristotelian translators of the fifteenth century were Greeks who acquired Latin without the advantages of cultural proximity that Bruni enjoyed as

[17] Weiss (1977: 227–77); Bruni (1987: 15–46, 255–64); Geanakoplos (1989: 9–12); Hankins (1990a: i. 40–81; ii. 367–400); below, Ch. 4, n. 3. Primary sources for Salutati are Salutati (1891–11; 1913; 1947; 1951; 1957; 1985); for secondary works see Iannizzotto (1959); Ullman (1963); Kessler (1968); Witt (1976; 1977; 1983); De Rosa (1980); Trinkaus (1989a).

[18] Translation in Bruni (1987: 264–7, 294, 387–8); Hankins (1990a: i. 54–8, 64–6).

[19] Translation in Bruni (1987: 197–201, 208–213); Copenhaver (1988b: 92–6); Cicero, *Tusculan Disputations* 1. 10. 22; *Academica* 2. 38. 119.

an Italian. The same cultural circumstances made Bruni a born enemy of scholasticism with no patience for the technical rigours of logic and physics recently come south to Italy from the England of the Oxford Calculators. Bruni agreed with Petrarch and Valla that the philosophy of the uncouth north was barren and its language outlandish; the very names of the barbarous Merton doctors—Swineshead, Heytesbury, Dumbleton—grated on the Italian ear as much as their neologized Latin and logical jargon offended the classicist eye. Given the dispositions of his time and place, Bruni's Aristotle had to take a form quite unlike the Philosopher of the medieval universities.

In certain respects, religion being the great exception, Bruni had more in common philosophically with Cicero than with Swineshead. As chancellor of Florence, he shared Cicero's commitment to affairs of state, and like his ancient hero he applied his oratorical gifts and rhetorical skills to political ends. If not unique in this respect among Aristotelian thinkers of his day, he was certainly unusual, and, in order to emulate Cicero's oratorical politics while professing loyalty to Peripatetic philosophy, Bruni had to trim his Aristotle to a Ciceronian pattern—particularly in trying to find a balanced position in the ancient debate on the active and contemplative lives. Doubtless he owed as much to Cicero's letters, speeches, oratorical treatises, and writings on ethics as to the broader range of philosophy in the Aristotelian Corpus. Bruni's philosophical perspective was narrow, skewed, and personalized, yet from this point of view he saw an Aristotle—most of all, the author of the *Nicomachean Ethics*, *Oeconomics*, and *Politics*—who still spoke persuasively to the citizens of quattrocento Florence.

In these three works Aristotle taught lessons of personal, familial, and civic virtue that Bruni found relevant to his times. Thomas Aquinas had made the same teachings useful for the thirteenth century, but Thomas was a celibate friar who lived in the communal discipline of religion with duties and opportunities unlike those that Bruni met as a married layperson and citizen. Thomas, named the Angelic Doctor, earned his sainthood and his philosophical glory in a career defined under the aspect of eternity, while Bruni won his chancellorship, as

well as a great measure of fame, by facing political and economic responsibilities in the evolving temporal order of Florentine commerce and statecraft. In Bruni's context, Aristotle's
Oeconomics—a work on household or estate management—
took on new meaning and value. For laypersons worried about
the changing roles of spouses, children, and servants in the
early modern family, Bruni's version of the text that he called
De re familiari was of great interest and became an immense
success. Except among some recalcitrant university philosophers, his new translation and commentary soon eclipsed the
medieval versions and remained the standard through the sixteenth century. On the evidence of surviving manuscripts (over
two hundred) and early printed editions (fifteen incunabula), it
was vastly more popular, for example, than Leon Battista
Alberti's original vernacular treatise *On the Family*. Modern
scholarship has generally treated the *Oeconomics* as spurious,
and medieval readers who regarded it as Aristotle's were not
enthusiastic about it. But in the Renaissance, because Bruni's
translation was aesthetically attractive and because the increasingly secular context of the Italian city-states created a new
audience for it, the *Oeconomics* became widely influential and
set Aristotle's seal of approval on important new attitudes
about the status of women, wealth, marriage, and business. A
work previously of middling interest to university people found
a wider readership—a 'public' in the modern sense—after
Bruni put it in better Latin. For most of the fifteenth century,
the universities remained wary of Bruni's *Oeconomics*, as in
general they were suspicious of humanist innovations in Aristotelian studies; but gradually even the professors relented,
and during the sixteenth century this and other parts of the
Peripatetic system became best known in their new humanist
garb.

The author of the first book of the *Oeconomics* introduced
his work by explaining how 'economics and politics differ'. In
Greek his opening words were *hê oikonomikê kai hê politikê
diapherei*, rendered in Latin by a thirteenth-century scholar as
yconomica et politica differt but by Bruni as *res familiaris et res
publica inter se differunt*. The medieval translator's intention

was to make his Latin correspond word for word with the Greek, without great regard for classical diction or syntax. Even though ancient Latin authors had used *oeconomicus* and *politicus*, Bruni knew that these were unusual terms, Greek borrowings alien to the Roman genius, words whose roots (*oikos* for 'house', *polis* for 'city') were not Latin and hence drew no instinctive response from a Greekless Latin or Italian reader. Instead, Bruni chose expressions—*res publica* and *res familiaris*—which accurately reflected the conceptual distinctions in the first lines of the *Oeconomics* in a Latin much closer to its classical state than the language of the medieval translator. However, just because Bruni's phrases were key terms for Cicero and Livy, they implied a community of political interests between Greece and Rome that Aristotle could never have imagined.[20] In other words, Bruni's wish to use the classical languages in pure and original forms unstained by Gothic barbarism encouraged a vision of the ancient world with no strong sense of discrimination between the various periods and places of antiquity. This vision was ideological inasmuch as it answered Bruni's political needs: in the case of the *Oeconomics*, if a Ciceronian vocabulary made Aristotle's ideas more pleasing to the Florentine republic, so much the better. On the other hand, Bruni's vision was also historical, for he sincerely wanted an accurate picture of a past that medieval ignorance had obscured. The critical point for Renaissance philosophy is that Bruni's historical programme had the defects of its virtues, and those virtues were above all philological. To make Aristotle an actor in the drama of classical politics as humanism conceived of it, Bruni wrote him a Romanized script that in some respects was anachronistic. In terms of fidelity to Latin usage, his *res familiaris* was a great gain over the medieval *yconomica*, which none the less was truer to Aristotle just because it was a Latin graecism that did *not* invoke Roman realities.

[20] Santinello (1962); Gadol (1969); Ponte (1981); Aristotle (1984: vol. i, p. xiii; ii. 2130); Bruni (1987: 300–17); Aristotle, *Oeconomics* 1343^{a}1; Cicero, *Familiar Letters* 1. 9. 5; *On Old Age* 7. 22; *Against Catiline* 1. 2. 4; Livy 8. 4. 12, 25. 7. 4.

Words like *yconomica*, *oligarchia*, and *democratia* look familiar enough to the modern reader, but they jarred Bruni's humanist sensibility in several ways: first, in departing from authoritative classical usage; second, in their lexical and etymological obscurity; and finally, in seeming ugly. This last judgement followed from extending the principle of authority into the sphere of aesthetics, wherein the humanist canon of mimesis regulated literary and other forms of creativity by judging their success in emulating classical models. Mimesis was an ancient idea well-known to the Middle Ages, but Petrarch, Bruni, Valla, and other humanists established new norms for its expression that unquestionably enriched the scanty historical insights available to medieval thinkers. One consequence of their new aesthetic historicism was the assumption that any ancient text was likely to be more beautiful than an analogous product of the Dark Ages; another was the ensuing conviction that good contemporary writing, including philosophical translation, should conform to superior classical standards. Having heard Cicero's persuasive oratory and having seen the elegance of Plato's dialogues, Bruni and other humanists concluded that all language, even philosophical language, should strive for beauty as a good in itself but also as a means to rhetorical ends.

The first important philosophical product of these new attitudes was Bruni's *Nicomachean Ethics*, whose preface contained provocative criticisms of earlier versions while insisting on the beauty of Aristotle's prose and on the fitness of Latin to reproduce his Greek accurately without the coarse contrivances of medieval translators. Criticism came quickly, and Bruni replied about ten years later with an influential treatise *On Correct Translation*, only to face another, fiercer assault a few years afterward from a Spanish churchman, Alfonso of Cartagena. The most discussed items in the '*Ethics* controversy' were Bruni's misunderstanding of the Greek term *tagathon*, an unusual spelling which he took to mean 'supreme good' in a place where Aristotle meant only 'good', and his reformulation of a rule he had learned from Chrysoloras, that the translator should render meanings before worrying about words. At a deeper level his quarrel with Alfonso and other critics concerned the relation of language to text. Alfonso, who knew no Greek, thought of Aristotle's text as expressing truths unconstrained by time and place and hence unbound by any particular language, but Bruni and other humanists treated every text as a contingent artefact of the particular language in which it happened to be written. For Bruni, a faithful translation of Aristotle required fidelity not only to his Greek but also to norms of Latinity discovered in other ancient texts. For Alfonso, however, such scholarly and literary duties were irrelevant to the truths expressed imperfectly in any given text; he argued that the real object of translation was *ratio*, a metachronic structure that transcends history and philology. Bruni saw translation very differently, as a movement from *lingua Graeca* to *lingua Latina*, where both terms of the transaction were embedded in historical particulars. For this reason, he required the translator to master the broader cultural context in which a text had emerged. To understand Aristotle fully, one must know the world in which Aristotle lived as well as the language that he and other Greeks spoke.[21]

This new way of reading ancient texts entailed changes not only in the method of translation but also in the mode of interpretation. Where medieval commentators had by and large limited themselves to the immediate body of conceptual problems as given or implied in a philosophical text, Bruni enlarged the scope of commentary to help the reader see the text in wider historical and philological perspective. At the beginning of the *Oeconomics*, for example, where the text cites a line from Hesiod, Bruni takes great pains not only to identify the poet but also to exculpate Aristotle's misogyny by showing how he misunderstood Hesiod's use of the word *gunê* ('woman').[22] By the sixteenth century the more expansive philological commentaries in Bruni's manner merged with the traditional philosophical style of annotation in a fusion of medieval and

---

[21] Bruni (1987: 201–12, 217–29); Copenhaver (1988*b*: 89–100); Aristotle, *Nicomachaean Ethics* 1094ᵃ1–3.

[22] Bruni (1987: 304, 311); Aristotle, *Oeconomics* 1343ᵃ20–4; Hesiod, *Works and Days* 405.

humanist expositions of Aristotle. Although Bruni was neither an original philosopher nor a great mind of any kind, his work as expositor and translator helped bring about momentous changes in the reading and writing of philosophy, not to speak of other disciplines. He represents the kind of Renaissance philosopher who saw the discipline as necessarily allied to history, rhetoric, and philology, but who expressed little or no curiosity about scientific, metaphysical, or epistemological issues. Despite his lack of interest in these core concerns of the Peripatetic tradition, Bruni was an important Aristotelian in his time; his way of doing philosophy must be taken into account if we are to grasp Renaissance Aristotelianism in all its variety.

When Bruni's Greekless critic, Alfonso, heard the great humanist's translation of an oration by Demosthenes read aloud in 1426, several years before he encountered Bruni's *Ethics*, he admired it, probably because it was a text of no professional concern to him. George of Trebizond (Trapezuntius), whose native language was Greek and who became an eminent Latinist, was harder on Bruni's version of Demosthenes' speech *On the Crown*, one of many Greek works that George himself translated in the years before and after Bruni's death in 1444.[23] On the whole, however, George admired Bruni, whose *Life of Cicero* inspired his own work of 1421 *On the Praises of Cicero*. When he wrote this treatise on the patron saint of civic oratory, Trapezuntius had been in Italy only about five years, having come to Venice in 1416 around the age of twenty at the invitation of Francesco Barbaro. Except for a stay in his native Crete for a few years after 1423, he spent the first two decades of his Italian career mainly in Venice, first learning Latin, then teaching it. He left for Bologna, Florence, and eventually Rome in 1437 after quarrelling with another eminent teacher, Guarino Guarini of Verona.

---

[23] The following section on George of Trebizond is indebted mainly to Monfasani (1976) and Trapezuntius (1984), ed. Monfasani; see also Vasoli (1968a: 81–99); Lojacono (1985); Bruni (1987: 203–4); Geanakoplos (1989: 17–21, 68–90); Hankins (1990a: i. 165–263; ii. 429–48).

In Florence and Ferrara he probably visited other Byzantine scholars who attended the Council convened there in the late 1430s to unite the Greek and Latin churches. Finally, in 1440, he found a post in the Roman curia that supported so many humanists, and he spent the thirty-three years remaining to him as a creature of papal generosity, which waned as often as it waxed. Patronage in the best of circumstances makes an unsteady living; Trapezuntius, one of the more ambitious, pugnacious, and flamboyant figures in the history of philosophy, pressed his benefactors to the limit, and sometimes further.

George's first twelve years in Rome were his best in that city, during the reigns of Eugenius IV·and Nicholas V, the popes for whom he produced most of his translations. More plentiful than Bruni's and even more controversial, his Latin versions were mainly patristic or philosophical, especially the *libri naturales* of Aristotle, which he completed by 1452 and issued in a comprehensive collection in 1455. Of Plato's dialogues he rendered the *Laws* and *Epinomis* in 1451 and the *Parmenides* in 1459; each was important in its way, and the bulk of the three exceeded the output of any Plato translator before Ficino. In 1451 the first two translations caused him to write a letter to Francesco Barbaro that advanced the development of the political theory of mixed constitutions, of which the Venetian was the most famous current example. In 1459 he dedicated his *Parmenides* to Nicholas of Cusa, whose metaphysical curiosity could not be satisfied by the abbreviation found in William of Moerbeke's translation of Proclus' commentary on the dialogue. George's complex theory of translation, which required literal renderings for sacred or 'sublime' texts but permitted freer translation of others, allowed him to produce a Latin *Laws* that can only have been meant to disgrace Plato, a motive compatible with George's later attacks on the ascetic, disembodied authoritarianism of the *Laws*. George's *Parmenides* translation was literal and more precise, but no match for the dialogue's metaphysical depths. During his most active time as a translator, Trapezuntius also ruled the teaching of humanities in the holy city, but his grip on fame and papal favour began to loosen in 1449–50 when Theodore Gaza, another learned Byzantine who had been at Florence, came to Rome from Ferrara. After public clashes with Gaza, George gradually found himself an ex-member of the club that surrounded Basil Bessarion, the Greek cardinal, and in 1451, after vying with Lorenzo Valla for a teaching post, he decided to withdraw from the competition. In the same year worse trouble came when he suggested to Nicholas V that someone check his new translation of Ptolemy's *Almagest*. When the reader had harsh words for his work, George irritated Nicholas and Bessarion by refusing to revise. Having let his curial support dwindle, he saw it dry up altogether in 1452 when he came to blows with another papal secretary, Poggio Bracciolini. The disgraceful brawl put him in jail and eventually forced him to leave Rome for Naples.

It was not George's translation of Ptolemy but the accompanying commentary that started the quarrels that drove him from Rome; but there is no question that his versions of Greek texts invited hostility. He made himself doubly vulnerable to critics by applying two standards, one to offend those who insisted on close rendering, another to annoy those who objected to literalism. Without aping the word-for-word style of medieval translators whom he respected, he took a literal approach to 'sublime' works like the *Parmenides* and to technical philosophical texts like those of Aristotle, but he preferred a freer style for the apologetic and homiletic works of the Fathers. The latter principle tempted him to play fast and loose with the *Preparation for the Gospel* by Eusebius; he cannot be blamed if the Greek manuscript from which he worked omitted one whole book out of fifteen in this long treatise, a major source for early Christian attitudes to philosophy, but he treated the text that he had with scant respect for the original. The opposite rule of literalism for technical writing brought him into renewed conflict with Gaza, who retranslated the Aristotelian *libri naturales* for Pope Nicholas after George's fall from grace. George had almost finished Latinizing the pseudo-Aristotelian *Problemata* before leaving Rome in 1452; news of a rival version by Gaza in 1454 moved him to finish his own *Problems* in that year. Two years later he wrote a *Protection Against the Perversion of Aristotle's Problems by a Certain Theodore Cages*, in which he complained that Gaza sacrificed accuracy to preserve Latinity and that this yielded a text too imprecise for close study. Better for a philosophical translation to be inelegant than inexact, he maintained, preferring even a clumsy medieval product if it rendered the Greek more strictly than a refined but clouded humanist effort.[24]

One of George's complaints about Gaza's disrespect for the medieval versions was that he undermined the textual and terminological basis of the philosophical and theological systems of the great scholastics, especially Albertus and Aquinas. In effect, he treated Gaza as the fellow-traveller of a conspiracy aimed at Christian theology and its Aristotelian infrastructure; as the great Satan of this plot he named George Gemistos Plethon, who had been a Greek delegate at Ferrara and Florence. While at the Council, Plethon wrote a book in Greek *On the Differences between the Platonic and Aristotelian Philosophies*.[25] George accused Plethon of being a pagan, and he seems at least to have strayed from orthodoxy; Plethon's *Book of Laws* and his *Summary of Zoroastrian and Platonic Doctrine* advocated a Hellenism steeped in Neoplatonic theology and gave instructions for pagan worship. Naturally, Plethon preferred Plato to Aristotle, refuting the Stagirite's criticisms of his teacher and showing why Christians should favour Plato on religious grounds. His leading Greek disciple was Bessarion, who had won his cardinal's hat by supporting the cause of union but whose office ceased to protect Trapezuntius after

---

[24] Monfasani (1976: 71–82, 150–78); for Gaza, see also Stein (1889); Taylor (1925a; 1925b); Mohler (1943–9); Labowsky (1968); Geanakoplos (1989: 68–90); Hankins (1990a: i. 203–11).
[25] *De differentiis* is translated in Woodhouse (1986: 191–214); besides Monfasani (1976), see also Taylor (1921); Anastos (1948); Knös (1950); Masai (1956); Garin (1958: 153–219); Tavardon (1977); and Kristeller (1979b: 150–68) on Plethon; for Bessarion see Mohler (1923–42); Labowsky (1961–8; 1979); *Centenario . . . Bessarione* (1973); *Il Cardinale Bessarione* (1974); Coccia (1974); *Miscellanea marciana* (1976); Neuhausen and Trapp (1979); Bianca (1980); Stormon (1980); Monfasani (1981a; 1983a); below, Ch. 3, n. 15.

the ruckus with Poggio in 1452. George linked Gaza's anti-medievalism with Plethon's alleged neo-paganism as twin treasons against the faith. One bizarre basis of his suspicions emerged in 1453, when Constantinople fell to the Turks and within a month he had written *On the Truth of the Faith of Christians to the Emir*; the emir was the conqueror, Mehmed II. It was not unusual that George fantasized about converting Mehmed and adapting Islam to Christianity, but it was impolitic of him to address Europe's most feared enemy as king of kings by divine right and, in a later work of 1467, to picture him as the 'divine Manuel', not an Ishmaelite Antichrist but a Christian emperor who would conquer Rome itself and then move on to Ceylon and Britain. Shortly before writing these reckless words, George had actually travelled to Constantinople to present his works to the emir, and on the return trip he tried to steal the entire corpse of a recent, if dubious, martyr. His international escapades landed him in jail again on his return to Rome in 1466.[26]

In one sense, differences as transient as those between Greek and Latin churches or Platonic and Aristotelian philosophies might have vanished in the perspective of George's chiliastic prophecies, but the fact is that he found a role for Platonic forces of evil in his vision of history as grand conspiracy: he divined that Plato had bequeathed his perversions to none other than Mohammed, from whom they passed eventually to Plethon and his student Bessarion. This genealogy of darkness appeared in 1458 in George's Latin treatise on the *Comparison of the Philosophies of Aristotle and Plato*, which was one of several reactions from Byzantine scholars to Plethon's Greek *De differentiis* of 1439. The Plato of George's first book is too dazed and deceitful to be instructive, unlike Aristotle, the orderly pedagogue; Book II shows Platonism to be incompatible with Christianity, described as much closer to Aristotle's monotheism than to Plato's polytheist perversities; Aristotle in Book III is an upstanding citizen and moral paragon, while Plato is a libertine degenerate. If George's polemic sounds too

[26] Monfasani (1976: 125–36, 183–94); Hankins (1990*a*: i. 193–208).

wild to be credible, note that he was clever enough to buttress his charges with the newest devices of humanist philology, which made an impressive cover for his blunders and slanders.

In hoping to distance Aristotle from Christian dogma on immortality, providence, creation, and other issues, Plethon had already drawn from a contrary tradition reaching back to the Neoplatonists and beyond, but his Greek treatise had almost no detectable impact on Latin writers of the fifteenth century. Byzantine scholars in the East began to respond within a few years of Plethon's writing, and their *émigré* compatriots in the West joined them by the late 1450s, when Bessarion and Trapezuntius crossed swords, at first on the relatively restricted topic of nature and art. In 1458 the cardinal published a direct attack on Trapezuntius in a longish work on this subject; George issued his *Comparison* in the same year and pursued the fight over the next decade, at the end of which, in 1469, Bessarion published a Latin response *Against Plato's Calumniator*, although three Greek versions had been prepared over the previous ten years. Bessarion, who cared enough about Aristotle to produce a durable translation of the *Metaphysics* by 1450, refused to accept the idea that Plato and his disciple were deeply at odds. Their differences were verbal, although Plato's teaching was better suited to Christianity; his works were also better written, better informed, and of better moral fibre than his student's. To refute the cardinal's arguments, George sought support from scholastic allies, but no help arrived, and in Italy the noise of applause for Bessarion eventually covered his rival's protests. For a time, however, events worked in George's favour when Paul II—who as Pietro Barbo had been George's student—rose to the papal throne in 1464, but George's international adventures cancelled this advantage until 1468, when the pope brought charges of sodomy, heresy, and sedition against Bartolomeo Platina, Pomponio Leto, and others associated with the Roman Academy. Some of Leto's circle were also friends of Bessarion, whose Platonism thus became more vulnerable to George's charges of immorality. Bessarion's response in the *Calumniator* did nothing to quash his enemy, but when he and George both died around

1472, their passing ended this first phase of the controversy about Plato and Aristotle.[27]

George was not born an anti-Platonist. In fact, although he leaned toward Aristotle and away from Plato early in his career, he expressed no real malice toward Plato until he published the *Comparison* in 1458, and in that work he explains that it was the *Gorgias* that turned him against Plato. An early *Oration on the Praises of Eloquence* uses the arguments of the sophist Gorgias against Plato's Socratic attack on rhetoric. Thus, the ingredients of anti-Platonism showed in George's thought before he wrote his *Five Books of Rhetoric* in 1433–4; his movement toward the Western church in the 1420s as well as his perception of Plato's disloyalty to Pericles and other Greek heroes may have helped inspire his anti-Platonism, but his original insight into the anti-rhetorical animus of Platonic philosophy was reason enough.[28] Although he eventually produced a popular translation of Aristotle's *Rhetoric*, it was not Aristotle but Hermogenes of Tarsus, a rhetorician of the second century CE, whom he chose as his guide in rhetorical theory and its philosophical appendages. Hermogenes left a number of works that were assembled during the sixth century into a manual that became the main authority on rhetoric in the Byzantine world; his two chief contributions were an intricate analysis of style and, more important for the history of philosophy, an equally complex theory of *stasis*, or *status* in Latin, so called from the point at which a court case was said to 'stand' when deliberations first reached a critical issue.

Aristotle did not deal with *stasis*, and in his work *On Invention* Cicero actually gave it a third name, *constitutio*, taking his material from an earlier Greek work, now lost, by Hermagoras of Temnos. Hermagoras taught that a jurist could begin *finding* (*invenire* in Latin, hence the name 'invention' for the part of rhetoric at issue) material by considering the first *stasis* in the case, which is a *stasis* of *fact* if a defendant rejects a charge

---

[27] Monfasani (1976: 156–66, 201–29); Hankins (1990a: i. 208–17, 236–45).

[28] Monfasani (1976: 6, 18–19, 258–61); Hankins (1990a: i. 167–74).

outright, as when someone accused of burglary simply denies taking anything. *Stasis* of *quality* arises if the alleged burglar admits taking something but claims justification, and *stasis* of *definition* turns on whether one can define the action as burglary. Finally, a *stasis* of *transference* occurs if the accused calls the court's jurisdiction into question. Following Hermagoras, Cicero advised the orator who had explained the *constitutio* or *status* of a case to urge the court toward favourable judgement by selecting a particular line of argument and looking in the right places (*loci*, or *topoi* in Greek) for material to support it. In the *Rhetoric* and the *Topics*, Aristotle had written about various kinds of places or topics, which came to be called dialectical or rhetorical, common or particular; Cicero devoted a whole work to their interpretation, also called the *Topics*. Common topics include terms like genus, species, difference, cause, effect, and others of philosophical interest; hence, questions of logic or dialectic confronted the rhetorician as he searched in various places for the makings of his arguments. Cicero listed abstract dialectical places in his *Topica*, but in *De inventione* and elsewhere he also gave more concrete advice in topical form, suggesting four *loci*, for example, to capture a court's goodwill. The places where the orator should look to inspire benevolence were his own noble or at least sympathetic character, the hateful nature of the other side, the esteemed person of the judge, or, failing all else, the merits of the case.[29]

Hermogenes, whose textbook Trapezuntius identified as his quickest path to glory in the West as early as 1420, used the same four divisions of *stasis* (fact, definition, quality, transference) that Cicero had found in Hermagoras, but he transformed the *staseis* profoundly by organizing them in a hierarchy formed by *diaeresis* or division. Beginning with an issue that may be certain or uncertain, defined or undefined, qualified or unqualified, the orator finds its *stasis* by moving through the nested dichotomies shown in Fig. 1. This simple scheme of subordinated divisions was an ancestor of the pedagogical

[29] Monfasani (1976: 248–55); G. Kennedy (1980: 82–105).

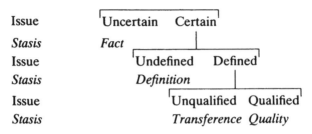

Issue	Uncertain Certain	
Stasis	*Fact*	
Issue	Undefined Defined	
Stasis	*Definition*	
Issue	Unqualified Qualified	
Stasis	*Transference Quality*	

FIG. I.

method made famous (but not invented) by Johann Sturm, Peter Ramus, and others in the sixteenth century. Although Trapezuntius ignored *diairesis*, he introduced Hermogenes to the West and hence deserves credit (or blame) for having helped spark the fad that filled so many thousands of school texts with the bifurcating charts of the Ramists. Having left the hierarchy of *staseis* out of his rhetoric, George did not forget the topics, which he presented both in the usual Latin form and also in the Greek manner. Although his favourite subject was style or *elocutio*, he gave a great deal of attention to argument as well, and his theory of argument paid more attention to topics as dialectical abstractions than as concrete oratorical opportunities. In this regard, he was influenced by Peter of Spain and other medieval logicians. He thought of the humanities as a preparation for persuasive speech in public life, and hence he excluded philosophy, seeing in it no need for eloquence. He considered philosophy a poor education for civic life, yet he respected scholasticism for its own technical strengths. His goals for rhetoric were technical as well; the orator was to apply his art to political ends of the narrowest kind. George did not mean his *Rhetoric* to build character or break new artistic ground. It was a tool for lawyers and politicians, and readers found it handy enough to pay for ten printed editions through the middle of the sixteenth century, when direct access to Greek or Latin versions of Hermogenes made it redundant.[30]

[30] Monfasani (1976: 255–99, 318–27); G. Kennedy (1980: 103–4); see also Patterson (1970).

Much more popular was the little book on logic that George published in 1440, the *Introduction to Dialectic*, the first logic in humanist dress. The *Isagoge* saw fifty-seven editions, almost all in the six decades before 1567; during this period it became the companion to Rudolf Agricola's bestseller *On Dialectical Invention*, which was finished around 1479, published in 1515, and rose to peak demand shortly before mid-century. As its title implies, Agricola's larger work focuses on invention, the location of arguments, rather than on their judgement or evaluation, which was the subject left to George's *Introduction* as adjunct to Agricola. Lefèvre d'Étaples saw the *Isagoge* as a vehicle for humanist reform of logic, but George's goals were more modest. In order to help the orator reason, invent, define, and divide, he wanted to isolate only the required parts of dialectic and put them in a short handbook of demonstrative reasoning for quick consumption. Shrinking the domain of logic had long been part of the humanist cause, from Petrarch through Bruni and Valla to Juan Luis Vives and other sixteenth-century writers, but George did not share their programmatic dislike of scholasticism. Philosophy has its own technical discourse, he maintained, which grammarians may not restrict on philological grounds. He used Paul of Venice and earlier medieval logicians, and he included at least brief reference to some of the more advanced features of later medieval logic. His dialectic has no overt metaphysical content, but this was also true of much scholastic logic of the time. Having covered the *loci* in detail in his *Rhetoric*, he only mentioned them in the *Isagoge*, and he emphasized the new logic of propositions— in contrast to the older Aristotelian logic of classes—when discussing how topics find arguments that must be assembled in inferential order. Unlike Agricola, he had no wish to make invention a part of dialectic.[31] His larger aims remained rhetorical, but when he reached the limits of oratorical interest, he recommended Aristotle and the Peripatetics for more help on logic than an orator's handbook could give. Within the domain of philosophy, George's views contrast most strongly

---

[31] Ashworth (1974: 10, 14, 19); Monfasani (1976: 300–17, 328–37; 1990).

with the teachings (discussed below) of his brilliant and equally
belligerent contemporary, Lorenzo Valla.[32] Moral philosophy
aside, his humanist writings matched Valla's in scope, surpassed them in impact, but fell short in originality. Unlike Valla,
Trapezuntius was a humanist who combined philological expertise with fidelity to Aristotle and respect for scholasticism.

Calling them Goths and barbarians, Jacques Lefèvre d'Étaples
had less patience for medieval thinkers, though he shared their
desire to harness Aristotelian philosophy to the burdens of
Christian faith.[33] In 1508 he edited George of Trebizond's
Isagoge, which reappeared in his version fourteen more times
by 1560, and George's manual was only one of Lefèvre's
logical publications; he also brought out an *Art of Suppositions*
in 1500 and an edition of Aristotle's *Organon* in 1501. But his
most important contribution to logic was his earliest, the
Logical Introductions of 1496, to which Josse Clichtove added
an excellent *Commentary* in 1500; with and without Clichtove's
commentary, the *Introductiones logicales* appeared twenty-six
times by mid-century. Lefèvre, who until 1508 spent about
twenty years teaching in the arts faculty of the University of
Paris, specialized in books designed to clear the student's path
through the philosophical jungle of the arts curriculum. His
first printed work, *Paraphrases of the Whole of Aristotle's
Natural Philosophy*, appeared in 1492, followed by *Introductions* to the *Metaphysics* and *Nicomachean Ethics* in 1494; in
various forms the latter work saw nearly fifty editions and
printings. Lefèvre enjoyed great success as an author. In the
half-century after 1492, his works were edited or reprinted
more than three hundred and fifty times, and about a third of
them, either translations or teaching texts, focused on Aristotle.
Like Bruni, Trapezuntius, Ermolao Barbaro, and others whom

---

[32] Below, pp. 209–27.

[33] On Lefèvre see Renaudet (1953; 1969); Vasoli (1968a: 183–213;) Rice
(1969; 1970; 1971; 1976); Simone (1969: 155–78); Heller (1972); Bedouelle
(1976); Gosselin (1976: 49–63); Copenhaver (1977); Cavazza (1982); Hughes
(1984); Pantin (1988); for Lefèvre's opinion of medieval logic, see his prefatory letter to the 1496 *Introductiones logicales* in *Lefèvre* (1972: 38–41, with
Rice's introd. pp. xi–xxv). See also Copenhaver (1978a); Ashworth (1986).

he admired, Lefèvre proved that 'humanist Aristotelian' is a meaningful term; moreover, he wanted to give a new force to reformed Peripateticism by making it a step toward spiritual rebirth as well as cultural renewal.

The aim of the early *Logical Introductions* was humbler than the evangelical purposes to which Lefèvre gave the latter part his life. His prefatory letter is more than customarily apologetic, comparing the work to 'quick travel-money sent in advance' to students about to enter foreign territory. The best reason Lefèvre can give for mastering the current style of logic is that students who ignore it will be thought ignorant: when in barbary, do as the barbarians do. Listing the divisions of the 'outlandish and vulgar literature' that he despised, he mentions 'suppositions, ampliations, restrictions, appellations, exponibles, insolubles [and] obligations'.[34] Most of these terms are headings in the seventh part of the most popular logic text of Lefèvre's day, the *Logical Summaries* of Peter of Spain, a thirteenth-century work of which Renaissance readers demanded more than one hundred and sixty printings. The first six sections of the *Summulae logicales* correspond more or less to Aristotle's *Organon*, but the seventh, the *Parva logicalia* or *Little Logicals*, deals with issues outside the range of the Aristotelian Corpus, and this departure was one cause of Lefèvre's unease.[35] He wanted to restore Aristotle, through the Greek text, to a purer state than the Middle Ages had known, a task that would require scraping away the accretions still surrounding his *Logical Introductions*. Lefèvre felt that for the sake of his students he had to cover some of the alien ground where humanist feet should not tread. But his embarrassment went deeper than mere worry about inconsistency. To gauge the depth of his discomfort, one may note how the same items presented in Lefèvre's book became comic in the writings of François Rabelais.

Lefèvre's base in Paris was the College of Cardinal Lemoine,

[34] Lefèvre (1972: 39).
[35] Kneale and Kneale (1962: 234–5); Peter of Spain (1972: pp. ix–lxi, lxxxviii–c); Ashworth (1974: 1–4); Noreña (1975: 1–12); Kenny and Pinborg (1982: 17–19); Ong (1983: 53–91).

home to many of the faculty who wished to reorient the university in directions marked out by Italian humanists. Around the turn of the century, while Lefèvre was still teaching, the College of Montaigu stood at the opposite point of the cultural compass. Montaigu's leader was Jean Standonck, a rigorist ascetic and clerical reformer who rescued the fortunes of his college while making it a puritanical bootcamp, hellish even by late medieval standards, for the needy students who were his special charges. In 1495 one of Montaigu's victims was Erasmus, who complained of Standonck as one

whose intentions were beyond reproach but [who was] . . . entirely lacking in judgement. . . . [To make sure that students] did not have too soft a life, he [used] . . . bedding so hard, diet so coarse and scanty, sleepless nights and labors so burdensome, that within a year he had succeeded in killing many . . . ; and others . . . he reduced to blindness, nervous breakdowns, or leprosy. . . . I omit the astonishingly savage floggings, even of the innocent. . . . How many rotten eggs used to be eaten there! How much bad wine drunk! Perhaps these conditions have been corrected; but too late, obviously, for those who have died or carry a diseased body about.[36]

Erasmus immortalized the place that he called Vinegar College (*Mons aceta* instead of *acuta*) in his *Colloquies*, a work first published in 1518 and better remembered than all the treatises of Jean Mair or Major, who came from Scotland via Cambridge to Paris in the early 1490s, became Master of Arts in 1494 and began theological studies at Montaigu a year later, when Erasmus also arrived. Mair, who stayed in Paris until 1517 and returned there twice from Scotland before his death in 1550, made Montaigu the centre of the Parisian revival of nominalist scholasticism or terminism, so called for its fascination with the properties of terms (*termini*) that make up propositions. Gathering a large circle of Scots and Iberian disciples to extend his influence, Mair published original works, such as his *Liber terminorum* of 1501, but he also edited and commented on medieval texts, as in his *Commentaries on the Summulae of Peter of Spain* of 1505. After earning his fame as a logician,

[36] Erasmus (1965a: 351–3 [Thompson trans.]); Renaudet (1953: 171–83, 260–80, 302–13).

Mair went on to other important studies in ethics, politics, history, and theology. In his long career in France and Scotland, he had the distinction of teaching not only John Calvin, John Knox, and George Buchanan, but also Ignatius of Loyola.[37] While few have read his work since the terminist movement evaporated in the first quarter of the sixteenth century, many more have seen his name attached to a book not of his making: Majoris *De modo faciendi boudinos*.

Major, *On Making Sausages* was the brainchild of Rabelais, who put it in a list of books—mostly invented, some real— seen by the giant Pantagruel when he came to Paris from Orléans and inspected the renowned Library of Saint Victor. Other books in the long and hilarious catalogue are: Tartaret, *On How to Shit*; Bricot, *On Differences among Soups*; Beda, *On the Excellence of Tripes*; and, without attribution, *Whether a Chimera, Humming in the Void, Can Dine on Second Intentions, a Most Delicate Question Debated for Ten Weeks at the Council of Constance*. In the midst of gullet and toilet jokes, the last anonymous title clarifies the others. Mair and his students debated endlessly about chimeras (non-entities with meaningful names) and second intentions (names of names, in Mair's brief description) in a refined and intricate logic that Rabelais found obscure and illiterate. As for the authors identified: Pierre Tataret spoke for Scotist realism at Paris when Mair advocated nominalism; Noël Beda succeeded Standonck as master of Montaigu; and Bricot might be either Thomas, a nominalist of the generation before Mair, or Guillaume, who persecuted Johann Reuchlin, a humanist pioneer of Jewish studies for Christians. (Mair himself sat on the infamous Paris commission that condemned Reuchlin in 1514.)[38] When Rabelais belittled these thinkers, he had the butt of his humour well in his sights, as one can see from his tale of Gargantua, Pantagruel's father, who stole the bells of Notre-Dame.

---

[37] Mair (1892: pp. xxix–cxxx); Élie (1950–1); Renaudet (1953: 366–70, 404–9, 456–72, 591–7, 647–60, 698–701); Burns (1954); Oakley (1962; 1965); Torrance (1969–70); Noreña (1975: 12–20); Broadie (1985: 1–6). Torrance stresses Mair's debts to Scotus as well as to Ockham, and characterizes his teaching as a 'combination of logical analysis and empirical realism' (p. 261).

[38] Rabelais (1973: 238–44); Screech (1979: 60–3); see also Frame (1977).

Gargantua's theft of the bells put the disputatious Parisians in an uproar, and 'after having therefored pro and con, they concluded in Baralipton to send the oldest and ablest of the faculty to Gargantua'. Although some faculty would have sent 'an orator instead of a sophist', it was Master Janotus de Bragmardo who went—hooded, glutted, and sprinkled with holy water. After much slinging of bad Latin, the lewd old cougher made his point not rhetorically but syllogistically, one-upping the syllogism in Baralipton (a mood of the disputed fourth figure; see below) that started his embassy to the giant:

Omnis clocha clochabilis, in clocherio clochando clochans clochative, clochare facit clochabiliter clochantes. Paris habet clochas. Ergo gluc.

Every bellable bell, belling bell-like in the belfry by belling, makes bellings bell bellishly. Paris has bells. Therefore, gluc.

Unable to recall features of his syllogism as basic as figure and mood (which Rabelais correctly identifies as Darii, the third mood of the first figure), Janotus is none the less delighted with himself. Down to the final *gluc*, which mocks the non-sense words (*buf, baf, blitiri*) that represented non-signifying terms in terminist logic, the syllogism is an exquisite send-up of the tortured speech that Mair's school had to use because their Latin did double duty as natural language and as thinly formalized metalanguage. The travesty becomes even more pointed when Gargantua's tutors decide to reward Janotus for splitting their sides with laughter. His main prize is a length of cloth, but when Janotus carries it off, the artless master (*maistre inerte*) Bandouille objects to the indignity of so great a person's hauling his own load. Janotus will have none of it. 'Ha! Jackass', he shouts, 'Jackass! You don't conclude in mood and figure. What good are the suppositions of the *Little Logicals?* In place of what [*pro quo*] does the cloth go [*supponit*]?' 'Confusedly and distributively', answers Bandouille. 'Ass', re-torts Janotus, 'I'm not asking in what way [*quo modo*] but in place of what [*pro quo*] it goes. It goes in the place of my shins, jackass, and so I myself shall bear it just as the subject [*suppositum*] carries the predicate [*adpositum*].' The fun in this joke is the doctrine of supposition, the hub of terminist logic, the first of six parts in Peter of Spain's *Little Logicals*, and also first in the list of ugly words that made Lefèvre squirm in his *Logical Introductions*.[39]

The terminists' theory of supposition grew out of their view of signification (*significatio*, which served for 'meaning' and 'reference' as well as 'representation'), based on a hierarchy of mental, spoken, and written signs.[40] *Canis natat* (LS_1) and 'a/ the dog swims' (ES_1) are Latin and English sentences in good grammatical form, but the Latin sentence LS_1 is not a well-formed proposition in the logic of Peter of Spain or John Mair. Since all propositions need three terms—subject, predicate, and copula—the logician's task in this case is to unpack the two-word sentence into a three-term proposition, a harder job in Latin because its ordinary present-tense verbs lack auxiliary forms like '*is* swimming.' The terminists meant their logical analysis to replace written or spoken phrases with logical propositions (DP_n) also expressed in strings of Latin words but corresponding more closely to mental propositions (MP_n) which, unlike speech and writing, signify autonomously; i.e. the English and Latin sentences ES_1 and LS_1 have no signification unless they correspond to a mental proposition MP_1, which signifies in its own right. Strings of letters, syllables, and words in any sentences LS_n or ES_n relate to their significations as linguistic accident to linguistic substance; such relations can change in numerous ways that the terminists loved to puzzle out. In sentence LS_1, for example, *canis* refers to a more restricted class, dogs able to swim, than the same word outside the context of LS_1. Thus, the terminists said that terms and propositions written or spoken in conventional languages could be *imposed*—that they could lose or gain a signification. But, because mental terms (MT) and propositions are modifications of mind, within the sphere of language MT_n and MP_n are not changeable substance/accident composites. As a linguistic entity, the mental term MT_1 does not *become* another mental

[39] Rabelais (1973: 88–95); Screech (1979: 150–62); Broadie (1985: 39); above, nn. 29–30; below, pp. 224–30.
[40] Kneale and Kneale (1962: 246–74); Ashworth (1974: 4–8, 26–89; 1988); Broadie (1985: 7–76; 1987: 1–31).

term MT_2; instead, one modification of mind stops and another starts.

Beginning with their sophisticated account of signification, the terminists treated supposition as the key feature of terms *as* they appear in one proposition or another. To say that a term (T) *supposes* for a concept (C) means that the term's appearance in some particular proposition (P_a) entails a distinction between two *linguistically* identical but logically different terms (T_{1a} and T_{1b}), such that term T_{1a} has supposition S_{1a} in proposition P_a. Taken independently or in another propositional context (P_b), a term (T_{1b}) *linguistically* indistinguishable from T_{1a} may signify differently and have a different supposition (S_{1b}). When Janotus harries the artless master for criticizing his carrying the cloth, he asks: *panus pro quo supponit?* Taken as a question in ordinary rather than logical language, his bad Latin means 'where does the cloth go [when worn]?' But as a good terminist, the hapless Bandouille has every right to think that Janotus wants to know the supposition of the term *panus* or 'cloth', literally 'for what does "cloth" suppose?' Janotus explodes in fury at Bandouille's inept and abstracted resort to the *Little Logicals*, as Lefèvre had vented his frustration at having to cover Peter of Spain's curriculum in his own *Logical Introductions*. As Lefèvre's list shows, supposition was only the broadest of several appendices to Aristotle's original logic.[41] John Mair's treatment of *ampliation* as a special case of supposition provides just one example of how the terminists and their predecessors expanded their logic and exasperated the humanists. Ampliation is the analysis of supposition from the point of view of time and modality; it is the supposition of terms predicated of subjects through verbs not in the indicative mood of the present tense. Mair used ampliation to make sense of odd propositions on the pattern of 'an old man will be a boy', but critics of Lefèvre's type saw such efforts as vicious nonsense. Mair's analysis of tense structure expanded these paradoxes into expressions on the pattern of 'one who is or will be an old man will be a boy', by which he

---

[41] Rabelais (1973: 94–5); above, nn. 29–30.

seems to have meant something like 'an old man *will have been* a boy'.[42]

Supposition, ampliation, restriction, appellation, and the other parts of the *Little Logicals* clarified thought for Mair but perverted speech for Lefèvre. In its extreme form the gulf between the two Parisian masters can be sensed in Mair's dictum that 'science has no need of fine language', a fair inference from the terminist theory of signification.[43] If Lefèvre knew them, Mair's words must have seemed hostile and preposterous. Lefèvre valued Peripatetic logic only as the beginning of a larger programme of learning whose motives were chiefly pedagogical, where Mair's were largely professional. By the time the two men began teaching at Paris in the 1490s, logic carried the weight of nearly three centuries of growth and refinement since Peter of Spain had finished his textbook. Early fifteenth-century scholars had codified the work of Ockham, Buridan, Burley, and others, and at the end of the century Mair's predecessors at Paris added another intricate layer to this monument of abstraction. Terminist logic was not kind to the teenagers who studied the arts in Paris. Teachers like Lefèvre, who respected Aristotelianism primarily as moral philosophy, metaphysics, or natural philosophy, resented the logicians as competitors for curricular space. Metaphysics and ethics had to share the third of a three-year arts curriculum with natural philosophy; the second year went to the logic of Porphyry and Aristotle; the whole first year to Peter of Spain. As Mair and his talented students elevated nominalism to some of its greatest achievements in logic, they also pushed their curriculum toward destruction at the hands of other professors who wanted time to teach other parts of philosophy to students unhampered by a hypertechnical logic.

Thus, one dimension of Lefèvre's humanist Aristotelianism was a pedagogy that cared for students; another was his humanist respect for the classical languages; and a third was the religious instinct that caused Noël Beda to call him a

---

[42] Broadie (1985: 76–88; 1987: 31–7).
[43] Renaudet (1953: 464).

'theologizing humanist'.[44] Lefèvre and his students improved the Latin Aristotle read in northern Europe either by reissuing earlier versions done by Bruni and others in fifteenth-century Italy or by making their own translations, which as a rule took the medieval Latin as a basis for revision in order to preserve as much of the traditional understanding of the text as humanist principles (e.g. no transliterated Greek) permitted. Except to criticize them, Lefèvre took little notice of ancient or medieval commentators, and his own commentaries discarded the scholastic *quaestio* in favour of a philological style that hewed closer to the language of the text and looked into its historical circumstances. His many introductions to Aristotle's thought and paraphrases of his works digested Peripatetic doctrine to make it easy fare for students. In 1492 he began his publishing career with a resounding pledge of loyalty to the Stagirite, lauding him as 'chief of all philosophers' and praising his doctrine as 'useful, beautiful and holy'. That Lefèvre rejected the Epicureans and castigated the same Hermetic writings that he edited was normal in so pious a Christian, but, in light of his devotion to Dionysius the Areopagite and Nicholas of Cusa, it is surprising that he also denounced the Platonists as 'bitter enemies of the faith'.[45]

Another discordant note in Lefèvre's attitude toward Platonism was his interest in its Florentine revivers, Marsilio Ficino and Giovanni Pico. He made his first trip to Italy in 1491-2 because he wanted to meet Pico, and he republished Ficino's translation of the *Hermetica* in 1494 and 1505. More important, it was the *prisca theologia*—Ficino's and Pico's myth of philosophy's origins in an ancient Eastern theology—that enabled Lefèvre to treat Aristotelianism not just as a useful and beautiful system but also as a holy one. In the preface to his *Introduction* to the *Metaphysics* (1494), he traced the beginnings of 'divine philosophy' to 'Egyptian priests and Chaldaean magi' who passed on their wisdom to the philosophers, of whom 'those who emphasize ideas are Platonists, while those

---

[44] Rice (1970); also in Lefèvre (1972: pp. xxiii–xxiv); Ashworth (1974: 5–8); Noreña (1975: 2–5); below, Ch. 4, n. 8.
[45] Lefèvre (1972: pp. xi–xxiv, 1); Rice (1970: 138–44).

who pursue divine and eternal reasons are Aristotelians, and their theology agrees and conjoins with Christian wisdom in a great harmony and affinity'. Although he departed from Ficino in preferring Aristotle to Plato, Lefèvre resembled the great Florentine in reaching beneath the surface of a philosophical text for its deepest meaning. This hermeneutic strategy, whose ancestry is more Neoplatonic than Peripatetic, enabled him to locate grades of spiritual progress within Aristotle's system — rising from natural philosophy through moral philosophy to metaphysics — and then to identify the system itself as only the first of three stages, the two higher levels being a patristic reading of scripture and a final ascent to mystical theology with Cusanus and Dionysius. In his own work, Lefèvre finished with the philosophers, the Fathers, and the mystics by 1520; he gave the last sixteen years of his life to biblical studies, a hot but risky field in the early years of the Reformation. His evangelical leanings put him in danger for a few years after 1523, but royal authority protected him in his last decade.[46]

More loyal than Lefèvre to the matter and form of scholastic thought was his close contemporary, Pietro Pomponazzi, another famous — some would say notorious — Aristotelian of their day.[47] Born in Mantua in 1462, around the same time as Lefèvre and about ten years before Trapezuntius died, Pomponazzi remained active through the third decade of the next century. Although the new humanist methods that Bruni promoted had spread to the universities by Pomponazzi's day, elegance and erudition did not interest him, yet he still profited in various ways from the revival of antiquity. Pomponazzi stood at a crossroads in the history of Aristotelianism. On the

---

[46] Lefèvre (1972: pp. xii–xiv, xxii–xxiv, 21); Rice (1970: 140–4).

[47] Fiorentino (1868); Kristeller (1951a; 1955–6; 1956: 279–86; 1961a: 35–42, 134–8; 1964a: 72–90; 1972b: 37–42; 1983a; 1990a: 102–110); Di Napoli (1963); Nardi (1965); Poppi (1970b), (1988: 653–60); Cassirer (1974: i. 98–120); Zanier (1975b); Graiff (1976; 1979); Schmitt (1983a: 98–102); Garin (1985); Pine (1986); Kessler (1988: 485–507); Lohr (1988: 597–604). For primary sources, see Pomponazzi (1567; 1954; 1957; 1966–70; 1970); the treatise *On the Immortality of the Soul* is translated in Cassirer, Kristeller, and Randall (1948: 257–381).

one hand, he studied logicians and natural philosophers of the fourteenth century who were *passé* for most of his Italian colleagues; these medieval doctors were still known in Galileo's time and beyond, but Pomponazzi was one of the last in Italy to regard them as central to his inquiries. On the other hand, some of Pomponazzi's philosophical peers—his adversary Agostino Nifo, for example—were taking up Greek as a direct route to a more genuine Aristotle. Encouraged by Ermolao Barbaro the younger, Angelo Poliziano lectured in Florence on Aristotle's Greek text and sided with Cicero against John Argyropoulos on a key point of terminology in his *Miscellanea* of 1489. A few years later, cracks in the fortress of Latin Aristotelianism at Padua encouraged the hiring of Niccolò Leonico Tomeo, an Italian-born Greek, to lecture on the Greek Aristotle. Demetrius Chalcondyles had begun teaching Greek poetry and grammar in Padua nearly three decades earlier, and Aristotle was probably also one of his subjects. His successor, Marcus Musurus, taught the Greek poets and playwrights after 1503 while helping Aldo Manuzio follow up his Aristotle edition with other Greek books, including the ancient commentators as well as Plato.[48] Much of this was lost on Pomponazzi, who never mastered Greek. His Latin was closer to Swineshead's than to Cicero's, but he responded philosophically to the achievements of humanism, as when he applied recently revived Neoplatonic teachings on the soul to the hotly disputed problem of immortality. He spoke warmly of Lefèvre as an authority on Dionysius the Areopagite, but if he had known how the Parisian used Aristotle's metaphysics as a conduit to mysticism, it is hard to imagine that his admiration would not have cooled.

Pomponazzi began his studies at Padua in 1484; then he taught there with great success for twenty years, moving only briefly to Ferrara; he settled at Bologna in 1511, where he worked until his death in 1525. Nicolaus Copernicus and

---

[48] On Nifo see Nardi (1958); Poppi (1970a); Mahoney (1968; 1970a; 1970b; 1971a; 1971b; 1976c; 1983; 1986); Zambelli (1975); L. Jardine (1981); see also Geanakoplos (1962: 111–67; 1974; 1976: 231–64; 1989: 24–9, 52–3, 60–1, 114–29); Grafton (1988a: 48–50).

Thomas Linacre both came to Padua during Pomponazzi's tenure, in the same years when Paduan professors pioneered new approaches to human anatomy in medical education, a development that culminated in Vesalius' researches at Padua later in the century. During the twelve decades or so between Pomponazzi's arrival and Galileo's departure in 1610, the learned community that Shakespeare called 'fair Padua, nursery of arts', achieved a distinction in scientific and medical studies unmatched elsewhere in Europe. Thus, Pomponazzi's career in northern Italy brought him close to the most exciting advances of his time in science and medicine. In keeping with the nature of his university appointments, he approached Aristotle from a perspective quite distant from Bruni's humanism or Lefèvre's theologizing. Bruni saw Aristotle almost uniquely as an authority on moral philosophy; Lefèvre used him as a stepping-stone to divinity; but Pomponazzi's Aristotelianism developed entirely within the framework of natural philosophy, assuming that one understands natural philosophy to include the psychological and epistemological issues raised by Aristotle's *De anima* and, by extension, the metaphysical, ethical, and theological consequences of interpreting that work in a Christian context. Pomponazzi published a number of books on Aristotle's *libri naturales* or on topics growing out of them; he also left a substantial body of manuscripts, some still unpublished. When a moral or theological problem arises in these works, its motivations come from natural philosophy, and Pomponazzi's answers to such questions have a decidedly naturalistic ring. One issue that attracted a good deal of his attention in later life was the problem of miracles. Pomponazzi excluded miracles less rigorously than Hume, but his whole strategy was to find purely natural causes for effects that seemed to be supernatural. By leaving no room within philosophy for faith or supernatural agency, he provoked criticism from religious quarters and aroused suspicions among believers that colour his reputation to this day.[49]

[49] Shakespeare, *The Taming of the Shrew* I. ii. 2; Randall (1961); Poppi (1970*a*); Siraisi (1973); Schmitt (1984: ch. 1); Pine (1986: 110–11); above, n. 13.

In his own century and later, even in the era of Leibniz, Kant, or Hegel, Pomponazzi's fame (or notoriety) endured because he prominently revived an old philosophical challenge to an indispensable Christian dogma, the immortality of the soul. Aristotle says in *De anima* that part of the human soul, the *psuchê* that enlivens the body, is mortal, perishing with the body, while another part continues to exist eternally even after the body dies. But Aristotle fails to say whether the immortal part of the soul preserves its individuality after death; perhaps, as some of his greatest students were to argue, the soul enters into a state of unitary immortality for mankind in general, so that whatever survives has no personal identity and, hence, no stake in an after-life of pain or pleasure dependent on individual moral choices. The crucial passage of *De anima* is obscure, even when elucidated by other relevant texts, and its interpretation had long baffled Aristotle's expositors.[50] Ancient pagan commentators found the Philosopher's meaning elusive, and medieval Christian readers saw this vexed question as more and more perplexing. By referring to the resurrection of the body and to an eternity of reward or punishment, the first Christian creeds testified to the development of a doctrine of personal immortality in the primitive church. These early Christian views were heavily influenced by Neoplatonic readings of Plato, who taught that the human soul is immaterial and the human person immortal. Once purged of concomitant elements (such as metempsychosis) that were religiously unacceptable, a Platonic psychology and eschatology became the core of later Christian doctrine on the fate of the individual soul. Meanwhile, in the second century CE, Alexander of Aphrodisias wrote commentaries on *De anima* that were to conflict with Christian teaching on the soul, and, in the twelfth century, Averroes proposed another line of interpretation that was equally offensive. Beginning in the thirteenth century, scholastic philosophers and theologians in Paris and elsewhere debated this question hotly and often. Although their argu-

---

[50] Aristotle, *On the Soul* 413^{b}25–9, 415^{b}1–7, 429^{a}18–21, 430^{a}20–6; Lloyd (1968: 184–7, 195–201); Pine (1986: 75–7).

ments continued long after his death, Thomas Aquinas offered a compromise that satisfied many Catholic authorities, whatever its fidelity to Aristotle's original intentions. He described the higher intellective soul both as the form of the body and as a substance separable from it. Thomas regarded the claim that the individual human soul (at least the highest part of it) is immortal as a *philosophically* sound position in accord with Aristotle. After the early fourteenth century the controversy simmered, but then it boiled over again at Padua in the late fifteenth century, when Pomponazzi was a student.[51]

From early in his career at Padua, Pomponazzi found himself at odds with Nicoletto Vernia and his students. Vernia began his public career with an Averroist *Question on the Unity of the Intellect* but was compelled by church authority in 1489 to retract his Averroism and eventually to prepare another work *Against the Perverse Opinion of Averroes on the Unity of the Intellect and the Happiness of the Soul*. A succession of north Italian professors (Blasius of Parma, Paul of Venice, and others) had prepared the way for Vernia, as Vernia anticipated some of Pomponazzi's positions, especially in making use of the ancient Aristotelian commentators and also of Neoplatonic ideas. Pomponazzi succeeded Vernia at Padua in 1499 as professor of philosophy, remaining in that position for ten years and at first presenting a thoroughly Averroist version of Aristotle. Very soon, however, he began to develop a more independent line of his own on the soul. By 1516, when he finished his famous work *On the Immortality of the Soul*, his efforts to discover how a single soul could simultaneously sustain many different vital functions had led him to question Averroes, Thomas, and Ficino, and finally to move closer to Alexander of Aphrodisias, but under strong Neoplatonic influence. Since all parties agreed that the soul's powers of growth (vegetative) and perception (sensitive) must perish with the body, only its powers of thought (intellective) might require immortality; but Pomponazzi showed that even mind

[51] Copleston (1960–6: ii. 375–87, 423–41); Lohr (1982: 87–94); Kuksewicz (1982a: 595–6; 1982b); Mahoney (1982c: 611–15); Pine (1986: 78–90).

needs matter to do its intellective work and hence must cease to be when the body dies. No mental act, no matter how lofty or abstract, occurs without connection to matter via images or phantasms; hence, mind cannot survive the destruction of the body that sustains it. Inspired by the Neoplatonic notion of degrees of being between matter and non-matter, Pomponazzi eventually described the soul as matter's highest form; philosophy could go no further, and as for the soul's immortality, this was a philosophically 'neutral' issue insoluble by reason and ultimately the province of revelation. Meanwhile, in 1512 the Roman Catholic church had convened a great meeting, the Fifth Lateran Council, primarily to deal with complaints of ecclesiastical corruption and to consider plans for church reform. In its main purpose the council failed; Martin Luther began his revolt in 1517, the very year the council ended. But in 1513, pulling the reins on the wrong horse as the team was about to bolt, the church solemnly decreed that the immortality of the individual human soul was a truth of religion that philosophers must teach and make clear.[52]

Pomponazzi's denial that philosophy can prove immortality was by no means original; others had often said as much, even an authority as revered as Duns Scotus, and his troubling conclusion emerged in *De immortalitate* only after a long exchange of argument and counterargument in the scholastic style. The fact remains, however, that the promulgation of the Lateran decree put Pomponazzi in special danger of heresy charges, which his enemies were glad to make. At the same time (and somewhat foreshadowing Galileo's tactics in the *Discourse*), Pomponazzi may have deliberately provoked the *cucullati*, the hooded monks, by making a Dominican speak for controversial points in his treatise, thus embarrassing the head of this powerful order, Thomas de Vio, who had also declared *against* the Lateran position but only *before* the actual decision of the council. In any event, Pomponazzi did not insist that the soul is mortal, only that tools of reason used by

---

[52] Pine (1986: 55–65, 86–95, 99–102); on Vernia see Mahoney (1968; 1976b; 1978a; 1982a; 1982b; 1983; 1986); see also Kessler (1988: 485–96).

philosophers cannot prove its immortality. After much complicated analysis, he concluded that the human soul has an intermediate status between material and immaterial entities, ending on a theme that echoes and transforms the Neoplatonism of Marsilio Ficino and Giovanni Pico, whose works date from only a generation earlier. The soul is mortal in one sense, in another sense immortal.

The immortality of the soul is a neutral problem. . . . No natural reasons can . . . [prove] that the soul is immortal, . . . still less . . . mortal. . . . Wherefore we shall say, as Plato said . . . , that to be certain of anything, when many are in doubt, is for God alone. . . . Moreover, every art ought to proceed by things proper and fitting to that art, . . . as Aristotle says. . . . But that the soul is immortal is an article of faith . . . proved by what is proper to faith, . . . revelation and canonical scripture. . . . Other reasons are foreign, and . . . [do] not prove what is intended. Hence it is not surprising if philosophers disagree . . . about the immortality of the soul. . . . Plato wrote so many and such great things about . . . immortality, . . . yet I think that he did not possess certainty. . . . But those that go the way of the faithful remain firm and unshaken. . . . And therefore these are the things that must be said in this matter, yet always submitting myself in this and other matters to the Apostolic See.[53]

As many arguments support immortality as refute it, and philosophy has no sure answer. For assurances of immortality one must look to faith and ecclesiastical authority.

To take the measure or to test the sincerity of Pomponazzi's fideism, one must consider the conditions of ecclesiastical culture and theological doctrine in which he reached his conclusions. Throughout the fourteenth century the power of church hierarchy in Europe had been severely tested by the removal of the popes to Avignon, by the domination of French interests, and, finally, by scandalous disputes over the succession to the throne of St Peter, but with its success at the Council of Constance in the early fifteenth century, the papacy recovered for a time from decades of schism and confusion. The church's central authority not only prevailed against various institutional

[53] Translation in Cassirer, Kristeller, and Randall (1948: 377–81); Pine (1986: 109–12).

disruptions but also restrained any intellectual dissent that might have been provoked by thinkers as creative as Ramon Lull. The Thomist view of church power and of the relation between philosophical and revealed truth flourished in this context; by the same token, Thomas's account of Aristotle's epistemology shored up ecclesiastical authority by denying the sufficiency of interior illumination, the inner light that was to guide so many dissident spirits of the Reformation. North of the Alps, a confident scholasticism had established metaphysics as a science useful to the church, and had developed metaphysical support for Christian teachings on creation, immortality and other topics at odds with Aristotelian positions. When the friars came to Italy to establish Scotist and Thomist chairs of philosophy, they brought their theologized metaphysics with them, and it deeply offended the sensibilities of the Italian natural philosophers in Pomponazzi's tradition. Thus, in denying a philosophical basis to the doctrine of immortality, Pomponazzi was proclaiming the autonomy of his profession, advocating secular philosophy in a Christian culture, but he was also roiling the intellectual waters beneath the expensive, delicate ship of late medieval theology. In fact, some critics, noting Pomponazzi's clever arguments not only *against* demonstrable immortality but also *on behalf of* mortality, have doubted his sincerity in leaving the issue philosophically undecided. On the soul, on miracles, on demons and angels and other topics, he reached heterodox conclusions, yet no biographical evidence proves that he professed his faith cynically. As he died, he said that he would go happily 'where all mortals go', leaving an ambiguous testament that will not settle the argument.[54] May it not be that in contending honestly with difficult and dangerous questions, questions that he could not resolve, he simply located the boundary between faith and reason differently from the way most of his contemporaries dared or, indeed, otherwise than church officials would have liked?

Pomponazzi spent much of his career at Padua, whose faculty

[54] Gilson (1986: 217–25); Kristeller (1964a: 84–90); Lohr (1988: 596–606); cf. Pine (1986: 3–39, 48–53, 103, 109, 119–23, 344–68, with quotation on p. 51).

included not only its long-standing complement of natural philosophers and logicians, who shared his wish to explicate Aristotle without accommodating theological interests, but also theologians and metaphysicians whose orientation was conspicuously religious. Dominican Thomists and Franciscan Scotists were his teachers, colleagues, and adversaries. Before its author died in 1525, *De immortalitate* had provoked eight different published refutations; the most important rebuttals came in 1518 from Agostino Nifo, a student of Vernia, and in 1519 from Ambrogio Flandino, an Augustinian. The Pomponazzi affair was one of the *causes célèbres* of Renaissance philosophy, and its effects reverberated through the next century. No wonder that when Pomponazzi finished his treatises *On Fate* and *On Causes of Natural Effects or on Spells* in 1520 he withheld them from publication. In the latter work Pomponazzi eliminated all non-natural agency from physical causation, denying, in other words, the traditional Christian view of angels, demons, and even miracles attested in scripture. Having eliminated these supernatural forces, Pomponazzi replaced them with divine action as transmitted through the celestial intelligences and ultimately through astrological influences. Pomponazzi preferred stars and planets to demons and angels because he regarded the heavens as *natural* causes of earthly effects. His naturalist defence of astrological and occult powers jars modern sensibilities, just as he outraged contemporary opinion by suggesting that religion itself, even the Christian religion, can be understood as the result of world cycles plotted by astrologers. In the five books of *De fato*, he threatened orthodox belief on another key point, the freedom of the will, presenting a thoroughly determinist picture of the world along Stoic lines in Books I and II, but in the last three providing a milder Thomist account of predestination compatible with Christian ethics. Here, as elsewhere in his work, Pomponazzi's presentation of the Christian position has convinced some readers that he wanted to weaken the church's case.[55] That we will ever be sure of his intentions is unlikely, but we can be

[55] Di Napoli (1973: 85–159); Pine (1986: 275–343); Poppi (1988: 653–60).

Aristotelianism

certain that his achievement in Aristotelian natural philosophy was memorable.

Of Francesco de Vitoria's accomplishments in moral and legal philosophy we can say the same.[56] Vitoria was born in Burgos around 1492, a momentous year for the New World whose impact on the Old he was greatly to influence. In 1509 he came as a novice Dominican friar to the Convent of St Jacques in Paris, where his early work as an arts student included Greek and other humanist instruction, preparing him broadly for higher studies in philosophy and theology. While still very young he seems to have helped Pierre Crockaert, restorer of the *via antiqua* in Paris, with an important new edition of the *Secunda secundae* of Thomas Aquinas, a large section of the *Summa theologica* that deals with 'special ethics' or particular moral issues. After finishing his licentiate and doctorate in theology in 1522, Vitoria returned to Spain and quickly rose to the first chair of theology at Salamanca, where he taught until he died in 1546. Publishing almost nothing in his lifetime, Vitoria devoted himself to a remarkably effective career of teaching that made him a major force in shaping the 'School of Salamanca' in its earlier Dominican and later Jesuit phases. In ordinary lectures he commented on the great *Summa* of Aquinas, emphasizing applied moral philosophy and slighting traditional scholastic interests in logic, metaphysics, and natural philosophy; what little we know of this main body of his teaching comes indirectly from the notes of his students. Vitoria's extraordinary lectures or *relectiones*, delivered between 1527 and 1540 on thirteen pressing moral problems of the day, saw frequent posthumous publication; they covered a wide variety of subjects, ranging from homicide, marriage, and magic to church–state relations and the familiar contest between papal and conciliar authority. It was chiefly these topical *relectiones* that earned Vitoria the title of *doctor resolutissimus*

---

[56] Getino (1930); Beltrán de Heredia (1939); García Villoslada (1938); González (1946); Hanke (1959); Hamilton (1963); Noreña (1975: 36–149); Fernández-Santamaria (1977: 58–119); Pagden (1982: 24–37, 59–118).

or 'doctor most steadfast' when he addressed sensitive questions with small regard for the risk of official reprisal. His reputation as a sympathetic critic of Erasmian humanism, no easy label for a Spanish Dominican to wear, helps explain his engagement in contemporary moral debates and his readiness to take controversial stands.

As the leading Dominican theologian of Salamanca, Vitoria was expected not only to educate his students but also from time to time to advise the Spanish monarchy and its ministers on affairs of state and Christian conscience. Beginning in 1504, canon and civil lawyers, theologians, and other academic experts had reassured the most Catholic kings in a series of consultations or *juntas* that the conquest and enslavement of the indigenous peoples of the Americas were well founded in law and morality. Some Dominicans, especially the missionaries who had witnessed the suffering of Indians at the hands of the *conquistadores*, complained about the brutality of Spanish imperialism; but the findings of the first *juntas* supported government policy, whose original basis was a papal bull of 1493 that transferred to Spain rights in the New World granted earlier to Portugal. Since the pope's authority to make such arrangements involved him in temporal jurisdictions, this claim naturally offended those who wished to confine papal powers to the spiritual realm. Thus, in order to find a firmer foundation for Spanish policy, it was expedient for a *junta* in 1521 to invoke a different principle, the theory of natural slavery recently set forth in a commentary on the *Sentences* of Peter Lombard by John Mair, who took his ideas from Aristotle's *Politics*.[57]

In the first pages of the *Politics* and elsewhere, Aristotle treated the human condition not as a fixed essence belonging equally to all members of the biological species but as a *telos*, a state of completion or perfection, against which individuals might be judged as attaining the fullness of humanity more or less completely. Aristotle measured the spectrum of the more human and the less human psychologically, describing states of

[57] Noreña (1975: 1–20, 37–68, 87–92, 97–101); Pagden (1982: 37–41).

soul governed in the best people by intellect, in the worst by
appetite. This view of biological mankind as graded between
ideally intellectual humans and bestially appetitive not-so-
humans enabled Aristotle to claim that when 'there is such a
difference as that between soul and body or between men and
animals . . ., the lower sort are by nature slaves, and it is
better for them . . . [to] be under the rule of a master'. Seizing
on this and other pronouncements of the Stagirite, apologists
for Spanish colonial policy asserted not only that Indians were
slaves by nature but also that enslavement would help them
become more human by forced association with European
masters—a Christian scholastic vision of the white man's burden whose appalling arrogance needs to be seen in its time and
place. Faced with whole new worlds of humanity and nature in
the Americas, Europeans scurried for the handiest categories
as they groped to comprehend the novelties of conquest, and
naturally they found many answers ready for the taking in the
prevailing Peripatetic philosophy. Aristotle had not only devised the convenient concept of natural slavery, he had also
reinforced the older Greek notion of the barbarian, recalling
how 'the poets . . . thought that the barbarian and the slave
were by nature one'. Having identified the uncultured barbarian with the half-human natural slave, Aristotle gave his
Renaissance expositors the license they sought to enslave people
whose religion was not Christian and whose behaviour was
not European.[58] What better proofs could there be of barbarism and natural unfitness for the pursuit of virtue in civil
society?

These arguments and other rationalizations of Spanish policy
in the Americas found their harshest voice in Juan Ginés de
Sepúlveda, an Italianized and dogmatic minister of the crown
who wrote his *Democrates secundus* around 1544, only to see it
swiftly condemned and denied publication by the Universities
of Salamanca and Alcalá. Sepúlveda's interesting polemic also

[58] Pagden (1982: 10–24, 41–50); Aristotle, *Politics* 1252^{a}24–1255^{b}39,
1259^{b}16–1260^{b}20, 1332^{a}39–1334^{b}26, 1337^{a}33–1338^{b}38 (Jowett trans.);
Nicomachean Ethics 1095^{a}14–30, 1142^{b}34–1143^{a}4, 1145^{a}26–33, 1148^{b}15–
1149^{a}21; *Parts of Animals* 673^{a}19–26; *Wonderful Things Heard* 836^{a}6–19.

aroused the wrath of Bartolomé de Las Casas, a Dominican missionary bishop who became his century's most celebrated advocate of humane treatment for the Indians. Inasmuch as his book remained suppressed, Sepúlveda lost his case against the Indians in the famous debate with Las Casas at the Valladolid *junta* of 1550–1, but government policy did not change dramatically in response to this academic spectacle. Spain's American empire continued to evolve along political and economic lines of least resistance.[59] Within the academic province of moral philosophy, the basis for opposition to Sepúlveda had been established by Vitoria; as early as 1534 he showed impatience with the barbaric treatment of native Americans by Europeans who so ruthlessly manipulated the taxonomy of civilization and barbarism.

In 1521 Tenochtitlán and the Aztec empire of Montezuma fell to the forces of Hernan Cortés. Eleven years later Francisco Pizarro imprisoned and then killed the Inca Atahualpa, and by late 1533 Pizarro had taken Cuzco, the Inca capital. The two Francisco de Montejos, father and son, campaigned against the Maya in Yucatán from 1527 until the fall of the peninsula in 1546. In conquering these Indian kingdoms the Spanish encountered cultures whose structure and complexity matched European expectations better than the smaller and simpler societies ravaged in the earlier Caribbean phase of empire-building. The tragedies of Peru and Mexico belied the claims of Sepúlveda and others who saw Indians as mentally deficient savages incapable of social, civil, or cultural achievement. The murder of Atahualpa especially enraged Vitoria, who wrote in 1534 that 'if Peruvian natives were monkeys instead of human beings, I would recognize that they could not be victims of "injustice". However, being our fellow-men and subjects of the Emperor, I cannot . . . excuse the *conquistadores* . . . [or] praise their . . . massacres and their pillages.'[60]

---

[59] Andrés Marcos (1947); Losada (1948–9); Bruton (1953); Giménez Fernández (1962); Hanke (1974); Mechoulan (1974); Noreña (1975: 97–101); Pagden (1982: 109–45); cf. Fernández-Santamaria (1977: 163–236), who takes a less negative view of Sepúlveda.
[60] Translation of a letter written by Vitoria in 1534, in Noreña (1975: 63).

Vitoria's most effective statements against imperial policy came in his two *relectiones* of 1539 *On the Indies* and *On the Right of War*, particularly the former. In the first part of the *Relectio de Indis*, he refuted four arguments that denied the Indians political autonomy. That Indians were sinners he found irrelevant: only John Wyclif and other heretics made grace a prerequisite of political dominion, which in Vitoria's Thomist politics was a natural consequence of human sociability. Likewise, the description of Indians as infidels evaporated with the scholastic distinction between vincible and invincible ignorance. Evidence of civil, social, economic, and cultural order in Indian societies disposed of the two remaining arguments, that Indians were either mentally defective humans or else irrational subhuman creatures of some other kind, fit only for slavery. Although Vitoria debated these points pro and con in the scholastic manner, his clear belief, already institutionalized in the bull *Sublimis deus* issued by Paul III in 1537, was that the Indians were not slaves by nature. His view was less brutal in its motives and implications than Sepúlveda's, yet it demeaned the Indians as children—if not slaves—of nature, classifying them as underdeveloped humans whose mental powers had not progressed fully from potency to act. The missionaries who had first condemned the *conquistadores* wanted fully human souls to convert and new Christian subjects for the empire. Their intentions were nobler than those of the *encomenderos* for whom the Indians were only so much chattel labour, free people only in the abstract terms of a grant of *encomienda*; but the missionaries still paid small respect to cultural autonomy or individual liberty. As for Vitoria, he knew that the tide of empire was irreversible in the Americas, and on religious grounds he had to regard Christianization of the Indians as good and necessary. He drew the line only at forced conversion, denying any right of violence against Indians who simply refused the gospel, but admitting force readily and perhaps cynically when needed to defend agents of the faith against the aggression of their unwilling beneficiaries.[61]

[61] Noreña (1975: 74–122); Fernández-Santamaria (1977: 75–87); Pagden (1982: 57–108).

Vitoria was a priest who used his command of Aristotelian philosophy to impugn the justice of Spanish conquests that subdued half a hemisphere. Jacopo Zabarella was a lay Aristotelian whose accomplishments in logic, epistemology, and psychology caused a stir only in the narrower world of the university. If the moral theologian Vitoria showed small interest in natural philosophy, Zabarella, a logician and natural philosopher, expressed his Aristotelianism in a contrary manner. He tried to keep Aristotle's authority independent of theology and subject to rational criticism: 'I will never be satisfied with Aristotle's authority alone', he wrote; 'I will always rely upon reason . . . and . . . imitate Aristotle in using reason.'[62] Born in Padua in 1533, Zabarella died there in 1589, having been granted the doctorate by his city's university at the age of twenty, whereupon he immediately began almost four decades of teaching and writing philosophy in Padua. Although a generation separated the beginning of his career from the end of Pomponazzi's, Zabarella worked in the same tradition of natural philosophy and logic, the secular Aristotelianism of the north Italian universities. For a few years he taught logic in Padua's lowest-paid position, then moved to the second chair of natural philosophy, and finally won the first chair in that field, the loftiest and most lucrative philosophical post in the university. Italian universities paid their medical professors better, however, and held them in greater esteem, so many philosophers, who had often earned medical degrees along the way, also taught medicine. Gabriele Falloppia, Andrea Cesalpino, and Ulisse Aldrovandi were all famous physicians of Zabarella's day who taught philosophy before proceeding to chairs of medicine, but Zabarella himself chose not to teach medicine. He belonged to the same faculty that taught medicine, however, and most of his students encoun-

[62] Translation in Schmitt (1983a: 10-12, 16-18, 30-32, 153); on Zabarella see also Edwards (1960; 1969); Gilbert (1960: 164-79, 211-18); Randall (1961: 48-68); Dal Pra (1966); Bottin (1972); Poppi (1972); Wallace (1972-4: 139-55); Crescini (1972); Cassirer (1974: i. 136-44); Jardine (1974a: 54-8); Schmitt (1981: ch. 8); Ashworth (1988: 145-6, 169-72); Park (1988: 479-84); Kessler (1988: 530-34); N. Jardine (1988: 686-93).

tered philosophy while preparing for medical careers. The professional climate of his university was thus quite hospitable to Zabarella's zeal for natural philosophy.

The Paduan passion for science was a continuing theme in its history, well in place long before Pomponazzi arrived; but the university had also evolved in the fifty-three years between his death and the publication of Zabarella's most important work, the *Opera logica* of 1578. Zabarella's education, unlike Pomponazzi's, was thoroughly humanist, and he put it to good use in explicating Aristotle. When he felt the need to analyse an Aristotelian text in its original language, he did not hesitate to use Greek words and phrases in his commentary. In one case, for example, he shows that certain logical distinctions are hard to make in Latin because that language lacks a definite article: the difference between 'a man' and 'the man' in English or *un uomo* and *l'uomo* in Italian corresponds more or less to *anthrôpos* and *ho anthrôpos* in Greek, but the Latin *homo* must cover both cases. In appreciating such distinctions, Zabarella had learned from Bruni and Valla, but he also inherited scholastic habits of mind from Aquinas and Pietro d'Abano, the latter an eminent Paduan physician of the early fourteenth century. Although logic, method, and natural philosophy were Zabarella's great loves, he shared with Bruni and other humanists a taste for the rhetorical and literary side of Aristotle's works. He wrote no treatises on these subjects like those of his Paduan contemporary, Antonio Riccobono, but he discussed the role of rhetoric and poetics in the larger philosophical encyclopedia. Like other Aristotelians who taught in the Italian universities, he was active in several Paduan academies devoted to broader cultural pursuits. By action and by inclination, he joined the scientific impulse of the Paduan tradition to the humanist love for letters without contradiction or inconsistency.

Zabarella wrote commentaries on several Aristotelian texts, most notably the *Posterior Analytics*, the *De anima*, and the *Physics*. More widely read, however, were his *Opera logica* of 1578 and a 1590 collection of short treatises *On Scientific Subjects* (*De rebus naturalibus*). His natural-philosophical works were among the finest products of late Renaissance Aristotelianism, but he is best remembered as a logician. Given his obligations as a teacher, it comes as no surprise that Zabarella saw logic and method as approaches to medical and scientific problems, and in this sense his *Opera logica* represent the culmination of a very long development within Latin Aristotelianism. Along with his extensive, learned, and penetrating commentary on the *Posterior Analytics*, which was Aristotle's primary statement on what we would call 'scientific method', the *Opera logica* also include two brief but much discussed treatises *On Methods* and *On Regress*. The similarity between these works of Zabarella and certain questions pursued by Galileo has long been recognized, and in his concern with scientific demonstration one can see a link to the interests of Bacon as well as Galileo. More clearly than most philosophers of the scholastic type, he acknowledged the need for an empirical connection in scientific knowledge, and he took great pains to delineate the various stages of scientific demonstration. In his treatise *On Methods*, he uses the phrase *scientificae methodi*, but it would be wrong to take these words as meaning 'scientific methods' in the modern sense.[63]

The methods that Zabarella had in mind were based on his interpretation of the *Posterior Analytics* by way of Aristotle's Greek and Muslim commentators. A major topic in Peripatetic discussions of demonstration was the problem called *regressus* or demonstrative regression, which arose from Aristotle's distinction in the *Posterior Analytics* between demonstrating the *dioti* (the 'wherefore' or *propter quid* in Latin) and demonstrating the *hoti* (the 'that' or *quia*). The former procedure, which the Latins called *methodus compositiva* or *demonstrativa*, involved inference from a known cause to its unknown effect; the reverse process from effect to cause was the *methodus resolutiva*.[64] Aristotle permitted the middle term (see below) of a demonstrative syllogism to express either cause or effect,

[63] Gilbert (1960: 171); Randall (1961: 49, 61); Wallace (1972–4: 144–5).
[64] Aristotle, *Posterior Analytics* 78ᵃ22–9; Crombie (1953: 24–9, 55–90, 296–308); Gilbert (1960: 104–7, 167–7); Randall (1961: 50–2; 1968); Cassirer (1974: i. 136–43).

likewise for the major term, yielding two basic arrangements, of which one may be symbolized as follows:

All *NE* are *NT*.
All *P* are *NE*.
Therefore, all *P* are *NT*.

This shorthand represents Aristotle's view that heavenly bodies which do not twinkle (*NT* bodies) are those near the earth (*NE*), so that nearness to the earth causes the non-twinkling of the planets (*P*). In this case, when the middle term of the syllogism (*NE*) stands in a causal relation to the major term (*NT*), demonstration proceeds a priori by composition, while resolution follows the opposite a posteriori path when the middle term (now *NT*) is the effect and the major term (now *NE*) is the cause:

All *NT* are *NE*.
All *P* are *NT*.
Therefore, all *P* are *NE*.

Zabarella believed that the first or compositive method leads to knowledge of substance, so planets may be defined as heavenly bodies that do not twinkle; resolution only provides information about accidents, such as that planets happen to be near the earth. Together the two patterns of reasoning cover all cases of demonstration. But since effects are better known *to us* than their causes, while causes are better known *in themselves* than their effects, the best possible demonstration must involve middle terms of both types: it must 'regress' or move from one to the other, from resolution to composition. Unlike some of his predecessors — Agostino Nifo, for example — Zabarella invested great epistemological confidence in this double method, concluding that logic is a powerful instrument that can produce new demonstrative knowledge of causes. Yielding the sceptics no quarter, he distinguished the two *methods* leading to new knowledge from mere *procedures* that only reshuffle knowledge that already exists. The joint product of the resolutive and compositive methods is the construction of natural philosophy, whose aim is to know the states of bodies as they can be observed. Despite his appreciation of experience, Zabarella treated induction as a weaker kind of resolutive method, not as a distinct type of inference. He regarded sensible images as stimuli that cause the *possible* intellect, a passive phase of mind, to receive from the mind of God signs of universals presented to it by the *agent* intellect, mind's active phase. Hence, there is no genuine inference in induction, only a kind of feedback or movement between two analogous structures of information, from observed individuals as tokens of universals to other tokens of the same universals presented by the agent intellect to mind.[65]

Despite his weak view of induction, Zabarella had great confidence in observation and experience, respecting the Thomist principle that nothing comes into the intellect except by way of the senses.[66] The concreteness of Zabarella's epistemology as well as the technical refinement and rigour of his logic were the strengths of his philosophical achievement, whose major defects lay in the areas of mathematics and method. Most important, Zabarella failed entirely to appreciate the role of mathematics in understanding nature. But the incomprehension of mathematics was a weakness of Aristotelian natural philosophy in general, not just of Zabarella's version. Medicine and biology—which, despite William Harvey's work on circulation, would long remain impervious to quantification—continued to preoccupy Zabarella and other Italian Aristotelians just at the moment when Galileo and Kepler were about to make their great breakthroughs in mathematicized physical science. Moreover, even those Peripatetic philosophers who shared Zabarella's openness to experience had few productive ideas about organizing the data of sensation in scientifically useful ways. Bacon's attempts to construct a discipline of observation were little better in their direct benefits for the practice of natural philosophy, but at least they proclaimed an empiricist ideal that proved more inspiring than Zabarella's efforts to reform Peripatetic methodology.

---

[65] Aristotle, *Posterior Analytics* 71^{b}6–72^{a}5, 78^{a}22–^{b}2; Randall (1961: 53–60); L. Jardine (1974*a*: 54–8); N. Jardine (1988: 686–93).

[66] Schmitt (1981: ch. 8); above, Ch. 1, n. 38.

History has been kinder to Bacon than to Zabarella, but less generous with John Case, Britain's leading Aristotelian at the end of the sixteenth century.[67] Case's obscurity results in part from the generally impoverished condition of academic philosophy in the British Isles between the last quarter of the fourteenth century, when the great days of Oxford's Merton College came to an end, and the last quarter of the sixteenth, when Case's generation effected a reawakening of Peripatetic thought. From the late fourteenth until the early sixteenth century, the influence of the Merton school worked more powerfully in Italy and the centre of the Continent than in England, where philosophy at Oxford and Cambridge became routinized and derivative. Only John Mair, a Scots Franciscan who did his best work at Paris at the opening of the sixteenth century, recalled the level of excitement provoked by Walter Burley in later medieval England. After 1525, even England's attenuated Aristotelianism dried up when humanist rhetoric displaced scholastic logic in the curriculum and vigorous Protestant theologies washed over the arid subtleties of Scotus. The Spain of Vitoria, the Germany of Melanchthon, the France of Lefèvre, and the Italy of Pomponazzi nurtured new variants of the Peripatetic tradition, but scholasticism in England all but vanished in the middle quarters of the sixteenth century. The publication of English logic-books illustrates this trend.[68] The last truly medieval logic text was printed in England in 1530, one of about twenty such works published in the previous fifty years. Readers then waited fifteen years for the first edition of John Seton's popular *Dialectica*, whose appeal rested on its adherence to the anti-scholastic views of Valla and Rudolf Agricola. Next in 1551 came Thomas Wilson's *Rule of Reason*, a very successful vernacular logic. Until 1570, when Richard Stanyhurst published his *Harmonia seu catena dialectica* in London, editions of Seton or Wilson were all that England had to offer, and only after this time did frequent publication in logic begin again. At least twenty-four logic

[67] Schmitt (1983*b*).
[68] Howell (1956); Ashworth (1974: 2–3; 1988: 143–53, 162–3); Schmitt (1983*b*: 13–76); L. Jardine (1988: 181).

texts appeared in England in the 1580s. Twenty of them were in Latin; one was John Case's *Summa veterum interpretum* of 1584, which went through seven other editions in Oxford and Frankfurt by 1622.

Born near Oxford around 1546, Case spent his whole adult life serving the university in one way or another until he died in 1600. He entered St John's College in 1564, ten years after its foundation, and his undergraduate education seems to have mixed the new humanism with the tired scholasticism of the time, leading him to the BA in 1567, the MA in 1572, and a fellowship in the same year. In 1574 he lost his fellowship when he found it prudent to marry the widow of the keeper of Bocardo, Oxford's prison; he turned to making a living by private teaching at home, the calling that fed him for at least fifteen years thereafter. He took his MD in 1589, and during the same year income from a church benefice improved his financial picture, which had grown solid enough by 1584 to allow him to make a sizeable gift of money to St John's. 1584 also saw his first publication, the work on logic mentioned above, the *Summary of the Old Interpreters of Aristotle's Whole Dialectic*, and eight other published works followed by 1599. Thirty-eight editions of his books eventually appeared in England and Germany, the latest in 1629; he dedicated them to Robert Dudley, Earl of Leicester, Sir Christopher Hatton, Sir Thomas Egerton, and Thomas Sackville, Lord Buckhurst, all of whom connected him with the world of Elizabethan court patronage. Except for a few school texts, his books were more often reprinted than any other British works of philosophy of the sixteenth century. They represent the acme of revived Aristotelianism in Renaissance England.

Like most Peripatetics in northern Europe of the sixteenth century, Case was more interested in moral philosophy and dialectic than in metaphysics or natural philosophy, and this choice was in keeping with the educational programme of the English universities, which at this time were less concerned with the higher faculties of law, medicine, and theology than with the broader mission of the arts curriculum in its post-humanist version. Case's *Summa veterum interpretum* of 1584, for example, is a sketchy beginner's logic oriented toward the rhetorical task of persuasion in moral discourse; it slights the problems of demonstrative inference explored in depth by Zabarella and others who emphasized natural philosophy and medicine. Two other works are even more elementary: the *ABCedarium moralis philosophiae* of 1596 is a primer on moral philosophy for very young readers; and the *Ancilla philosophiae* of 1599 is its counterpart in natural philosophy. Case's other Aristotelian treatises aim at a more advanced readership. Four are expositions of Aristotle's moral and political works. The *Mirror of Moral Questions* comments on the *Nicomachean Ethics*; the *Reflection of the Moral Mirror* analyzes the *Magna Moralia*; the *Sphere of the Commonwealth* treats the *Politics*; and the *Treasury of Economy* deals with the *Oeconomics*. Of these the most important was the *Sphaera Civitatis* of 1588, launched in the Armada year to attract a European audience to an English political philosophy. Case's treatment of Aristotle's *Physics*, the *Lapis philosophicus* or *Philosopher's Stone* of 1599, was an equally original offering in natural philosophy.[69]

Case organized his books methodically and with didactic intent, following the argument of the corresponding Aristotelian texts book by book but not covering every topic introduced in the original. His chief tool of analysis was the familiar medieval *quaestio*, usually followed by a handy summary in the form of a *tabula* or bifurcating outline of the kind popularized (though not invented) by the Ramists. Case's motives, set forth in the prefaces to his books, were those of a teacher, but he also wished to make his own mark on philosophy. To this end, he consulted an impressive range of sources, contemporary and medieval, and he was not afraid to follow where his inquiries led. Although some accused Case of being a secret papist at a time when Catholicism was dangerous and unpopular in England, he seems to have kept the Anglican faith, which did not prevent him from making Thomas Aquinas his most cited author. His lists of authorities also name Scotus, Buridan, and Burley among the medieval doctors, as well as

[69] Schmitt (1983*b*: 77–105).

Francisco de Toledo, Juan de Celaya, Benito Pereira, Sepúlveda, and the Jesuits of Coimbra among the moderns. When commenting on Aristotle's *Oeconomics*, he used Bruni's translation, and he also depended on the humanist Aristotelianism of Donato Acciaiuoli, Lefèvre d'Étaples, Pier Vettori, and Giulio Pace. His choice of reading was eclectic, like much of the Peripateticism of his day, and it was at least open-minded, if not in the advance guard of Renaissance thought. Above all, Case's philosophy was forthrightly Aristotelian, as he wrote in the preface to his *Ancilla*: 'Since without Aristotle every short-cut [*compendium*] in philosophy is a detour [*dispendium*], let me bring Aristotle to your attention as the only one who does philosophy, when the vain and varied opinions of this age have been left behind.'[70]

Case's loyalty to Aristotle permitted him, in the spirit of his age, to consult other philosophers as well, especially the ancient schools and sages revealed by the researches of the humanists. He adopted the common scheme of the *prisca theologia* or 'ancient theology' as an account of the earliest history of philosophy, tracing its genealogy backward from Aristotle and Plato through the pre-Socratics to the fabled wisdom of Egypt and Chaldaea. Where he saw the need, he applied Platonic or Neoplatonic solutions to problems that arose in a generally Aristotelian context. On the other hand, his vituperative criticisms of Machiavelli and Paracelsus were motivated not only by the material errors that he discerned in their writings but also by the threat that they posed as original critics of the traditional world-view sustained by—and sustaining—the Peripatetic philosophy of the schools. Case was conservative, but not doctrinaire. In the *Lapis philosophicus* he took an innovative view of the art/nature relation that left more room than many Peripatetics would allow for the alchemical art to improve on nature. He was no humanist himself, but he read Aristotle in the framework created by humanism, deciding points of interpretation from the form of Greek words, for example, or rejecting the *De mundo* as

[70] Case (1599: 1); Schmitt (1983*b*: 139–63).

inauthentic for philological reasons. Philological analysis of Aristotle touched his own work closely in the case of the *Oeconomics*, whose first and third books he regarded as genuine, while isolating the second as spurious on grounds of doxographic and stylistic evidence previously set forth by Lefèvre.[71]

Case was an unusual figure in his own country, but a characteristic type on the larger stage of Protestant northern Europe. More effectively than any other Englishman, he combined traditions of scholastic and humanist Aristotelianism that had been separate in the previous century. He paid more attention to history and philology than any scholastic, but he maintained scholastic forms of organization and inquiry in his expositions of Aristotle. It was Case who brought the new humanist-scholastic Aristotle to Renaissance Oxford, reviving interest in standard philosophical questions which had found few substantive answers in England since the Reformation and preparing the intellectual revival that began early in the next century. Case left a body of philosophical works more comprehensive in coverage and more serious in intent than any English university philosopher since Burley. If, from a broader perspective, one takes philosophy to include new currents in political and theological speculation outside the university tradition, his only rivals or betters were John Colet, Thomas More, Thomas Cranmer, Richard Hooker, and a few other original thinkers of the Tudor period. Case bequeathed a renewed sense of Peripatetic philosophical discipline to the next generation of Englishmen, the most adventurous of whom, most notably Francis Bacon, were to abandon it more decisively than Case's predecessors.

[71] Schmitt (1983*b*: 164–7, 172–8, 181–6, 191–216).

3

Platonism

Aristotle remained the dominant force in early modern philosophy before Descartes, and in some respects early modern thinkers knew Aristotle as the medieval schools had known him. When Renaissance philosophers recovered Aristotle's Greek and put it in better Latin, they still preserved much of the scholastic apparatus for understanding his ideas. One strong challenge to scholastic Aristotelianism came from the recovery of other ancient philosophies that could claim equal intellectual authority, and it was Aristotle's teacher, Plato, for whom such claims were most credible. The career of Platonic philosophy in the early modern period differed from the contemporary development of Aristotelianism in at least two ways: Renaissance Platonism, clearly a product of humanism, marked a sharper break with medieval philosophy; and one person, Marsilio Ficino, can be called the moving spirit of the Platonic revival. Despite his extraordinary mastery of Greek and his extensive knowledge of ancient texts long unread in the West, Ficino was no humanist in the strict sense of the term; he was a philosopher, not a philologist. But the enormous success of his translations and interpretations of the Greek works of Plato and the Neoplatonists presupposed the humanist revival of antiquity as the prevailing intention of the high culture of quattrocento Florence, where Plato was reborn and whence his fame soon spread all over Europe.

In the earliest period of Italian humanism, in the fourteenth century, some thinkers who knew little about Plato none the less preferred him to Aristotle. In 1367, for example, Petrarch wrote an invective *On His Own Ignorance and That of Others* that spared Aristotle himself from the harshest charges brought against Aristotelian scholastics, but Petrarch still found Plato

'praised by greater people, Aristotle by a larger number ...
[because] Plato and the Platonists ascended higher in matters
of divinity; although neither could go where he wanted, ...
Plato came closer.' Explicitly following St Augustine, Petrarch
made Christian dogma the touchstone of philosophical truth,
and on this criterion some important Aristotelian positions—
an eternal world, an improvident God, a human soul with no
clear claim to immortality—had long since run afoul of credal
obligation and religious conviction.[1] Platonism better accommodated these and other Christian doctrines, especially Platonism as modified by Plotinus and his successors and as adapted
by the Church Fathers for various theological purposes. Plato
was especially influential among the theologians and apologists
of the East who wrote in Greek, such as Clement, Origen, and
pseudo-Dionysius, but Latin authors read in the medieval West
also saw the advantage of buttressing their faith with Platonic
wisdom. Platonism seemed so hospitable to Christian teaching
on creation, immortality, and the afterlife that the Church
Fathers paid Plato the dubious compliment of believing him to
have lifted his ideas from Moses and other biblical sages.

   The revival of antiquity and the new Greek philology prepared the humanists for a richer debate than the Fathers or the
schoolmen had conducted, not only about Plato's religion but
also about his social, political, and philosophical doctrines: his
élitist educational programme; his abdication from a politics of
the here and now; his elevation of intuition over reason; and
his account of reason's vulnerability to Socratic scepticism. On
these grounds and more, some found Platonism persuasive,
but against such attractions one must set a number of problems
that could only perplex a Christian thinker. Why should an
upwardly mobile scholar or bureaucrat sympathize with Plato's
élitism? Were humanists not troubled by his scorn for poets
and rhetoricians? Plato's advocacy of communism and adver-
tisement of homosexuality invited political and social complaint. Even his renowned piety seemed out of tune with a
philosophy that made matter eternal, the human soul pre-

---

[1] Petrarch (1975: 1118); Cassirer, Kristeller, and Randall (1948: 111).

existent and migratory, and the gods and demons many, power-ful, and worthy of worship. As the Renaissance came to know Plato better, discussion of his thought could not have been other than complex and divided, and the controversy had been prepared by an anti-Platonic tradition long sustained by pagans and Christians alike. As early modern thinkers developed new modes of reading unknown to antiquity and the Middle Ages, Plato's compatibility with Christianity remained the leading question.[2]

A main channel for Platonic currents in Western medieval theology was Augustine. When Petrarch cited the *City of God* as putting Plato 'nearer the truth than that whole ancient troop of philosophers', he was repeating a familiar formula.[3] Passages in Plato's dialogues about homosexual love or the transmigra-tion of souls might offend Christians, and Augustine himself was often critical of Platonism, yet the spiritual, other-worldly motivation of Plato's thought covered a multitude of lesser sins. In many ways Christians found Platonic philosophy safer and more attractive than Aristotelianism, and this greater com-patibility raises a question as interesting as it is unanswerable: how might Western intellectual history have changed if Plato's dialogues had re-entered Europe along with Aristotle's treatises in the high Middle Ages? The question can only help us speculate, but we can recognize the historical complications and ideological tensions that characterized the actual relations between Christianity and a more attenuated Platonism. Augus-tine attributed his movement toward conversion partially to 'some books of the Platonists translated from Greek into Latin [in which] . . . I read, not of course in these words, "In the beginning was the Word and the Word was with God and the Word was God"'. Augustine saw a number of Platonic teach-ings reflected in the language of John's Gospel; but in the end 'that "the Word was made flesh and dwelt among us" I did not read there', nor did he see several other items indispensable to

[2] Hankins (1990*a*: i. 5–26).
[3] Petrarch (1975: 1104); Cassirer, Kristeller, and Randall (1948: 101); Augustine, *City of God* 8. 5–11; Kristeller (1956: 355–72; 1961*a*: 55–8; 1964*a*: 8–13); Wilkins (1961: 8–13, 144–51, 197–8); Garin (1965*a*: 24–7).

Christian belief.[4] At best, Platonism for Augustine was an incomplete inducement to a higher truth, a defect consistently recognized by Platonizing Christians who caused or called attention to other problems as well.

It was probably in the fifth century but after Augustine's time that an unknown author influenced by the Neoplatonism of the period of Proclus wrote four Greek works titled *Divine Names*, *Mystical Theology*, *Celestial Hierarchy*, and *Ecclesiastical Hierarchy*, along with ten surviving letters. Taking the scriptural pseudonym Dionysius, this writer acquired apostolic authority when he assumed the identity of the person named in Acts 17:34 as converted by Paul's speech before the Areopagus in Athens, and in the ninth century the translations of Hilduin and John Scotus Eriugena gave pseudo-Dionysius a Latin readership. Taking its main inspiration from Proclus, the affirmative theology of the *Divine Names* aims to know God by analogy with those features of creation deemed compatible with his perfections, while the negative way of the *Mystical Theology* paints a minimalist portrait of God by stripping visible creaturely imperfections from its abstract picture of transcendent divinity. The Neoplatonism of the Dionysian works exposed them to charges of heterodoxy, especially on Christological and trinitarian issues, and as early as the sixth century challenges to their textual authenticity also arose. The most convincing criticism came in the 1440s from Lorenzo Valla, who in his *Collation of the New Testament* subjected them to the same philological tests that uncovered the forged Donation of Constantine. Erasmus and others accepted Valla's doubts about the Areopagite, but this did not stop figures as well informed as Lefèvre d'Étaples and John Colet from propagating the fervour for Dionysius that had marked Western theology from Eriugena to Aquinas and Nicholas of Cusa. Boethius, who lived through the first quarter of the sixth century, was another early medieval author whose problematic credentials as a Christian did not weaken his influence. Often called the first scholastic, he invented a Latin terminology for

---

[4] Augustine, *Confessions* 7. 9. 13–14 (Chadwick trans.).

medieval philosophers when he applied Aristotelian categories to the problem of the Trinity and undertook a vast but incomplete project of translating Aristotle into Latin. He also wanted to translate Plato, and in his wish to reconcile Plato with Aristotle he anticipated an important impulse in Renaissance thought. He read Porphyry and other Neoplatonists, and the tenor of his enormously influential *Consolation of Philosophy* is Platonic—as, for example, when he uses the *Timaeus* to establish the goodness of creation as God's gift.[5]

Valla and other critics of scholasticism distrusted Boethius as the originator of a misguided philosophy that perverted language and corrupted its ancient purity; but Petrarch, having written a book *On Remedies for Both Kinds of Fortune* whose motivation recalls that of the *Consolation*, admired Boethius as an imitator of Augustine. Petrarch also defended Plato against his own scholastic enemies who 'claim that Plato wrote nothing but one or two little books'. His counter was that he had 'sixteen books by Plato or more at home. . . . Let them come and see our library, which is not unlettered though it belongs to an illiterate. . . . They will note not only several in Greek but also some turned into Latin. . . . What part of Plato's books is this? I have seen many with my own eyes.' Petrarch, who campaigned to have himself crowned poet laureate in Rome on Easter Sunday of 1341, called himself illiterate only to contrast his attainments ironically with those of his professedly learned detractors; but in one sense his failure ever to reach his goal of learning Greek kept him an unlettered spectator of the most important remains of antiquity. He owned a partial Greek codex of Plato and struggled to read Homer, but he was only a little less isolated from the genuine texts than his medieval predecessors, as he confessed in writing his thanks when given a Greek Homer in 1348:

[5] Laistner (1966: 85–91, 323–9); Copleston (1960–6: ii. 91–135); Minio-Paluello (1970); Sheldon-Williams (1970: 457–72, 518–33); Liebeschütz (1970: 538–55, 576–93); Gersh (1978; 1986: ii. 647–718); Ebbesen (1982: 101–10, 121–7); Lohr (1982: 80–8); Monfasani (1987c); Watts (1987); Gregory (1988: 54–6, 70–80); Wetherbee (1988: 24–33, 42–9); Stump (1989: 31–66); Chadwick (1990).

'Your Homer is dumb to me, or rather I am deaf to him. Yet I delight in the mere sight of him.'[6]

Knowledge of Plato in the West had been confined to a few fragmentary glimpses since the time of Augustine, who learned Greek in school but seems not to have read Plato in the original. The direct Latin tradition available in Augustine's time included versions of the *Protagoras* and *Timaeus* 17–47 by Cicero and the *Phaedo* by Apuleius, but only a fragment of Cicero's *Timaeus* circulated after the early sixth century and then only in a limited way; even the humanists ignored it until the late fifteenth century. Calcidius had translated a longer piece of the *Timaeus*, probably in the fourth century, and had added a commentary that brought his work great renown throughout the medieval period. In the twelfth century, Aristippus of Catania added the *Meno* and *Phaedo* in rigidly literal versions, and a part of the *Parmenides* appeared with Proclus' commentary, embedded in the thirteenth-century translation by William of Moerbeke, who rendered other works of Proclus as well. Meanwhile Christian and pagan authors had long supported an indirect Platonic tradition. Augustine's role was central because of his philosophical depth and his familiarity with a wide range of materials from late antiquity; but Ambrose, Lactantius, and other Latin fathers were also valuable, as were Clement, Origen, Basil, and other Greeks in Latin translation. Boethius may have been Christian, but he read Plato from a point of view that respected pagan conventions. Pagan or Christian, Calcidius was paramount because of his commentary, more influential than Macrobius or Martianus Capella. Cicero, Apuleius, Valerius Maximus, Servius, and many other non-Christian authors known to medieval readers carried their share of the Platonic legacy, which entered the early medieval encyclopedia with Cassiodorus and Isidore in the sixth and seventh centuries and reasserted its philosophical energies with Eriugena in the ninth. The part of the *Timaeus* that Calcidius analyzed stimulated the great revival of Platonism centered on

---

[6] Petrarch (1975: 1118–20); Cassirer, Kristeller, and Randall (1948: 112–13); trans. of 1348 letter in Wilkins (1961: 135–6, 171–3, 207–8); Weiss (1977: 150–92); Geanakoplos (1988: 350–4); below, p. 262, on Martin of Braga.

the cathedrals of Chartres and Paris in the twelfth century. Peter Abelard, Bernardus Silvestris, William of Conches, and others awakened indirect memories of Neoplatonic schemes of interpretation, especially the allegorical exegesis that took any views contrary to its chosen theological line as incentives to peel away textual surfaces hiding some deeper truth. Compatibilities between the biblical story of creation and the cosmology of the *Timaeus* alerted Christian readers to listen for other resonances between Platonic and Mosaic scriptures. Once issued the licence of Calcidian hermeneutics, medieval Platonists wasted no time in moving beyond the immediate cosmological content of the *Timaeus* to compose moral and political variations on the grand themes of microcosm and macrocosm.

Thus, before absorbing new Aristotelian texts in the thirteenth century, medieval philosophy went through a Platonist phase during the period often called the 'twelfth-century Renaissance', and even in its full vigour scholasticism was more open to Platonic influence than one might think. Some of Proclus was translated, commentaries followed, and works actually of Neoplatonic origin were attributed to Aristotle; the influential *Book of Causes*, for example, can be traced to Proclus. Given the quantity of Platonic material transmitted through Moslem authorities or otherwise in the air in medieval universities, it is not surprising that parts of Thomist metaphysics owe more to Augustine, Proclus, or Plotinus than to Aristotle.[7] But some important features of the Platonic tradition could not be appreciated until the original texts were recovered and their historical relations to one another were clarified. The second part of this task is still under way, and the work could start only when Ficino and his successors uncovered the primary evidence and began to interpret it. In our time, when most readers of Plato still do not know that Ficino first made him accessible in Western Europe, we take for granted the complexity of the Platonic tradition in its historical development over a millennium; when Justinian closed the Platonic school of Athens in 529 and the Platonic inheritance

---

[7] Dillon (1977: 401–8); Klibansky (1981); Gersh (1986: i. 1–25; ii. 779–807); Gregory (1988: 54–80); Hankins (1987*b*; 1990*a*: i. 4–5); Kristeller (1987); above, Ch. 1, n. 11.

of Alexandria passed to the Muslims in 641, more than ten centuries had passed since the Athenians killed Socrates.

During these thousand years, Platonism evolved from the teachings of its founder through the Old Academy of his first successors, the New Academy of the next sceptical generations, the newly dogmatic Middle Platonism of the three hundred years before Plotinus, and the Neoplatonism of the four centuries following.[8] Plato's thought was itself complex enough to have kept his interpreters busy to this day deciding which was the real or the mature or the sincere Plato: the sceptic or the dogmatist, the pragmatic statesman or the abstruse theologian, the Socratic Plato or the Platonic Plato? As early modern thinkers sensed their alienation from medieval culture and their kinship with antiquity, they shaped the contours of a temporal perspective that allows us to take for granted the principles of change and development without which so long-lived a cultural construct as Platonism will always remain opaque to historical inquiry. But in Ficino's day the philological and historical labour had only begun. If we wish to imagine the Platonic tradition from a Renaissance point of view, we would do better to think of our own popular conception of the deep past of ancient Egypt, with its long parade of indistinct dynasties, than of recent epochs in which historical change is more visible. As we shall see, Ficino actually diminished the historicity of Platonism by superimposing a mythic genealogy, the idea of an ancient theology rooted in Mosaic times, on the real historical connections that he knew only in bare outline distorted by chronological error. Since it was Ficino who fashioned the early modern idea of a Platonic tradition more unitary and more sympathetic to Christianity than we now know it to have been, we should be wary if friends of Plato might wish to dismiss early modern Aristotelianism as a ponderous monolithic dogma. No early modern Aristotelian rivalled Ficino in his impact on the history of philosophy; but by the same token the Aristotelianisms of the Renaissance were more varied than Platonism as Ficino depicted it.

Renaissance thinkers knew that Plato, Plotinus, and Proclus

[8] Above, Ch. 1, n. 12.

were different philosophers separated by time and doctrinal difference, but for early modern people historical distance was less well defined in quantity or quality than it is for us. The fact that Christianity was closer in time and doctrine to Neoplatonism than to any other phase of the tradition made it tempting to turn the varieties of Platonic thought into a harmonious chorus of pious *Platonici*. Despite Ficino's impulse to Christianize Plato himself, problems of trinitarian theology were resolved better by the Plotinian hypostases of One, Soul, and Mind than by Plato's less schematic theology, and the Neoplatonic conception of philosophy as a way toward union with God supplied Christian mystics with some of their richest inspiration. Christians and Neoplatonists had so much in common that it was natural for Ficino and others to view Platonism from a Neoplatonic perspective as a unified tradition. A Neoplatonic stance implied less interest in Plato's politics than in his metaphysics, little notice of the ironically diffident Socrates but great readiness to construct intricate theological hierarchies; it also meant that the *Phaedrus*, *Symposium*, *Timaeus*, and *Parmenides* would be more important than the *Euthyphro* or *Theaetetus*. Platonism in its Neoplatonic version produced theologies that removed God's transcendent reality so far from the illusory matter of the lower world that elaborately graded spiritual hierarchies soon arose to fill the ontological vacuum. Neoplatonists also aimed at clear metaphysical principles—the pre-eminence of unity, the priority of cause over effect, the conception of grades of reality as grades of consciousness—that distinguished their systems from Plato's thought not only in leading to doctrinal differences but also in promoting a dogmatic programme of philosophy. It is hard to imagine Plato writing a work as didactic as Proclus' *Elements of Theology* or even the more discursive *Theology of Plato*; Ficino's *Platonic Theology* has much more in common with the schematic Proclus than with the fluent Plato, even though Ficino appreciated Plato's literary gifts and admired his playful spirit.[9]

---

[9] Tigerstedt (1969; 1974; 1977); Lloyd (1970; 1990); Merlan (1970); Wallis (1972: 1–15); Coulter (1976); Dillon (1977: 43–69); Witt (1977); Gersh (1978); Allen (1984*a*; 1986); Lamberton (1986).

Ficino and other Renaissance students of Plato were disposed
by their experience of Neoplatonism and their belief in Christianity to take a syncretist approach to the Platonic tradition,
whose development over a period of centuries when other
philosophies and religions came into their own naturally tempted many thinkers to work eclectically toward an improved
Platonism. In the Hellenistic and imperial periods, Platonists
took advantage of progress in logic and natural philosophy
made by Stoics and Peripatetics. They also heard promises of a
better life in this world or the next made by Neopythagoreans,
Gnostics, initiates of mystery religions, alchemists, astrologers,
and theurgists. Theurgy, a pragmatic magical technique for
attaining the divine union that Plotinus had sought through
philosophy and contemplation, was of great interest to the
later Neoplatonists, who were avid readers of the *Chaldaean
Oracles*, purportedly a collection of wisdom from the world
east of Greece that would supply the diligent seeker with a
road-map to the godhead. The supposition of a mysterious
'oriental' origin for such arcane doctrines, set in the framework of Pythagorean and other philosophical doxographies,
gave the Platonic tradition the aura of a secret society whose
teachings passed from generation to generation of initiates,
unsullied by outsiders. Much extravagant speculation arose
from this semi-fabulous historiography, much of it far from
Plato's intentions, perhaps, yet of great importance to Renaissance Platonists.

Evidence that Plato was heir to an esoteric ancient theology
was available not only in Diogenes Laertius, Apuleius, and
other classical sources but also in the writings of the Church
Fathers; none the less, the *prisca theologia* became a major
element in Western historiography only in the later fifteenth
century, when Ficino and Giovanni Pico made it famous.[10]
Although Pico and Ficino were not professional humanists,
their promotion of the ancient theology took for granted a
broader assumption of humanism: that the place to find wisdom

[10] Walker (1972); Schmitt (1981: chs. 1, 2); Hankins (1990*a*: ii. 460–4);
above, Ch. 1, n. 1; below, n. 18.

was in the distant past. This principle was the common property of Platonists like Ficino and Pico and of the many classicizing scholars of the earlier Renaissance, whose knowledge of Plato was skimpier and whose interest in philosophy was as a rule quite limited. During the first half of the century, when Leonardo Bruni turned away from Plato to Aristotle, humanists in the city of Florence paid little attention to philosophy except as it might answer ethical questions. Bruni himself concentrated on Aristotle's major works of moral philosophy, which were also translated by Giannozzo Manetti, best known for having written a treatise in 1452-3 on the fashionable 'dignity of man' theme, developed earlier by Antonio da Barga and Bartolomeo Facio. In contrast to the cynicism of the *Two Books on the Misery of the Human Condition* composed in 1455 by Poggio Bracciolini, Manetti's four books *On the Dignity and Excellence of Man* took an optimistic view of humankind as active and inventive, not pitted against a jealous deity like the Greek Prometheus but made in the image of a triune God whose powers of intellect, memory, and will are reflected in the faculties of the human soul. A remarkable feature of Manetti's work is its first book in praise of the body, which shows an unusual grasp of Aristotelian natural philosophy and Galenic medicine, thus confirming Manetti's reputation as 'a fine scholar in Greek, Latin and Hebrew, eminent in moral and natural philosophy, and a theologian equal to any of his time'. The unusual items in this contemporary encomium are Hebrew, theology, and especially natural philosophy. More typical of Florentine humanism before Ficino's time was Poggio's frank admission to a young scholar in the mid-1450s: 'I am wanting in the art of philosophy.'[11]

In 1454 the Peace of Lodi brought a new stability to the Italian city-state system, but peace and security for the Floren-

---

[11] Field (1988: 42-4); Bracciolini (1964-9: iii. 174-5); Vespasiano da Bisticci (1963: 372 (George and Waters trans.)); Kristeller (1956: 261-86; 1961a: 120-39; 1972b: 1-21; 1988b: 271-6); Holmes (1969: 1-35, 68-167); Trinkaus (1970: i. 210-70); Di Napoli (1973: 31-84); below, n. 32. On Poggio see also Shepherd (1837); Walser (1914); Rubinstein (1958-64); Tateo (1961); Castelli (1980); Flores (1980); Fubini and Caroti (1980); Trinkaus (1989b); on Manetti see also Wittschier (1968); Fioravanti (1983).

tines briefly spelled trouble for Cosimo de' Medici, the political boss whose grip on the city's affairs had grown ever tighter since his return from exile in 1434. The years after 1455 were difficult for Cosimo and his party, which recovered its control over Florence's electoral politics only in 1458. Poggio, the most prominent humanist spokesman for the Medici, lost the chancellorship in 1456.[12] During this turbulent period, controversy also disturbed the University of Florence. Carlo Marsuppini, another eminent humanist who had been chancellor before Poggio and after Bruni, taught classical literature and moral philosophy in the university, which had been closed intermittently since its foundation in 1321. When Marsuppini died in 1453, Donato Acciaiuoli and other young Florentines from powerful families wanted him replaced by a teacher of equal skill and stature, but the city officials, during this interlude of anti-Medici sentiment, proposed lesser appointments that blocked the ambitions of Acciaiuoli and his friends. Manetti was unavailable because of tax troubles with the city; Poggio was no teacher and too busy besides; and the Medici disliked another obvious choice, Francesco Filelfo, the great Hellenist and polemicist. In the end, a compromise settled part of the job on Cristoforo Landino, who eventually became famous as a Platonizing moralist and interpreter of Virgil and Dante; the other post in philosophy went to the Byzantine Aristotelian, John Argyropoulos, who accepted his appointment in 1456–7 and lectured on Aristotle for the next fifteen years.

The first Byzantine scholar to influence Italian humanism significantly was Manuel Chrysoloras, whose teaching in Florence for three years after 1397 formed the earliest generation of Western Hellenists, including Bruni, Roberto Rossi, and Niccolò Niccoli. By 1402 Chrysoloras and Uberto Decembrio had finished their rough rendering of the *Republic*, which, on the evidence of Decembrio's later *Six Books on the Republic* (*c.* 1420), would seem to have appealed to its first Western translator as a defence of the signorial rule that Uberto knew

[12] Field (1988: 10–35); Martines (1963; 1968); Rubinstein (1966); Kent (1978); A. Brown (1979; 1986).

in the Milan of the Visconti. Uberto's son, Pier Candido, became secretary to Filippo Maria Visconti in 1419, and he was still in the agitated duke's employ when he finished his revised Latin *Republic* twenty years later. The younger Decembrio had to face critics who doubted Plato's moral and theological rectitude as well as his educational usefulness, and in refuting them he was more aggressive but less skilful than Bruni had been, using every possible device of suppression and interpretation to make the *Republic* an ahistorical ground-plan for a timeless Christian polity. Meanwhile, Bruni's more sophisticated misreadings of the dialogues continued until 1435, by which time Francesco Filelfo and other less famous scholars had begun to turn more of Plato into Latin. Besides Bruni and Ficino, a dozen quattrocento humanists translated, wholly or in part, the *Letters*, the *Epinomis*, various pseudonymous works, and half the dialogues now commonly treated as genuine: the *Apology*, *Crito*, *Phaedo*, *Charmides*, *Lysis*, *Euthyphro*, *Ion*, *Gorgias*, *Phaedrus*, *Symposium*, *Republic*, *Parmenides*, and *Laws*. A year after Chrysoloras died in 1415, George of Trebizond arrived in Venice, and during the middle years of the century he added three dialogues of Plato to his long list of Aristotle translations. Theodore Gaza, who displaced George as Aristotle translator for Pope Nicholas but contributed little to the Latin Plato, came to Italy just after the Council of Ferrara and Florence in 1438–9, where Plethon had declared himself Plato's champion against Aristotle. When Ficino later claimed that the idea of a Platonic Academy came to Cosimo from Plethon, he may have meant only that Plethon had given Cosimo a Greek codex of Plato. A greater influence on Ficino was Plethon's favourite student, Cardinal Bessarion, who tried to save Plato for Christianity and defend him against the calumnies of Trapezuntius without defaming Aristotle. As the controversy between Trapezuntius and Bessarion reached its height, Argyropoulos began his work in Florence, where for fifteen years he did little but teach Aristotle and translate him into Latin.[13]

[13] Field (1988: 35–126); cf. Burckhardt (1990: 145–6); Garin (1954: 211–87; 1958: 155–90; 1976: 89–129); Geanakoplos (1989: 91–113); Hankins

Like many other Byzantines, Argyropoulos first came to Italy because of the Council; then he studied at Padua and finally returned to Constantinople, only to flee again in 1453 when that ancient city fell to the Turks. Argyropoulos became Aristotle's most influential translator in the fifteenth century; unlike Bruni, he moved beyond the ethical works to logic, metaphysics, and natural philosophy; and, unlike Trapezuntius, he aimed for a freer and more fluent Latin better suited to an Italian audience. Although he took Bessarion's side against Trapezuntius and gave Plato an honourable place in the history of philosophy, Argyropoulos remained convinced of Aristotle's primacy and had little sympathy for the 'ancient theologians' who preceded Socrates and fascinated Ficino and his circle. What Argyropoulos had to offer Florence, both in his teaching and in his translating, was the first systematic exposition of the whole range of Aristotle's works in a setting attractive to recipients of humanist education. What he had in common with Ficino was a more serious inquiry into *all* the requirements of philosophical discourse than had been possible within the constraints of the earlier humanist programme, with its limited focus on ethics and politics. In other words, Argyropoulos presented the full Greek Aristotle to intellectually ambitious Florentines at the same time as Ficino revealed all of Plato to them in Latin. That both philosophies appealed to this audience is evident in the later career of Donato Acciaiuoli, who spent five years methodically taking notes on Argyropoulos' lectures and then worked some of them into a commentary on the *Nicomachean Ethics* in 1463–4. While Acciaiuoli's commentary is not explicitly Ficinian, it treats the question of friendship in a manner compatible with Ficino's views on love and also with the interests of the Medici party in a harmonious political order.[14]

Bessarion's attempt in the *Calumniator* to defend Plato against charges of homosexual immorality came even closer to

(1990*a*: i. 89–95, 105–48, 163–5; ii. 436–40, 819–22; 1990*b*; 1991); on Argyropoulos, see also Lampros (1910); Garin (1937*b*); Cammelli (1941–54: ii); Vasoli (1959); Seigel (1969); Verde (1974); above, Ch. 2, nn. 24–7, 48.

[14] Field (1988: 45–51, 123–33, 202–30).

Ficino's doctrine of Platonic love. This feat of exegetical sublimation was but one use of a hermeneutic that Bessarion had taken from his teacher Plethon. A native of Trebizond, Bessarion became a Basilian monk in 1423 at the age of twenty and soon rose in the imperial service; he was entrusted with diplomatic work even before he studied with Plethon in the early 1430s.[15] He may have helped persuade John VIII Paleologus to agree to the celebrated Council of Union, the event that first brought him to Venice in 1438 as an 'orator' or spokesman for the Greeks before the great assembly. The Council reached its climax in Florence's Duomo in the summer of 1439 when the Greeks, worried as much by the Turks as by Christology, agreed to union. In the chief theological dispute, which contested the credal formula for genetic relations among the persons of the Trinity, Bessarion began as an ardent advocate of the Greek view, and he never lost his native distrust of scholastic dialectic in theology. But by combining the Dionysian negative theology with the metaphysics of Proclus and the philology of Byzantine and Latin scholars, he was able to argue for theological and ecclesiastical accord with the West, as ultimately expressed in the Council's declaration of 'one faith in a variety of rites'. To convince himself and his compatriots that compromise was possible, he insisted that the suspect Latin logic could not truly upset Greek belief based on faculties of intuition and experiences of illumination superior to discursive reason. Bessarion thus added a genuinely Neoplatonic dimension to the humanist critique of dialectic as it had been known since Petrarch's time.

Bessarion became a cardinal in 1439, at the age of thirty-six, but catastrophe marred the triumphs of his early career when Constantinople fell to the Turks in 1453, causing him to redouble his efforts to save Greek philosophy by finding a Western haven for it in Venice, where his remarkable library became a treasury of Greek manuscripts preserving the Platonism of late antiquity. From the perspective of Bessarion's adaptable

[15] For Bessarion, see above, Ch. 2, n. 25; Kristeller (1972*b*: 86–109); see Hankins (1990*a*: i. 217–63) for what follows here; on the Council, see Geanakoplos (1989: 224–54).

Christianity, the ancient Neoplatonists seemed to verify Plethon's claims for an ancient theology in which Plato was a precursor of Christ. The Fathers charged that Plato had stolen his wisdom from Moses; the schoolmen boasted that the Peripatetic system was of a higher order than Plato's incoherent fables; but Plethon's ancient theology allowed Bessarion to honour Plato as the greatest in a line of holy sages who had made straight the way of the Lord. Although three of four books of his *Calumniator* simply adopt the structure of the polemic that they answer—the *Comparatio* of Trapezuntius—and look back to the Greek debates incited by Plethon, one of the four looks ahead to the *Platonic Theology* of Ficino, whose Neoplatonic hermeneutics Bessarion inspired.

In Neoplatonism Bessarion found a method that had the power of ancient *auctoritas*; it also had the advantage of seeing Plato as both praiseworthy and often in accord with Aristotle. Given the enormous Western investment in Aristotelianism, a Platonism that did not require a complete break with the Peripatetic tradition would be more expedient than Plethon's more exclusive position. Bessarion's readings of Plato on any particular point may excite little philosophical interest, but his *way* of reading deserves more attention and had considerable effect, especially on Ficino. Unlike the scholastics, who were quicker to make distinctions than to discover agreement, Bessarion listened for harmony among his authorities—a consensus that, when taken chronologically, justified the search for an ancient theology and, when understood doctrinally, encouraged eirenic and even syncretist approaches to theology and philosophy. Bessarion also read the ancient texts with the humanist's philological eye, rescuing Plato with crude historicist apologetic by arguing that his errors on pre-existent and migratory souls were inevitable *in their time* if Plato was to maintain the higher principle of immortality. But the cardinal's most important contribution to Platonic philosophy was to revive the Neoplatonic view of the dialogues, seeing them not as profane texts to be understood literally but as sacred mysteries to be deciphered.

This was no work for dialecticians; it needed initiates acquainted with the chains of correspondence that bind an object low in the order of being to the higher entity that it signifies; it required masters of mystagogic language who know that human tongues utter only the mundane facts that imprison bodies and imperil souls, never speaking the sublime sentences that address the Mind and tell the way to union with the One. If a thought is truly worth thinking, its very loftiness makes it obscure to embodied mortals—if discourse of reason measures obscurity. Critics who call Plato's doctrine of recollection heretical, for example, or who recoil from his descriptions of homosexual love are simply incapable of hearing the divine truths beneath the surfaces of human speech. Pederastic passages in the *Symposium* or *Phaedrus* are lower figures for the higher metaphysical love wherein God embraces and unifies all creation. Likewise, Platonic recollection must be understood not in the order of time but in the order of being; the recollecting soul turns within itself and toward its creator, not backward to some past store of memory. Such were the methods and findings of Neoplatonic exegesis that Bessarion passed on to Marsilio Ficino.

Marsilio Ficino

While Bessarion was preparing the Greek versions of the *Calumniator* and Acciaiuoli was writing on Aristotle, Ficino was beginning to translate Plato. In 1462, two years before he died, Cosimo gave Ficino a Greek manuscript of Plato, and in 1463 he added the means to study it at leisure—the proceeds from a farm near Careggi, where the Medici kept a villa. But having a space at the Medici's country place did not isolate Ficino from the life of his city. He continued to live and work mostly in Florence, though the symbolism of Medici patronage and the opportunity of withdrawal that it provided were obviously meaningful in their time and place. After recovering from an unhappy and disorderly decade, the Medici financed Ficino to work out his philosophy of Platonic love and concord; it requires no cynicism to see the ideological component of this arrangement. Ficino's work not only entailed a profounder commitment to the whole compass of philosophy than anything attempted in Bruni's generation; it also glorified the contemplative life and professed an ascetic contempt for the material world not in keeping with the pragmatic interests of the civic humanists. But to see the Aristotelian Argyropoulos as champion of the active life and the Platonist Ficino as prophet of contemplative quietism is too simple. For one thing, Argyropoulos seems to have intended no activist propaganda in his teaching, and, even more important, Ficino's theory of the contemplative life kept his philosophy attractive to the politically and economically vigorous Florentines who supported him. Always urging the ascent of the soul, Ficino presented the contemplative life as the final step in a hierarchy of human action that led people to surpass the active life without utterly denying it; lived well, the active life becomes a step on the way to escaping matter and uniting with God. It was the genius of Neoplatonism to open channels between the divine and the mundane that transcended the world while preserving it as a platform for ascent to the godhead. Ficino, who knew this better than anyone, worked out a philosophy of love that might appeal to the Medici by persuading the Florentines that the closest communion was among their souls, closer certainly than any union of bodies or commerce of material things, closer even than the junction between any one person's soul and body. Love between embodied individuals is a secondary but valued effect of the love of each person for God, toward whom all souls finally converge. Ficino's townsmen could vie with one another for the welfare of the body or particular pleasures, as long as material strife and physical enjoyment were ultimately sublimated in the flight of souls above.[16]

Ficino was born in Figline near Florence in 1433. His father, a physician who treated the Medici, seems to have intended the same career for his son, who studied logic, natural philosophy, and the humanities at the University of Florence in the

---

[16] Field (1988: 3–5, 45–51, 60–4, 104–6, 176–7, 181–201); Kristeller (1988a: 263–88); Nelson (1958); Fubini (1984); Allen (forthcoming).

1450s. Years before the Medici discovered him, Ficino's brilliance attracted other patrons, even some enemies of the Medici. His first philosophical works of the mid-1450s were predictably scholastic treatments of logical, metaphysical, and natural-philosophical topics, but even these early efforts show him leaning toward Plato. His *Institutiones ad Platonicam disciplinam* of 1456 is lost, but a letter of 1455 on familial love uses pseudo-Dionysius to describe the joining of souls in the divine oneness. He began Greek in 1456, and in 1457 he was reading Lucretius and other sources of Epicurean philosophy that helped him to respect pleasures that rise upward toward contemplation and to appreciate the concept of a hierarchy of passions. By the early 1460s he was ready to take up the monumental task that Cosimo assigned him, and he tells us that he read ten of the translated dialogues to the dying magnate in the summer of 1464. All the works of Plato that Ficino translated were ready before the end of the decade, at least in draft, but they were printed only in 1484, accompanied by 'arguments' or short commentaries, but lacking most of the six fuller commentaries collected for separate publication in 1496. About half of what Ficino put into Latin depended to one degree or another on earlier translators, especially Bruni, Bessarion, and Trapezuntius, but he outdid all his predecessors in the precision of his renderings, in his respect for Plato's full texts—whatever their doctrinal blemishes—and in his philosophical insight. Ficino's Latin is faithful to Plato's meaning but a far cry from his elegant Greek, and the intentions of his translation were of a piece with his Neoplatonic reading of Plato. We may gauge the impact of the *Platonis opera omnia* on the Renaissance from its more than thirty printings (including three major revisions) in the sixteenth century.[17]

---

[17] Kristeller (1956: 35–97; 1961a: 48–69); Allen (1989: 15–17, 31–34); Hankins (1990a: i. 267–78, 300–12, 341–2; ii. 465–72, 499–82). Kristeller (1986a) is a comprehensive bibliography on Ficino; with its 11 appendices it runs to nearly 200 pages. The Latin works are still read in Ficino (1959), which is a reprint of the standard 16th-c. edition, and in Kristeller (1937), but see the editions and translations by Allen, Gentile, Jayne, Kaske and Clark, Marcel, and others in the bibliography under Ficino; for the letters translated

In 1462 Ficino had already received his first Plato manuscript from Cosimo when his new patron interrupted him with something he found more momentous. Cosimo had obtained a fourteenth-century Greek text of the first fourteen discourses of the *Corpus Hermeticum*, an eclectic and incoherent collection of pious philosophy actually written in the early centuries of the Christian era but believed by Cosimo, Ficino, and their contemporaries to be the work of Hermes Trismegistus, a Greek version of the Egyptian god Thoth, whom they dated just after the time of Moses. More important, they made Hermes the author of a pagan tradition of divine knowledge, an ancient theology which paralleled and confirmed the revealed truth of scripture and whose Egyptian provenance reinforced the tales of Plato's travels in Egypt. Ficino went quickly to work on this treasury of primeval wisdom, soon producing a Latin version that still holds up under scrutiny if one considers the defects of the text available to him. Why Ficino and Cosimo thought it best to turn away from Plato and toward Hermes for a time becomes clear in Ficino's preface to the work he called

by the London School of Economic Science, see Ficino (1975–), but Ficino (1990) begins Gentile's edition of the Latin texts. The fundamental account of Ficino's philosophy is Kristeller (1988*a*), the most recent Italian version of the 1938 study whose English version is Kristeller (1964*c*). On the philosophy, see also: Kristeller (1939; 1955*a*; 1959; 1961*b*; 1964*a*: 37–53; 1964*b*; 1965*b*; 1966; 1968*b*; 1972*b*: 8–13, 31–40, 54–8, 103–9; 1974: 29–91; 1979*b*: 50–65, 151–63, 169–210; 1983*b*; 1983*d*; 1985*c*; 1990*a*: 89–110); Garin (1939; 1942; 1951; 1965*a*: 78–128; 1983*a*; 1983*b*; 1985; 1986; 1988); Festugière (1941); Cassirer (1945; 1963; 1974: i. 80–98); Chastel (1954; 1961); Saitta (1954); Walker (1958*a*: 3–72; 1958*b*; 1986); Klein (1956; 1960); Sicherl (1957; 1962); Schiavone (1957); Rotondo (1958); Seznec (1961); Klibansky, Panofsky, and Saxl (1964); Yates (1964: 1–83); Wind (1967); Devereux (1969; 1975); Trinkaus (1970: ii. 461–504; 1986); Sensi (1971–2); Tarabochia Canavero (1971–2); Gombrich (1972); Zambelli (1973*a*; 1973*b*); Collins (1974); Allen (1975; 1977; 1980*a*; 1980*b*; 1980*c*; 1981; 1982*a*; 1982*b*; 1984*a*; 1984*b*; 1986; 1987; 1988; 1989; forthcoming); Allen and White (1981); Pintaudi (1977); Purnell (1977; 1986); Zanier (1977); Gentile (1981; 1983; 1986; 1987); Mahoney (1982*a*; 1982*b*; 1986; 1987); Kaske (1982; 1986); Gentile *et al.* (1984); Castelli *et al.* (1984); Fubini (1984; 1987); Copenhaver (1984; 1986; 1987*a*; 1988*a*; 1988*c*; 1990; 1992); Eisenbichler and Pugliese (1986); Garfagnini (1986); Gilson (1986: 89–101); Hankins (1986; 1990*a*; 1990*b*; 1991); Klutstein (1986; 1987); Couliano (1987); Hankins, Monfasani, and Purnell (1987); Buhler (1990); Bullard (1990). The standard biography is Marcel (1958).

a *Book on the Power and Wisdom of God, Whose Title is Pimander*:

At the time when Moses was born flourished Atlas the astrologer, brother of the natural philosopher Prometheus and maternal grandfather of the elder Mercurius, whose grandson was Mercurius Trismegistus. . . . They called him Trismegistus or thrice-greatest because he was the greatest philosopher and the greatest priest and the greatest king. . . . Among philosophers he first turned from physical and mathematical topics to contemplation of things divine, and he was the first to discuss with great wisdom the majesty of God, the order of demons and the transformations of souls. Thus, he was called the first author of theology, and Orpheus followed him, taking second place in the ancient theology. After Aglaophemus, Pythagoras came next in theological succession, having been initiated into the rites of Orpheus, and he was followed by Philolaus, teacher of our divine Plato. In this way, from a wondrous line of six theologians emerged a single system of ancient theology, harmonious in every part, which traced its origins to Mercurius and reached absolute perfection with the divine Plato. Mercurius wrote many books pertaining to the knowledge of divinity, . . . often speaking not only as philosopher but as prophet. . . . He foresaw the ruin of the old religion, the rise of the new faith, the coming of Christ, the judgement to come, the resurrection of the race, the glory of the blessed, and the torments of the damned.[18]

Ficino later modified the pedigree of the *prisca theologia* by heading the list with Zoroaster and dropping Philolaus, but the idea remained powerful with him and with other European intellectuals for the next two centuries. He finished the job of translating the fourteen discourses of Hermes in 1463; they were printed, though poorly, in 1471, two years after the first edition of the Latin *Asclepius*, the only part of the *Corpus Hermeticum* known to the Middle Ages. Much improved in its next printing of 1472, Ficino's *Pimander* remained the most

---

[18] Ficino (1959: 1836; 1975: 50–1); Kristeller (1956: 221–57); Hankins (1990a: ii. 460–4); on the *Hermetica* and related topics, see above, n. 10; also Kristeller (1960); Garin (1961a: 143–54; 1988); Yates (1964); Perrone Compagni (1975; 1978); Purnell (1976; 1977; 1987); Westman and McGuire (1977); Vickers (1979); Allen (1980c; 1988); Copenhaver (1987a; 1988a; 1990; 1992); Faivre (1988); Merkel and Debus (1988); Grafton (1991: 145–77).

influential presentation of the *Hermetica* until the nineteenth century. By the mid-sixteenth century, it had seen two dozen editions and had stimulated vernacular versions in French, Dutch, Spanish, and, most important, in the Italian of Tommaso Benci, also completed in 1463 when Ficino was available to supervise it.

Ficino's ambitions for the ancient theology—which had attracted him from the mid-1450s, even before he could take note of Plethon's admiration for Zoroaster—were more than doxographic. He thought of the history of philosophy not just as a linear transmission of ideas but also as a recurring struggle in which wisdom or faith, philosophy or theology, reason or eloquence might rise or fall as lights of the human spirit. Before Christ came, even the biblical prophets and pagan wise men could not fully grasp the wisdom that God granted only to the inspired few, but the Christian era opened new resources of interpretation to mankind, as when—so Ficino believed— the ancient Neoplatonists used the Areopagite and other Christian authorities to penetrate the secrets of their own Platonic philosophy. Augustine, Origen, and other Fathers of the church then learned from the Neoplatonists, but the subsequent demise of pious philosophy (*pia philosophia*) in the medieval period revealed another jarring rhythm in history. People sometimes enjoyed religious truth in periods of wisdom when the advance of piety coincided with the progress of philosophy, but sometimes the truth was veiled and philosophy parted from religion. 'O you happy times', exclaimed Ficino,

which have kept sound this divine bond of wisdom and religion, . . . [but how] unhappy when . . . separation and wretched divorce occurs . . . between wisdom and decency . . . [and] teaching is left largely to the profane. . . . I beg you, let us now free philosophy, God's holy gift, from impiety . . . [and] do all we can to save holy religion from detestable ignorance.

Ficino wrote so passionately because he believed that the providential mission of *pia philosophia* was to lead humanity toward a 'learned faith' (*docta religio*); Platonic education would help humans recall the Good above and within, thus moving them to justice in the active life and uniting them through the contemplative life in the peace and concord of mutual love in God.[19]

Between 1469 and 1474, after finishing his translations of Plato and seeing his *Pimander* through two editions, Ficino composed his longest original work, the eighteen books of *Platonic Theology on the Immortality of Souls*, dedicated to Lorenzo de' Medici. The first chapter of the first book immediately ties the topic of immortality to a central theme of Ficino's thought, the ascent of the soul. He maintains that, although man's worship of God puts him closer to divinity than any other mortal thing, to allow death to thwart the human yearning for immortality would make mankind the most wretched of creatures, thus violating the order given the world by its creator. The 'author of beatitude' would not so whimsically deny the intentions of his own providence or frustrate the very nature of his most glorious mortal creation. With this assurance, Ficino exhorts his readers to 'loose the chains of these earthly shackles forthwith and fly more freely to the aethereal region, guided by God and lifted on Platonic wings, where in happiness we shall immediately contemplate the excellence of our kind'. Despite the fervent prose and the reference to the Platonists, the inspiration and content of what follows in the *Platonic Theology* is as much patristic and scholastic as classical, depending not only on Plato, Plotinus, and Proclus but also on Augustine and Aquinas. Some of Ficino's reasons for making the soul immortal were familiar to medieval theology, which supplied many chapters of his treatise with material on the faculties of the soul, the attributes of God, the order of nature, and the errors of philosophers. Other themes emerged from Ficino's revision of Neoplatonic categories for adaptation to Christian theology. Thus, the soul's indissolubility follows from its central place in the ontological order below divine and angelic being but above the qualitative and corporeal; if the soul perishes, the whole hierarchy dissolves.[20]

---

[19] Ficino (1959: 1); Hankins (1990a: i. 282–6).
[20] Ficino (1964–70: i. 38–9); Kristeller (1964a: 43–7; 1972b: 31–7; 1974: 73–91; 1988a: 23–5, 265–82, 350–96).

An important and distinctly Neoplatonic element in the *Platonic Theology* is the hierarchy of reality that guarantees man's immortality and constitutes the order through which the soul will rise when it escapes its bodily prison. Rational soul itself occupies the middle place in the series of five whose two higher levels Ficino called 'angelic mind' and 'divine sun' in the first chapter of this long treatise; all three stand above the two lower kinds of being, the 'active quality' that gives some form to matter and the 'dull mass of bodies' that lie beneath. The upper reaches of this hierarchy correspond to the three hypostases—One, Mind, and Soul—which according to Plotinus are the divine part of reality. Because Plotinus did not sort his hypostases neatly or consistently, naming four, five, or six at one time or another, it was left to his successors, chiefly Iamblichus and Proclus, to fill in the details of their relations with each other and with things below. Proclus left the clearest metaphysical blueprints in his *Elements of Theology* and *Platonic Theology*, whose fivefold schemes influenced Ficino's sequence of God, angel, soul, quality, and body, in which soul's centrality gave it a role that weakened the position of angelic being in the upper part of the hierarchy and of quality in the lower. Ficino accepted the Neoplatonic axioms governing accounts of the being that intervenes between the One and Good above and Evil and Not-being below. The One and Good transcends being; Not-being and Evil, as mere negations of the good that exists, have no being. Everything between these extremes must be good and existent in some degree, but in some measure must also admit differences of being and not-being, filling up a hierarchy graded according to such principles as the superiority of one to many, of cause to effect, of rest to motion, and of whole to part. It follows from this last rule, applied to particular living beings observed in the world, that the cosmos as a whole must be ensouled, since soul is higher than the soulless. And from soul's middle place in the ranks of reality Ficino derived metaphysical reinforcement for the claims of human dignity so often made by his humanist contemporaries on moral, theological, or literary grounds. Ficino's cosmology generally mirrored the familiar world-picture of

Aristotle and Ptolemy that put the earth in the centre of the cosmos, a fitting stage for God's noblest work; if man's rational and immortal soul is central ontologically as well, metaphysics will enhance man's physical claim to be the focus of creation. Macrocosm and microcosm, world-soul and human soul, affect one another through symmetries of psychic correspondence and mutually sustain an optimistic view of man's ability to fulfill an immortal destiny in a cosmos divinely ordered for human ends.[21]

Ficino especially emphasized one rule governing the hierarchy of being. It appears as follows in the *Platonic Theology*:

The first in any genus is the beginning [*principium*] of the whole genus. What is the beginning of other things contains the things that follow. Therefore, what is first in its genus lacks nothing that belongs to its genus. If the sun, for example, is first among bodies that give light, it wants no degree of light, though the rest of the light-giving bodies beneath it, such as stars and elements, do not receive light in all its fullness.

Every genus contains one highest member and one only, which causes all other members of the genus to belong to it—to possess the features that characterize the genus. God causes this first member (*primum*) of the genus, which in turn causes the rest of the genus. The *primum* is the upper bound of the genus, with respect to whose features the *primum* is pure, perfect, and complete. In fact, the *primum* has no features except those of its genus, since any other feature would make it impure with respect to the genus. If the *primum* is the upper limit of the genus, the lower limit is the member that least belongs to the genus, bearing its features in the smallest degree. Such a scheme easily suggests the notion of grades between upper and lower bounds, places ordered like points on a line connecting two extremes, or elements varying as different mixtures of generic perfection and privation. Many partial genera —those made of natural species, for example—occupy some

---

[21] Kristeller (1964*a*: 42–3; 1988*a*: 26–123, 204–12, 311–27, 381–96); Trinkaus (1970: ii. 475–87); Wallis (1972: 90–3, 110–34, 146–58); Allen (1975; 1982*a*; 1989: 49–82).

finite part of reality, but there are also universal genera, the true, the beautiful, and so on, that involve some aspect of being as a whole. Ficino sometimes calls God the *primum* whose genus is Being itself, but thus to make God a limit on the hierarchy gives rise to certain problems.[22]

Augustine, Proclus, pseudo-Dionysius, the author of the *Book of Causes*, and many other medieval thinkers had developed a metaphysical scheme in which God at one extreme and matter or non-being at the other stood as two end-points against which the location of all other entities in the continuum of being could be plotted. This spatial metaphor for metaphysical grades was an old idea when Ficino came upon it. Two of his contemporaries, Cardinal Bessarion and George of Trebizond, had also debated it. In order to bolster his charge that Plato put a host of redundant middle deities between God and his human creation, George argued that no entity could be any closer than another to its infinite creator. Bessarion replied that the creator's power must bear some proportion to the creation and that the creative God might thus be considered perfect and supreme rather than infinite, attributes suitable to a deity who measures the degrees of being. In answering Trapezuntius, Bessarion had cited two Christian authorities—Augustine and Aquinas—admired by Ficino, who in turn accepted Bessarion's position and discussed it in several of his works. In the *Platonic Theology*, for example, he maintains that God is supreme in the genus of all Being, arguing that we can neither rise nor fall through the grades of being without coming to some limit, which at the upper bound is God. Any genus lacking a higher limit or *primum* would have no order or measure; neither known to mind nor desired by appetite, it would lie beyond the reach of science and morals alike. In deciding that an infinite God can measure his creation, Ficino was especially exercised by the contrary and 'barbaric' views of Paul of Venice, who confined measurement to the 'zero grade of being' (*non gradus entis*). Arguments resembling Ficino's views or contradicting them continued through the sixteenth century, interesting Peripatetics as well as Platonists, and they foreshadowed seventeenth- and eighteenth-century conceptions of the 'great chain of being'.[23]

Ficino's ideas about the 'first in any genus' and divinely measured grades of being combined concepts familiar to medieval philosophers with newer ideas discovered in Neoplatonic texts. Ficino also blended his new readings of Plato and the Neoplatonists with more traditional materials in the catalogue of fifteen immortality proofs that fill Book V of the *Platonic Theology*. The following summary passage from the fourth proof on soul's superiority to matter shows a stylistic current that runs through the whole work, and would not be out of place in a scholastic disputation:

Let us review. Unless it is changed into nothing, matter cannot be changed from what it is; but nature does not allow anything to be changed into nothing; therefore, matter does not perish. Much less will the very natural force that is mistress of nature perish. Its mistress is the efficient force that forms it. The force that forms it is what first moves it. The source of movement is the rational soul, whose servants are the qualities that move matter as instruments.

The Latin is correct but simple and unadorned; the prose would have left Bruni cold, and the content would not have surprised Aquinas. However, because Plato's *Phaedrus* was unavailable to him, Thomas could not have appreciated the links between the eighth section of that dialogue and the analysis of the soul's self-motion that opens Ficino's fifth book. And because he had no Greek, Thomas lacked any philological perspective on Plato's claim that 'all soul [*psuchê pasa*] is immortal; for that which is ever in motion is immortal'. Did Plato's term *pasa* refer here to *all* soul in general or to *every* soul in particular? In his commentary on the *Phaedrus*, published in 1496 but completed a few years earlier, Ficino took up this point with all the expertise of a pioneering Hellenist

---

[23] Mahoney (1982*a*: 165–72, 186–94; 1982*b*: 173–7; 1987: 223–5); cf. Lovejoy (1936) and, for other critiques of his *Great Chain of Being*, see Gordon-Bournique (1987); Oakley (1987); Wilson (1987).

and all the experience of a lifetime of Platonic studies, not least his knowledge of Hermias and other ancient commentators. He concluded 'that Socrates said, not that every soul is immortal, but that all soul is immortal: that is, only that soul is immortal that is all and totally soul. . . . Such is any rational soul.' Thus, in a characteristically Neoplatonic way, Ficino established the immortality of *each* human soul by asserting its participation in *all* soul as a kind that excludes any being other than soul and, hence, any being other than the immortal.[24]

Ficino's incomplete commentary on the *Phaedrus*, written twenty years after the *Platonic Theology*, is richer than the earlier work in the hermeneutic novelties that made Platonic philosophy so attractive to the broader literary readership of the Renaissance. To a certain extent, Plato himself guaranteed strong literary interest by writing a dialogue in which advocates of philosophy and rhetoric debate the capacity of their disciplines to give an account of love, a one-sided contest when philosophy is conceived as 'the culture of the soul' and love as the soul's desire for its truest end. Plato, as great an ironist as his teacher, invents a speech for the orator Lysias that makes the case for rhetoric unpersuasively, while the Socratic arguments for philosophy owe much of their power to literary forms and figures. Imagery especially—above all the great image of the human soul as an unmatched pair of good and evil horses 'in a team of winged steeds and their winged charioteer' —makes Socrates eloquent, as Ficino well understood, for he wrote that 'Socrates here plays not a philosophical so much as a poetical role'. Ficino believed that Platonic texts contained mysteries of Christian doctrine that could be comprehended and communicated only by special interpreters—lovers, poets, priests, and prophets—rapt in an ecstasy that unites them with God. Like David, Solomon, and Orpheus, Plato took his inspiration from God and the divine ideas, which moved him to write such poetry as the *Phaedrus* contains. Although Plato subordinated poetic to erotic madness in the *Phaedrus* and

---

[24] Plato, *Phaedrus* 245C; Ficino (1964–70: i. 174–5, 180; 1981: 15–21, 91 [Allen trans.]); Kristeller (1974: 73–91); Allen (1984*b*: 69, 77–85, 228–58).

elsewhere, Ficino interpreted the *Phaedrus* as pre-eminently a work of poetic philosophy.[25]

Ficino's original research in the Neoplatonic philosophers acquainted him with a tradition reaching back to the fourth century BCE which regarded Homer and other great poets as theologians who use their art to teach about the gods in an obscure manner that needs interpretation. The required hermeneutic itself came to be seen as a kind of theology. Stoics as well as Platonists worked at puzzling out the theological hints in poetry that said one thing yet meant another, but the mythopoeic character of the Platonic dialogues was an especially strong inducement for Plato's school to interest itself in allegorizing, which at first meant almost any interpretation that looked beyond the bare literal meaning of a text. Porphyry and Proclus were avid allegorizers; Porphyry's *Cave of the Nymphs*, an analysis of eleven lines from the thirteenth book of the *Odyssey*, is the longest surviving example of the method as applied to Homer, but the same technique permeates all Neoplatonic exegesis after Plotinus.[26] Petrarch, Salutati, and other early humanists had begun to realize that a Platonic interpretation of pagan poetry could find a deeper monotheism beneath the polytheist veils of ancient literature, thereby justifying the prominence of classical letters in humanist education. With his much deeper knowledge of Neoplatonism, it was natural for Ficino to try his own hand at interpreting Plato allegorically, as he does with great effect in the *Phaedrus* commentary, for example.

Socrates meets Phaedrus at the opening of the dialogue outside the city in a sylvan setting near the banks of a river, where Boreas, god of the north wind, was said to have ravished a nymph. When Phaedrus asks him about the myth, Socrates mentions a possible explanation only to dismiss it as a waste of time for someone who has more important work to do in knowing himself. Some modern critics have taken even less interest in such details of Plato's work, which many philoso-

---

[25] Plato, *Phaedrus* 237D, 246A; Ficino (1981: 74 [Allen trans.]); Guthrie (1962–81: iv. 420–1); Hackforth (1972: 9, 69); Allen (1984b: 41–67).

phers will easily pass over as mere ornament. One modern commentator writes that 'since a diversity of meanings was possible in every case, . . . it was to little purpose to devote one's energy to excogitating them'.[27] Ficino's attitude, like that of the ancient Neoplatonists, was more respectful of the text as Plato left it. Three times in the dialogue, Socrates takes the trouble to mention the cicadas singing in the hot summer air as he and Phaedrus talk, and Ficino concluded that 'the fable of the cicadas demands we treat it as an allegory'. He noted that these insects, like windy Boreas, are beings of the air who 'live by song'; they also undergo a kind of regeneration. Thus, they represent music and rebirth, reminding Ficino of philosophers who quit their earthy bodies for a higher existence as aerial demons especially attuned to musical sounds in the airy medium. As aerial demons, the cicadas come low in the hierarchy of spiritual beings who inhabit various levels of air, aether, and fire up through the stellar seats of the highest demons, yet they are good spirits, 'singers and interpreters' who convey the influence of the Muses. 'Under the good demons', noted Ficino, 'are bad demons by whose traps and lures . . . souls are detained in bodily delights and do not turn back . . . to . . . their celestial home'. Although he emphasized the beneficence of the demonic hierarchy, Ficino, like any good Christian, had to acknowledge that evil powers also lurked in the realm of the spirits.[28]

Ficino sacralized Platonism to adapt it to Christianity, but he did not treat the dialogues with the full reverence due to scripture, and he sometimes criticized the Neoplatonists for weaving their allegories through the flimsiest threads of text. He agreed, however, that in its depths the Platonic philosophy concealed a theology; that Plato used allegory to hide theological mysteries; and that an allegorical hermeneutic could resolve apparent difficulties caused by Plato's esoteric ways.

---

[26] Trinkaus (1970: ii. 683–721); Wallis (1972: 22–5, 96–8, 134–7); Witt (1977); Lamberton (1986); Hankins (1990a: i. 29–40); above, n. 9.

[27] Plato, *Phaedrus* 227–30; Hackforth (1972: 26), commenting on earlier views of J. Tate.

[28] Plato, *Phaedrus* 230C, 258E-259D, 262D; Ficino (1981: 192–9 [Allen trans.]); Allen (1984b: 3–31).

Ficino combined his Neoplatonic interpretation with humanist methods that searched the texts for moral examples, ringing sentences, and miscellaneous literary data; but he was no more aware that Plato might be reconstructed by historical criticism than he was inclined to pass the dialogues through the sieve of scholastic dialectic. Above all, he needed to make Plato useful to his faith, and so his Platonism became a species of Christian apologetic, suited to a century when Savonarola would inherit the anti-Platonism of George of Trebizond and, a few years earlier, a lecture that Ficino gave in a Florentine church horrified a powerful clergyman: 'Having entered the house of the angels, I was amazed to see what is supposed to be God's house filled with a chorus of seated laity, changing a place of prayer [*oratorium*] into a lecture hall [*gymnasium*], and the altar-seat kept for the priest alone . . . turned over to a philosopher.' Ficino's apologetic answered the time-honoured complaints against Platonism. As the author of a poetic theology, Plato could not and should not have written in pedagogic order with scholastic clarity; he wrote to move his reader toward a wisdom beyond human comprehension. Critics of Plato's moral teaching fail to grasp the correspondences between higher and lower, heavenly and earthly orders of being. If Plato seems to condone what Christians find illicit—homosexual love, for instance—then we may be sure he had in mind some higher activity and that our pious worries apply only at lower levels. Those who doubt Plato's religious probity must remember that true theology lies beyond dialectic, and that his ability even to approach such mysteries as the Trinity, however obscurely, should cause us to honour him as a poet and prophet.[29]

Under the influence of Florentine humanism, Ficino naturally understood Plato's theology as the foremost of many attractions in the dialogues—not, however, as their sole value, as Neoplatonic commentary implied. Ficino's literary culture disposed him also to appreciate Plato's gifts of rhetoric, logic, mytho-

---

[29] Kristeller (1937: ii. 234; 1956: 111, n. 45) identifies Ficino as the target of the churchman's remarks; Allen (1984a); Hankins (1990a: i. 18–33, 341–66).

logy, irony, even humour, though these were features of his language that for the Neoplatonists were at best decorative, if not distracting. On the other hand, the Neoplatonic quest for a Platonic theology moved Ficino beyond the humanist hunt for maxims, morals, and philological data. He saw Plato's works as a unified body of thought, coherent in purpose and structure, and inviting lines of interpretation that resolved particular doctrinal problems by appealing to the meaning of the Corpus as a whole. In the broadest sense, Plato's aim was educational, to provide the religious and moral instruction that would convince people to purify themselves and then to choose a higher life in pursuit of the Good. If the reader fails to discern this intention in one dialogue or another, Ficino will offer a number of explanations to show how Plato adapted his message to various subordinate and more manifest ends. Sometimes he chose a subject or a method because his audience was more or less mature in spirit. One text might be more superficial than another in order to appeal to lower levels of understanding, perhaps as literary bait to lure readers toward deeper but less appealing truths. Unlike the Neoplatonists, who considered each dialogue as devoted to one end or object (*skopos*, *telos*), Ficino looked for some sign of the profoundest truths in every dialogue, so that the themes of all the texts were related to one another symphonically or poetically, not dialectically as in a scholastic *summa*.[30]

Since the Enlightenment, philosophy has taken up the common burden of secular education, to bring people more and better knowledge and ways of knowing, often without reference to moral consequences. Ficino's philosophy, as his contemporaries would have expected, had a different purpose, not just to help people know more but to make them wiser, to make them better in the moral sense, not just more efficient intellectually. Since his intentions were moral and religious, it comes as no surprise that Ficino did not portray Socrates as a wily proto-sceptic but rather as a heathen saint, whose doubts about human knowing foretold the negative theology of pseudo-

[30] Hankins (1990*a*: i. 328–41, 364–6).

Dionysius. Ficino's Plato, likewise, was no dyspeptic critic of the failed Athenian *polis* that murdered his teacher but rather a pious guide of souls seeking the heavenly city. More than the versions of Bruni and his successors, Ficino's translations of the dialogues respected Plato, preserving even his most troubling passages, almost never bowdlerizing or distorting to hide doctrinal embarrassment. But Ficino's larger philosophical purpose, as expressed in the commentaries, arguments, and autonomous works, had more in common with Augustine than with any modern student of Plato. Ficino fashioned his Plato to serve the faith, but it was the faith as he understood it, not entirely in keeping with credal orthodoxy or ecclesiastical jurisdiction. In the most general terms, Ficino propagated a learned and inward spirituality which could only threaten external structures of creed, worship, and church government on the eve of their being tested in the furnace of the Reformation. More specifically, this internalization of religion naturally inclined Ficino to dislike official ritual (though he invented some rites of his own) and vulgar superstition; but his most celebrated heterodoxies, real or imputed, had to do with syncretism, astrology, and magic, all of them well in touch with respectable philosophical beliefs, whatever their status in moral theology. Ficino, an ordained priest, was no pagan, but if by 'syncretism' one means applying pagan mythology to Christian purposes and finding a place for ancient gods and demons in one's ontology and cosmology, then Ficino qualifies as a syncretist. That he vigorously advocated astrology and natural magic is certain, even though he knew that licit natural magic might lead to sinful demonic magic.[31]

The danger presented by evil demons became a major problem in one of Ficino's most popular works, his *Three Books on Life* of 1489, the third of which, the book *On Arranging One's Life According to the Heavens*, was the most influential Renaissance treatment of the theory of magic. That a distinguished philosopher should write about magic may strike the modern reader as perverse, but before and after Ficino's time—until

[31] Ibid. 274–82, 321–8, 360–6.

the middle of the seventeenth century, in fact—educated people wanted to find philosophical reasons for believing in magic, astrology, demonology, and other varieties of occultism that were normal features of intellectual life in early modern Europe. Ficino's main interest in the third book *On Life* was in *natural* magic, ways of using plants, stones, musical sounds, and other natural objects as sources of unusual power without any appeal to personal, supernatural agents such as demons or angels. He found good philosophical support for natural magic not only in Aristotelian physics and metaphysics, which had long been used for this purpose by authorities as orthodox as Aquinas, but also in his new Neoplatonic sources, especially Plotinus, Iamblichus, Proclus, Synesius, and the *Chaldaean Oracles*. Scholastic thinkers had found a relatively clear way of drawing the line between innocent natural magic and damnable demonic magic: as long as magical recipes recommended no signs or messages that could be addressed only to intelligent spiritual agents, the magus avoided the sin of demonolatry. But the metaphysics that underlay the magic of the Neoplatonists blurred this critical distinction. Iamblichus described natural objects as so tightly connected with personal beings higher in the ontological hierarchy that the latter were involved automatically in any magical operation that began with the former. Ficino admitted this problem by ending *De vita* ambiguously, with a chapter that leaves one wondering what he really thought of the theurgy described in the 'god-making' sections of the Hermetic *Asclepius*. Although magic is not a major topic of the Greek *Hermetica* translated by Ficino in 1463, the Latin *Asclepius* devotes two sections to statues designed to receive demons attracted by magical art. Because Iamblichus associated theurgy with other techniques for the ascent of the soul that was always Ficino's aim, and because the *Asclepius* hallowed this practice with the authority of Hermes Trismegistus, Ficino faced real conflicts with Christian prohibitions of demonic magic. No wonder his work on the theory of magic ends indecisively.[32]

[32] *Asclepius* 23–4, 37–8; Ficino (1989: 385–93, with Kaske's introd.); Walker (1958*a*: 45–53; 1958*b*; 1985; 1986); Copenhaver (1984: 549–54; 1986;

The popular *Three Books on Life*, which had seen more than thirty editions by the middle of the seventeenth century, was a relatively late work, published ten years before Ficino died in 1499, though there was much to follow in his last decade. His translation of Plotinus and commentary on the *Enneads* appeared only in 1492, followed in 1497 by an important collection of translations of Iamblichus, Proclus, Porphyry, and other Neoplatonists. Six of his seven larger commentaries on the *Timaeus*, *Symposium*, *Philebus*, *Phaedrus*, *Parmenides*, *Sophist*, and *Republic* VIII were published together in 1496, though some of them had been written three decades earlier and two were printed with the *Platonis opera omnia* of 1484. His translations and commentaries alone would have assured Ficino a distinguished place in the history of philosophy; their influence continued through the nineteenth century, a remarkable run that kept Ficino's Plato the most important Plato for several centuries. But besides his translations and commentaries and books of letters, many of which are really brief philosophical essays, Ficino left other original works in addition to the *Platonic Theology* and the *Three Books on Life*. After he took holy orders in 1473, for example, he published an apologetic work *On the Christian Religion* in 1474 that upheld his faith against Judaism and Islam while maintaining a kind of religious universalism on the basis of the concord between Platonic philosophy and Christian revelation. His other works addressed various topics in moral philosophy, natural philosophy, medicine, and other fields; most were in Latin, though a few appeared in Italian.[33]

His writings were the most enduring part of Ficino's achievement, but there was more to him than his books; his personal influence in Florence and among a European range of corres-

1987*a*; 1988*a*; 1988*c*: 274–85; 1990); Allen (1988; 1989: 108–16, 168–204). On magic, astrology, and occultism more broadly, see also Garin (1954: 150–91; 1960; 1961*a*: 155–65; 1983*a*); Castelli (1960); Tateo (1960); Müller-Jahncke (1973; 1985); Zambelli (1973*a*; 1973*b*; 1975; 1976; 1977; 1978; 1986; 1988); *Magia, astrologia* (1974); Zanier (1975*b*; 1977; 1983*a*); Vickers (1979; 1984); Webster (1982); Garfagnini (1983); North (1986); above, n. 18.

[33] For a list of Ficino's works see Kristeller (1937: vol. i, pp. lxxvii–clxvii), supplemented by Kristeller (1986*a*: 20, 136–58); Hankins (1990*a*: ii. 483–5).

pondents was also enormous. More celebrated than well founded was his reputation for reviving a Platonic Academy of Florence, whose precise nature remains unclear. Lorenzo the statesman, the philosophers Giovanni Pico and Francesco da Diacceto, the humanist poets Angelo Poliziano and Cristoforo Landino, and other celebrated politicians and intellectuals were certainly well known to Ficino, but their connection to the great Platonist seems not to have been institutionalized in any regular way outside the religious confraternities and other loose gatherings long active in Florence. Ficino thought that the original Academy was not a formally organized school, and his own version was probably an informal assembly of his students, some of whom would also have been attending the Florentine Studio. We know little of what went on in their discussions, which seem to have had no firm institutional setting or regular schedule. In some sense, no doubt, Ficino wished to revive the glories of Plato's Academy. Plotinus had honoured the custom of celebrating 7 November as the anniversary of Plato's birth and death, and Ficino and his *complatonici* may have met once or twice on this grand occasion; he immortalized such a celebration for the year 1468 in the setting of his commentary on the *Symposium*, but his description of the event may have been less historical than ideological.[34] In any case, there were other public or semi-public events that sometimes engaged Ficino as Plato's paraclete in the rich cultural life of his city; but most of his work, collected in two massive folio volumes published in 1561 and again in 1576 and 1641, was the solitary labour of scholarship and contemplation. Fortunately, because his publishing career corresponded with the first, incunabular decades of the new print technology, he was the first major European philosopher whose works could spread widely and swiftly in his own lifetime. In this and other respects, Ficino's philosophical career was very much a product of the Renaissance, as he himself suggested in a frequently

[34] Ficino (1959: 1320–1); Marcel (1958: 335–40); Kristeller (1956: 99–122, 287–336; 1965a: 89–101); Field (1988: 3–18, 56–8, 107–9, 120–4, 171–4, 195–201); Hankins (1990a: i. 208, 296–300, ii. 436; 1990b; 1991).

cited letter of 1492 where he mentioned the invention of printing as one reason why

one who cares to consider the brilliant discoveries of this age will scarcely doubt that ours is an age [of gold], for . . . it brought back into the light the liberal disciplines that had nearly been extinguished—grammar, poetry, oratory, painting, sculpture, architecture, music. . . . And it happened in Florence . . . [where] Platonic learning was recalled from darkness into light.[35]

If Florence enjoyed an age of gold in the quattrocento, it minted no coin brighter than the refined spirituality of Ficino's refurbished Platonism.

Giovanni Pico and Nicholas of Cusa

Since the time of Burckhardt and Walter Pater, students of the Renaissance have seen Giovanni Pico della Mirandola as the most brilliant of the torch-bearers who lit the passage of modern culture 'from darkness into light'. Writing in 1873, Pater scandalized the Oxford dons by inspiring their students with a collection of essays, mostly art-historical, on *The Renaissance*, wherein he concluded that 'the service of philosophy . . . towards the human spirit, is to rouse, to startle it to a life of constant and eager observation. . . . Not the fruit of experience, but experience itself, is the end. . . . To burn always with this hard, gemlike flame, to maintain this ecstasy, is success in life.' Although Pater ended his book with this philosophical manifesto, mocked by his critics and suppressed in a later edition, only one philosopher rated a full essay in his collection—Giovanni Pico. Ill at ease with earnest Victorian Christianity, Pater admired Pico as 'one of the last who seriously and sincerely entertained the claim on men's faith of the pagan religions', and in Pico's famous *Oration on the Dignity of Man* he rejoiced to see that

this high dignity of man . . . was supposed to belong to him, not as renewed by a religious system, but by his own natural right. The

[35] Ficino (1959: 944); Kristeller (1986a: 26; 1988a: 13).

proclamation of it was a counterpoise to the increasing tendency of medieval religion to depreciate man's nature, . . . to make it ashamed of itself. . . . It helped man onward to that reassertion of himself, that rehabilitation of human nature, the body, the senses, the heart, the intelligence, which the Renaissance fulfills.

In Pater's eyes Pico was a neo-pagan aesthete and therefore 'a true *humanist*. For the essence of humanism is . . . that nothing which has ever interested living men and women can wholly lose its vitality, . . . nothing about which they have ever been passionate. . . .'[36] In 1926, writing from the different moral perspective of neo-Kantian thought, Ernst Cassirer dedicated *The Individual and the Cosmos in Renaissance Philosophy* to Aby Warburg, founder of the Institute that bears his name and still acts as a focus of Renaissance studies. The first chapter of this influential book deals with Nicholas of Cusa (Cusanus), the German canon lawyer, theologian, bishop, and cardinal of the Roman church whom Cassirer called 'the first modern thinker' because he recognized the epistemological problem implicit in the duty of finite human creatures to know an infinite creator. Cassirer believed that Cusanus approached this puzzle in a spirit of 'religious humanism and religious optimism' which, transposed from a neo-pagan frame of reference, sounds much like Pater on Pico:

human culture has found its true theodicy. Culture confirms the freedom of the human spirit, which is the seal of its divinity. The spirit of asceticism is overcome; mistrust of the world disappears. . . . Even sensible nature and sense-knowledge are no longer merely base things, because . . . they provide the first impulse and stimulus for all intellectual activity. .

Unsurprisingly, Cassirer heard echoes of Cusanus in Pico's *Oration*, in which he discovered 'the whole intent of the Renaissance and its entire concept of knowledge, . . . the polarity . . . [that requires] of man's will and knowledge . . . that they be completely *turned towards* the world and yet completely *distinguish* themselves from it.' Cassirer found the themes of

[36] Burckhardt (1990: 135, 145–7, 228–9, 302–3, 327–9, 350–1); Pater (1910: 41–3, 49, 236); cf. above, pp. 154–9; Ch. 1, n. 16.

Pico's *Oration* of 1486 in Cusanus' work *On Conjectures*, written around 1443, and in both he saw the 'basic propositions' needed 'whenever humanism sought to be more than just a scholarly movement, whenever it sought to give itself a philosophical form'.[37]

Debate on these two Renaissance thinkers—Pico especially—continues today. Pico knew about Cusanus and wanted to see his library, but there is no textual evidence of the direct influence that Cassirer claimed.[38] Still less would any current student of Pico sustain Pater's verdict of neo-paganism. Pico's theological adventures may have been imprudent and provocative, but there was no insincerity in his wanting to die in a friar's habit nor any inconsistency in the friendship with Fra Savonarola that guided his final years. Most important, the meaning of Pico's *Oration* still evades the learned consensus which has settled these other points; it may be that the form, content, and history of this best-known of all Renaissance philosophical texts have doomed it to ambiguity.[39] Not yet twenty-four years old, Pico wrote the *Oration* in the autumn of 1486 to introduce his most audacious project, the nine hundred *Conclusiones* or theses that he planned to defend publicly in Rome early in the next year. Worried about the heterodoxy of a few of Pico's theses and perhaps about the sheer daring of his plan, Pope Innocent VIII forestalled the public disputation by appointing a commission to investigate the *Conclusions*, but not before Pico had them printed. When the commission found

[37] Cassirer (1963: 10, 44, 84–88); see also Cassirer (1968).
[38] Kristeller (1965a: 66); Watts (1982: 11–12).
[39] For the collected works see Pico (1572); editions and translations of separate works have been prepared by Garin, Kieszkowski, and Jayne; see Pico (1942; 1946–52; 1973; 1984). English translations of the most important works are available in Cassirer, Kristeller, and Randall (1948); Breen (1952); and Pico (1965). Garin (1937a) remains the standard work, and Craven (1981) discusses more recent interpretations, adding views of his own. See also Dorez and Thuasne (1897); Baron (1927); Kibre (1936); Anagnine (1937); Garin (1942; 1950; 1961a: 231–89; 1965a: 101–13; 1965b; 1967a: 185–217); Nardi (1958); Walker (1958a: 54–9; 1972); Monnerjahn (1960); Secret (1964: 1–43; 1965; 1976); Kristeller (1964a: 54–71; 1965a; 1975); Yates (1964: 84–116; 1965); Dell'Acqua and Münster (1965); Di Napoli (1965); *L'Opera* (1965); Marcel (1965); Raith (1967); Waddington (1973); Lubac (1974); Crouzel (1977); Zanier (1981); Wirszubski (1989).

three theses heretical and ten others suspect, Pico hastily drafted an *Apologia* that was no apology and published it as well, provoking the pope to condemn the whole set of *Conclusions*. Although the *Apology* repeated a large portion of the *Oration*, the complete text was published only in 1496, two years after Pico died, and it acquired the title *On the Dignity of Man* only in 1557.

To Pico it was simply the *Oration* that introduced the *Conclusions*. If the latter were related to the quodlibetal disputations that permitted medieval scholars to debate any topic of their choice, the former was in the tradition of the academic inaugural speech, whose first part customarily praised the speaker's discipline—in Pico's case, philosophy—and whose second part defended the speaker's approach to that discipline. The genre and occasion of the *Oration* provide clues to its meaning. It was a work of oratory meant to persuade an audience on first hearing, not a technical philosophical treatise meant to demonstrate a position through close reading. Its rhetorical impact explains such reactions as Pater's, who found it so convincing that he read his own attitudes into it; but Pico's oratorical genius did not make his *Oration* mere rhetoric. The question of man's worth was a large one in quattrocento Italy; it had moved Gianozzo Manetti and other humanists to take a brighter view of mankind than that expressed in the twelfth-century work *On the Misery of the Human Condition* by Lotario dei Segni, who became pope as Innocent III but never added a promised companion-treatise *On the Excellence of Man*.[40] Having worked hard at philosophy for six years before he wrote the *Oration*, Pico must have understood that eventually his speech would be read as a serious philosophical statement on a controversial issue.

However, the topic of human dignity occupies only the first third of the first half of the *Oration*. Unlike Ficino, who had added a metaphysical dimension to man's cosmological centrality as lord of earthly creation, Pico argued that God had empowered humanity to transcend its central position. Spinning

[40] Trinkaus (1970: i. 173–78; ii. 505–26); above, n. 11.

his own fable of genesis, he pictured God telling Adam before
the Fall that, unlike all other creatures, he had no fixed place
or form or function. 'To him is it given', wrote Pico, 'to have
what he wishes, to be what he wants.'[41] Exercising his free
will, the sinless Adam could elect either a lower bestial existence or a higher life of divinity. Whether Pico had in mind
man's ontological freedom to shape his own nature or his
moral freedom to choose a higher path is debatable. In any
case, Pico's advice was to emulate the Cherubim, the second
highest rank of angels. Stationed below the Seraphim, who
burn in the hot love of God, the Cherubim are angels of
contemplation, as the Thrones below them are angels of judgement. Philosophy teaches humans to live like these intellectual
angels, who can rise up to divine peace or descend to the
world of activity. Pico's philosophy was a graded way of life,
not simply a technique or a discipline; its goal was death, the
soul's union with all other souls joined in the highest mind.
The soul rises to harmony through preliminary steps that Pico
described on a Stoic pattern, reaching back to Chrysippus by
way of Plutarch: moral philosophy tames the passions; dialectic
calms the storms of discursive reason; then natural philosophy
addresses differences of opinion about the worlds of mankind
and nature.[42] At the end of this progression comes the peace
of theology, described by Pico as an *epopteia* or mystic initia-
tion following the expiations of dialectic and moral philosophy.
Extolling this fourfold Cherubic life, a procession of biblical,
Greek, and Eastern sages moves through the latter half of the
first part of the *Oration*—Moses, Plato, Pythagoras, and other
ancient theologians.

In the second part of the *Oration*, Pico defended his decision
to take up the contemplative life of philosophy and to declare
his intentions in a public presentation of theses selected from
as many sources as he could find. 'Pledged to no one's words,'
he proclaimed, 'I have decided to let myself roam through all
the masters of philosophy, to look at every scrap of opinion

[41] Pico (1942: 106); Cassirer, Kristeller, and Randall (1948: 225).
[42] Craven (1981: 36); Long and Sedley (1987: i. 26).

and to know all the schools', and in each of them he found some piece of the larger truth he wished to construct. Pico's eclecticism was another, methodological aspect of the onto-logical or moral freedom announced earlier in the *Oration*, and he meant its chief product to be a work on the 'concord of Plato and Aristotle' such as many philosophers had desired since late antiquity.[43] He wanted to harmonize not only Plato and Aristotle but also other thinkers generally supposed to be at odds, such as Aquinas and Scotus or Averroes and Avicenna, and this concordism was to be one of several contributions to philosophy which Pico regarded as his most original and adver-tised as such in closing the *Oration*. Others were Pythagorean numerology, Orphic and Chaldaean teachings, a theory of natural and demonic magic, and Cabala in the service of Chris-tianity. Pico's wish to build philosophy from so wide a range of materials presupposed Ficino's vision of Platonism as the pro-duct of an ancient Egyptian theology and as compatible with Christianity; but Pico's syncretism was more ambitious than Ficino's in several respects. While Ficino knew little about Cabala, a system of Jewish mysticism and hermeneutics that developed in the Middle Ages, Pico studied Cabala as exten-sively as his linguistic skills permitted and treated it as another channel of esoteric wisdom parallel to the *prisca theologia*. Pico was also less devoted to Plato than Ficino was and much friendlier to Aristotle and his commentators, both ancient and medieval, in this respect echoing Bessarion's concordism rather than the anti-Platonism of Trapezuntius.

Pico's Aristotelianism is evident in the nine hundred *Con-clusions*, which fall into six groups, only the last two labelled as representing his own opinion. The number (almost five hundred) and variety of these theses *secundum opinionem propriam* make it hard to know exactly what Pico meant by giving them that name. He dedicated three of the previous four sets to ancient and medieval Peripatetics, most of all to

[43] Pico (1942: 138–40, 144); Cassirer, Kristeller, and Randall (1948: 242, 245).
[44] Pico (1973: 50, with comments on sources in Kieszkowski's introd. 9–26); Kristeller (1965a: 54–75).

Averroes, Albertus, Aquinas, and Scotus. Along with the *Hermetica*, the *Chaldaean Oracles*, and the Pythagoreans, Pico listed Plotinus, Porphyry, and Iamblichus as authorities for his fourth, Platonic group of theses, but his favorite Platonist was Proclus, from whom he took fifty-five theses, adding another forty-seven 'according to the teaching of the wise Hebrew Cabalists'.[44] The thirteen theses that troubled the church covered a variety of issues: whether Origen is saved, how the cross is venerated, how the eucharist works, whether faith is free, whether God can assume an irrational nature—this last a favourite conundrum of the *via moderna*. The three items called heretical also involved typical philosophical questions. By proposing that Christ was not really present when he descended into Hell, Pico raised the problem of location for incorporeal entities, and in denying that mortal sins were punished forever his concern was the disproportion between finite causes and infinite effects. His most troublesome claim, however, was that 'there is no science that gives us more certainty of Christ's divinity than magic and Cabala'. Perhaps Pico meant to clarify the authority of the divine miracles that Christ worked by contrasting them with the lesser wonders of magic and Cabala, but his judges naturally took this gnomic statement as a threat to the divine science of theology, which Pico seemingly debased by comparing it to the dark arts of wizards and Jews. To protect himself he distinguished in the *Apology* and *Conclusions* between 'practical' Cabala as a way of doing magic by manipulating divine names and 'speculative' Cabala as a path to metaphysical and theological contemplation through meditation on the emanated divine attributes or *Sephiroth* (see below).[45]

The *Oration*, the *Conclusions*, and the *Apology* were the climactic products of Pico's early career, forcing him finally to flee from Italy and ending in his arrest in France in 1488, after which he was allowed to return to Florence, where he spent the last few years of his life. In all likelihood, he visited Florence and met Ficino as early as 1479, just two years after

---

[45] Pico (1973: 79); Craven (1981: 47–75).

he began galloping through several Italian universities. First he
tried law at Bologna, then humanities at Ferrara, and in 1480
he came to rest in the Padua of Nicoletto Vernia, though it
was another Averroist Aristotelian, Elia Del Medigo, who
most strongly influenced Pico's absorption of Peripatetic philosophy. Del Medigo was a Jew who translated Averroes from
Hebrew for Pico. A philosopher in his own right in the medieval Jewish tradition, Del Medigo disliked Cabala but still
introduced it to Pico, finding some Cabalist works for him and
providing lists of other texts. But Averroism was Del Medigo's
most important gift to Pico, who never forgot it: the second of
his forty-one 'conclusions according to Averroes' maintains
that 'the intellective soul in all people is one'.[46]

The culmination of Pico's scholastic period was his stay at
the University of Paris in 1485–6, but even before this trip he
declared his sympathy for medieval philosophy in a letter to
the Venetian humanist, Ermolao Barbaro. Barbaro, a humanist
Aristotelian who did important work on the Greek commentators, wrote to Pico in April of 1485 to stress the importance of
good Latin style in philosophy, and in passing he criticized the
northern scholastics as 'dull, rude, uncultured barbarians'. In
June Pico shot back an elegant defence of the inelegant schoolmen, reminding Barbaro that he had 'spent six years on those
barbarians . . . [and had] lost in Thomas, John Scotus, Albert,
and Averroes the best years of my life'. Pico stressed the
conflict between oratory and philosophy and criticized rhetoric
as superficial and deceptive. Philosophy requires a specialized
terminology that cannot always be beautiful. Its speech must
be brief, clear, thorough, accurate, and serious; philosophy
has as much right to its linguistic conventions as the ancient
Romans had to theirs. Rhetoric may work for political or
moral issues that arise in the public arena, but ornamental
language will obscure the deeper truths of physics and metaphysics. For Barbaro, writing in the Petrarchan tradition, language was an end in itself, but for Pico language was merely

[46] Pico (1973: 34); Garin (1937a: 3–29, 65–8); cf. Kristeller (1965a: 63–4);
Sirat (1985: 405–7); Ruderman (1988: 385–7, 401).

the philosopher's tool, and a blunt instrument to boot. Pico recalled the ideal of Pythagorean silence, claiming that the ancient sage would have used no speech at all if he could have communicated in a way less impeded by the senses and more suited to philosophy's immaterial objects. Like the Stoics, he regarded the phonetic vehicle of language as corporeal, its semantic content as incorporeal; thus, the philosopher's concern should be inward immaterial reason (*ratio*), not sensible embodied speech (*oratio*). Against Barbaro, Pico took a position resembling Alfonso of Cartagena's against Bruni or George of Trebizond's against Gaza, but, ironically, he dressed it in the best classical style. The studied Latinity of his prose and the careful structure of his rhetoric are the best proofs that Pico understood and, within certain limits, appreciated the classicism that he attacked in Barbaro; and the best evidence that his esteem for scholasticism was real is the prominence of medieval Aristotelianism in the *Conclusions*. One side of Pico's universalism was his openness to scholastic thinkers typically rejected by humanists as barbarians; another side was his curiosity about other systems of thought all but unknown to European Christians.[47]

As early as 1480 Pico began to learn a little about Cabala from Elia Del Medigo in Padua, but he met his Hebrew teacher years later in Florence—Samuel ben Nissim Abulfaraj, a Sicilian rabbi known after his conversion as Guglielmo Raimondo Moncada or Flavius Mithridates. Flavius, who had worked earlier in the curia of Pope Sixtus IV, translated thousands of pages of Cabala for Pico, who displayed his new learning in one hundred and eighteen Cabalist theses arranged in two groups and published with the other *Conclusions* in 1486. The sources to which Flavius gave Pico access include the twelfth-century *Book of Splendour*, Abraham Abulafia's thirteenth century commentaries on Maimonides, and Menahem Recanati's fourteenth-century interpretation of the Torah. Since Pico had the benefit of this material only for a few months

---

[47] Translation in Breen (1952: 393, 395); Gray (1968: 209–13); Long (1986: 131–9); Vickers (1988a: 184–96).

before he wrote the *Conclusions*, it is unsurprising that the Cabalist theses are no more coherent than the others; yet they develop themes that were to fascinate Christian Cabalists for centuries to come. In the first set of theses on Cabala, Recanati was the main inspiration for Pico's speculations on the *Sephiroth*, the ten powers that emanate from the hidden God and reveal the divine attributes. Abulafia was the chief source of his analysis—more visible in the second set of theses—of sacred names, especially the names of God which, in Pico's view, prove that Jesus is the Messiah and disclose the trinitarian God of Christianity in the Hebrew Bible. Cabala taught Pico that every feature of the Torah is meaningful and that special hermeneutic devices (such as gematria, a way of interpreting Hebrew words according to the numerical value of their letters) can penetrate its secrets. But when he wrote his conclusions on Cabala, Pico's grasp of Hebrew cannot have been strong enough to free him from dependence on the translations made by Flavius, who changed the meanings of the texts that he rendered and sometimes augmented the originals in ways that would have dismayed their authors. Flavius convinced Pico that the Aristotelian Maimonides was a Cabalist, that Abulafia anticipated Cusanus on the coincidence of opposites (see below), and, above all, that Recanati read trinitarian and Christological meanings into the Pentateuch. Pico's greatest innovation in Cabala was to derive the name of Jesus from the holiest Hebrew name of God as if it encoded a Christian secret, but he owed such insights to his tampering translator.[48]

Pico took Cabalist hermeneutics seriously, and he made Cabala an important component of his syncretist philosophy. He was one of very few Christian thinkers since the Patristic period who saw real value in Jewish thought of post-biblical times. But his use of Cabala shared the hostile, proselytising intentions of the apologetic literature written mainly in Spain by converts after the twelfth century. Petrus Alfonsus, Raymond Martini, Abner of Burgos, and many others through

---

[48] Secret (1964: 24–37; 1965); Ruderman (1988: 401–3); Wirszubski (1989); on Cabala and Judaica in general, see Blau (1944); Cassuto (1965); Scholem (1954; 1974; 1987); Zika (1976); Kristeller (1985b); Idel (1988).

Pico's time applied their knowledge of Jewish exegesis and philosophy to Christian ends. That Pico was complicit in such motives is clear from remarks in his *Heptaplus*, a commentary on Genesis 1:1–27 written in 1489, in which he assures his 'Christian brothers' of the usefulness of Cabala: 'You will be equipped with the most powerful weapons against the Hebrews' stony hearts, and they will be drawn from their own armories.'[49] The Christianization of Cabalist *ideas* was well known in the *converso* literature long before Pico, but—thanks to Flavius—he pioneered in using Cabalist *methods* to find new ways of certifying Christian belief. In the year before he finished the *Heptaplus* and after his troubles with the church, Pico had met another important Jewish figure, Yohanan Alemanno, who himself had been influenced by the oratorical humanist speculations of Judah Messer Leon. Alemanno had thus been prepared to receive Greek philosophical ideas from Pico, as Pico continued to explore Jewish thought with him, especially from Alemanno's interpretation of the Song of Songs. The *Heptaplus* is a brief but intricate work. It uses a Cabalist and Neoplatonic scheme of three worlds—ultramundane, celestial, and sublunary, with the human world added as a fourth—to justify a sevenfold system of cosmology corresponding to the six days of creation and the seventh of rest. Biblical motifs such as the three-part design of the tabernacle and the structure of the seven-branched candlestick illuminate Pico's scheme throughout, and the work ends with an appendix showing how gematria can decode the first word of the Hebrew text of Genesis to discover a Christian message.[50]

In the fourth and fifth 'expositions' of the *Heptaplus*, Pico discusses the human condition in a way that some expositors find less daring than the *Oration*, suggesting that Pico had perhaps been chastened by the church's punitive stroke. Pico makes man's body and soul correspond to earth and heaven, and to join these two extremes he puts a spiritual substance

---

[49] Pico (1942: 346–60; 1965: 158–65); Secret (1964: 8–21); Ruderman (1988: 395–6).
[50] Sirat (1985: 402–4, 410–12); Ruderman (1988: 391, 394–5, 403–7); Wirszubski (1989: 161–7).

between them. In the intellective and sensitive faculties of the soul he finds analogies for the biblical waters above and below heaven. 'Mankind is not so much a fourth world, like some new creature', he argues, 'as the bond and union of the three already described.' These words seem to recall the anthropology of the *Oration*, in which humanity lacks a proper nature and must find it by ranging through the rest of creation. But Pico also says that 'mankind contains all things in itself as their centre'. Did he thereby revert to binding Adam's children to the axle of the world? Perhaps this question pushes Pico's language, with its high oratorical charge, too far in the direction of consistency and terminological precision. In any case, there is no doubt that the *Heptaplus* expresses an optimistic view of human dignity. Its key chapter on human excellence begins with the words of the creator—'Let us make mankind in our own image'—and closes with the same Hermetic maxim that had opened the *Oration*—'A great miracle, Asclepius, is mankind!'[51]

Even if the *Heptaplus* is a tamer work than the *Oration*, *Conclusions*, and *Apology*, it was still imprudent of Pico to flaunt his Christian Cabala so soon after his encounter with the church. Ficino and other Florentines had good cause to worry that their brilliant young colleague would go too far. Since the early 1480s, Pico had hoped to meld Ficino's thought with a unified philosophy that would overcome sectarian discord, and he had urged Ficino to press on with his Platonic researches, especially the long, exacting labour of translating and interpreting Plotinus. Neither in his views on particular Platonic texts nor in his more ambitious syncretism did Pico hesitate to differ with Ficino, who was his elder and his friend but not his teacher in any strong sense. In his *Commento* (1486) on the love poem of Girolamo Benivieni, for example, Pico took an independent line on the *Symposium*, the object of one of Ficino's most influential Plato commentaries. But Pico's most prominent dispute with the older philosopher began when

---

[51] *Asclepius* 6; Pico (1942: 300–4; 1965: 134–5); Cassirer, Kristeller, and Randall (1948: 223); Craven (1981: 29–36).

Lorenzo de' Medici disagreed with Angelo Poliziano on the relation between Plato and Aristotle. Poliziano, an eminent humanist poet who taught in the Florentine Studio for fourteen years before his death in 1494, was also an influential expositor of Aristotle. His discussion of the *Nicomachean Ethics* had moved Lorenzo to correct Aristotle from a Platonist—in other words, a Ficinian—point of view, and in 1491 Pico replied in a short tract *De ente et uno*, the only surviving part of a projected treatise on the *Concord of Plato and Aristotle*.

The topic of this little work is evident in its title, *On Being and the One*. While Ficino maintained with Plotinus that the One is above being, Aristotelians denied the distinction, and Pico tried to show that the argument for equivalence between being and unity taken from Aristotle's *Metaphysics* was truer to Plato than the contrary Neoplatonic view. 'Those who believe that Aristotle disagrees with Plato disagree with me,' he wrote, 'for I make a concord of both philosophies.' To prove his case, he had first to dispose of several passages in the *Parmenides* that seemed to uphold Ficino's Plotinian position; he did so by denying any serious doctrinal value to the dialogue, dismissing it as 'nothing but a dialectical exercise of some sort'. Then he turned to the *Sophist* for positive evidence that unity and being are the same. Ficino rebuked Pico, though quietly and obliquely, in his *Parmenides* commentary of 1492–4, wishing that the 'wondrous [*mirandus*] young man' had paid better attention to him and to Plato before parting so rashly with sound Platonic teaching. Oddly enough, Ficino found the best proof that the *Parmenides* expressed a profound theology setting unity above being in Dionysius the Areopagite, whom Pico cited for the opposite purpose in *De ente*. Pico's fondness for Neoplatonic sources and his wish to befriend Aristotle not by defending him against the Platonists but by blurring his distinctiveness could not please rigidly Peripatetic critics, one of whom, Antonio Cittadini of Faenza, attacked the *De ente* more openly than Ficino had done.[52]

---

[52] Pico (1942: 386–90; 1965: 37–9); Ficino (1959: 1164); Garin (1937a: 34–42); Allen (1986).

In the last years of his life, Pico worked on a refutation of predictive astrology, which even in its unfinished form is his largest work by far; some critics have seen the defence of human freedom against astral determinism as its main philosophical point, but one must recall that Ficino, Pomponazzi, and many other leading philosophers shared a broader interest in magic and astrology, whose final status in Pico's mind remains an unsettled question. Amid rumours of poisoning, Pico died on 17 November 1494, two months after Poliziano and on the very day when the invading French army of Charles VIII entered Florence, already deserted by Piero de' Medici and soon to endure four years of cathartic theocracy under Savonarola, who had vested the young prince in the habit of the Dominican tertiaries on the eve of his death.[53] Although Ficino survived Pico by five years, the coincidence of the latter's death with the departure of the Medici has come to symbolize the end of the 'golden age' that Ficino saw in Florence. Pico's birth in 1463, around the time when Ficino began to translate Plato, established another conjunction that has served to fix the two thinkers in the historical imagination as jointly raising Renaissance philosophy to its apex. By now, however, it will be clear that the genius of Ficino's Platonism was far from coextensive with the spirit of early modern philosophy, a much broader and more complex body of thought whose commonest concerns were Peripatetic and whose dominant texture was eclectic. By the same token, it will be obvious that Pico was not a Platonist in the same way that Ficino was. Platonism was a major source, but only one source among many, of Pico's hopes for a universal philosophical peace, and there was more room in his system than in Ficino's for distinctly Aristotelian and Averroist ingredients, as for many others as well.

Nicholas of Cusa, often linked with Pico and likewise called a

[53] Baron (1927); Garin (1937a: 42–8, 169–193; 1960: 34–7); Walker (1958a: 54–9); Cassirer (1963: 114–22; 1974: i. 153–71); Kristeller (1964a: 68); Yates (1964: 84–116; 1965); Copenhaver (1988c: 267–74); cf. Craven (1981: 131–54).

Platonist, is another figure who strains the usual categories.[54] Cusanus died in 1464, the year after Pico was born, at the age of sixty-three. Born Nicholas Krebs in the town of Cues near Trier in the western part of Germany, he was educated in philosophy, law, and theology at Heidelberg, Padua, and Cologne, an excellent preparation for his rapid rise as a churchman. After 1431, he came to prominence at the Council of Basle as a conciliarist but eventually changed his views as opinion shifted in favour of papal authority. He was ordained priest after 1436 and became bishop and cardinal in time for the jubilee year of 1450, working tirelessly in the cause of church reform. At Basle he met Italian humanists who worked for the papacy, and in 1437 he went to Byzantium as one of the delegation assigned to invite the Greeks to the Council of Ferrara and Florence in 1438–9. Greek manuscripts formed part of the large and famous library that he collected, but he made his most celebrated find in 1429, when he recovered twelve comedies of Plautus forgotten in the Middle Ages. Near the age of forty, when he completed his best known book, *On Learned Ignorance* (*De docta ignorantia*), Cusanus added a second career of philosophical and theological writing to his busy life in ecclesiastical politics. In addition to letters and sermons, he finished about forty works on various subjects ranging from church government to mathematics; more than half are of philosophical interest.

Like Pico and Ficino, Cusanus left the university after his student days; freedom from professorial duties doubtless helped him develop as an eclectic and original thinker. His familiarity with early Christian literature extended to the Greek Fathers,

---

[54] Much of Cusanus is still untranslated; for the Latin texts see Cusanus (1967); translations by Heron, Dolan, Hopkins, Fuhrer, and Watts appear in Cusanus (1954; 1962; 1986; 1989); and Hopkins (1979; 1980; 1981*a*; 1981*b*; 1983*b*). A good recent treatment of the philosophy, followed here, is Watts (1982); see also Vansteenberghe (1920); Bett (1932); Gandillac (1942; 1982); Copleston (1960–6: iii. 231–47); Cranz (1953; 1974); McTighe (1958; 1970); Colomer (1961); Garin (1961*b*); *Nicolò Cusano* (1961); Sigmund (1963); Watanabe (1963); Lübke (1968); *Nicolò Cusano* (1970); Santinello (1970); Senger (1971); Schnauer (1972); Flasch (1973); Cassirer (1974: i. 21–72); Biechler (1975); Hopkins (1983*a*); Stadler (1983); Lohr (1988).

and he had extensive knowledge of scholastic law, theology and philosophy, particularly the tradition known to his contemporaries as the 'old way' (*via antiqua*) in the version traceable to Albertus Magnus. Thomas Aquinas, Thomas Bradwardine, and Ramon Lull were also favourite authorities, as were the Scotist Franciscans. Although nominalism is evident at many points in his work, Cusanus does not seem to have followed the more recent scholastic controversies of the generations after Ockham. He read Aristotle in humanist as well as medieval versions, and he covered the whole Platonic tradition as it was known before Ficino. Pseudo-Dionysius was his great inspiration, but he also depended on Augustine, Proclus, Calcidius, Eriugena, Anselm, Thierry of Chartres, and others. The mystical theologies of Meister Eckhardt, Hildegard of Bingen, Hugh of St Victor, and Bonaventura reinforced his Dionysian Platonism. He confined Aristotle's usefulness to questions of ethics and physics, and worked to find a replacement for Peripatetic metaphysics as the basis of theology. Cusanus fits the broad context of European intellectual history better than the immediate situation of his own time, where it has been easier to locate analogies with his ideas than to identify precise influences, in either direction. In some general sense, and after recognizing his strongly anti-Platonic views on some issues, one must acknowledge Cusanus as a major figure in the Platonic tradition who found a new voice for Lullian and Dionysian ideas and kept them alive for Bruno and later German thinkers.

He finished his first and most famous philosophical work in 1440, *On Learned Ignorance*, a brilliant reformulation of the Dionysian negative theology whose three books show that man's intellectual distance from God and the universe can be bridged only in the transcendent mystery of Christ's incarnation. People spontaneously express their need to know by comparing the more known with the less known, but even the most abstract and precise reflections on counting and measuring end in a crisis of incommensurability. Like a polygon approaching the circle as limit, each approximation of truth will always fall short of the next; divine and cosmic infinities remain out of alignment with man's finite conceptions. Only a Socratic conviction of ignorance can halt the vertigo of epistemic disproportion. Like the Petrarchan humanists, Cusanus prayed to be freed from the chattering logic of the schools, the rambling noise of discursive reasoning, but like Pico he looked for rescue in a deeper silence, not in more elegant language: 'mystical theology leads to respite and silence, where we are granted a vision of an invisible God, while the knowledge that trains us for conflict . . . [and] hopes for victory in words . . . is far from that which hurries us on to God, who is our peace.'[55] Since God is incomprehensible, humanity knows divinity incomprehensibly through symbols, metaphors, and enigmas; but even the best of them, derived from mathematics and geometry, are mere likenesses that bear no true proportion to their divine model. Thus, even the claim that God is the *coincidentia oppositorum*, the meeting of opposites in an abyss that swallows up all minima, maxima, and contradictions, even this statement of the divine paradox fails just because it is a finite, human assertion about an infinite God.

Estranged from the creator, mankind is also strange to other creatures because objects in the world lack the common proportion that would make them knowable. Cusanus equated knowing with comparing or measuring, and he could find no true measure either between humans and God or between humanity and the rest of the universe. Only Christ, the undying God who became man and died, gives mankind hope in the quest to know the divine. Like Christ, who resolved the disjunction between humanity and divinity in his own person, the human creature is a juncture of higher and lower natures, a microcosm or little world who recapitulates the infinities of the great world. But by depending on merely human capacities of mind, mankind will remain exiled from God and the cosmos. Only faith in Christ will bring the prodigal home.

Understanding begins with faith, . . . [which] enfolds every intelligible thing in itself. . . . Since God is unrecognizable in this world, where

---

[55] Cusanus (1967: i. 104–5 [*Apologia* 7–8]); Watts (1982: 41); above, pp. 28–30, 129–32, 170–1.

reason, opinion or learning lead us from the more known through symbols to the less known, only where arguments stop and faith starts do we grasp him. Faith carries us in simplicity beyond all reason and intelligence up to the third heaven of simplest intellectuality ... so that in the body we may contemplate him incorporeally ... in a heavenly and incomprehensible way, and we see that he cannot be comprehended because of the immensity of his excellence. And this is that same learned ignorance....[56]

Ignorance becomes learned when people confess it forthrightly and accept its implications, the clearest of which is that a mystical faith must displace reasoned discourse as the path to God.

Within four years of completing *De docta ignorantia*, Cusanus finished its companion piece, *De conjecturis*, which turns the seemingly sceptical view that all human claims are conjectures, approximations of truth at best, into a more optimistic vision of man's intellectual status. Cusanus interpreted the biblical story of creation, particularly the description of the human creature as made in God's image and likeness, to mean that mankind stands in the same relation to the rational products of his mind as God stands to real objects in the world. God created real things; humans create conjectures. On this basis, Cusanus proposes a conjectural art, a system of mathematical metaphors, to bring man's understanding closer to the structure of divinely created realities, of which his own rational constructs are conjectural likenesses. In order to illustrate the mental exercises that he prescribed, Cusanus provided one of his characteristic diagrams (see Fig. 2).[57]

The scheme derives from Pythagorean, Neoplatonic, and Christian numerological speculations on the quaternary, or first four integers, whose sum is ten. One hundred is the sum of each of these integers multiplied by ten, one thousand the sum of each multiplied by one hundred. From these patterns Cusanus derived further relationships (Fig. 3) meant to show how lower orders of being and thought (below the line) unfold

[56] Cusanus (1967: i. 92–3 [*De docta ignorantia* 3. 11]; 1962: 87–8); Watts (1982: 83–4).
[57] Cusanus (1967: i. 120–35 [*De conjecturis*]); Watts (1982: 93–101).

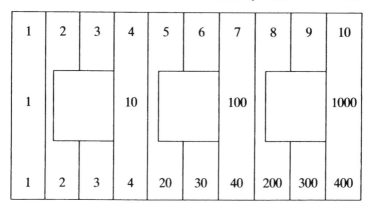

Fig. 2.

from divine unity (above the line). The conjectural art itself exemplifies human creativity, weakened by its divorce from infinity yet wielding great power within a finite domain. The fact that a person can keep thinking anything at all shows that the thinker is immortal; thought, a function of soul, replicates itself perpetually and requires a perpetual faculty. This meditation on mankind's creativity leads Cusanus to orate on human dignity:

Man is God, then, but not in an absolute sense, for he is man; thus, he is a human God. Man is also a world, but he is not all things through contraction, for he is man; therefore, man is a microcosm—a human world, at any rate. . . . Man can be a human God, then, and as God in a human manner he can be a human angel, a human beast . . . or whatever else. Within man's potency all things exist in their way.

1	1	divine mind	point	
2	10	intelligence	line	synthesis
3	100	soul	plane	distinction, judgement
4	1000	body	solid	perception

Fig. 3.

The language is as strong as Pico's and anticipates him by almost half a century.[58]

In 1450 Cusanus produced three dialogues known collectively as the *Idiota* from their protagonist, a simple Artisan who gets the better of an Orator and a Philosopher in conversations on the Christian standing of worldly wisdom. The biblical account (in the book of Wisdom) of creation as an act of numbering and ordering sanctifies the profane counting and weighing of the market-place, where the layman's banal but immediate experience makes a better way to wisdom than the mediated knowledge of the learned. The Idiot's work of shaping a crude wooden spoon shows the relation of human to divine craftsmanship, of copy to paradigm, while also suggesting that human art transcends created nature in forming objects without natural models. The divine artist made real things; the human makes notional artefacts; but within its bounds man's work is active and creative. Awareness of his mental failings, directed inwardly as the religious experience of humility, makes the Idiot's ignorance not only learned but also holy. The image of the carved spoon, which perfectly expresses the Idiot's oxymoronic mundane creativity, is one of a number of poetic devices that Cusanus uses to ease the tension between mystical and philosophical discourse.

Perhaps the most striking case is a work of 1453 *On the Vision of God*, which explores ancient themes of light and vision as metaphors for reciprocal knowledge between God and humanity. Stimulated by queries from monks about mystical theology, Cusanus chose an icon of Christ as his key metaphor. Referring to well-known images and sending the monks an example of the picture he had in mind, he compared God's omniscient concern for each person with the gaze of a painted Christ whose eyes seem to follow the movements of all observers. Like the Idiot's spoon, the monks' icon is an artificial object of common experience, but it makes an even more powerful metaphor because its image embodies the divine love

[58] Cusanus (1967: i. 173 [*De conjecturis*]); Watts (1982: 101–16); above, nn. 41, 42, 51.

that keeps mankind restless, seeking rest in a remote God. The creative and provident motions of an unmoved God are the antinomies presented in a dialogue, *De possest*, of 1460. 'I take an example known to us all from common practice,' wrote Cusanus,

the top that boys play with. . . . The stronger the boy's arm, the quicker the top spins, so that it seems to stand and rest while it moves the more. . . . Now you understand better how to harmonize the theologians, of whom one says that the wisdom which is God is more movable than any mobile thing, . . . while another says that a fixed first principle stands at rest, immobile, though it allows everything to be moved.

In one of his last works, *On a Game of Ball*, written in 1463, Cusanus returned to the same family of metaphors. Comparing a ball's movement to the soul's animation of the body, he likened the soul's capacity for free invention to the game itself, making play a distinctly human activity and a sign of cultural creativity.[59]

Another late work, the *De beryllo* of 1458, uses the 'beryl' — actually a kind of refracting device — to show how divine unity produces diversity, just as a lens bends a straight ray of light through different angles. Pursuing his fascination with the geometry of light and vision, Cusanus made a point in this work of challenging Plato on the metaphysics of mathematical forms, taking the strong anti-realist position that numbers and geometrical figures are not extramental realities. They are rational constructs whose analytical power confirms 'the saying of Protagoras that man is the measure of things', as well as the Hermetic claim that man is another god.[60] In general, Cusanus moved in his later thought toward a brighter view of the human condition than that implied by the epistemological darkness of the early *De docta ignorantia*, where universals are granted a limited sort of existence outside the mind. In some

[59] Cusanus (1967: ii. 650–2 [*Trialogus de possest*]); Hopkins (1980: 82–7); Watts (1982: 25–30, 153–63, 189–97).
[60] Aristotle, *Metaphysics* 1053^{a}35; Cusanus (1967: ii. 710, 734 [*De beryllo*]); Watts (1982: 171–88); Trinkaus (1983: 169–91).

very loose way, Platonist ontology and optimist anthropology seem to have been inversely related for Cusanus; as his vision of mankind became more active and creative, the human mind took up a greater burden of responsibility for the reality of its contents. Throughout his life, Cusanus voiced his disagreements with Plato not only on universals but on other issues as well, such as the power of fate, the creation of the world, the existence of a world-soul, and the designation and definition of the first principle. He was as far from being a doctrinaire Platonist as Pico was, though the Dionysian strain of Platonism colours his whole outlook more than any single influence detectable in Pico's writings.[61] Both, in some sense, were Platonists, in whom the flames of poetry or oratory sometimes burned hotter than the pale fire of philosophy, and both were warmed by an ardent faith to praise humans as God's most creative creatures. Cusanus was definitely more pious than Giordano Bruno, the cinquecento thinker whom he most deeply influenced, and his unconventional theology was certainly more orthodox than the views of Baruch Spinoza, another great philosopher of a later day whom he also anticipated in some respects.

Pious, perennial, and Platonic philosophies: Francesco Patrizi

Once Pico and Ficino had established the *prisca theologia* as a leading motif in Renaissance conceptions of the past, later thinkers became interested in the larger implications of the ancient theology, both political and historical. Christian Europe had never been a tolerant society, and for a long time the religious frenzies sparked by the Reformation made people even less forgiving of each other's heterodoxies. In this climate, to have welcomed new and alien elements within one's belief-system must count as a step, however halting or unwitting, toward religious and intellectual toleration. When Pico harmonized Plato and Aristotle, he earned the nickname 'Prince

[61] Copleston (1960–6: iii. 244–7); Watts (1982: 68–71, 76, 134–7, 147, 177–9, 184–203).

of Concord' (*Princeps Concordiae*), a pun on the name of a small territory owned by his family. Later, in 1525, a Venetian Franciscan named Francesco Giorgio or Zorzi published his speculations *On the Harmony of the World*, which tried to uncover a unity within the cosmos beneath its apparent multiplicity. Zorzi's Hermetic pieties were a long way from the philosophical elegance of Leibniz's metaphysics, but there was a community of motivation and a (complicated) line of influence between the two.[62] One of the intervening high points was a work published in 1540, whose title, *On Perennial Philosophy*, gave later advocates of syncretism their favourite slogan.

Its author was Agostino Steuco, an Italian Augustinian and polyglot biblical scholar. While a young man he worked as librarian for Cardinal Domenico Grimani, who had acquired Pico's books; he became bishop and Vatican librarian in 1538 and represented Pope Paul III at the Council of Trent. At the beginning of *De perenni philosophia*, Steuco extended the meaning of the ancient theology by claiming that there is 'one principle of all things, of which there has always been one and the same knowledge among all peoples'. A comprehensive unity of thought linking all peoples together is what Steuco meant by 'perennial philosophy, [which] reaches back even to the origin of the human race'.[63] Since Ficino's ancient theology was Steuco's point of departure, his atemporal history of thought naturally took on a Platonic colouration. He saw no real historical change, only intellectual continuities binding all cultures in a Christian matrix, and he admitted no clear distinction between philosophy and theology, blending them in the manner of the later Neoplatonists. Steuco thus formulated one of the defining statements of Renaissance Christian Platonism, but his wish to listen for a deeper unison beneath cultural and intellectual discord was out of tune with an age of doctrinal combat and religious war.

[62] Vicentini (1954); Walker (1958a: 112–19); Secret (1964: 126–39); Maillard (1971); Vasoli (1974: 131–403; 1986; 1988a); Yates (1969; 1979: 29–36); Schmitt (1981: chs. 1, 2); Perrone Compagni (1982).

[63] Steuco (1972, with Schmitt's introd. pp. v–xiv); Ebert (1929–30); Freudenberger (1935); Di Napoli (1973: 245–77); Schmitt (1981: chs. 1, 2); Crociata (1987).

Dogmatists on both sides of the confessional trenches could shelter in a university curriculum as unitary as that of the sixteenth century. Within its limits, the Peripatetic tradition had become eclectic, and Aristotelians often disagreed among themselves, but the institutionalization of Aristotelian philosophy in the universities could only inhibit the growth of rival systems. Moreover, since Plato wrote dramatically rather than systematically, his dialogues made poor pedagogic fodder, and the medical students of Italian universities were used to a richer diet of logic and natural philosophy than he provided. Ficino, Pico, and Steuco all attended universities, but only Ficino actually taught in one, and then only briefly; when they were students, it was all but impossible to learn Platonism in any of Europe's centers of higher education. In time the situation improved, but the universities kept Aristotle paramount and seldom opened their doors to Platonic teaching. On the few occasions when Plato was admitted, it was usually a teacher of Greek, not a philosopher, who expounded his dialogues. Because Greek literature was not part of the venerable medieval curriculum, its professors could be more hospitable to new texts—as with the *Poetics*, an Aristotelian novelty. After the late fifteenth century, a few professors at Leipzig, Padua, Pavia and Paris taught one or more Platonic dialogues. Plato lasted longer at Paris, whose influence extended throughout Europe, and from the early sixteenth century one hears echoes of this new philosophical voice in such quarters as the poetry of the Pléiade and the prolific popularizations of Symphorien Champier. Jerome Aleander taught Plato in Paris as early as 1508, and Adrien Turnebus lectured in the Collège Royal on the *Phaedo* and *Timaeus* after 1547, around the time when his colleagues Peter Ramus and Omer Talon took up the sceptical Platonism of the New Academy. By mid-century, Parisian professors were teaching Plato—as they did Aristotle—from Greek texts.

Italy gave Platonism its first full billing as a university subject. Francesco da Diacetto compared Plato to Aristotle early in the sixteenth century at Pisa. Ferrara and Pisa established separate posts for the teaching of Plato in the 1570s, and

Rome followed suit before the end of the century. Among those who taught the subject were two of the foremost Platonists of the day, Francesco Patrizi and Jacopo Mazzoni. Mazzoni was a man of many parts. He succeeded Francesco Verino as lecturer on Plato at Pisa in 1588, continuing a tradition that survived through 1620. His own death prevented him from following Patrizi at Rome when the latter died shortly before him in 1597. As a Platonist Mazzoni followed the concordist tradition of Steuco and his predecessors. His major philosophical works try to bring Plato and Aristotle into agreement, but he also wrote on literary topics, including Dante. What Mazzoni actually taught his students in Pisa and Rome about Plato is unclear, but we do know that at Pisa he became friendly with Galileo and kept in touch with him later. The connection may be an important one for those who detect a Platonic strain in Galileo's mathematical physics. Mazzoni's status as 'official' Platonist was significant in its own right, but his influence in a Peripatetic world was quite limited. In the latter half of the sixteenth century, however, a number of syncretist Aristotelians were smuggling Platonic contraband into their courses. Zabarella berated one such miscreant, Francesco Piccolomini, for interpreting logic too Platonically. Several Italian Aristotelians went so far as to write commentaries on Plato's *Republic* or *Timaeus*, and some university mathematicians were more pleased by Plato's praise of mathematics than by Aristotle's hasty denial of that subject's efficacy in natural philosophy.[64]

After Ficino, Cusanus, and Pico, the most imposing Platonist of the Renaissance was Francesco Patrizi.[65] Born in the far north-east of Italy at Cherso in 1529, almost a century after Ficino, Patrizi could read Plato more easily because in the mean time a great deal of philological work had been done by

[64] Kristeller (1956: 287–336; 1961a: 60–4); Purnell (1971; 1972); Schmitt (1981: ch. 3).

[65] Donazzolo (1912); Arcari (1935); Brickman (1941); Menapace Brisca (1952); *Onoranze a . . . Patrizi* (1957); Kristeller (1964a: 110–26); Muccillo (1975; 1981; 1986); Purnell (1976); Maechling (1977); Henry (1979); Bolzoni (1980); Vasoli (1980; 1983b: 559–83; 1988a); Antonaci (1984); Wilmott (1984; 1985); Kraye (1986). For the main Latin works, see Patrizi (1581; 1591).

humanist scholars. When Ficino translated Plato, he had to compile his own dictionary and work from manuscript; the first printed Greek text of Plato appeared only in 1514. By Patrizi's time, not only Plato but also most extant Greek literature had been published, permitting sophisticated comparison of texts and giving access to various sources of historical information. Patrizi lived a fuller life than most philosophers, and in his travels to Cyprus, Spain, and elsewhere he accumulated a large library. Well-educated in Italy and Germany, he also perfected his Greek in journeys to the eastern Mediterranean. Like many of his contemporaries, he approached philosophy from a humanist perspective; indeed, history and philology dominate much of his work, whose pedantry Bruno found repulsive. His first philosophical education at Padua around the middle of the century was, inevitably, Aristotelian, but in an autobiographical sketch he recalled his conversion to Plato in this Peripatetic stronghold. Disappointed in his search for a good teacher and happier with medicine than with philosophy, he followed a friar's suggestion and read Ficino's *Platonic Theology*, which put him irrevocably on a Platonic path. Since the friar was a Franciscan, another Franciscan of the Veneto — Zorzi — may lurk in the background of Patrizi's inspiration. Giulio Camillo, an expert on the art of memory, was a kindred spirit certainly known to Patrizi in this period.[66] In any event, his discovery of Plato made Patrizi a zealot; his passions were quite foreign to the generous spirit of Ficino and Pico, and his guiding motive was an aversion to everything Aristotelian.

In 1571, Patrizi published the first instalment of his *Discussiones peripateticae*, whose seemingly innocent title masks its destructive intent; the root of the word *discussio* in classical Latin suggests 'shaking apart', not 'conversation'.[67] While tutoring the nephew of a powerful Venetian churchman, he decided to give his young student a truer picture of the life,

---

[66] Walker (1958a: 141–2); Yates (1966: 129–72); Vasoli (1983b: 561–6; 1986; 1988a: 129–34).

[67] All of the first volume of Antonaci (1984–) is devoted to the *Discussiones* and their background.

works, and influence of Aristotle than could be found in the hagiographic summaries read in the schools. In the latter part of the decade he added three more books on Aristotle's sources, on the discord between Aristotle and Plato, and on the defects of particular Aristotelian doctrines, and he published the enlarged work in 1581. Patrizi claimed to be a disinterested scholar, guided only by facts, innocent of any prejudice against Aristotle; but the *Discussiones* have the glint of hard-edged polemic. He saw Aristotelian thought as a threat to Christianity, an impious philosophy to be discarded in favour of Platonic piety. He also regarded the Peripatetic tradition as servile, inimical to philosophical freedom. Aristotle's first disciples — Theophrastus, Strato, Galen, and others — had independent views, but after Alexander of Aphrodisias the tradition degenerated into slavishness. Patrizi's opinion of medieval Aristotelianism was generally low, although he made some distinctions, preferring Avicenna to Averroes, for example, as a more autonomous thinker.

In the first book of the *Discussiones*, Patrizi disposed of Aristotle's good name by finding him dissolute in his life, disloyal to Plato, and even hostile to Alexander, in whose untimely death he may have conspired. As for Aristotle's works, only four of six hundred and forty-six titles that Patrizi found attributed to him were incontestably genuine, and none of these was a standard university text. In deciding questions of authenticity, Patrizi developed clear criteria that show a strong critical sense well-informed by history and philology. He was especially energetic in covering the whole range of relevant ancient literature in Greek, and he had no patience with those who read Aristotle in fragments, focusing on a few parts of a few works and forgetting the Corpus as a whole, not to speak of its larger literary context. After studying the vexed question of Aristotle's exoteric and esoteric works, he identified the former as those that Aristotle gave to the public, the latter as texts meant for private teaching purposes in the Lyceum. In grouping the works, he was less interested in chronology than in doctrine, arranging them in eight sets according to the greater or lesser generality of their contents. This new placement of texts created patterns and juxtapositions unlike anything known to the Peripatetic tradition.

The second and third books of the *Discussiones* include Patrizi's version of the mythic ancient theology as well as his original interpretation of the more historical pre-Socratic thinkers. In both cases his intention was polemical, to destroy Aristotle's authority as historian of ancient philosophy and to exclude him from the mainstream of *pia philosophia*, the Platonic piety that Patrizi found better suited than Aristotelianism to Christianity. The same motives are visible in the dedication to Pope Gregory XIV of Patrizi's other major work of philosophy, the *Nova de universis philosophia*, first published in 1591 and revised in 1593, four years before he died.[68] He told Gregory that there were four pious philosophies, those of Zoroaster, Hermes, and Plato in addition to his own, and he urged the pope to use his system instead of Aristotle's in all Catholic schools and universities, especially those run by the Jesuits. 'It has become fixed in the minds of common people,' he complained,

and many of the learned as well, that most of those who do philosophy have neither good nor pious feelings about the Catholic faith or else believe incorrectly or not at all, and philosophers have become the butt of a joke common everywhere: 'He's a philosopher; he doesn't believe in God.' For they see in all the schools of Europe, in all the monasteries, that Aristotelian philosophy alone is highly valued and taught with great interest. But they learn and they know that only this philosophy . . . takes away God's omnipotence and providence.[69]

Applying his knowledge of Philo, Josephus, and other Greek sources ignored by the Peripatetics, Patrizi reaffirmed the historiography proposed by Ficino in the previous century. Zoroaster, taken to be a son of Noah, and the Chaldaean Abraham passed on a holier wisdom to Hermes Trismegistus and the Egyptians, from whom Orpheus took it to Greece. Orpheus

---

[68] Antonaci's first volume (1984) does not cover the *Nova de universis philosophia*, but there is a summary in Brickman (1941) and in Kristeller (1964a).

[69] Vasoli (1983b: 575–6) quotes from the preface to the *Nova de universis philosophia*.

was the first Greek theologian, followed by Thales in mathematics, Democritus in natural philosophy, and Pythagoras in moral philosophy. From Orpheus and the others the Eleatics learned their theology, which was not at all the materialism that Aristotle attributed to Xenophanes, Parmenides, Melissus, and Zeno. What little Aristotle got right in his own philosophy also came from Orpheus, and he was certainly wrong to materialize the soul of Empedocles or the fire of Anaxagoras, which Patrizi interpreted allegorically as spiritual principles.

Patrizi found the evidence for his reconstruction of the origins of philosophy in Diogenes Laertius, in the Neoplatonic commentaries of Simplicius and Philoponus, and also in various texts now regarded as pseudo-Aristotelian. Of the last, the most important for Patrizi was the pseudo-Aristotelian *Theology*, which he rejected as spurious in the *Discussiones* but then published as genuine in an appendix to his *New Philosophy* along with the *Chaldaean Oracles* and *Hermetica*, even though the authenticity of the latter had been challenged by other critics. The *Theology* is a collection of excerpts from Plotinus in a ninth-century Arabic version discovered earlier in the sixteenth century, but Patrizi concluded that it contained Aristotle's record of Plato's private talks on Egyptian wisdom. His final evaluation of the *Theology* had two important results: it uncovered a channel for the transmission of Plato's secret teaching to Plotinus; and it reconnected at least one work by Aristotle with the ancient theology, from which the *Discussiones* had cut him off entirely.[70] To appreciate the scope and flavour of the work in which Patrizi filled this critical gap between the Peripatetic tradition and *pia philosophia*, one need only read its long and immodest title:

A New Philosophy of Universes contained in fifty books, in which one rises to the first cause by the Aristotelian method, not through motion but through light [lux] and brightness [lumen]; then, by a certain new and special method, all of divinity comes into view; finally, the universe is derived from God, its creator, by the Platonic method. . . . To these books are added the Oracles of Zoroaster . . . , the treatises and frag-

[70] Kraye (1986).

ments of Hermes Trismegistus . . . [and] Asclepius . . . [and] the mystic philosophy of the Egyptians dictated by Plato and taken down by Aristotle. . . .

Despite Patrizi's dedication to Pope Gregory and a subsequent invitation from Clement VIII to take up a chair of Platonic philosophy at the Sapienza in Rome, the Congregation of the Index condemned the work, worried, no doubt, by its religious universalism and also by its undermining of the Peripatetic basis of Catholic dogma.

Patrizi's style in all his books, whether Latin or Italian, is dense and learned, strewn with quotations from classical sources. Brevity and clarity meant little to him in works not meant for the faint-hearted or uninformed. His *New Philosophy* was some time in preparation; the final printing appeared in 1593, by which time the Roman watchdogs had begun to bark and troubles with the censors left his project somewhat short of what he intended. The *New Philosophy* has four parts, each glorified by a Greek name: *Panaugia*, *Panarchia*, *Pampsychia*, and *Pancosmia*; or All-Splendour, All-Principle, All-Soul, and All-World. The subject of *Panaugia* is light, long treated as a metaphysical principle by Platonists. God, the first light (*prima lux*), produces the illumination (*lumen*) that terminates in lucent, transparent, and, finally, opaque bodies. The original divine *lux* is incorporeal, as suggested by its power to penetrate instantaneously, but the *lumen* diffused through the world is both incorporeal and corporeal, extended yet unresisting. Optics describes the activity of light, whose types are graded hierarchically, like those of darkness, understood as a real entity rather than a privation of light. Another hierarchy is that of the principles set forth in *Panarchia*. *Un'omnia*, the One-All, is the ultimate source that produces three levels of nine principles in all. The four that remain within the One—unity, essence, life, and mind—are insensible, incorporeal and indestructible, but contrary properties weaken the condition of the four that lie below, outside the One—nature, quality, form and body. Soul lies between in fifth place as intermediary. Patrizi's system is more complicated than its sources, of which Plotinus, Proclus, and Ficino were the most important; his command of Platonic texts surpassed any Western effort since antiquity, except Ficino's.

Pampsychia, the third and briefest of the four sections, is an extrapolation from *Panarchia*, which also deals with soul, *anima* and *animus*, particular souls and soul as such. If light is a corporeal incorporeal, soul is an incorporeal corporeal, and hence well suited to mediate between material and immaterial being. Soul is both one and many, and the world itself is ensouled. The fourth part of the work, *Pancosmia*, is the most original. In it Patrizi criticized a number of Aristotelian doctrines and proposed a novel philosophy of nature that links him with such sixteenth-century naturalists as Telesio and Bruno and also looks forward to Gassendi and other seventeenth-century figures. As with Pico and Cusanus, Patrizi's originality makes it hard to find the right pigeon-hole for him; though he was a fervent Platonist, his curiosity about nature made him an unusual one. Rejecting the Aristotelian elements, he suggested his own set of four: *spatium* (space), *lumen* (light), *calor* (heat), and *fluor* (fluid or flux), simple substances that combine in different proportions to form a hierarchy of mixed bodies: heaven, ether, air, stars, water, and earth. When light radiates through space, it encounters *fluor* as a principle of resistance and finally produces bodily objects. The original difference between embodied objects and the incorporeal space that contains them is that the former possess resistance (the Epicurean *antitupia*), while the latter offers no resistance to things moving through it.

Space comes first in the order of time and being. It is prior to all other things and a condition of their existence; therefore, the mathematical properties of space are more basic than the physical properties of the bodies that it contains. Although he produced more numerology than quantitative analysis, Patrizi raised mathematics to a higher theoretical status than Peripatetics commonly granted it. In particular, his distinction between mathematical space and physical body would surface later in objections made by Newton, Leibniz, and others to the Cartesian concept of extension. Patrizi also used empirical arguments against Aristotle, though his examples are not original or based on firsthand experience. At the least, when he contradicted Aristotelian doctrine on the vacuum with the common experience of a bellows, he helped make a place in natural philosophy for empirical reference. Most important, his concept of space, which allowed for vacua and physical infinity, was a real advance on the Aristotelian notion of *topos* or 'place' and influenced later developments in cosmology. The word that Patrizi used, *spatium*, is the same term that appeared in Latin translations of Philoponus which criticized the Aristotelian doctrine and which were certainly known to Patrizi. It was also the word that Newton used a century later. Patrizi's concept of a light-filled cosmic space had more in common with Proclus than with Newton, but it is worth noting that his richly speculative system had its effect on the seventeenth-century reform of natural philosophy.[71]

In the Renaissance, no ancient revival had more impact on the history of philosophy than the recovery of Platonism, once granted that the Peripatetic tradition needed no such rebirth. No other renewal of an ancient school had a textual base large enough to support the growth of a coherent, wide-reaching, and independent philosophical system—a system like Patrizi's, in other words. For at least three reasons, the new Platonism of Ficino and his successors must be seen as central to any discussion of European intellectual history during the period in question. First, the rich doctrinal content and formal elegance of Neoplatonic Platonism made it at least a plausible competitor with Peripateticism. What the Neoplatonists lacked in systematic logic and natural philosophy, they made up for with a stronger appeal to creativity. They gave more latitude to all kinds of speculation, from aesthetics and mythology to cosmology and theology. After Ficino, anyone who disliked Aristotle could turn to Plato. Few took the opportunity, but some of those who did—Zorzi, Steuco, Mazzoni, Patrizi—made their mark. The second strength of Platonism was its extra-philosophical influence. Despite his harsh words for poetry, Plato

---

[71] Henry (1979); Schmitt (1981: ch. 7); Long and Sedley (1987: i. 34–5).

initiated a tradition that poets admired, from Petrarch, Landino, and Benivieni to Michelangelo, Ronsard, and Spencer. The same is true of his treatment of music, which played a key role in Ficino's magic and eventually inspired the Orphic narratives of early opera. Finally, certain attitudes and methods of the new science were more Platonic than Aristotelian. The habit of idealizing physics, which was fundamental to the new science of the seventeenth century, came more easily to the Platonic mentality than to the Peripatetic. Even more important was Platonic praise of mathematics. For Aristotle, physics and mathematics did not really mix, while Plato gave good grounds for a mathematical analysis of nature. Platonism never vanquished Aristotelianism in the Renaissance, but it acquired great cultural strength.

4

Stoics, Sceptics, Epicureans, and Other Innovators

Humanism, authority, and uncertainty

Humanists gave three gifts to philosophy in the Renaissance: new methods, new information, and new doubts. The recovery of so much Greek and Roman learning meant that there were more choices to make in the quest for wisdom, and that discriminations would be sharper as history, philology, and philosophy became finer instruments. Thinkers and schools that had been little more than names for medieval readers took on fuller identities; the clearer the distinctions among them, the more obvious it became that the ancients often disagreed with one another. Despite the yearning for a single truth, intellectual authority in the Middle Ages had never been unitary; Peter Abelard wrote his book on *Yes and No*, and debates on universals and scores of other topics made scholasticism proverbially disputatious. But the humanists who blamed the schoolmen for their contentiousness uncovered older texts that multiplied and hardened philosophical discord. The quarrels that Plethon started about Plato and Aristotle were one aspect of these new divisions, and Bessarion's response was a sign of the common nostalgia for harmony. Conciliation came harder when two titans of classical thought, Aristotle and Plato, were revealed in relatively reliable Greek and then fixed in print and sold all over Europe. As scholars learned more about antiquity, they found more to disagree about. One of the reclaimed texts that spread the divisive news about classical thought, the *Lives* of Diogenes Laertius, was a doxography, a work that highlighted changes and differences of opinion (*doxa*) among its subjects, and as humanists uncovered more data on the various Hellenistic schools—Stoics, Epicureans, Academics, and others—the depth of their disharmony became obvious and troubling. The Middle Ages had to connect faith with ancient reason mainly in the person of Aristotle, but now that there were more giants for the dwarfs to ride upon, travel became treacherous. In an age so given to deference, dissent among the authorities caused scandal and bred despair. Yet it encouraged braver thinkers to assert and sometimes to die for the philosophical liberty that we now hold dear.

Thanks to these bolder spirits, a new critical temper entered philosophy. This transformation justifies the picture of the Renaissance as an age of adventure and originality, but powerful contrary forces were also at work. To legitimize criticism, early modern people typically felt obliged to make one authority the cause of objections to another, and the starting-points for their doubts were texts hallowed by age and custom. Thus, in literary culture the classics sowed the seeds of their own destruction, just as the Bible planted a thousand theological doubts once large numbers of ordinary Christians began to read it from different points of view. Since Aristotle dominated early modern philosophy, it was most often Peripatetic dogma that took the brunt of contradiction from philosophical systems newly opened up. The Middle Ages knew some of the same Latin authors who undercut certainty in the Renaissance; Cicero and Seneca, for example, were always familiar names. But in late antiquity a process of selection—partly physical, partly cultural—began a winnowing of the ancient documents that left them fragmented and thinly scattered for medieval readers. Renaissance humanists regathered the dispersed texts and amplified their disruptive potential by requiring that they be read, not as isolated proof-texts for one Christian position or another, but as parts of a larger, non-Christian whole with its own cultural integrity. Only in the context of a deliberately historical philology did the classics gain their full power as engines of discord in early modern culture. In the Middle Ages, antiquity was less hurtful because its presence was vague and diffuse, but even a dull sword can cut both ways. Except for Aristotle, the classical texts were less potent for every medieval use, whether to buttress the establishment or to undermine it. Everyone knew that Plato upheld the immortality of the soul, but no one could cite the precise structure or wording of his arguments. On the other hand, Nicholas of Autrecourt learned enough from Aristotle's physics about atomism to see its advantages over Peripatetic matter theory, but in the fourteenth century he lacked the more potent ammunition that would be recovered with Lucretius and Diogenes in the next century. On physical and metaphysical questions, what Nicholas saw in Aristotle was dangerous enough to move the papacy to extract a recantation from him in 1347.[1]

While at the Council of Constance in 1417, Poggio Bracciolini made a troublesome find, the unfinished didactic poem *On the Nature of Things* by Lucretius, a contemporary of Cicero. This long Latin poem is the most informative source on the atomist philosophy of Epicurus, who died in 270 BCE. Lucretius explains the nature of the universe in order to quiet the fears that give rise to religion. Those who understand nature's vital cycles will not dread death. Nature is nothing but atoms moving in the void, and all natural kinds, including the human, are material aggregates formed from the chance swerve of atoms in their various shapes and sizes. In certain combinations, atoms give rise to life and sense, but Epicurus showed that man's mind and soul are nothing more than very fine material particles, and therefore mortal. Death ends life altogether, so we should fear no after-life. The gods exist, but they did not create us, and they care nothing for us. Our world and everything in it arose from an accidental meeting of atoms in nothingness. The gods, also made of atoms, are immortal, tranquil, and content, and so should mortals be if they truly understood that the human condition is material. Such a philosophy could scarcely elicit Christian sympathies, and during the Middle Ages, when Lucretius, Diogenes, and other sources were unavailable or little known, 'Epicurean' was only a conventional label for the most contemptible atheist materialism and hedonist dissipation, a caricature of a system which taught

[1] Weinberg (1948; 1967: 266–93); Crombie (1959: ii. 35–40); Copleston (1960–6: iii. 135–48); Murdoch (1982: 575–7); Elford (1988: 313–17).

that pleasure comes from avoiding pain in a life of austere temperance. A Dominican friar of the fourteenth century left this typical description:

Epicurus the Athenian . . . left many brilliant writings . . . , but he erred more than all other philosophers, . . . for he denied God's providence, . . . [and] said that God does not care for humans, . . . that the world existed always, . . . that pleasure is the highest good and that the soul perishes with the body.

By the early fifteenth century, the humanist Cosimo Raimondi could point to controversy about the real views of Epicurus and even argue that pleasure (*voluptas*) of body as well as soul is a legitimate good that requires corporeal along with spiritual well-being. Later, the young Ficino interested himself in an interpretation of Epicurean *voluptas* that identified it with God's cosmic love as a kind of life-force shared by all humanity, and Filelfo wrote in praise of bodily pleasure as a good in itself. By around 1469, a maturer Ficino had finished his *Philebus* commentary, in which he still approved of pleasure when constrained by wisdom and joined to the satisfaction of intellect and will.[2]

The commoner way to sanitize Epicurus was to make him as ascetic as the Stoics, another ancient school that became better known in the Renaissance, and since equanimity was an aim of both these philosophies, attempts at conciliating them could be convincing. Bruni's unimpressive *Introduction to Moral Philosophy*, written around 1425 and digested mainly from a few works of Cicero, made a good preface for printed editions of Aristotle's ethical works through the next century because it took a Peripatetic stance on the nature of the good, but Bruni also summarized Stoic and Epicurean views in this little dialogue. Accepting Aristotle's claim that happiness (*eudaimonia/*

[2] The quotation is anonymous; see Garin (1961*a*: 72–92, esp. 77); also Gabotto (1889); Radetti (1889); Timmermans (1938); Allen (1944); Garin (1959; 1965*a*: 47–50); Jungkuntz (1962); Wind (1967: 34–5, 44–52, 62–71, 141–51); *Epicurisme* (1969); Pagnoni (1974); Raimondi (1974); Ficino (1975, with Allen's commentary on 15–18, 20, 26–8, 56); Kraye (1979; 1981; 1988: 374–86); Flores (1980); Reeve (1980); Kristeller (1988*a*: 14, 189–92, 298–301, 319; 1988*b*: 279–80).

beatitas) is the highest end, he then asked what happiness is. The Stoics considered 'virtue alone . . . sufficient for happiness: neither imprisonment, nor torture, nor any pain . . . could stand in the way of the happy life. . . . This is the sort of thing the Stoics usually teach. I rather doubt it's true,' he added, 'but it certainly is a stout and manly creed.' As for the Epicureans, they 'maintained that pleasure was the final and ultimate end', but they also advised 'the wise man . . . [to] endure small pains in order to avoid the greater' and thereby find the 'tranquillity of mind brought about by emptying oneself of all one's troubles'. Bruni goes on to say that Aristotelians subordinated virtue to happiness as the soul's welfare. Having heard these descriptions, his partner in the dialogue finds that he likes all three moral systems, and Bruni concurs. 'Those doctrines . . . have endured,' he comments, 'and although they may battle over words, they are . . . very close.' Stoics correctly emphasize virtue; their differences with the Peripatetics over the status of external bodily goods are mainly verbal. Epicureans are right to claim that pleasure is needed for happiness. 'All of them seem to say the same things, or nearly so, at least about the highest good.'[3] The key element in Bruni's brief for reconciliation is that all three points of view 'have endured'. His genial classicism was still intoxicated with antiquity: the more old texts the better, whatever they may say. This exaggerates Bruni's docility, of course, for he was not afraid to criticize Plato or distort Aristotle; but it reveals something about the time that he lived in, when one new textual discovery followed another, year after year. It was the age of philological innocence.

Juan Luis Vives lived a sadder life in a harder time.[4] He was born in 1492, when the Catholic kings who sent Columbus to

---

[3] Translation in Bruni (1987: 270–3); above, Ch. 2, n. 18.

[4] For the Latin writings, see Vives (1782–5) with more recent edns. and translations by Fantazzi, Guerlac, Lenkeith, Tobriner, and others in Vives (1968; 1974; 1979*a*; 1979*b*; 1987; 1989; 1991); and Cassirer, Kristeller, and Randall (1948: 385–93). For the secondary literature see Kater (1908); Bonilla y San Martin (1929); Sancipriano (1957); Colish (1962); Vasoli (1968*a*: 214–46); Noreña (1970; 1975: 20–35; 1989); Cassirer (1974: i. 120–30); Buck (1981*a*); Waswo (1987: 113–33).

the New World drove the Jews from Spain. Thirty years later, the Inquisition sent his *converso* father to the stake; then his mother was exhumed to be burned; and his sisters lost all rights to their parents' property. Vives, tormented by these griefs, remained a leading Christian humanist, perhaps a finer Christian than Erasmus. After a short stay in Valencia, where Antonio de Nebrija was importing humanism from Italy, he went to Paris in 1509. He was one of several distinguished Spaniards studying at the College of Montaigu when John Mair was in his prime, but, like Erasmus, he approved neither the puritan regime nor the nominalist curriculum nor the intractable students. Montaigu's only positive influence on Vives was to introduce him to the simple spirituality of the Brethren of the Common Life, which Jean Standonck had brought with him from the Low Countries. In 1512 Vives left for Bruges, and he spent most of his life there as a private teacher, with longer and shorter excursions to England and Louvain, where he began to lecture occasionally in 1520. Many of his friends were Christian humanists and disciples of Erasmus, whom Vives first met in 1516. His major Erasmian project was an edition, with commentary, of Augustine's *City of God*, containing criticisms of popes, friars, scholastics, sacraments, and other Catholic institutions that brought Vives repeated condemnations and a place on the Index. Although his relationship with Erasmus cooled by 1518, it continued until 1534, not always pleasantly. News of his father's trial in 1522 brought Vives graver worries. Despite his family's troubles, he never returned to Spain, and in 1523 he travelled to England and Oxford, where he made valuable friendships in the circle of Thomas More that led to his becoming a confidant of Catherine of Aragon. Vives spent happy intervals teaching in Oxford's Corpus Christi College, a new humanist foundation of 1516, but Catherine's troubles ended his English connection in 1528, when Henry VIII cut off his money and he found himself back in Bruges, unemployed. For twelve years until he died in 1540 he scraped for a living, but this difficult period produced some of his finest writing.

Vives wrote bestsellers, especially in the field of education, that saw hundreds of editions in several languages in the sixteenth and seventeenth centuries. He was a humanist critic of philosophy read more widely than most philosophers of the period. As an educator he promoted better conditions for women and poor people; he wanted them well supervised in secular schools run by professionals competent to teach language, moral development, and various practical skills. His main contributions to philosophy were attempts to reform logic and to present a fuller history of the ancient discipline. More than most humanists of the previous century, he was open to the view that past experience permits improvement in the present state of learning: 'if only we put our minds to it, we can generally formulate better opinions about matters of life and nature than Aristotle, Plato or any of the ancients.' A scholar must be modest, but not timid: 'the comparison that some people make is false and foolish, . . . that we are carried further as dwarfs on the shoulders of giants. It's not so: we are not dwarfs, and those people were not giants; all are of the same stature.' Age is no guarantee of wisdom, though some say that 'the older anyone is, the greater . . . his name and credit. Why? Was Aristotle not later than Anaxagoras, Cicero later than Cato?'[5] These questions show that Vives had gained enough temporal perspective to make critical distinctions among the ancients, and he firmly believed that philosophy was impotent if it lacked this historical depth. His college in Paris had banned the humanist subjects that Lefèvre and others advocated, but Vives turned bitterly against the terminism of Montaigu as educationally useless because it was philologically and historically barren. 'If they put in some history, false and foolishly told,' he complained, they say 'it's not my field. . . . What is your field, then? To get nothing right?'[6]

Vives found the times he lived in so dismal that things were bound to brighten up; the reform of letters was the first gleam of a new dawn. One improvement in the human condition was a richer sense of intellectual history, for which Vives drew a

[5] Vives (1782–5: vi. 6–7, 38–42); Noreña (1970: 152–5).
[6] Vives (1782–5: vi. 62–3); Noreña (1970: 158–9).

baseline in the time before Socrates, dividing the pre-Socratic thinkers into three groups: first, the Druids, Brahmins, and other un-Hellenic sages who gave wisdom to Orpheus and other figures of Greek legend; then the Greeks from Thales to Pythagoras who studied nature and worked apart in two schools, the Ionic and Italic. The study of nature grew ever more detailed and wearisome until Socrates turned from physical to moral questions, and then 'philosophy divided itself into various factions and streams . . . , derived from Socrates as if from a sacred . . . fountain'—Dogmatists, Sceptics, Stoics, Epicureans, and others, much as Cicero had described them. Vives' treatment of the Epicureans is not much fairer than the medieval slander: 'they stand belligerently for pleasure, and subject to it even virtue, . . . shamefully ordering the mistress of the universe to enslave herself to brutish instincts.'[7] For religious reasons Vives was kinder to Plato, but, at least in the early works of 1518 and 1520 *On the Origins, Sects, and Praises of Philosophy* and *Against the Pseudodialecticians*, Aristotle reigns. His philosophy is a coherent whole written in good Greek and well suited to teaching, especially in the critical area of language. The modern Peripatetics, worst of all the terminists whom Vives knew at Montaigu, squandered Aristotle's bequest of a linguistically sensitive and morally useful philosophy. Influenced by Valla and Rudolf Agricola, though never a mouthpiece for Valla's more strident complaints, Vives wanted a reformed logic suited to the needs of education.

In his later treatise *On the Disciplines* of 1531, he protested that the logicians have 'strayed into infinity in all their dialectic but especially in the *Little Logicals*. . . . In Paris they spend two years on dialectic, barely a year on the rest of philosophy —nature, morals and metaphysics.'[8] If Peter of Spain gave correct laws for language, then Cicero and many other Latin authors must have been wrong. For Vives, 'correct' discourse depends solely on the experience of reading competent ancient writers, with no allowance for formalization or any other departure from ordinary language—where 'ordinary' indicates

---

[7] Vives (1987: 38–41 [Roberts trans.]).
[8] Vives (1979a: 143); Noreña (1975: 2–5); above, Ch. 2, n. 44.

literary prose, not the unrecorded speech of the Roman streets. What irked him most were artificial propositions of the kind used by Mair and his followers to test problems of quantity, ambiguity, reference, and so forth. Logical monsters like the following were his worst nightmare: 'Only any non-donkey *C* of anyone except Sortes and another *C* belonging to this same person begin contingently to be black.' Vives knew that his own learned Latin was a far cry from the common vernaculars, but he used the difference between Latin and Spanish or Flemish only to bait the dialecticians, who cranked out reams of freakish sentences about Sortes and Brownie, the ubiquitous little ass who brayed in so many scholastic syllogisms. 'Lucky for these people that they still dispute . . . in some semblance of Latin,' he snickered, 'for if such madness were understood by the common people, the whole mob of workers would hoot them out of town.'[9] He ruled Mair's mutant sentences out of court because he could not accept them as Latin, and the logic that he demanded was to be 'a Latin dialectic, [whose] words will take their meaning from Latin tradition and custom, not from our own'. Contrast this ultimatum with the words of a widely used logic book now in print: 'the preferred status of English in this book is a matter only of the authors' convenience; the subsequent treatment would apply as well to French, German or Coptic.' Such a thought would have astounded Vives, who maintained that logic regulates language rather than thought, and that logical rules or examples cannot be so far abstracted from the particular language governed by them that normal speech conventions no longer apply. Mair, of course, did not write grotesquely to be perverse or obtuse. He was after a rigour believed to come only from technical manipulations of language not meant for daily use. 'I hope to die if any of them knows what this rigour is,' Vives snarled, defining rigour differently as the strictest adherence to classical usage, not *abstracted* from cogitation in the manner of a logician but *collected* from reading in the manner of a naturalist.[10]

  [9] Vives (1979*a*: 52–5, 76–7); Copenhaver (1988*b*: 100–6).
  [10] Vives (1979*a*: 66–9, 134–5); Kalish, Montague, and Mar (1980: 3); above, Ch. 2, nn. 39–42; below, pp. 217–30.

In 1531 Vives wrote a brief treatise *On First Philosophy*, a compendium of Peripatetic fundamentals meant only as a provisional and conjectural gesture toward curricular requirements that students could not avoid. The *Censura de Aristotelis operibus* of 1538 was a simple catalogue of the Aristotelian Corpus. These utilitarian works in no sense contradicted the stiff anti-Aristotelian posture of *De disciplinis*, where he indeed censured Aristotle—not just his Peripatetic followers—for moral and doctrinal lapses. The Stagirite dealt dishonestly with his predecessors and distorted history in order to deter criticism. His metaphysics is murky, his natural philosophy sketchy and superficial, his moral philosophy too closely tied to worldly goods, and his logic too far removed from practical use. Vives rated knowledge in moral and pragmatic terms and decried the prideful isolation of philosophy from the needs of mankind and the glory of God. Inquiry for its own sake he considered sinful. To be credible and worthwhile, knowledge must serve some Providential end. 'Human inquiry comes to conjectural conclusions,' he claimed, 'for we do not deserve certain knowledge [*scientia*], stained by sin as we are and hence burdened with the great weight of the body; nor do we need it, for we see that man is ordained lord and master of everything in the sublunary world.' Real knowledge needs to be *deserved*, not just discovered, and in its fallen state mankind lacks the necessary worth. Ignorance and uncertainty are moral faults that we owe to Adam's sin. Our defective senses cannot be trusted to report the truth, especially when warped by evil passions, but all our natural knowledge comes through sensation, so we have no real certainty. To brighten the darkness, however, God allows a 'natural light' to illuminate our minds, which is how we can see our place in the order of things without demonstrative proof. Vives found philosophical grounds for this insight in the Stoic doctrine of common notions (*koinai ennoiai*) or preconceptions (*prolêpseis*) as reported by Cicero. He thought of these notions not as distinct claims about the world but rather as generalized attitudes shared by all schools of philosophy. To discover these broad points of view one needs the help of the best and the brightest, the *summi auctores*

of old.[11] One cannot call Vives a sceptic. His Christian humanism made him relax his grip on certainty, but he tempered his
doubts by appealing to common notions shared by all the
right-thinking ancients. In the end, he reverts to a slightly
cynical version of Bruni's genteel classicism and of the élitist
pedagogy that it implies.

To speak, read, and write the 'ordinary' language that Vives
made the norm of all discourse required a thorough and costly
education in the classics. Vives wanted to broaden the reach of
such schooling to persons usually shut out—women and the
poor, especially—but for all its good intentions the humanist
programme could never be populist.[12] One extreme expression
of the contrary, aristocratic instinct in humanism was the
Ciceronian controversy of the 1520s and after. Scholars quarrelled over the limits of normative usage: how far might one
stray from the diction and syntax enshrined in classical texts?
which classical texts? what is a classic? A fashionable answer
to such questions was that Cicero, the prince of eloquence,
should surely be the arbiter of language, and so some scholars
shunned all words and all syntactic structures not found in
Cicero's works. This ban applied even to the Church's Latin,
where one must write *flamen* for 'pope' and *proconsul* for
'bishop'; Jesus becomes *Apollo* and the Virgin Mary is *Diana*.
Erasmus, who had himself translated the *Logos* ('Word') of
the Greek New Testament as *Sermo* instead of the traditional
Verbum, found this pedantry pagan as well as foolish, and he
said so in his *Ciceronianus* of 1528, in which he also reviewed
leading Latin writers of the day for style. Vives forgave his
colleague for skipping him altogether, but Erasmus gained few
friends from this broadside. Etienne Dolet and Julius Caesar
Scaliger attacked his betrayal of Cicero, whom the humanists
had made their icon in the eternal dispute between rhetoric

[11] Cicero, *Academica* 2. 7. 21, 30–1; Vives (1782–5: iii. 188); Noreña
(1970: 238–53); Long (1986: 123–4); Long and Sedley (1987: i. 236–53).
[12] Grafton and Jardine (1986: pp. xi–xvi, 56–7, 210–20) see the rise of
classicism not as 'the natural triumph of virtue over vice' but as something
more problematic, culturally and politically.
[13] Erasmus (1908; 1965b: pp. xxxii–xlix, 148); Bainton (1969: 204–10);
O'Rourke Boyle (1977: 3–37); Chomarat (1981).

and philosophy. Cicero's philosophical excursions seemed to show that the orator had the best of the dialectician even on the latter's turf.[13] These issues were much on the mind of Mario Nizolio as he compiled his massive *Observations on Marcus Tullius Cicero*, published in 1535. The *Observationes* is a Latin dictionary of about 20,000 entries, all from Cicero's works. It was the tool that could implement the Ciceronian agenda in its most militant form, and even Peripatetic philosophy was not secure. Joachim Périon tried to put all of Aristotle into Ciceronian Latin, and nearly did it.

Born in Boretto on the river Po in 1488, Nizolio had entered the service of a noble family in Brescia by 1522 and stayed with them until 1540, when he left to seek a university post in Milan.[14] Instead, the faculty chose Marco Antonio Maioragio, a much younger philosopher and lawyer of Aristotelian background. Later, between 1546 and 1548, Nizolio exchanged polemics with Maioragio when the latter charged that the Stoic paradoxes found in Cicero's works were not genuinely Socratic and that, in any case, Cicero was a mere orator, not a real philosopher. Maioragio compared Cicero's ideas unfavourably with Plato's; Nizolio replied by restating George of Trebizond's case against Plato. He also recalled how Trapezuntius showed that the logician had no better hold on techniques of argument than the rhetorician. As the controversy continued, Nizolio's language grew more extreme, and on grounds of linguistic incompetence he accused Maioragio of lacking any skill in philosophical discourse. He also took Maioragio's liking for Plato and his advocate Bessarion as a symptom of mental illness. Besides Trapezuntius, Nizolio referred to Gianfrancesco Pico to prove that certain works of Aristotle were inauthentic, and to Agricola to buttress his case for the power of rhetorical argument. Of the five parts of rhetoric—invention, disposition, style, delivery, and memory—dialectic knows only the first, and of the six parts of invention the four that touch on logic

[14] Nizolio (1956, with Breen's introd., pp. xv–lxxv); Sabbadini (1885); Rossi (1953*a*; 1953*b*); Breen (1954; 1955*a*; 1955*b*; 1958); Garin (1965*a*: 156–8); Vasoli (1968*a*: 606–63); Nizzoli (1970); Cassirer (1974: i, 149–53); Wesseler (1974).

are better served by rhetoric. Therefore, the orator has absolutely no need of the dialectician; discourse is entirely free of philosophy.

In 1548 Nizolio defended Cicero's honour again, this time against the late Celio Calcagnini of Ferrara, whose *Disquisitions* against Cicero had appeared posthumously in 1544. Nizolio had taken his oratorical suppression of philosophy to extremes in his attacks on Maioragio, but his *Defences* against Calcagnini leaned even harder on the integrity of philosophy. If any problem can be said to *belong* to philosophy, it is the problem of universals, but Nizolio ingeniously proposed to solve it by applying the rhetorical figure of speech called *synecdoche*, which usually refers to a more complete term by one less complete—genus by species, for example, or whole by part, as when an actor walks the *boards* rather than the *stage*. Nizolio claimed that propositions of the form 'man is a rational animal' are expressed in synecdoche because whatever is predicated of the singular term 'man' really belongs to all 'men' in the plural. The part stands for the whole. 'Man' is not a universal; it is a turn of phrase, a decorative substitute for the plural 'men'. Rhetoric shows that the nominalists are right. Philosophy is expendable. The unlikely origin of this amazing argument was Calcagnini's obscure complaint that the title of Cicero's work *On Duties* ought to have been singular, *De officio* instead of *De officiis*, surely not one of the great issues of anyone's time. 'I say ... that Cicero could have entitled his book in either way,' replied Nizolio.

It is common among the great men ... to use the singular number for the plural, ... the part for the whole. Grammarians call this synecdoche.... [And] that singular number is figurative.... When one uses the plural number ... it is not figurative but literal.... When we say, Man is a rational mortal animal, one man stands for all men.... In view of all this there is no need of ... those things which dialecticians and philosophers call universals.... They have not been brought forth from the nature itself of things but from their false and empty imaginations.... Universals ... do exist, but not in the manner ... assigned to them by the dialecticians.

Leibniz, who respected Nizolio as a critic of philosophical

terminology while differing with his position on universals, acknowledged the value of this argument against confusing poetic metaphor with philosophical analysis.[15] Nizolio's aims were even more aggressive, however. His discussion of synecdoche was only one proof that grammar and rhetoric must replace metaphysics and formal logic in every respect. Philosophy has declined almost continuously since Socrates fought with Gorgias; Cicero brought one of the few moments of respite when he rejoined eloquence to wisdom. Nizolio laid out his rhetorical reform programme fully in his sizable treatise of 1553, *On the True Principles and True Method of Philosophizing, Against the Pseudophilosophers*, which Leibniz thought worthy of editing more than a hundred years later.[16] Nizolio's most original forerunner in this radical project of anti-philosophy was Lorenzo Valla.

Lorenzo Valla: language against logic

Valla was born in Rome around 1407 to a family of jurists with good connections at the papal court, where eventually he found employment after four decades of preparation and service to lesser masters.[17] His early education in Rome, which then

[15] Nizolio (1956: pp. liii–lvi, lxxiii [Breen trans.]); Nizzoli (1970: 56–7); Leibniz (1969: 121–30); Aiton (1985: 30–2).
[16] Nizolio (1956: pp. lxiii–lxxv); Nizzoli (1970: 58–73); Monfasani (1988: 208–11).
[17] For the collected Latin works see Valla (1962), a reprint; recent edns. and translations by Anfossi, Coleman, Hieatt, Lorch, Perosa, Pugliese, Trinkaus, and Zippel appear in Valla (1922; 1934; 1953; 1970*a*; 1970*b*; 1977; 1982; 1984; 1985); and Cassirer, Kristeller and Randall (1948: 147–82). Besides the introductions to these edns., for other important secondary literature, see Gabotto (1889); Barozzi and Sabbadini (1891); Mancini (1891); Casacci (1926); Timmermans (1938); Gaeta (1955); Kristeller (1964*a*: 19–36); Garin (1965*a*: 50–6); Gray (1965); Seigel (1968: 137–69); Vasoli (1968*a*: 28–77); Fois (1969); Trinkaus (1970: i. 103–70, 200–10; ii. 571–8, 633–8, 674–82; 1983: 151–9, 214–20, 263–73, 385–96, 441–6; 1988*a*; 1988*b*; 1989*b*); Di Napoli (1971); Camporeale (1972; 1976; 1988); Giannantonio (1972); Levine (1973); Gerl (1974); Fubini (1975); Setz (1975); Lorch (1976; 1985; 1988); Jardine (1977; 1981; 1983); Panizza (1978); Kessler (1980); Gravelle (1981; 1982; 1988; 1989); Perreiah (1982); Bentley (1983: 32–69); Kahn (1983; 1985); Monfasani (1983*b*; 1989; 1990); Struever (1983); Antonazzi (1985); Grafton and Jardine (1986: 65–82); Vickers (1986); Waswo (1987: 88–113; 1989).

lacked a university, was private and self-directed, but it was good enough to include Greek and other humanist attainments. Although he had no university degree, Valla taught in the early 1430s at Pavia, where the philosophy of Oxford and Paris had become fashionable; but even more than Petrarch and Bruni he learned to despise scholasticism in all its guises, legal, theological, and philosophical. Valla launched his long career as a polemicist at Pavia by befriending teachers of law who wished to cleanse their discipline of Aristotelianism, and his combative habits soon forced him to leave the university. Beginning in 1435, he spent thirteen years working for Alfonso of Aragon, who at the time ruled Sicily and also had designs on Naples. Alfonso's ambitions brought him into conflict with the pope, and their rivalry was the occasion of Valla's best-remembered work, the *Declamation on the Falsely Credited and Fabricated Donation of Constantine*, written in 1440 to refute papal claims to Western hegemony and Italian territory. The document in question, actually a product of the eighth century, recorded the emperor's gift of land and political authority to Pope Sylvester in the early fourth century, after Sylvester had miraculously cured Constantine of leprosy. Arguing from defective documentation, implausible motivations, and anachronisms of language, style, and fact, Valla proved the *Donation* a forgery, prefacing his *Declamation* with strong but careful language that religious reformers of the next century would exploit: 'I dare not say', he threatened, 'that, on instruction from me, others should prune the rank growth in the Papal See, Christ's vineyard, of its excessive branches.'[18] Ulrich von Hutten and others were happy to take the hint, which Valla offered in the narrower context of territorial politics but which also reflected a broad feature of his work, his wish to heal the religious ills of his day with the medicine of philology.

Alfonso got what he wanted in Naples by 1442. Valla stayed with him six more years, until a move to Rome in 1448 ended the most productive phase of his career. While translating

[18] Valla (1922: 24–5); Setz (1975); Antonazzi (1985); Camporeale (1988).

Greek historians for Nicholas V and defeating George of Trebizond in a contest for a chair of rhetoric, Valla continued to revise earlier works and added some new ones, including the responses to the *Invectives* that Poggio began to hurl at him in 1452. Ill will had divided the two scholars since the early 1430s, when Valla made Poggio, Bruni, and other famous humanists speakers in his dialogue *On Pleasure*, revised in 1433 and retitled *On the True Good and the False*.[19] To the time-honoured question about the nature of the good Valla gave a startling answer: *voluptas* or pleasure, a choice that upset not only Christian expectations but also the superficial Stoicism often favoured by the very humanist notables whom he made speak his lines. After a Stoic spokesman's unconvincing plea for virtue as its own reward in the face of bitter natural necessity, Valla introduced his Epicurean (originally the poet Antonio Beccadelli or Panormita; later Maffeo Vegio, also a poet and a priest), who made the case for pleasure as utility within the confines of mortal life. This abbreviated Epicureanism was more faithful to Valla's own ideal of practical oratorical virtue than to the views of Epicurus, but its presentation provided plenty of provocative material on the joys of sensuality. A passage condoning adultery, for example, maintains that 'it makes no difference at all whether a woman has sex with her husband or her lover. Take away the distinction of that perverse term "wedlock", and you have made one and the same thing of wedlock and adultery.' The dialogic structure of the work and its rhetorical subtlety shift the onus of such opinions from the author to his interlocutors.[20] But Valla was no prisoner of propriety. He dismissed the Aristotelian scheme of virtue as a mean between vices, and he preferred Epicurean to Stoic ethics because it revealed the emptiness of self-contained moral rectitude (*honestas*). Christians need God and the theological virtues of faith, hope and charity (*caritas*) that God gives them. Hence, Christian virtue can only be a means

---

[19] Valla (1970*a*; 1977, with introds. by Lorch, pp. xv-lxxvi and 7–46); Lorch (1988: 341–7); Kristeller (1964*a*: 27–33); Trinkaus (1970: i. 103–50; 1988*a*: 337).
[20] Valla (1977: 118–19); Panizza (1978); cf. Vickers (1986).

to some greater good, which Valla located in divine love (*caritas*) as the ultimate pleasure (*voluptas*) for humans whose immortal destiny carries them beyond the material boundaries of the Epicurean cosmos. From Epicurean materials he fashioned a Christian hedonism.

Between 1435 and 1443, Valla wrote another moral dialogue, *On Free Will*, that tested the compatibility of God's foreknowledge and man's moral liberty. He argued that knowing a future state of affairs, that something *will be*, implies causality no more than knowing that something *is*, a present condition: realizing that night will fall does not make the sun set. To understand the trickier condition of divine foreknowledge, he used the distinction between Apollo's wisdom and Jupiter's will to show that the two faculties can be separate, even in a single deity. In the end, we cannot know what causes God to will our destinies, to harden some hearts but not others. Citing St Paul on the folly of human wisdom, Valla concluded that 'we stand by faith, not by the probability of reason'. Religion provides the only answer; no salvation lies in philosophy, a seed-bed of heresy, and rhetoric is a better aid to faith than dialectic.[21] Despite his evident passion for philosophy, this pious anti-intellectualism was a constant in Valla's work. As a humanist living in an age of religious crisis, he wanted to reform Christianity by restoring it to the simpler and purer state that he found in the scriptures and the Fathers. He saw the development of philosophical theology between Boethius and Aquinas as a catastrophe from which contemporary theologians had not recovered; he wanted to replace scholasticism with a rhetorical theology capable of turning the human heart toward Christ. Time and again he challenged cardinal points of Christian belief—the superiority of the monastic life, the special efficacy of religious vows, the usefulness of sacramental theology—in the conviction that his own linguistically acute faith was closer to Gospel purity. In 1444 he quarrelled with a famous Franciscan preacher who made particular apostles res-

[21] Cassirer, Kristeller, and Randall (1948: 179–81 [Trinkaus trans., with introd., 147–54]); Rom. 12: 16; 1 Cor. 8: 1; II Cor. 12: 7; Trinkaus (1970: i. 165–7); Kristeller (1964a: 26–7); Kahn (1983).

ponsible for verses of the Apostles' Creed, but this was only the most public, not the most serious, of several affronts to conventional Christianity that brought him before the Inquisition of Naples in that year. In 1457, the year of his death, Valla turned an 'encomium' of Thomas Aquinas delivered to a gathering of Roman Dominicans into a denunciation of scholasticism and a call for an unphilosophical theology like that of the Church Fathers.[22]

A year or two before his encounter with the Inquisition, Valla had finished the first version of the work that Erasmus published in 1505 as *Annotations on the New Testament*; Valla called it a *Collation of the New Testament* because it compared the Greek text to the Latin Vulgate in a number of different manuscripts. He found the venerable Latin version wanting in style, clarity, and accuracy, and he wished to provide the makings of a better translation by applying new humanist techniques of textual criticism even to the sacred page. Because he aimed always to improve the Latin version, his analysis of the Greek was not complete or coherent enough to establish a new text of the original, but he did show that serious study of the New Testament must begin with the Greek. In scrutinizing hundreds of words and phrases of the Latin and comparing them to the Greek originals, he inevitably turned up linguistic difficulties in sensitive passages which had long buttressed key points of doctrine. In II Cor. 7 : 10, for example, where the Authorized Version has 'godly sorrow worketh repentance to salvation', he found that the Latin word for 'repentance' is *poenitentia*, connoting disgust or regret, while the Greek text has *metanoia*, which he found less negative in nuance, meaning simply 'change of mind or heart'. In disputes over the sacrament of penance and the forgiveness of sins that were to pit Protestant against Catholic, much turned on this distinction, because the passage in question was a proof-text for church dogma on the sacrament. One can scarcely exaggerate Valla's courage in probing the language of a book as sacrosanct as the

Bible, long revered as God's word in the most literal sense. No wonder that a scholar brave enough to rewrite scripture also dared to submit the deepest issues of philosophical theology to philological tests.[23]

Valla's originality made enemies not only in the theological arena but also in the field of his greatest expertise, in humanist philology, where he found the approach of his senior colleagues too tame. While Poggio, Bruni, Guarino, and others treated the classics as establishing a normative linguistic ideal, Valla regarded even ancient texts as contingent historical artefacts, and discriminated among them as better and worse examples of the linguistic usage (*consuetudo*) that he made his constant guide. Poggio found reprehensible the principle that Valla honoured unswervingly, that it was better 'to speak good Latin than good grammar', meaning that no rationally constructed set of grammatical rules could replace the examples of good usage that must be discovered empirically in the ancient texts. Valla collected such instances of diction and syntax in the work that was most famous in his own day and often reprinted afterward, the *Elegances of the Latin Language*, a treatise on grammar as the Renaissance understood that term —the fundamentals of Latin. Poggio mocked Valla for wasting his time on so juvenile a topic and rebuked him for rejecting so many worthy masters—Boethius, Priscian, Augustine, Jerome—in favour of a sole authority, Quintilian, who finished his twelve books *On the Education of the Orator* around 95 CE. Valla had bigger game in mind than Poggio knew, for even within the limits of the *Elegantiae* he raised linguistic questions of great weight philosophically and theologically. It might seem that such topics as the proper use of possessive pronouns and adjectives (*meus/mei, tuus/tui*, etc.) could delight only a schoolmaster, but Valla's treatment of these issues threatened the logic and metaphysics taught in the universities of his day. To mention only one way in which Valla undermined scholastic philosophy: by putting philological strictures,

[23] Trinkaus (1970: ii. 571–8); Di Napoli (1971: 101–11, 129–36); Camporeale (1972: 277–403); Bentley (1983: 32–69); Rummel (1985: 89–102).

empirically derived, on the use and form of possessive words (*meus* or *mei*, for instance), he ruled out certain forms of expression that were essential to an important division of logic, the doctrine of supposition. By declaring it impossible to say things in Latin except as ancient *consuetudo* permits, Valla made nonsense of the discourse, especially logical and metaphysical discourse, that medieval and early modern philosophers found intelligible and indispensable. In effect, he asked philosophy to be silent about the things it could not say in good Latin.[24]

It might be tempting to dismiss Valla as a pedant, an aesthete, or an antiquarian, especially since his leading light as an anti-philosopher was the orator Quintilian, who has rated little attention in histories of philosophy. Like other humanists, Valla also admired Cicero, not only for his eloquence but also as a transmitter of ancient philosophy. But it was Quintilian, not Cicero, who made Valla the scourge of school philosophy. Quintilian's *Institutio oratoria*—rediscovered, ironically, by Poggio in 1416—was a comprehensive programme for the Roman orator's education from the grammatical basics to the last rhetorical refinements, with a good deal of moral philosophy and logic added for good measure. Like Valla, Quintilian had small respect for the philosophers that he knew, and he paid allegiance to no particular school, but he had to confront serious philosophical questions in order to complete his educational programme. In effect, given the systematic nature of Quintilian's effort, Poggio's discovery had presented Valla a plausible—if not effective—opportunity to displace scholasticism as doctrine and as curriculum. Valla seized the day, trying, in a bold reversal of medieval priorities, to curb philosophy's pretensions by absorbing it within a rhetoric that he found better suited to the highest end of human language, persuading people to accept the Gospel. Valla had recognized Quintilian's significance from the first; his earliest project, now lost, was *On the Comparison of Cicero and Quintilian*. Quinti-

---

[24] Valla (1962: 45–50 [*Elegantiae* 2.1]); Camporeale (1972: 89–108, 180–92, 207–8); Grafton and Jardine (1986: 65–82); Waswo (1987: 91–3); below, pp. 353–7.

lian's *Institutio*, especially the fifth book on techniques of rhetorical proof, was also a fundamental component of Valla's most important philosophical work, the *Dialectical Disputations*.[25]

The title *Dialecticae disputationes*, although commonly applied to all versions of the work, belongs properly to sixteenth-century printings of the *first* revision that Valla may have made as early as 1441 of his *Repastinatio dialecticae et philosophiae*, which was finished by 1439 and had probably been stimulated by his earlier experience of scholasticism at Pavia. The eventual title of this original version, *The Retrenching of Dialectic and Philosophy*, suggests its ambitions, which Valla thought it prudent to curtail in the substantial expansions and excisions of the *first* revision, titled no less arrogantly *The Repair of All Dialectic and of the Fundamentals of Philosophy as a Whole*. He produced a *second*, less extensive revision in the eight years before he died in 1457. The context of this last version was his sinecure in the papal bureaucracy and his final battle with Poggio. The original version was a product of the year 1439, when the Council of Florence decreed union between the Greek and Latin churches and tried to settle the theological issues dividing them. The middle version, which was the *first* revision and the only text in print until a few years ago, followed Valla's appearance before the Inquisition in 1444.[26] In other words, the version that provoked the church to censure Valla was the original *Repastinatio*, which is perhaps the best witness of the three to its author's genius; but the other texts, especially the third, now available in a critical edition, are also of great philosophical value.

Had Valla never written the *Dialectical Disputations*, we would remember him for *De voluptate* and *De libero arbitrio* as a creative moral philosopher, but it is unlikely that the philological *Elegantiae* or the scriptural *Adnotationes* would have attracted much philosophical attention in their own right.

[25] Kennedy (1969); Di Napoli (1971: 57–63); Camporeale (1972: 89–100).
[26] Camporeale (1972: 12–16); Zippel's introd. in Valla (1982: pp. ix–cxxiv); Monfasani (1984).

It is the *Disputations* that reveal the importance of all the rest of Valla's work outside moral philosophy, the usual province of humanism in his time. As Professor Kristeller has written, Valla was the first to apply humanism to problems of great philosophical scope elsewhere than in ethics, and he did so in a truly revolutionary manner. He wanted to embrace the whole science of language in an aggrandized rhetoric no longer limited to persuasive argument but also including demonstration. In doing so, he denied logic any autonomous status, reducing it to a tool of oratory, and he implicitly dismissed most of metaphysics as a symptom of sick Latin. Unlike most humanist critics of scholasticism, he did not simply ridicule the prose of the Peripatetics or pick at a particular Aristotelian doctrine. Although his views on metaphysics have been called 'the rhetorical equivalent of nominalism', he tried to annihilate the whole linguistic basis of scholastic philosophy and to replace what he felt to be corrupt terminology and perverse habits of mind with his own anti-philosophical lexicon and methodology.[27]

Valla may be the only person ever denounced from the pulpit for having written against the ten predicaments. When speaking of metaphysics, Peripatetic philosophers regarded the predicaments or categories as the ten most general modes of being—substance, quantity, quality, relation, place, time, position, state, action, and affection; for logical purposes, they treated the same words as naming the largest classes of independently meaningful terms that could be predicated of a subject in a proposition. In Book I of the first version of the *Dialectical Disputations*, after a rousing declaration of the liberty of philosophizing against the servile Aristotelians, Valla gave twelve chapters to his case against the predicaments and the transcendentals, the five or six features of being (*ens*) treated as convertible with being itself and hence extending beyond any of the predicaments; those that Valla wished to eliminate were the *one*, the *good*, the *true*, *being* and *something*, leaving only *res*, the versatile Latin word for 'thing'.

[27] Kristeller (1964*a*: 33–6); Trinkaus (1970: i. 150–5; 1988*a*: 340–3); Camporeale (1972: 76–87); cf. Seigel (1968: 137–69); Waswo (1987: 94–5); below, n. 35, on reactions to Waswo's account of Valla's views on language.

Valla's reading of the Latin classics convinced him that *res* was the only term capacious enough to transcend all others, and he criticized Aristotle for having ignored its Greek analogue, *pragma*, as a basis of metaphysics. Instead, Aristotle had chosen 'being as being' for his point of departure, a phrase that Valla found inept because it implies that being might be other than what it is, i.e. that it might exist *as* something other than being. He rejected *ens*, a Latin word for 'being', as a faulty attempt to duplicate the key participial form in Aristotle's phrase, *to on hê on*, and he showed grammatically why *ens* is a poor surrogate for *on*. Grammar also indicates that the Latin words for 'the true' and 'the good', *verum* and *bonum*, are no more substantive than *veritas* or *bonitas*, abstractions that name distinct moral and logical qualities and hence cannot be convertible with undifferentiated and unqualified being.[28]

Likewise, since numbers can be other than one, *unum* can hardly transcend the categories of quantity or quality. However, Aristotle treated unity not as a number but as the beginning of number. To discredit what he regarded as idle Peripatetic abstraction, Valla countered with a homely story of

two women who shared twelve hens and one rooster among them. They agreed that one would have the eggs on days when the number laid was even, but that the other would get them when the number was odd. 'Say that sometimes single eggs were laid. To which would the egg go; to neither?' 'No, to the one who was due the odd number of eggs.' Therefore, one egg makes a number.

Belittling Aristotle by patronizing women, Valla showed how ordinary language gives meaning to number-words when it uses them to count concrete objects. 'Therefore,' he concluded, 'foolish women sometimes know the meaning of words better than great philosophers. Women put words to use; philosophers play with them.'[29] That common speech is the matrix of meaning was one of Valla's primary findings. Another was that

---

[28] Valla (1982: ii. 359–70, 377); Aristotle, *Metaphysics* 1003^{b}19–23; Di Napoli (1971: 63–80); Camporeale (1972: 153–71).

[29] Valla (1982: i. 18–19; ii. 380–1); Aristotle, *Metaphysics* 1052^{a}22–5, 1088^{a}4–10; Waswo (1987: 95–7).

grammar dissolves metaphysics, as in his discussion of *essentia* and *esse*, members of the same family of Latin words that produced the dubious *ens*. To define a key metaphysical term, the *form* that shapes the otherwise indefinite *matter* of natural objects, Thomists used *esse*, the infinitive 'to be', to distinguish actual existence (*esse*) from essence (*essentia*) as a potency: the usual definition was that 'form is *what gives existence* to a thing'—*forma est quae dat esse rei*. Valla's objection was grammatical. If I ask what (*quid*) form is, he argued, and you say that form is what (*quae*) gives existence, your phrase, *quae dat esse*, supplies no antecedent for the pronoun *quae* except *forma*, the word to be defined. Good Latin would not beg the question. Better to replace *quae* with *quod*, also meaning 'what' or 'which' but implying an antecedent *id* or *illud*, giving 'that which' in the form *id quod* or *illud quod*, which Valla had already shown to be equivalent to *illa res quae*, 'that thing which'. He had two aims in this elaborate exercise. One was to expose the metaphysical circle buried in the traditional definition of form; analysis revealed that 'form is that thing (*res*) which gives existence to a thing (*res*),' suggesting that if form is a *res*, and form is what gives existence to *res*, then form seems to give existence to itself. Another point was to bring the discussion back to the word *res*, the beacon of Valla's search for clear language and the only transcendental term.[30]

Valla reduced the transcendentals to *res* alone, and he trimmed the predicaments to three: substance, quality, and action. Any proposition needs at least two terms, a noun and a verb; the verb signifies action; the noun signifies qualified rather than bare substance. On this basis, Valla covered the terms of any proposition with three predicaments, not ten: substance and quality for nouns, action for verbs. He maintained that any object, wood or stone or flesh, consists at least of substance and quality; at some point the disappearance of quality entails the disappearance of the object. The word 'man' has more to do with a complex of human qualities than with simple sub-

[30] Valla (1982: ii. 370–1, 381–2); Copleston (1960–6: ii. 332–5); below, Ch. 5, pp. 303–5.

stance. 'Man' falls not under one predicament but several, not just substance and quality but action as well, for even while resting any human is always acting. In general, predication requires the determination of substance and quality always, of action often, so that a better term for substance is 'consubstance'.[31] Valla mentioned consubstantials of three kinds— *soul*, *body*, and the combination of soul and body or *animal*, all uniting substance, quality, and action in one *res*. Valla knew that Bessarion and other Greek delegates to the Council of Ferrara and Florence used *consubstantialis* to describe relations among the members of the divine trinity. In dealing with soul as the first species of consubstantials, he began with a chapter titled 'What is God?' This was the thirteenth and pivotal part of the first book of the original *Dialectical Disputations*, preceded by the twelve that ripped the predicaments, the transcendentals, and other metaphysical planks from the platform of Latin theology. In this chapter Valla supported the Greek position on the most crucial theological issue debated at the Council, the *Filioque*. This brief Latin term, meaning 'and from the Son', expressed a Western view of trinitarian theology, that the Holy Spirit, the third member of the trinity, proceeded not just from the first member, the Father, but from the Son as well, the second member. The Greeks resisted inserting this term in the creed, and Valla supported them.[32]

Valla maintained that 'this whole issue, with which the theologians and philosophers torment themselves in dispute, is one of words', and he settled the question by substituting his own scheme of consubstantials for the traditional terminology. Above all, he objected to the equation of the terms 'person' (*persona*) and 'substance' that he found in Boethius; and he cleared the way for his solution by showing that it was neither inaccurate nor impious to attribute quality and action as well as substance to the deity, thus enabling him to describe God as a *res* and a consubstance.[33] Careful not to identify the mem-

---

[31] Valla (1982: ii. 401–2).

[32] Ibid. 402–8; Southern (1970: 61–7); Trinkaus (1970: i. 153–5); Di Napoli (1971: 148–63); Camporeale (1972: 235–76); Geanakoplos (1989: 224–54).

[33] Valla (1982: ii. 405); Camporeale (1972: 235–40).

bers of the trinity with their qualities or actions, he none the less distinguished three aspects of a single divine consubstance by the actions and qualities proper to each. Using a metaphor favored by the Neoplatonists and their Byzantine Christian heirs, he compared God to the sun, wherein the gleaming light (*vibratus*), the emitted light (*lux*), and the heat (*ardor*) stand for Father, Son, and Spirit. The Father's quality is life, power, and eternity; his action is to gleam, to be seen, and to emit. The Son is the wisdom that shines. The Spirit is the love that burns. 'Why should we dissimulate?' asked Valla.

Whence does this heat proceed, from the gleaming only or from the light as well? Unless my senses deceive me, it seems to proceed from the gleaming alone. . . . Can I say the same of the Holy Spirit? I assert nothing but ask that I be permitted only to inquire, like any common person, since I do not grasp those sharp and ingenious arguments of the disputing theologians.[34]

In fact, from the Latin point of view, it was clear that Valla had taken the wrong side on one of the most controverted topics in the history of Christian dogma; worse, as a saboteur in the great mill of Peripatetic metaphysics that drove Western theology, he had given the enemy a most insidious comfort.

In later versions of the *Dialectical Disputations*, after the Inquisition called him to account, Valla muffled his theological novelties, but without inhibiting his linguistic creativity. The chapter 'On the Qualities Known by the Senses' in Book I of the revised versions shows weakness as well as strength in Valla's method. Having ridiculed Aristotle's use of alphabetical signs for variable terms in propositions, he rejected any formal notation. Yet he badly needed some scheme of symbolism in this chapter, one of many places where his argument strains the limits of ordinary Latin prose; as early modern readers met it on the page, Valla's text lacked devices as basic as the use of quotation marks to distinguish a word from its referent. To show that '*res*' is a word (*vox*) that transcends the predicaments and 'signifies the meaning or sense of all other words', he began with distinctions between sound (*sonus*), word (*vox*),

[34] Valla (1982: ii. 406–7); Camporeale (1972: 235–40).

and meaning (*significatio*), such that sound speaks only to the ear and meaning only to the mind, while words address mind and ear alike. If a spoken word (*vox*) is the image of a meaning, a written word (*litera*) is the image of a *vox*, and both are terms (*vocabula*) that represent concepts. A term spoken or written is also substance, quality, and action—a *res*, in other words. But just as the word 'wood' names wood and the word 'virtue' names virtue, so the word '*res*' names *res*, which leaves Valla at the summit of his minimal ontology and at the edge of his linguistic reach. A few sentences of the original, given below in the printed text (slightly emended) of 1540, may suggest Valla's dizzying effort to make ordinary Latin its own metalanguage, without benefit of formalism. After listing concrete and abstract objects paired with their names, all related as stone to 'stone' or substance to 'substance', he concluded that in the same relation

res significat rem; hoc significatur, illud huius est signum; illud non vox, hoc vox est; ideoque definitur: Res est vox sive vocabulum omnium vocabulorum significata suo complectens. Ergo vocabulum, inquies, est supra res quia res vocabulum est etiam. Sed significatum rei supra significatum vocabuli est, et ideo vocabulum res est et una res duntaxat. Illa autem vox omnes res significat, quemadmodum haec vox deus infra multas alias est, nam illam transcendit spiritus, ... substantia, ... essentia, ... aliquid et res; significationis autem dignitate cuncta alia transcendit.

'*res*' signifies *res*; the latter is signified, the former is a sign of the latter; the one is not a word (*vox*), the other is a word (*vox*); hence the definition: *res* is a word (*vox*) or term (*vocabulum*) embracing the things meant by all terms in its meaning. 'And so', you say, 'term is above *res*, for *res* is also a term.' But the meaning of '*res*' is above the meaning of 'term', and therefore a term is a *res* and one *res* only. That word (*vox*) signifies all *res*, just as this word (*vox*), 'God,' is below many others, for spirit, ... substance, ... essence, ... something and *res* transcend it, though in the dignity of its meaning it transcends all others.[35]

---

[35] Valla (1962: i. 676–7; 1982: i. 123–4); Waswo (1987: 105–8); for the reading *significata suo* in the 2nd sentence of the Latin, see Monfasani (1989: 310–11 n. 7, 318 nn. 38–9); Monfasani's critique of Waswo, Gerl, and Gravelle

The translation shows what Valla missed in the simple convention of quotation marks, even though he wrote in an inflected language. His scorn for the jargon of logicians deprived him of analytical tools that might have aided the reform of philosophical discourse. He believed, however, that formalized arguments lose inferential force when they shed their semantic and grammatical features.

In any case, Valla did not want to improve philosophy; he meant to shrink and hold it within the precincts of rhetoric, the art of language that he found better suited than philosophy to the evangelical needs of Christianity. His determination that rhetoric should swallow philosophy becomes clear in the second and third books of the *Dialectical Disputations*, which move beyond the various terms treated in the first book to larger structures made up of terms—propositions and arguments. In dealing with the broad issue of argumentation, Peripatetics assigned demonstrative reasoning to logic, leaving rhetoric the more elusive task of persuasion. Following Quintilian and Cicero, however, Valla discussed two kinds of demonstration, necessary and probable, allotting both types to rhetoric but limiting logic to necessary demonstration. Valla's rhetoric is broader than his logic. Scholastics divided dialectic from rhetoric, but Valla united them by subordinating the former to the latter. He took his cue from the standard division of rhetoric into five parts, the first of which is *invention*, the techniques used by the orator to find (*invenire*) his material. 'What else is dialectic', asked Valla, 'but a kind of affirmation and refutation? These are parts of invention, . . . one of the five parts of rhetoric. . . . The dialectician uses the syllogism naked, so to speak, but the orator uses it clothed, armed and adorned.' To establish the orator's mastery of demonstration as well as persuasion, Valla used his second book to eliminate what he took to be abuses in the scholastic analysis of propositions, clearing the way for a rhetorical theory of argument in his third book. Book two deals with the internal structure of

in this issue of the *Journal of the History of Ideas* is followed by replies from Waswo and Gravelle; see also Trinkaus (1988*b*).

the proposition, especially negation, modality, and syncategoremata (see below). In general, Valla wanted his propositions pruned of solecism and needless abstraction, and he tried
to simplify their construction by cutting the theoretical inventory, as when he reduced the modes of propositions, tradi-
tionally six, to three or four: true, possible, impossible, and
(perhaps) credible.[36]

The subject of the third book of the *Dialectical Disputations*
is argument in its two varieties, both seen as belonging to
rhetoric: necessary or demonstrative (apodictic) argument in
syllogistic form; and probable argument in the form of induction and epicheireme (see below). Valla retained more of
Aristotle's logic than of its Peripatetic derivatives, and he
made Boethius his primary opponent; but his main inspiration
was Quintilian, from whom he took long passages verbatim.
Boethius described induction as argument moving from particulars to universals, but Valla denied that enumeration of
contingent particulars could ever conclude in a necessary and
universal proposition. Inductive inference, or argument from
examples, always involves comparison of similar terms, an
analogical process that can lead only to probable conclusions.
But plausible conclusions can also be the product of rhetorical
deductive inference—in Valla's terminology an epicheireme
(more fully, *epicheirematis enthymema*), a rhetorical syllogism
with a probable conclusion, in contrast to the necessary conclusion of an apodictic syllogism. The terminology is important
but confusing, because Aristotle too had recognized the rhetorical syllogism along with rhetorical induction, but he called
the latter a paradigm and the former an enthymeme. Enthymeme (*syllogismi enthymema*), however, was Valla's term for
an elliptical apodictic argument, a demonstrative syllogism with
one or more of its parts missing.[37]

Besides shifting the major types of argument from Aristotle's
taxonomy to Quintilian's, Valla also extended his minimalist
programme for terms and propositions to the syllogism itself.

---

[36] Valla (1982: ii. 447); below, n. 38.
[37] Di Napoli (1971: 89–99); Camporeale (1972: 35–75, 82–5); G. A.
Kennedy (1980: 70–2, 76, 80–4).

The Peripatetic syllogism was a deductive inference *from* two (major and minor) propositions or premises, expressing class membership or predication, *to* a third proposition, called the conclusion, also expressing class membership or predication, as follows:

Every *B* belongs to *C*.
Every *C* belongs to *D*.
Therefore, every *B* belongs to *D*.

B, *C* and *D* represent variable terms which as independent expressions fall *under* the ten categories; terms like 'every', 'no', or 'some' are syncategorematic rather than categorical because they express relations *between* such terms. A categorical proposition asserts some relation between categorical terms by means of syncategorematic modifiers and a copula such as 'belongs to', 'is predicated of', or simply 'is'.[38] Thus, in contrast to the logic of propositions commonly taught today or the logic of topics promoted in the sixteenth century, Valla was faced with a logic of class terms, which he wished to make a better oratorical tool. Even though the contexts for oratory — the courtroom, the church, the political forum — would seldom encourage close attention to rigorous reasoning, Valla needed to bring the syllogism within the scope of rhetoric in order to liberate epistemic terrain from philosophy, which as mistress of logic guarded the gateway to the arts curriculum.

Most students in Valla's day still learned logic from Peter of Spain's *Summulae logicales*, the first six parts of which deal with issues directly derived from Aristotle's *Organon*. One part is syllogistic, organized according to the role of the middle term (*C* in the example above) as subject or predicate in the major and minor premises and yielding four possible *figures*, of which Aristotle allowed only three. Each figure can be further divided into *moods* according to the character of its propositions as universal and positive (symbolized by the letter *A*), universal and negative (*E*), particular and positive (*I*), or particular and negative (*O*). Then, in the first word of a famous

---

[38] Kneale and Kneale (1962: 67–81, 233–4); Noreña (1975: 6–12); Kretzmann (1982: 211–16); Spade (1982: 188–92); Broadie (1987: 3–17, 124–6).

mnemonic verse that originated in the thirteenth century, one
finds the name of the first mood of the first figure, B*a*rb*a*r*a*,
designating a syllogism all of whose propositions are universal
affirmatives (*A*) and whose middle term is the subject in the
major premiss but the predicate in the minor. By the same
process, C*e*l*a*r*e*nt becomes the name of the second mood of
the first figure, D*a*r*ii* of the third mood, and so on through
fourteen moods for the three usual figures—nineteen if one
includes the disputed fourth figure. These names helped students memorize the valid patterns of the syllogism, so that a
student who remembered C*e*s*a*r*e*, the first mood of the second
figure, knew that a syllogism of the following type is valid:

No *B* belongs to *C*.
Every *D* belongs to *C*.
Therefore, no *D* belongs to *B*.

Memory was important to the student who had to master Peter
of Spain's *Summulae*, because the complexities of syllogistic
were only one topic in the easier part of this widely used
textbook, which became harder in its seventh section, the
Little Logicals, on meaning, reference, quantification, and
other subjects not extensively covered by Aristotle.[39]

Valla, always aiming to disarm the philosopher and equip
the orator with a leaner logic, proposed to reduce the nineteen
moods of the syllogism to eight. His rejection of the fourth
figure is unsurprising, but he also condemned the whole third
figure, which always leads to a particular conclusion (*I* or *O*)
about an indefinite subject. He found this figure opposed to
the natural order of speech and useless for rhetorical purposes:
what good would it do a lawyer to argue so awkwardly that
some particular person is guilty or not guilty? Since even the
Peripatetics recognized the convertibility of the third figure to
the first, Valla saw no reason to preserve a redundant mon-
strosity that moved him to one of his purpler passages: 'No
man is a stone; some man is an animal; therefore, some animal
is not a stone. I can hardly keep myself from screaming,' he
screamed; 'O you family of Peripatetics, in love with trifles!

---

[39] Kneale and Kneale (1962: 54–7, 68–76, 232–3).

Have you ever heard anyone arguing like this, you nation of madmen?'[40] Although he gave much attention to apodictic argument, he distrusted the whole tradition of categorical syllogistic because of its artificiality and formalism. He also attacked hypothetical or conditional syllogisms, on which the hated Boethius had written a treatise, as an unnatural restriction on the many linguistic means of expressing conditionality, and he was equally suspicious of the a priori study of fallacies when the syntax and grammar of natural language afforded so many ways to go wrong. As always, customary usage learned from ancient texts was Valla's criterion for judging these medieval theories of argument, which fell far short of his humanist expectations. Language for Valla was culture, which always eludes any generalized prescriptions, just as the orator's need will always surpass the rules of argument meant to help him.

The simple method of Peter Ramus and its forerunners

Perhaps it was Valla's philosophical depth that limited his *Dialectical Disputations* to six appearances in print after 1496, when three much more teachable treatments of dialectic— George of Trebizond's *Isagoge*, Rudolf Agricola's *Dialectical Invention*, and the various works of Peter Ramus—ended Peter of Spain's long reign over the arts curriculum. Until the end of the third decade of the sixteenth century, Peter's *Summulae* remained hugely successful, but after 1530 only half a dozen printings were called for. So sharp a decline for so popular a book is hard to explain, but it coincided with the growing success of Agricola's treatise. In 1529 Johann Sturm introduced Agricola to the University of Paris, whose first year students had been called 'Summulists' from the textbook that filled their days with suppositions and ampliations. Agricola had written his *Dialectical Invention* in 1479, six years before he died, but it was published only in 1515. In five years after

[40] Valla (1962: ii. 739).

1538, fifteen of roughly seventy Renaissance editions appeared in Paris alone; Agricola's readership came from both Catholic and Protestant regions, mainly in northern Europe. Born in 1444 and educated in Erfurt, Louvain, and Cologne, Agricola travelled in the late 1460s to Italy to study with Battista Guarino in Ferrara, where he acquired the humanist zeal for persuasive speech and writing. Erasmus, the great champion of classical eloquence in Northern Europe, would later stress his intellectual descent from the Greek teacher, Alexander Hegius, who learned from Agricola, who came to represent the legitimating link between the previously barbarous North and the cultured South. As advocate of the humanist programme in education, Agricola treated dialectic as an instrument of communication rather than as a device for formal proof, and he cared more for the needs of students than for the queries of logic professors. Techniques of persuasion and probability were less rigorous in the ordinary logical sense than demonstration, but Agricola and other humanist teachers of logic could easily show that the critical verbal transactions of everyday life are seldom given to apodictic treatment. Influenced by the composition exercises of Aphthonius of Antioch and other ancient sources, Agricola provided graded exercises for oratorical education through repeated working of examples. His recipes for methodical pedagogy were so convincing that the discipline and rigour claimed for his teaching techniques became self-justifying—a new kind of rigour to please critics of the scholastic curriculum. Agricola's advice appealed to people like Lefèvre, Vives, Erasmus, or Rabelais who despaired of late medieval logic as a way of teaching or talking or reasoning. Because Agricola made a hit with the same Erasmian humanists who appreciated Valla, scholars have often assumed a strong link between the two. Though only a few manuscripts of the *Dialectical Disputations* circulated in Agricola's lifetime, he may well have read Valla, yet the differences between them were great. Valla made apodictic proof part of an expanded rhetoric; Agricola reduced rhetoric to stylistics and ignored rigorous demonstration. Valla reproduced Quintilian's remarks on the topics, adding nothing important of his own; Agricola put his own version of the topics at the centre of a dialectic meant to contain all discourse.[41]

Having laid out his twenty-four topics in the first book of his *Dialectical Invention*, Agricola defined dialectic at the start of the second book as 'the art of speaking with probability on any question whatever'.[42] Following a well-established tradition, he divided dialectic into *invention* for finding the places and *judgement* for putting arguments in good order by syllogistic and other means; he focused on invention, however, leaving a gap filled first by George of Trebizond's *Isagoge* and later by the Ramist theory of judgement. Although Cicero and Boethius had inspired a tradition of *logical* topics and invention, invention had always belonged primarily to *rhetoric*, but Agricola claimed it for his version of *dialectic*, teaching that rhetoric only embellishes arguments found by dialectic. Dialectic controls all features of language except style, and speaks to any problem: the effect of these sweeping claims was to erase the usual distinction between persuasion and proof. Agricola never really confronted problems of demonstrative inference, but he believed that his probable arguments could induce a certitude that we might call psychological rather than logical. His logic has been described aptly as a *place* or *topical* logic because it replaced the predicaments or categories with topics that seemed more effective instruments of speech. In the strictest sense, the work of Agricolan invention is to *find* a middle term (*R*) to join the extremes (*H, W*) in a Peripatetic syllogism. If I need to persuade my audience or my students that every *human being* (*H*) is a *worrier* (*W*), I must look in the right place for the middle term, *rational being* (*R*), that will enable me to say with conviction that

---

[41] Ashworth (1974: 2–4, 10–14; 1988: 143–6, 152–3); Monfasani (1990). For the Latin works, see Agricola (1703; 1967); and for secondary works see Allen (1906); van der Velden (1911); Faust (1922); Vasoli (1958b; 1968a: 147–82); Nauwelaerts (1963); Spitz (1963: 20–40); Heath (1971); Jardine (1974a: 29–35; 1988: 181–4; 1990); Kessler (1979); Weiss (1981); Mack (1983; 1985); Ong (1983: 58, 92–130); Cogan (1984); Grafton and Jardine (1986: 122–37); Akkerman and Vanderjagt (1988).

[42] Agricola (1967: 192); Ong (1983: 101).

Every *H* is an *R*.
Every *R* is a *W*.
Therefore, every *H* is a *W*.

Riffling through my topical checklist, I soon come to places like definition, genus, and species to remind me that human animals are rational and that reason is a worry. Agricola thought of these and other places—property, time, name, similarity, and so on—as little boxes or chests holding a treasury of persuasive instruments ready for handy insertion into arguments. His places were a scheme for inquiry into all particulars. He made invention encyclopedic, a method for asking questions about whatever may be found in the universe of specifics. Images involving location had always been part of the idea of topics, but Agricola's place logic happened to coincide with the new age of printing, when visual representations of abstract relations as structures in space could be reproduced more accurately and disseminated more widely than ever before. The Ramist obsession with tables and charts as dialectical maps had its origins in this coincidence. Ramists made these visual aids ubiquitous, but they did not invent them. Medieval manuscripts often presented their contents schematically; Lefèvre's crudely printed texts of the 1490s used charts to ease the strain of introductory logic; and in 1530 Bartholemew Latomus published one of the first examples—reproduced in Fig. 4 as a useful conspectus of place logic—in the direct Agricolan-Ramist line of ramifying charts.[43]

Petrus Ramus or Pierre de la Ramée was born in Picardy in 1515.[44] At the age of twelve or so he left an unhappy boyhood

[43] Ong (1983: 63–5, 74–91, 96–8, 104–112, 116–30); Jardine (1974*a*: 30–4); Cogan (1984: 163–7, 181–94).

[44] For the several hundred early modern edns. of the main Ramist works, see Ong (1958) as well as the summary in Ong (1983: 295–306); Ramus (1964*a*; 1970) and Ramus and Talon (1971) are reprints of 16th-c. edns.; Ramus (1986) is a modern version. Ong (1983) remains the standard work, corrected in some respects by such recent studies as Bruyère (1984) and Meerhoff (1986); see also Waddington (1855); Rossi (1953*c*); Hooykaas (1958); Gilbert (1960: 129–63); Risse (1964); Vasoli (1968*a*: 331–601); Walton (1970; 1971); Schmitt (1972*a*: 78–108); Cassirer (1974: i. 130–6); Jardine (1974*a*; 1988: 184–90); Ashworth (1974: 15–17); Sharratt (1975; 1976: 4–20; 1982; 1987); Margolin (1976*b*); Piano Mortari (1978); Schmidt-Biggemann (1983); Grafton and Jardine (1986: 161–200); *Pierre de la Ramée* (1986).

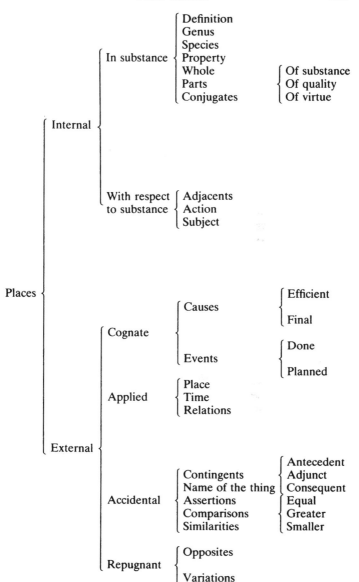

FIG. 4. *A table dividing the places.*

to begin a hard university life in Paris. He disliked the scholastic regimen but did well at it, proceeding to his MA in 1536, seven years after Sturm had given Paris not only Agricola but also Hermogenes, a more distant ancestor of logic by topical division. Years later, after Ramus died a Protestant martyr in the St Bartholemew's massacre of 1572, his religious and intellectual fame attracted biographers, who in the spirit of the times depicted him as a dauntless anti-Aristotelian. The story went round that he won his MA with the thesis that 'Whatever has been said by Aristotle is arbitrarily contrived', but, even if true, the tale tells little about Ramus' character or ideas. Defending a thesis was not a strict degree requirement, and weirder claims than Ramus allegedly made had been normal in the quodlibetal and sophistical literature for centuries.[45] In any event, as a new master the young Ramus was faced with teaching the same pack of logic-dazed adolescents from which he had just escaped. This hard fact of his employment, in the context of the new Agricolan dialectic, seems to have motivated his two brash publications of 1543, the *Divisions of Dialectic* and the *Remarks on Aristotle*, in which he denounced the arts curriculum and enraged his faculty colleagues. Within a year Francis I quashed the two books from the throne, warning Ramus not to teach philosophy without royal assent. Shifting his teaching to mathematics, he went briefly underground as a writer, issuing an update of the *Divisions of Dialectic* in 1546 under the name of Omer Talon, his long-time collaborator.

When Francis I died in 1547, Charles of Lorraine, the Guise cardinal, convinced the new king, Henry II, to forgive Ramus, who responded gratefully with a flood of book dedications. Now favoured at court, he rose to the first and only regius chair of eloquence and philosophy at the Collège Royal in 1551, and for most of the next twenty years his quarrelsome habits did no great harm to a brilliant career. His friend Talon became a priest before he died in 1562, but Ramus, who was never a cleric, was suspected of Protestant sympathies by this time,

---

[45] Ong (1983: 36–47).

though he gave no overt sign of his new religion until 1570. A *Commentary on the Christian Religion* published after his death reveals a Reformed faith of Zwingli's type, which alienated previous Catholic associates, while Protestants disliked his opinions on church government. Still, his murder in 1572 seems to have been accidental; Catherine de' Medici had wanted to shield him from the marauding mobs that she loosed on St Bartholemew's Day. His glory came from his books, but his teaching also won him acclaim; students came in herds to hear him thunder theatrically against the conventional texts taught by their conventional professors. People found him charming and liked his smile, though he was known to abuse students physically. Angry critics—Jacques Charpentier, Antonio de Gouveia, Joachim Périon, Adrien Turnebus, Jacob Schegk— abused him verbally for aberrant beliefs, but he turned their wrath against them by constantly revising his books to meet every shift in the tide of hostile opinion. His famous position on method, in particular, grew out of a response to Gouveia, who seems to have spotted the Ramist method before Ramus himself.[46]

His brief *Remarks on Aristotle* tore destructively through the *Organon*. Plato stood at the pinnacle of ancient dialectic, he claimed, but Aristotle fell and the Peripatetics sank lower in the mire of barbarism. Ramus proposed to rescue the arts of discourse by abandoning Aristotle's logic in favour of the one, true omnicompetent union of rhetoric (for style) and dialectic (for all other needs of discourse): 'to any fields or limits whatever of disputation . . . , to any subject you like, treated in any manner you choose, one and the same alliance of rhetoric and dialectic applies.' Ramus repeated his anti-Aristotelian programme in the *Divisions of Dialectic* and in the nearly identical *Dialectical Education* also published in 1543. He looked at dialectic from three points of view: as a natural human endowment, as an art that must be taught, and as a skill requiring practice. People are born with a natural dialectic that enables them to talk, argue, make distinctions, and reason together;

[46] Ibid. 16–35, 214–24.

the power common to all these innate faculties is one of discrimination or discernment. Art must assist nature if dialectical ability is to reach its full development.[47]

Like Agricola, Ramus divided the art of dialectic into invention and judgement, but he had little new to say about invention or places. Judgement, which Agricola had slighted, he described as a way of fitting together what invention has found in order to compare and evaluate. Judgement proceeds through three stages: first, arrange the findings of invention in propositions and syllogistic arguments; second, construct larger chains of argument by definition and division; third, rise to divinity through the grades of dialectic. Ramus wanted a dialectic well-suited to the classroom in its simplicity and clarity. He crusaded against ambiguity, believing that division, reduction, and summary are the essentials of reasoned speech; all else is decoration. 'The foundations of the arts', he wrote in the *Remarks on Aristotle*, 'are definitions, divisions or certain sure inferences from definitions and divisions; there is nothing else.' By the time he was ready to release his French *Dialectique* in 1555, Ramus had moved the fundamentals of definition and division to invention; first and second judgement had acquired grander labels, 'dianoetic' and 'axiomatic'; and the whole process of judgement had evolved into disposition or arrangement, the framework of the Ramist method.[48]

Largely because Ramism sparked intense controversy and flourished in spite of it, method was a familiar issue when Bacon and Descartes made so much of it in the next century. But philosophers had worried about method long before Ramus, who loved to display his own knowledge of ancient opinion on the question. Perhaps the most fruitful text was the section of Plato's *Phaedrus* in which Socrates clarifies the *methodos* of dialectic—division (*diairesis*) and collection (*sunagôgê*)—by comparing it to the useful and purposefully acquired *technê* (*ars* in Latin) of a Hippocratic physician. Aristotle's treatise on *Methodics* did not survive; nor did his com-

---

[47] Ramus (1964a: fo. 78); Ong (1983: 171–95, esp. 175).
[48] Ramus (1964a: fo. 58r); Jardine (1974a: 42–5); Ong (1983: 187–9, 250–2).

ments in the *Posterior Analytics* and *Topics* on apodictic and persuasive technique satisfy Renaissance thinkers, who felt the lack of an authoritative Peripatetic statement on method. The Stoic revival called attention to Zeno's definition of an art as an ordered set of *katalêpseis*, 'graspings' or 'cognitions'; although Cicero correctly rendered Zeno's Greek as *perceptiones* or 'percepts', *praeceptiones* or 'precepts' emerged in medieval texts, which thus encouraged a conception of method as a body or rules. Given the striking Socratic analogy between dialectic and medicine, Galen devoted a special treatise to Hippocratic and Platonic views on the matter, in which he suggested that any investigation should start with larger and easier problems; here, and in other works, his comments on clarity, analysis, resolution, and composition proved influential for early modern readers, though their effect was somewhat dampened by Galen's diffuse prose. Roman writers seldom used the Latin *methodus*; Cicero preferred *ratio* ('system'), but Quintilian once wrote *methodice* to mean something like 'correct technique'. Boethius added *methodus* to the Latin philosophical lexicon when translating Aristotle's *Topics*, and the word commonly stood for its Greek analogue in the medieval Latin Aristotle, until Bruni and other purists resorted to ingenious circumlocutions to purge the sin of transliteration. John of Salisbury, Albertus Magnus, and other medieval authorities had seen method as a way of bringing *scattered* materials *together* in some *brief* expression, a *compendium*, and, despite Socratic warnings to the contrary, Agostino Nifo and other early modern philosophers were still looking for short cuts when they hunted for a method.[49]

Before Ramus, the words bearing on the understanding of method that medieval and early modern readers were most likely to see appeared in the memorable (though partly spurious) first sentence of Peter of Spain's *Summulae*:

Dialectic is the art [*ars*] of arts and the knowledge [*scientia*] of

[49] Plato, *Phaedrus* 270B–E; Cicero, *Academica* 2. 30–1; Quintilian, *Oratorical Education* 1. 9. 1; Galen, *On the Doctrines of Hippocrates and Plato* 9.1–7; *Gilbert* (1960: pp. xxii–xxiii, 6, 3–66); Jardine (1974a: 29–58); Long and Sedley (1987: ii. 251–2).

branches-of-knowledge [*scientiae*], and it holds [*habere*] the way [*via*] to the foundations of all methods [*methodi*]. For dialectic alone disputes with probability [*probabiliter*] about the foundations of all other arts; hence, dialectic ought to come first in acquiring knowledge [*scientiae*].

Here, in the first verse of this bible of medieval logic, Ramus clearly had precedent for putting dialectic at the centre of discourse and for blurring the line between probable and demonstrative argument. He and his early modern predecessors —Sturm, Melanchthon, and others—also had reason to be confused by the jumbled relations among *ars*, *scientia*, and *methodus* suggested in this classic statement.[50] One perplexed observer of method was Antonio de Gouveia, an early critic of Ramus, who in his *Reply on behalf of Aristotle to the Calumnies of Peter Ramus* (1543) sensed that the 'second judgement' of the *Dialectical Education* had something to do with method. Gouveia referred Ramus to Galen, and Ramus answered in 1546—while still under the king's ban—with a revised and pseudonymous edition of the *Institutiones* which presents Ramist method in its earliest form. He defined method as arrangement (*dispositio*) either of teaching (*doctrina*) or of prudence, but then he discarded prudence as incoherent empirical experience of things, people, and events, leaving only the method of teaching for orderly disposition. Methodical arrangement is always the same: 'one needs only method and a sure way (*via*) of disposition', he asserted, 'which teaching (*doctrina*) shows us to be the one simple way of putting universal and general things first, specific and secondary things afterward.'[51]

Up until a final revision in 1572, Ramus continued to amplify his method with new rules and embellish it with the gingerbread of erudition, but the 1546 *Institutiones* had captured his programme in its stark triviality. Indeed, on one side of a leaf

---

[50] Peter of Spain (1972: 1 [with readings from De Rijk's apparatus]); Ong (1983: 53–63, 156–63, 182).

[51] Ramus, *Dialectici commentarii tres authore Audomardo Talaeo editi* (1546), pp. 83–4, cited at length in Ong (1983: 245–6, 363–4; see also 214–52).

at the end of the earlier 1543 version he had printed a tabular summary of the whole of dialectic that foreshadows the multitude of bifurcating tables to come and announces his compulsion for the quick, teachable answer to all questions.[52] Ramus ruthlessly domesticated the classical curriculum as conceived by Bruni and Vives. Older humanists had moral and intellectual aspirations, but he wanted results in the classroom, where philology and philosophy took a back seat to curricular pragmatism. Ramist teachers aimed to make their students competent citizens and capable workers, not better people. They trimmed excess information about language, history, and philosophy from the commentaries that they ransacked, and they reduced the remainder to a tight package of imitable models, memorable facts, stirring examples, and sleek sentences. Students read the classics not so much for their own value or even for moral application but as instances of dialectic, an expedient and austere procedure with great attractions: Ramism gave students orderly habits of thought, and it gave teachers easy patterns of instruction. If discourse could do so much, what need to claim the ethical benefits that seemed so remote from the actual effects of classicism? Tedious drill and practice promised to put more bread on the table than odiously sterile philology. In declaring his new method supreme, Ramus repudiated the scriptures of oratorical moralism. Citing Quintilian's famous definitions, he denied that the complete orator must be

a good man skilled in speaking, [equipped with such] . . . virtues of mind as justice, fortitude, temperance, prudence—likewise the whole of philosophy, knowledge of law and understanding of history. . . . I claim that such a definition of the orator seems defective. Why? Because the definition of any practitioner [*artifex*] is excessive if it includes more than the practice [*ars*] contains in its principles . . . , [and] rhetoric is not a practice [*ars*] that develops all the virtues of mind . . . [about which] moralists philosophize (*ethici philosophantur*).[53]

Ramus the Pedagogue vanquished Quintilian the Orator as

[52] Ramus (1964a: fo. 57r).

[53] Quintilian, *Oratorical Education* 1.pr.5–20, 12.1.1; Ramus (1970: 319–20 [sig. o2v]); Grafton and Jardine (1986: 161–200, esp. 192).

well as Aristotle the Philosopher; on his battle-flag he might have written that to conquer is to divide by two.

Under the title 'dialectic', which humanists preferred to 'logic', his books sold well in Latin, and they also won a good response in English and French. It was not his originality but his genius for layout and organization that put Ramus on top of the textbook market, master of the most popular method for conveying complex information to beginners. His books on dialectic presented the method as applicable to all fields of learning, while other works extended his ideas to specific subjects, particularly mathematics, where the influence of his technique was strong. It was above all the dichotomous tables, frequently seen in the earlier age of manuscripts and favoured by medical authors who published before Ramus, that he made his hallmark and raised to new levels of popularity. By the end of the sixteenth century, whole books on ethics, politics, and other topics, hundreds of pages long, consisted wholly of such tables. Academic books, especially those meant for classroom use, routinely appeared as blocks of ordinary prose linked every few pages by a summary and a table, condensing the intervening material into skeletal form, short and easy to remember. The point of this apparatus was to reduce the student's confusion and ease his labour. As a beginner in natural philosophy, for example, the student could divide *nature* into *organic* beings with vital souls and *inorganic* entities without souls, and *organic* beings could be further separated into *irrational* plants and animals and *rational* humans, and so on. The resulting synoptic scheme may be too trivial for the modern eye to notice, but in its own time it was a pedagogic marvel that many found more useful than traditional syllogistic reasoning. The Ramist method took over quickly in many areas, including the classrooms of Peripatetic professors, whose textbooks were often crammed with tables and diagrams. The glaringly visible Ramist method was perhaps the most obvious way in which the humanist revolution in persuasive and expository reasoning took hold in all spheres of intellectual life. Logic remained for the most part Aristotelian, and the *Organon* was still the bedrock text, but few new teaching manuals of

any kind were without humanist colouration of some kind.[54]
Logic became a softer and maybe a duller tool than it had
been in the Middle Ages, but the humanists also made it more
flexible and adaptable to the whole range of discourse. Medieval logic had been best suited to medicine and natural
philosophy, and after the Renaissance an improved mathematics would become the language of a new natural science. In
the mean time, in the age of Valla, Trapezuntius, Agricola,
and Ramus, logic served the interests of language as interpreted
by humanism.

The crisis of doubt

In the prologue to his *Quart Livre*, Rabelais tells the story of
Couillatris, a poor woodcutter who lost his axe and, 'because
necessity invented eloquence', prayed loudly to Jupiter to restore it. The great god, interrupted in council by this puny plea
while resolving the quarrels of the mighty, lists all the disputes
he has settled until he reaches one that has him stumped.
'What shall we make of this Rameau and this Galland? Backed
by their gophers, groupies, and yes-men, they throw the Academy of Paris into confusion. I'm greatly perplexed and haven't
yet decided whose part to take. Both seem good ballsy fellows
in their ways.' Jove's adviser, Priapus, recommends turning
the pair into stone gargoyles for the porch of Notre-Dame,
where passers-by can snuff torches and candles on them: the
punishment fits the crime because, in their ardour for fame,
they had 'lit the fire of faction . . . and division among the idle
scholars'. Pierre Galland published his *Oration for the School
of Paris against the New Academy of Peter Ramus* in 1551, the
year before the *Quart Livre* appeared, the same year when
Henri II restored Ramus to his academic dignities.[55] Galland's
attack on Ramus was a hot story at the time, perfect material
for Rabelais, but a closer look will show that the real advocate
of the 'New Academy' in Galland's title was not Ramus but

---

[54] Schmitt (1983*a*: 53–63, 121–33; 1988: 795–804); above, Ch. 1, n. 26.
[55] Rabelais (1973: 571–5); Screech (1979: 321–32).

Omer Talon. Except that he liked the style of Cicero's
Academica, Ramus had little to say about Academic scepticism,
but in 1547 and 1550 Talon had published one of the first and
best Renaissance editions of the *Academica* accompanied by
commentary and introduction. With Cicero as his guide, Talon
showed how philosophy can join forces with eloquence to
route credulity and dogmatism, especially doctrinaire Aristotelianism. Galland feared Talon's scepticism as subversive of
tradition and authority, and he denounced it as incompatible
with Christianity. In 1557 the *Dialogues against the New Academics* of Guy de Brués made roughly the same case in the
vernacular. Montaigne read the *Dialogues*. But Montaigne
also read Latin translations of Sextus Empiricus unavailable to
Talon and his critics: the *Outlines of Pyrrhonism*, published by
Henri Estienne in 1562, and *Against the Mathematicians*, issued
by Gentian Hervet in 1569. Estienne apparently lacked the wit
to look into the Pandora's box that he opened; he had no
inkling that the ideas he let loose would haunt philosophers
for centuries. Hervet, a humanist like Etienne, knew better
what he was about. He was a Catholic spokesman for the
church's Counter-Reformation programme who wanted to use
Sextus against the Huguenots, convinced as he was that their
beliefs were more vulnerable than his own to sceptical anti-
dogmatism.[56]

The printing of Sextus in the 1560s opened a new era in the
history of scepticism, which had begun in the late fourth century BCE with the teachings of Pyrrho of Elis. Pyrrho wrote
nothing, but his ideas were revived in the first century BCE
by Aenesidemus, who was also influenced by the sceptical
New Academy that began with Arcesilaus in the early third
century and culminated with Carneades in the late first century.
Before Antiochus of Ascalon took Plato's School back to the
dogmatism of the Old Academy, Cicero read the works of
Clitomachus, who succeeded Carneades as head of the Academy, and studied with Philo of Larissa, who followed Clito-

[56] Schmitt (1972a: 81–108; 1972b: 371–4, 380; 1989: chs. 13, 14); Cavini
(1977); Grafton (1988b: 790); Popkin (1979: 18–34; 1988: 679–81).

machus; these experiences underlie the *Academica*, *De natura deorum*, and other works in which Cicero deals with Academic scepticism. Later, in the second century CE, the physician Sextus used Pyrrhonian scepticism as passed on by Aenesidemus to blast medical and other dogmas of his day, shortly before Diogenes Laertius included a section on Pyrrho in his *Lives*. These works of Cicero, Diogenes, and Sextus preserve most of the surviving evidence on ancient scepticism, but they were little known before the Renaissance. William of Ockham and other fourteenth-century thinkers refuted intellectual certainties of various kinds, but their doubts seem to have had no connection with ancient scepticism. Even the word 'sceptic' was absent from the medieval vocabulary. Until Francesco Filelfo brought Greek manuscripts of Sextus from Constantinople in 1427, the only Latin text was a fourteenth-century version of the *Outlines* that survives in just three manuscripts; two partial Latin translations followed in the fifteenth century but attracted little interest. Fifteenth-century scholars read the new documents philologically rather than philosophically, focusing on new Greek words in the texts but caring little for the larger import of their meanings. Before the Estienne and Hervet versions, Sextus seems to have had only two serious students, Gianfrancesco Pico at the turn of the century and Francesco Robortello about fifty years later. By Pico's time, Traversari's translation of Diogenes from the 1430s circulated widely, though Diogenes had been at best a rarity when Walter Burley seems to have used him early in the previous century. Traversari's Latin was helpful—it seems to have put the word *scepticus* into circulation—but it was no substitute for the fuller story told by Sextus.[57]

Cicero's *Academica* were likewise no match for Sextus, but they represented a distinct tradition in scepticism, a negative dogmatism. Strictly speaking, Academics rule out the possibility of certain knowledge, while Pyrrhonists can neither affirm nor deny that certainty is possible, professing an undogmatic scep-

[57] Schmitt (1967; 1972a: 9–13; 1972b: 363–8, 375–9); Cassirer (1974: i. 172–220); Popkin (1979: pp. xiv–xvii); Popkin and Schmitt (1987); Burnyeat (1983); Long (1986: 75–80, 88–95, 106, 222–4, 229–31).

ticism that doubts sceptical judgement itself.[58] Cicero had enormous influence in the Middle Ages, yet his *Academica* were not widely read; medieval readers knew Ciceronian scepticism mainly as refuted by Augustine in his early work, *Against the Academics*, and as used by Lactantius against philosophical dogmatism. John of Salisbury and Henry of Ghent were uncommon medieval students of Academic scepticism, but after Petrarch listed the *Academica* among his favourite books in the 1330s, they found more readers: Salutati, Guarino, Poggio, Ficino, and others. As compared to most of Cicero, however, the *Academica* remained unpopular in the Renaissance, perhaps because the spectacle of Cicero's taking on *all* the major schools—Platonic, Aristotelian, Stoic, and Epicurean—made readers uneasy and gave offence everywhere. Cicero's philosophical works, including the *Academica*, appeared in a printed collection in 1471, but no separate text came out until 1535, no commentary until 1536. The *Academica* had their heyday in the middle decades of the sixteenth century, before Sextus became available, and in northern Europe rather than Italy. When Galland attacked Ramus in 1551, it was the charged atmosphere of the Reformation that led to Galland to distrust scepticism as a menace to religious dogma. The faithful had been divided on scepticism since Augustine, who feared it as an irreligious threat to Christian certitude, and Lactantius, who praised it as a pious weapon against heathen philosophy.[59]

These divisions continued during the Reformation, when scepticism was the furthest thing from atheism. Its typical use was on behalf of faith, particularly by Catholics, although friends and enemies of scepticism were to be found in both confessional camps. When he published his *Praise of Folly* in 1511, Erasmus had kind words for the 'Academics, ... least impudent of the philosophers, ... [who say] that nothing can be clearly known'. But in his battle with Luther over free will in the 1520s, he blanched at being called an Epicurean, an

[58] Popkin (1979: xiii–xv, 47); cf. Schmitt (1972*a*: 7–8).
[59] Schmitt (1972*a*: 14–19, 23–66); Popkin (1979: 23–33).

atheist, and a sceptic. The core issue in these Reformation debates was the criterion of religious belief, the 'rule of faith' shaken by Luther when he challenged Roman Catholic hierarchy and tradition with his canon of *sola Scriptura*: true religious conviction emerges *only* when the reading of *scripture* forces one to hold some article of faith. Although faith is an act of individual conscience, Luther insisted against Erasmus that it must be certain. When Erasmus longed for 'an undogmatic temper', Luther despised him as faint-hearted. 'Away, now, with Sceptics and Academics from the company of us Christians,' he wrote in 1525; 'let us have men ... twice as inflexible as very Stoics! ... Nothing is more ... characteristic among Christians than assertion. Take away assertions, and you take away Christianity.' In the next decade, Erasmus criticized Melanchthon's *Common Places* for too broad a ban on Academic suspension of judgement, and in successive editions of the *Loci communes* Melanchthon retreated, eventually permitting *epochê* (suspension of judgement) in philosophy but forbidding it in church doctrine, where faith has no need of philosophy. In 1553 John Calvin and his followers gave horrible witness to their theological certainty by burning Michael Servetus at the gates of Geneva for doubting the trinity. Sebastian Castellio, himself a Protestant, answered in 1554 with his treatise *On Heretics, Whether They Should Be Persecuted*, followed by an unpublished work of 1561 *On the Art of Doubting*. Castellio, convinced that error has rights, limited intervention against heresy to excommunication; no religious conviction justifies killing. Calvin's reply was the stony *Declaration of Orthodox Faith* of 1554, followed in the same year by the book in which Theodore Beza declared Castellio's policy of toleration to be the devil's work: *That Heretics Should be Punished by Civil Magistracy*.[60]

What Luther detested in Erasmus was a mild and discri-

---

[60] Erasmus (1941: 63 [Hudson trans.]); Luther (1961: 168-9 [Dillenberger trans.]); Castellio (1981, with introd. by Feist Hirsch); Leclerc (1955: i. 133-46, 312-42); Schmitt (1972a: 58-66); Friedman (1978: 11-20, 137-9); Skinner (1978: ii. 241-54); Popkin (1979: pp. xvi-17); O'Rourke Boyle (1983: 43-66); Trinkaus (1983: 274-301); Oberman (1989: 209-25).

minating fideism, a wish to suspend judgement on most matters
of religious controversy while following traditional authority
where understanding cannot reach. A rougher and more resolute fideism appeared in the *Invective Declamation on the
Uncertainty and Vanity of the Sciences*, written by Henry
Cornelius Agrippa von Nettesheim in 1526. Agrippa had many
targets in this disorderly diatribe: the corrupt clergy, his own
earlier belief in occultism, but, above all, false and un-Christian
confidence in reason in all the arts and sciences, which he
wanted to replace with grace and scripture.[61] Rabelais made
fun of Agrippa in the *Tiers Livre*, where he appears as Herr
Trippa, the double-talking magician who 'doesn't know the
first line of philosophy, which is "know thyself"'. Later in the
same book Rabelais introduced the evasive Trouillogan,
'ephectic [cf. *epochê*, above] and Pyrrhonian philosopher', who
merely fans Panurge's burning wish to know whether he should
marry. 'For God's sake, should I marry?' asks Panurge. 'Apparently,' answers Trouillogan.

P. And if I don't marry?
T. I see nothing inconvenient in it.
P. Nothing, you say?
T. Nothing, unless my sight deceives me. . . .
P. Shall I marry then?
T. Perhaps.
P. Will I like it?
T. Depends on how it goes.
P. If it goes well, as I hope, will I be happy?
T. Happy enough.
P. Turn things around; if it goes badly?
T. I have to go.
P. But please, advise me; what should I do?
T. What you like.

When Rabelais sketched the cagey sceptic between 1546 and
1552, he had only Cicero, Diogenes and contemporary inter-

[61] Prost (1881–2); Zambelli (1960; 1965; 1966; 1969; 1970; 1976); Nauert
(1965: 98–100, 157–99); Bowen (1972); Müller-Jahncke (1973); Korkowski
(1976); Popkin (1979: 21–6); Crahay (1980); Perrone Compagni (1982);
Backus (1983); Keefer (1988).

preters such as Agrippa to go on. Another modern critic available to him, but one whom he and Agrippa probably missed, was Gianfrancesco Pico della Mirandola, nephew, heir, and biographer of Giovanni Pico, and the only serious student of Sextus before the middle of the sixteenth century.[62]

His uncle and his uncle's circle of Florentine friends were important influences on the younger Pico, who also continued the older philosopher's devotion to Savonarola, even after Florence tired of him in 1498. Gianfrancesco lived longer than his uncle, from 1469 to 1533, but he spent much of his time fighting his relatives to keep the little princedom that he bought from Giovanni in 1491, so his published output of more than thirty works, about a third of them philosophical, is remarkable. Savonarola taught him to exclude reason from religion and to distrust philosophers as infidels, and Gianfrancesco modified the friar's views mainly by reinforcing them with his greater learning. As early as 1496, in one of his first works, *On the Study of Divine and Human Philosophy*, he distinguished divine philosophy, rooted in scripture, from human philosophy based on reason; he denied that Christians need human wisdom, which is as likely to hinder as to help the quest for salvation. By 1514 he had completed a longer and sterner work, *The Weighing of Empty Pagan Learning against True Christian Teaching, Divided into Six Books, of Which Three Oppose the Whole Sect of Philosophers in General, while the Others Attack the Aristotelian Sect Particularly, and with Aristotelian Weapons, but Christian Teaching is Asserted and Celebrated throughout the Whole*. As its title suggests, the *Examen*, published in 1520, hardened Pico's hostility to pagan philosophy. Just when Luther was making the Bible the sole rule of faith, Pico discredited every source of knowledge except scripture and condemned all attempts to find truth elsewhere as *vanitas*, emptiness; profane knowledge is at best a distraction from the work of salvation, as some of the greatest Fathers had taught. Pico's purpose was sincerely religious and only

---

[62] Rabelais (1973: 460–5, 498–504); Screech (1979: 235–8, 251–7); Zambelli (1960); cf. Schmitt (1967: 239–42).

incidentally philosophical; much of Renaissance scepticism remained true to his pious motives, though they were not fully appreciated for forty years after he wrote. By demolishing secular thought, Pico hoped to empty the human mind of reason and make it a clear channel for God's grace; man's only intellectual security lay in church authority. Convinced of Christianity's unique value, he turned his uncle's eirenic learning to contrary purposes, working skilfully with Greek manuscripts to make his humanism a potent weapon against religious error. While Giovanni Pico had looked for philosophical harmony in his erudition, Gianfrancesco sought discord and contradiction, proof that the pagan sages were not wise at all. 'It is more reasonable and useful to render the philosopher's dogmas uncertain', he concluded, 'than to conciliate them, as my uncle wanted.'[63]

Pico devoted most of his first three books to reproducing the arguments of Sextus Empiricus against the various schools of ancient philosophy; in Books IV and V he turned scepticism against Aristotle. His extensive borrowings from Sextus often come closer to translation than paraphrase or analysis, and his choices are therapeutic rather than theoretical. Aristotle had to go because he was the chief source of secular contagion among the faithful, and Sextus was the best medicine available. Pico regarded Christianity itself as immune to sceptical infection because it does not depend on the dogmatic philosophies that Sextus had refuted. Given his own doctrinaire Christianity, it was fair of him to refuse the name 'sceptic' for himself, even though he used Sextus to assail other dogmas. Book II of the *Examen* is the centre of Pico's general presentation of scepticism; the problem of the criterion and the *modes* or *tropes* of suspending judgement, which generally play on the relativity of various points of view, occupy the whole second book. In the latter half of the work, Aristotelian thought becomes the

[63] Pico (1601: 486); Schmitt (1967: 11–48) remains the best treatment of the younger Pico, on whom see also Schmitt (1970; 1972a); Walker (1958a: 146–51; 1972: 33–5, 58–62); Raith (1967); Cassirer (1974: i. 144–9); Secret (1976); Burke (1977: 32–52). See also the introductions by Schmitt and Park in G. F. Pico (1984).

leading instance of vain natural knowledge. Pico tackled Aristotle not because he was a Platonist but because Aristotle was the obligatory target for someone who aimed at the wholesale ruin of philosophy. Book IV is a general assault on the Peripatetic tradition, tracing Aristotle's primacy to the errors of Maimonides and Averroes and disputing it on all possible counts: inauthenticity, inconsistency, inaccuracy, irrationality, obscurity, and impiety. Book V concentrates the attack on Aristotle's demonstrative method, interpreting texts from the *Physics* and *Posterior Analytics* to make Aristotle more empiricist than he was and then turning the powerful sceptical critique of sense knowledge against him. 'Since Aristotle's teaching is based on sense, it is easily shown to be uncertain,' argued Pico; 'for not only is sense uncertain . . . , but quite often false, and in more ways than Aristotle thought it can deceive and be deceived. . . . It varies with different people and at various times in the same person.' Holding Aristotle to the Peripatetic axiom that the mind knows only through the senses, Pico relentlessly set out to disqualify sensation as a reliable conduit of information. From the *Outlines* of Sextus and other works, he armed himself with all the best sceptical arguments: a stick in water is not really bent, a mirage is not what it seems, the colour-blind see false colours, and the sheen on a pigeon's neck looks different from different angles. Such everyday experiences confirmed his distrust of the empiricism that he fathered on Aristotle. Finally, in Book VI, which makes original use of such unusual sources as John Philoponus and Hasdai Crescas, Pico rejected particular Aristotelian doctrines; in dealing with physics, for example, he took impressive arguments against Peripatetic teaching on motion, time, place, and the vacuum from Philoponus and Crescas. His objections to Aristotle's logic reinforced the case against sense knowledge; if neither reason nor sensation can be trusted, philosophy has no resources at all.[64]

Another sceptical opponent of Aristotle was the Portuguese physician Francisco Sanches. He published his *Quod nihil scitur*

---

[64] Aristotle, *Posterior Analytics* 100[a]10–14; *Physics* 184[a]16–25; Pico (1601: 687); Schmitt (1967: 49–159, esp. 75; 1989: ch. 8); Sirat (1985: 357–72).

in 1581, two decades after the Latin Sextus had begun to appear, yet he made no use of Sextus in an anti-Peripatetic polemic as ardent as Pico's but different in its motivations. Sanches was born in Spain near the Portuguese border in 1551. Eleven years later he moved with his family to Bordeaux, a common destination for Jews fleeing the rigours of Iberian Christianity; Montaigne's mother's family were Spanish Jews who had been in France for several generations. Whether Sanches was a Jew is unclear; he may have made a great point of his Catholic orthodoxy just because the religious climate in Bordeaux and Toulouse was so tense. In any case, he spent nine years after 1562 learning grammar, logic, and natural philosophy at Bordeaux's College of Guyenne, where Montaigne had studied a decade before under the headship of André de Gouveia, brother of the anti-Ramist Antonio. He may also have read medicine in Bordeaux before travelling to Rome in 1571 to spend two years at the Sapienza during its great days as a centre of medical empiricism and naturalist Aristotelianism. Before returning to France in 1573 to complete his medical studies at Montpellier, Sanches had learned to appreciate the Roman accent on observation in medicine and pharmacy and also to respect the methodological writings of Galen. He finished his doctoral work in 1574 and left the next year for Toulouse, where a job had become available. Although he won his chair in medicine only in 1612, he stayed in Toulouse for the rest of his life, practising medicine, lecturing in surgery, and, from 1585 or so, teaching philosophy until he died in 1623.[65]

His rather brief proclamation *That Nothing is Known* was the work of a young and insecurely employed philosopher-physician who aimed his doubts at the innards of Peripatetic dogma, particularly the doctrine of the demonstrative syllogism. He used the polemic of Vives *Against the Pseudodialecticians*, but he carried the critique of logic further in denying all certainty to syllogistic reasoning. Beginning with Aristotle's claim that knowledge is 'a habit of mind with an aptitude for demonstration', he showed that the usual technique leads into a maze of incomprehensible words—worst of all the vacuous 'being'—made even more meaningless by the logic of terms. 'Do you call this knowledge?' he protested; 'I call it ignorance.'[66] Aristotelianism is a shaky framework of bad definitions supporting circular arguments. Sterile syllogisms only shuffle the old data; formal logic is philosophical cobbling that yields nothing new. To replace the flimsy and fruitless formalism of the Peripatetics, he looked to Galen's tools of judgement and experience. Scepticism for Sanches was a weapon against Aristotle, not an autonomous philosophical theory, and the goal of his anti-Aristotelianism was a firmer foundation for medicine, conceived as a philosophical enterprise. Because he wanted a positive method for medicine, the constructive, probabilist strain in Academic scepticism appealed to him more than Pyrrhonism, and he also followed the contemporary literature on method produced by Niccolò Leoniceno and others. Despite his medical habit of accumulating, organizing, and testing observations, however, Sanches undermined the claims of experience with sceptical doubts about the powers of sense and mind.[67]

Comparing knowledge to vision, he asserted that 'knowledge is only of each individual thing, taken by itself, not of many things at once, just as a single act of seeing relates only to one particular object'. To accumulate such objects mentally is to remember, not to know them, but any epistemology based on recollection will lead to endless regress, which will also frustrate knowledge if one defines it as understanding through causes. Where does the vortex of caused causes stop? Aristotelian attempts to solve the problem with axioms or first principles will drown in the bottomless well of definition. Complete knowledge is knowledge of wholes, whose tiniest parts escape our comprehension.[68]

---

[66] Aristotle, *Nicomachaean Ethics* 1139^{b}31–5 (Thomson trans.); Sanches (1988: 178–82, 266 [Thomson trans.]).

[67] Limbrick's introd. in Sanches (1988: 53–67).

[68] Sanches (1988: 190–207 [Thomson trans.]).

For luckless humanity, there are two means of discovering truth, . . . experience and judgement. . . . Experience is in every instance deceitful and difficult . . . [and] reveals only the external aspect of events; in no way does it reveal the natures of things. As for judgement, it is applied to . . . experience; and . . . likewise can . . . only be applied to externals, but even this is done badly.

Sanches found small comfort in this allusion to the first aphorism of Hippocrates, still less in meditating on the faulty means that people use to transmit their flawed judgments in books too many to read and too poor to worry about. People keep changing what they think; inconsistency results from ignorance. Having given up the effort to learn from this mistaken wisdom, Sanches 'turned [his] . . . attention to things . . . and began to examine [them] . . . as if no proposition had ever been laid down by anyone. . . . How am I to avoid doubt', he asked 'if I cannot grasp the natures of things, from which true scientific knowledge has to come?' Even if he lived for centuries, he could 'have experience of only a few things, and faulty experience at that; still worse will be the judgments'. Finally, Sanches decided that his quest for knowledge only uncovered the obstacles that make it unattainable, even though he gave no rigorous proof that nothing is known. He ended his book with the single interrogative '*Quid?*' or 'What?'[69]

Michel de Montaigne, another questioner and the greatest Renaissance sceptic, was born near Bordeaux in 1533, before the wars of religion began, but by the time he entered the Parlement of Bordeaux as a councillor in the late 1550s the situation in France had grown explosive. His father, who became mayor of Bordeaux in 1557, died eleven years later, leaving his estate to his son. Before he died—so Montaigne tells us—he asked his son to translate a fifteenth-century Latin work on natural theology by Ramon Sibiuda that was troublesome enough to appear on the Index in 1558–9. The translation was Montaigne's first literary venture, but in 1571 he 'retired to the bosom of the learned virgins' to give himself entirely to

[69] Ibid. (278–90 [Thomson trans.]).

leisured thought and writing.[70] Through the last years of his life, political duty often interrupted this idyllic plan. He served two terms as mayor of Bordeaux when the region was badly troubled by religious strife, and he also worked as negotiator between the warring factions. The first complete edition of his three books of *Essais* appeared posthumously in 1595, three years after he died. The earliest essays date from the early 1570s, just after his first retirement, and the first edition in two books came out in 1580, followed by a three-book version in 1588. The 1595 text is larger by a quarter than the last lifetime edition because of manuscript notes added posthumously. Like Ramus, though perhaps less compulsively, Montaigne never stopped revising; one hallmark of the *Essais* is their evolving organic relation with the living person who wrote them. Another is their astounding erudition, including wide philosophical learning. Although he had a formal education in law, Montaigne did his philosophizing outside the university, as a private moral thinker in the tradition of Cicero, Petrarch, and Bruni. His independence from the academy no doubt made it easier for him to write in the vernacular and thus to join Bruno, his contemporary, in inaugurating the transformation of philosophical language that Descartes, Hobbes, and Kant would complete in the next centuries. Though his Greek was meagre, Montaigne was a talented Latinist, and, because much of ancient literature circulated by his time either in Latin or in the vernacular, he was able to stuff his essays with an enormous mass of allusion, quotation, and history from a wide variety of sources, all of them subject to his own original judgements. One measure of Montaigne's literary brilliance is that pedantry did not suffocate his prose. Naturally, he knew the older

[70] Montaigne (1965) is the Frame translation, the source of all quotations here; the reference to an inscription in Montaigne's study is from Frame's introduction, pp. ix–x; see also Montaigne (1962). The bibliography on Montaigne is large; see esp. Villey (1933; 1935); Strowski (1931; 1938); Frame (1955; 1965; 1969); Keller (1957); Brown (1963); Thibaudet (1963); Brush (1966); Dréano (1969); Boase (1970); Chinard (1970); Sayce (1972); Trinquet (1972); McGowan (1974); Limbrick (1977); Popkin (1979: 42–55); Burke (1981); McFarlane and Maclean (1982); Screech (1983); Friedrich (1984); Schiffman (1984).

sources of ancient scepticism in Cicero and Diogenes Laertius as well as their contemporary expositors, but he also read the newer material provided by the Latin Sextus, which emerged only ten years before he began to write.

Montaigne's most extensive presentation of scepticism is also his longest essay, composed between 1575 and 1580: he called it the 'Apology for Raymond Sebond', ostensibly a defence of the *Natural Theology or Book of Creatures* translated for his father and published in 1569. *Natural* (as distinct from *revealed*) theology infers God's existence and attributes from creatures by analogical and other rational arguments; the Index listed Sibiuda because he trusted reason too much in religion. In Montaigne's words, 'he undertakes by human and natural reasons to establish and prove against the atheists all the articles of the Christian religion. . . . I do not think it is possible to do better [than Sebond] in that argument', he added, meaning only that the *Natural Theology* would serve as well as any other effort in a futile genre.[71] Faith and grace must uphold religion; man's pygmy reason can help only a little, and never by itself. In good Pyrrhonist fashion, Montaigne showed that reason's weakness is as much a drag on Sibiuda's opponents as on his supporters. On the immense stage of the cosmos, the human is a 'miserable and puny creature'. Comparison with other animals, who reason, speak, learn, teach, and even display piety, reveals the vanity of our self-image; it was a favourite sceptical theme and a strong rebuke to humanist pretensions about human dignity. 'When I play with my cat,' he mused, 'who knows if I am not a pastime to her more than she is to me?' That animals even have a faculty of abstract reasoning is proved from their dreams. Many possess powers beyond man's comprehension, though they lack the unruly imaginations and redundant desires that lead to sin. Philosophers blocked from proving man's uniqueness on intellectual or moral grounds are reduced to aesthetics. Then,

---

[71] Montaigne (1965: 320); Lohr (1988: 543–5); for an understanding of the scepticism of the 'Apology' differing from mine, see Screech's introduction in Montaigne (1987: pp. ix–xxxiii).

even if the beasts . . . had all the virtue, knowledge, wisdom . . . of the Stoics, they would still be beasts, . . . [not] comparable to a wretched, wicked, senseless man. In short, whatever is not as we are is worth nothing. And God himself, to make himself appreciated, must resemble us.

Inverting the usual humanist line on man's creation in God's image, Montaigne concluded that the human form is shabby evidence of grandeur. If we were cranes, God would have long legs and a pointed beak, and Trismegistus would have an avian marvel to boast about.[72]

What people know may be useful to them, but not very useful. Learning will not dull the pain of gout. God's first command to Adam was to obey, not to know; the wish to know caused the first sin. Knowledge can lead to the pains of hell and to earthly torment as well; we fear and imagine all manner of things. 'In much wisdom is much grief', said the preacher. Religion needs simplicity and ignorance, but not insensibility. In recommending the Stoic remedy of annihilation to those who know life's agonies too well, philosophy shows its impotence. We learn from the nations of the New World that the simple and unlearned life is more pleasant and also more virtuous than ours. Docility is good; curiosity is evil. Socrates was wise to think himself ignorant, and Paul confounded the wisdom of this world.[73] The learned are like stalks of wheat: if their heads are really full, they bend low in humility; only empty heads stand high. If we attend to the testimony and experience of the best minds, we see that philosophy aims 'to seek out truth, knowledge and certainty' in one of three ways. Stoic, Epicurean, and Peripatetic dogmatists think they have found what philosophy seeks. Doctrinaire Academics believe that it cannot be found.

Pyrrho and other Skeptics or Epechists . . . say that they are still in search of the truth, . . . that those who think they have found it are infinitely mistaken; and that there is an overbold vanity in . . . [saying] that human powers are not capable of attaining it. . . . Ignorance that

[72] Montaigne (1965: 329, 331, 358, 395–7).
[73] Ibid. 366, 370; Eccles. 1: 17–18; 1 Cor. 1: 18–2:1.

knows itself . . . is not complete ignorance; to be that, it must be ignorant of itself. So that the profession of the Pyrrhonians is to waver, doubt and inquire, to be sure of nothing. . . . Now this attitude . . . , taking all things in without adherence or consent, leads them to their Ataraxy, . . . a peaceful and sedate condition, . . . exempt from . . . agitations. . . . They do not fear contradiction. . . . If you accept their proposition, they will just as gladly take the opposite one to maintain; it is all one to them; they have no preference. . . . And by this extremity of doubt that shakes its own foundations, they separate . . . themselves from many opinions . . . which . . . have upheld doubt and ignorance.

In the sphere of knowledge, the Pyrrhonists recommend suspension of judgement; in action, they advise following nature, law, and custom. Their tranquil prescription leaves the mind 'naked and empty', void of any heretical opinion and ready to be filled with God's grace. Pyrrhonian man is 'a blank tablet prepared to take from the finger of God such forms as he shall be pleased to engrave'.[74]

Aristotle, 'the prince of dogmatists', played the philosophical trick of making his hollow thoughts appear hard in order to hide their vanity, while Socrates, Parmenides, Xenophanes, and other doubters thought it wiser to question than to answer. Even Plato, who was ready to tell the big lie for the sake of a higher good, chose to write dialogues in order to express a variety of ideas. Philosophy amuses us until curiosity buries itself in idle and inconsistent opinion, as heard in the 'clatter of . . . philosophical brains' from Thales to Epicurus who tried to penetrate the mystery of the godhead instead of honouring God's incomprehensibility, as Paul did in Athens.[75] Like Cusanus, Montaigne had a keen sense of the disproportion between the divine condition and the human. 'The least-known things are the fittest to be deified; wherefore to make gods of ourselves . . . passes the utmost bounds of feeble-mindedness.' When we liken God to mankind, we limit and defile him. Furnished with human joys, paradise itself seems cheap. Bizarre and wicked deeds done in the name of religion turn

---

[74] Montaigne (1965: 371–2, 375).
[75] Ibid. 376, 383.

reverence into sacrilege when humans vulgarize the holy. Montaigne's ethnography taught him that, in worship as in all other respects, 'there are species of men ... who have very little resemblance to our kind'. If nature mocks our laws in this way, how absurd to think that God honours them.[76] Our speech is a frail instrument, soon shattered by paradox and semantic confusion if we try to catch God in a sieve of words. The Pyrrhonists anticipated the need for a negative or, better, an interrogative theology; they saw that they could not

express their general conception in any manner of speaking; for they would need a new language. Ours is wholly formed of affirmative propositions, which to them are utterly repugnant; so that when they say 'I doubt,' immediately you have them by the throat.... [Their] idea is more firmly grasped in the form of interrogation: 'What do I know?'—the words I bear as a motto, inscribed over a pair of scales.

Montaigne, who covered the beams of his study with quotations from Sextus, had his motto—*Que sais-je?*—cast as a medal with the scales on the obverse, to remind him always of the mismeasure between God and mankind and of the need to keep doubting.[77]

Pomponazzi and others had shown philosophy to be unsure of itself on questions of great theological moment, but Montaigne went further in distancing faith from reason. Having exposed the posturings of theology, Montaigne turned to natural philosophy and medicine. Anyone who considers astronomy for a moment 'would think we had had coach-makers ... up there ... [to] set up machines with various movements'; such constructs are 'dreams and fanatical follies'. A review of ancient cosmological opinion shows that one prime substance is as good as another, certainly as plausible as the matter and form of Aristotle, 'the god of scholastic knowledge'. People who consider Sibiuda's reasons defective should investigate the learning of physicians, who cannot account for the simplest bodily acts, the movement of a finger or a foot. Claims that expertise or first principles belong uniquely to various dis-

[76] Ibid. 383, 391.
[77] Ibid. 392–3.

ciplines are screens for ignorance. Only God can give us principles. No human assertion has more weight than another
unless weighed in the scales of reason. Aristotle's dogmas are
of no use to the cannibals, who do nicely with a physics of
common sense. Philosophy is a strange and less useful tool,
but quite pliable. In Italy, Montaigne once told a traveller
anxious to speak Italian that he should simply tack Italian
endings onto any Romance words that came to mind, and 'he
would never fail to hit some dialect. . . . I say the same thing
about philosophy; it has so many faces . . . that all our dreams
and reveries are found in it.' Given so many choices, Montaigne
found his own behaviour conforming to many styles of philosophy. 'What rule my life belonged to, I did not learn until
after it was . . . spent. A new figure: an unpremeditated and
accidental philosopher.'[78]

People want to reason well, yet they cannot say what reason
is or where it resides. If reason lives in the soul, is its home
immortal? One cannot tell what Aristotle or the other ancients
taught on this critical question. Weak and contradictory claims
about immortality show only that the subject is beyond man's
power, and teachings on the body are as confused as those on
the soul. In the face of this perplexity, Montaigne warned that
Pyrrhonist techniques were a 'final fencer's trick' and a 'des-
perate stroke' to be used rarely and cautiously; a proper time
would be when 'one of these new doctors tries to show off his
ingenuity . . . at the risk of his salvation and yours' by substituting philosophical dogma for the gift of faith. In ancient times
diversity of opinion created confusion, but now the rigid Peripatetic syllabus breeds credulity as well.[79] The learned now
dispute everything dogmatically, but their querulous certainties
would evaporate if they realized how little it takes to unsettle
our powers of perception and judgement. A sore toe or an
upset stomach can shake a world-view. Having seen how fickle
were his own states of mind, Montaigne claimed to have 'acci-
dentally engendered . . . a certain constancy of opinions. . . . I
do not change easily. . . . And since I am not capable of choos-

[78] Ibid. 400, 403, 408–9.
[79] Ibid. 418–20.

ing, I accept other people's choice and stay ... where God put me.' He once told a natural philosopher that he 'would rather follow facts than reason', but then he found that 'the Pyrrhonians ... ruin the apparent facts of experience'. Beliefs and customs change with time and space, so that 'the form of our being depends on ... the soil where we are born.' In morals and manners variation is especially great; the best each person can do is to follow local custom, but this leaves moral agency entirely unhinged. Except for the Pyrrhonists, philosophers have little help to give.[80]

Consider the noble cause that persuaded Metrocles to shift from Peripatetic reticence to Stoic candour. He farted 'while debating in the presence of his school, and ... was hiding for shame, until Crates went to visit him and, adding to his consolations and reasons the example of his own freedom, started a farting contest with him, by which he rid him of his scruple.' Philosophy as farting contest: this was Montaigne's emblem of reason disgraced and impotent.[81] Philosophy also divulged the scandal of the senses, which Montaigne called 'the greatest foundation and proof of our ignorance'. Epicureans maintain that if the senses perceive falsely, there is no knowledge; but the Stoics claim that sense perceptions yield no knowledge just because they are false; from these dogmatic premises Montaigne concluded 'that there is no knowledge'. After listing phenomena that trick each of the senses—an echo that comes from the wrong direction, a white scene that looks yellow to a jaundiced eye—he recalled the philosopher who blinded himself to avoid visual distraction. This catalogue of sensory deception introduces the problem of the criterion:

To judge the appearances ..., we would need a judicatory instrument; to verify this instrument, we need a demonstration; to verify the demonstration, an instrument: there we are in a circle. Since the senses cannot decide our dispute, being themselves full of uncertainty, it must be reason that does so. No reason can be established without another reason: there we go retreating back to infinity.

---

[80] Ibid. 428, 430, 433.
[81] Ibid. 440.

Sensation runs in a circle; reason regresses forever. In a world of coming-to-be and passing-away, the apprehension of being is as inconstant as water running through the fingers. Only God exists eternally and immutably. Seneca's wish that mankind should lift itself above the sordid human condition was 'a useful desire, but ... absurd.... [No man] can raise ... himself above himself and humanity.... He will rise if God by exception lends him a hand.... It is for our Christian faith, not for [Seneca's] Stoical virtue, to aspire to that divine and miraculous metamorphosis.'[82]

Montaigne's Pyrrhonist rejection of Stoicism in the 'Apology' and elsewhere in the second book of the *Essais* has — along with other evidence — persuaded some critics that his thinking evolved from humanist Stoicism in the first book through a sceptical crisis in book two toward an Epicurean resolution in the final book. Montaigne's *Essais* obviously grew with him, but their lines of development were too complex and their contours of expression too subtle to fit such easy patterns. 'That to Philosophize Is to Learn to Die' is an early essay from the period 1572–4, and its intention 'to teach us not to be afraid to die', is a sentiment worthy of a Stoic — or an Epicurean. In fact, the Garden is more visible than the Porch in the passage (reminiscent of Valla) from the same essay which maintains that 'in virtue itself the ultimate goal ... is voluptuousness. I like to beat their ears with that word.' Also Epicurean was Montaigne's wish, supported by two lines from Lucretius, that death 'find me planting my cabbages, but careless of death, and still more of my unfinished garden'.[83] In the late essay 'Of Experience' (1587–8) that closes the third volume, written nearly ten years after his refutation of Stoicism in the 'Apology', Montaigne spoke the lines of a Stoic sage in teaching that 'we must learn to endure what we cannot avoid'. In a decidedly un-Pyrrhonist vein, he also wrote that 'there is no desire more natural than the desire for knowledge.... When reason fails us, we use experience, ... a weaker and

[82] Ibid. 443, 447, 454, 457; Popkin (1979: 48–52).
[83] Montaigne (1965: pp. xii, 56, 62); Lucretius, *On the Nature of Things* 3. 900–1.

less dignified means. But truth is so great a thing that we must not disdain any medium that will lead us to it.' In this most mature phase of his thought, the experience that he had learned to trust was experience of himself, unmediated by any philosophical system. 'I study myself more than any other subject. That is my metaphysics,' he concluded, 'that is my physics.'[84]

Montaigne's essays are so powerfully compelling because of their grace and wit. He had the gift of electrifying a huge armature of classical citation that would crush a lesser stylist, and he knew how to update his erudition and make it newsworthy. Cultural relativism, for instance, had been an issue for Sextus, who emphasized the many differences among people separated by culture and geography in order to undermine the reader's confidence in the probity of his own behaviour. When Europeans feel hot, Ethiopians shiver; sexual, religious, and ceremonial usages differ so widely that one cannot speak of a uniform human nature. Montaigne's best-known treatment of this theme is the essay 'On Cannibals', written around the same time as the 'Apology'. To enliven the ancient *topos* of strange customs in faraway places, he describes the habits of New World people, including 'three of these men, ignorant of the price they will pay . . . for gaining knowledge of the corruptions of this side of the ocean, . . . [who] left the serenity of their own sky to come and see ours . . . at Rouen, at the time of the late King Charles IX' in 1562. Comparing the habits of these people to his own, Montaigne determined that 'each man calls barbarism whatever is not his own practice.' 'These nations . . . seem to me barbarous in this sense,' he conceded, 'that they have been fashioned very little by the human mind. . . . The laws of nature still rule them, very little corrupted by ours.' As for head-hunting, Montaigne was 'not sorry that we notice the barbarous horror of such acts, but . . . heartily sorry that, judging their faults rightly, we should be so blind to our own. . . . We may well call these people barbarians in respect to the rules of reason,' he wrote, 'but not in respect to ourselves, who surpass them in every kind of barbarity.' Montaigne

---

[84] Montaigne (1965: 814, 821, 835).

reported a long talk with one of the three visitors to Rouen, who impressed him with his martial bearing and his elegant modesty. 'All this is not too bad,' he concluded, 'but what's the use? They don't wear breeches.'[85] In his *Journals*, Montaigne recorded other personal experiences of alien customs in Italy and elsewhere in Europe, all of which convinced him that old moral certainties were toppling under the weight of new information flooding into Europe from the voyages of exploration and other journeys of mental discovery. The most important casualty of this transcultural crisis of confidence was religion, especially religion as the ground of morals. In the 'Apology' he admitted that 'we are Christians by the same title that we are Perigordians or Germans'. Faith is an accident of geography. This was strong talk for so thoroughly Christian a culture, whose more usual instincts were to bolster religious conviction with ethical prescriptions and other dogmas of philosophy. Montaigne hoped that his Pyrrhonism, like the ancient variety, would lead not to anomie but to *ataraxia*, the tranquility that was supposed to follow from suspended judgement. But like other utopian states of mind or world, this peace never came. Instead, scepticism caused more anxiety and gave philosophers plenty to brood about for a long time to come, especially in the next century, when Descartes and Pascal traced out the sceptical implications of Montaigne's thought.[86]

Justus Lipsius on a new moral code

In the section of the 'Apology' where he exposed the strife among philosophers on virtue and the greatest good, Montaigne recorded his wish that 'Justus Lipsius, the most learned man we have left, ... might ... compile into a register ... the opinions of ancient philosophy on ... our being and our conduct. ... What a fine and useful work that would be!'[87] By the time Montaigne added this passage to the 'Apology', Lipsius had published one of his two most successful works, the *Two*

[85] Ibid. 152–3, 155–6, 158–9.
[86] Ibid. 325.
[87] Ibid. 436.

Books on Constancy of 1584, but he had not yet completed the systematic surveys of ethics and physics which, at least as far as Stoic thought is concerned, fulfilled Montaigne's wish: his *Digest of Stoic Philosophy* and *Physics of the Stoics* both appeared in 1604 and took their place as the leading statements of the Renaissance revival of Stoicism. In the earlier *De constantia*, Lipsius had turned to Stoic moral philosophy as a refuge from the horrors of religious and civil war that ravaged the Low Countries in the last third of the sixteenth century, but later, in the *Digest* (*Manductio*) and *Physics* (*Physiologia*), he recognized that ethics and physics were inseparable aspects of Stoic philosophical inquiry because the injunction to live one's life in accord with nature requires knowledge of nature.[88] Even though the aims of the *Physiologia* are more ethical and theological than physical, Lipsius deserves credit for trying to reconstruct Stoic natural philosophy and reassert its centrality in Stoic thought. Even today, the ancient evidence on all of Stoic philosophy except ethics remains fragmentary; in the Middle Ages and early Renaissance the texts were even less accessible and intelligible, despite the fact that Stoicism had dominated philosophical discourse for more than four hundred years in the Hellenistic era.

Historians usually divide the long history of the Stoic school into Early, Middle, and Late periods, of which only the last is represented by anything more than fragmentary evidence. Seneca, Epictetus, and Marcus Aurelius lived in the first and second centuries CE under Roman rule, but only Seneca wrote in Latin, so it was Seneca, Cicero, and various patristic authors who transmitted Middle and Late Stoic doctrine to the Middle Ages. For medieval Christians, Stoic thought held a number of attractions: it was systematic in scope, earnest in morality, and reverent in theology. Seneca seemed so pious that a false correspondence with St. Paul was long attributed to him. Thus,

---

[88] Lipsius (1939) reprints a 16th-c. translation by Sir John Stradling of *De constantia*; otherwise, for the Latin works see Lipsius (1675) and (1978–). The Stradling translation contains an introduction by Rudolf Kirk. For other secondary literature see Faider (1922); Nordman (1932); Glaesener (1938); Ruysschaert (1949); Saunders (1955); Oestreich (1975; 1982); Zanta (1975); Abel (1978: 67–113).

even though their teachings on fate, matter, creation, and other topics conflicted with Christian doctrine, medieval writers could be much friendlier to the Stoics—such as they remembered them—than to the Epicureans. However, the Latin texts read in the Middle Ages had more to say about ethics than about logic or physics, and even when Epictetus and Marcus Aurelius became available in the fifteenth and sixteenth centuries, they added another layer of moral pronouncement to a picture of Stoicism that already exaggerated its ethical content and ignored or understated the logical, physical, and epistemological contributions of the Early and Middle Stoa. Influenced by Cynic ethics, Megarian logic, Academic theology, and Peripatetic method, Zeno had founded his own school at the beginning of the third century BCE; the school took its name from the *stoa* or 'porch' where Zeno taught. Through the late second century, his greatest successors were Cleanthes, who excelled in theology and physics, and Chrysippus, best remembered for logic, psychology, and comprehensive scholarship. Unattributed evidence of the Early Stoa is often thought to come from Chrysippus. The most renowned figures of the Middle Stoa were Panaetius of Rhodes and Posidonius of Apamea; Cicero knew Posidonius personally, and Panaetius greatly influenced him.[89]

In 1354 Petrarch began his long treatise *On Remedies for Both Kinds of Fortune*, imitating a sixth-century work by Martin of Braga then attributed to Seneca. Petrarch counselled the sage neither to revel in good luck nor despair in the bad. Fortune smiles for a thousand wayward reasons—birth, health, family, friends, means, and so on—but the same circumstances lead just as often to misery. A wise person will cool passions inflamed by either turn of fate and trust in a providential God for deliverance. Petrarch inaugurated a long Renaissance tradition of respect for Stoicism as a regimen of moral betterment useful to the philosophical Christian. But many early modern

[89] Verbeke (1983); Colish (1985: i. 1–79; ii. 1–9, 142–53, 234–41); Long (1986: 107–121, 150–2, 210–11, 216–18, 229–31). On Stoicism see also Screech (1956); Ettinghausen (1972); Spanneut (1973); Eymard d'Angers (1976); Lapidge (1988); and above, n. 88.

critics, who misinterpreted the Stoic view of the passions to mean that all emotion should be quenched, considered their medicine too bitter to swallow. Valla ridiculed the notion that virtue is a good in itself and denied that a Christian should be careless of pleasure and pain. Montaigne confessed that 'passions are as easy for me to avoid as they are hard for me to moderate. . . . He who cannot attain the noble impassibility of the Stoics, let him take refuge in . . . this plebeian stupidity of mine. What those men did by virtue, I train myself to do by disposition.' Christians saw much to admire in the Stoics, having learned from them such valuable lessons as the scheme of the four cardinal virtues worked out by Panaetius and passed on by Cicero, but they also had to face certain objections: making human virtue its own reward displaces divine love as the end of moral action; banning the passions casts doubt on the behaviour of a Christ who felt hot anger and wept salt tears; determinism threatens God's power and man's moral freedom. Critics from Salutati to Calvin saw these conflicts, which Justus Lipsius tried to resolve by creating the point of view now called 'Neo-Stoicism'.[90]

Joest Lips was a Catholic Fleming born in the neighbourhood of Brussels and Louvain in 1547. As an adolescent he studied with the Jesuits in Cologne, but soon moved on to the University of Louvain and travelled in Germany and Italy, where he met the humanist Marc-Antoine Muret. While still in his early twenties he published his first important philological work, the *Mixed Readings* of 1569, which cast his notes on a number of classical authors into fine Ciceronian periods — despite his association with the anti-Ciceronian Muret. In 1572, after Spanish troops commandeered his property in Belgium, he made the first of his notorious moves to another university and a new faith, accepting a chair of history and eloquence at Protestant Jena and shifting to the Lutheran confession, as such a post required. The pillaging Spaniards provoked Lipsius into anti-papist tirades, but even on the surface his typical attitude toward religion was indifference. At this stage of his

---

[90] Montaigne (1965: 780); Kraye (1988: 360–74).

life, he was a rising young classicist who found the wars of religion unhelpful to his career. A deeper look at his behaviour suggests that he was a Familist, like several other scholars connected with the publishing house of Christopher Plantin. The secretive Family of Love evolved from earlier Anabaptist origins into an anti-denominational, pacifist individualism, superbly adapted to the purposes of those rare spirits who found the religious venom of the later sixteenth century spiritually distasteful. Believing the true church to be invisible, Familists could pass lightly from one external observance to another, as Lipsius certainly did. His new colleagues at Jena were less adaptable, and denounced him as a crypto-Jesuit when he was named their dean. He left Jena for Cologne, married, and published important works on Tacitus and Plautus that finally convinced him to follow Muret in abandoning the Ciceronian ideal. This literary turnabout had philosophical consequences, because Muret had made the Stoic Seneca a stylish alternative to Cicero.[91]

Lipsius became doctor of laws at Catholic Louvain in 1576, but he was soon driven to Protestant territory again when soldiers looted his house a second time. By 1579 he was professor of history in Calvinist Leiden, where he stayed for thirteen years, always maintaining his connections with friends in Catholic regions. While at Leiden he witnessed Protestant hatred for the Roman church at its bitterest, and in this context he published his two most frequently printed books, *On Constancy* (1584) and *Six Books of Politics or Civil Doctrine* (1589). Drawing on Aristotle, Cicero, Tacitus, and other classical sources, Lipsius argued in the latter work for a policy of strict intolerance; no state can permit more than one religion, and public dissenters must be punished without mercy. He Christianized the goddess Fortune as representing God's will, but kept her as whimsical and irresistible as the Roman *Fortuna*. The only remedies are resolute faith and unwavering obedience to the powers that be. Even when oppressed by tyranny, a

---

[91] Ruysschaert (1949: 1–8, 43–7, 154–68); Saunders (1955: 1–18); Van Dorsten (1973: 26–36); Hamilton (1981).

subject's only lawful weapon is the shield of forbearance, never the sword of violence. Like Montaigne, Lipsius dreaded civil conflict more than despotism, and he was willing to pay the price. From its opening chapters, the dialogue *On Constancy* seeks a private remedy for public strife. When Lipsius tells his interlocutor how he fled the troubled Low Countries, it takes no time to convince him that 'travelling into forreine countreyes is not available against the inwarde malladies of the minde'. The Stoics teach that such palliatives are useless against the deeper passions, whose only cures are wisdom and constancy; right reason leads to constancy, while inconstancy arises from mere opinion. Evils that shake constancy through the passions of desire, joy, fear, and sorrow may be private or public, and public afflictions are the more fearful because they affect more people and seduce them into moral error.[92]

One source of public evil is intemperate love of any particular country or political order: 'if we respect the whole nature of man, all these earthlie countries are vaine . . . except only in respect of the body, and not of the minde or soule, . . . but heaven is our true or rightfull countrey.' Any evil that comes to an earthly land must be understood as God's providence to be obeyed, not as blind chance to be defied. To resist the divine plan is impious and foolish as well, no matter how awful the calamity: 'if there bee a God, there is also a Providence, . . . [and thus] a decree and order of thinges, and of that followeth a firme and sure necessitie of eventes . . . ; with what axe will you cut off this chaine?'[93] Although some accuse the Stoics of letting destiny rule divinity, Seneca and Panaetius have shown that Zeno and Chrysippus simply used the words 'destiny' and 'fate' to mean 'God'. 'No other sect of Philosophers avowed more the majesty and providence of God, nor drewe men neerer to heavenlie and eternall thinges' than the Stoics, from whom we learn that destiny is 'an eternal decree of God's providence'. None the less, the Christian must adjust the Stoic concept of destiny in several respects, by

---

[92] Lipsius (1939: 73); Ruysschaert (1949: 9–13); Saunders (1955: 18–33); Skinner (1978: ii. 277–84); Oestreich (1982: 17–20).

[93] Lipsius (1939: 98, 112); Oestreich (1982: 20–2).

making God clearly the ruler of fate and by allowing some contingency in events and assuring man's free will. Freedom, contingency, and moral responsibility are preserved in the order of *second causes*, far removed from the realm of *first causes* where destiny prevails. Likewise, Lipsius safeguards God's goodness in an evil world by distinguishing the ultimate causes of the catastrophes that surround us from the immediate but transitory effects that we experience as evil. God's will, which must be good, is the remote but primary cause of everything that happens to us, and his final intentions shape a good providential design. By and by, God's purposes will be revealed, and in the mean time we may thank him for our pains: they make us stronger, test our virtue, and set an example for others.[94]

Lipsius saw his miseries mount up again in 1590 when Dirck Coornhert published a long treatise in Dutch attacking his *Politics* on the issue of governmental enforcement of confessional unity. In his reply, *On One Religion* (1590), Lipsius maintained the religious authority of the secular arm, but he warned against too literal a reading of some of his inflammatory language, particularly the infamous advice to 'burn and cut— this is no place for clemency'. Coornhert was a liberal Catholic, but Protestants also despised Lipsius either as a spokesman for rigid Calvinism or as an agent of the Inquisition. The acrimony set Lipsius on his travels again. He left Leiden for Liège, won a pardon from the Spaniards, and mended his fences with the Jesuits; by 1592 he was teaching again in Louvain. The church disappointed him by putting the *Politics* and other works on the Index in 1593, even after he had submitted corrections. For a time he concentrated on history and philology, but then in 1604–5 he earned the contempt of Protestants and Catholics alike when he tried to display his loyalty to Rome in two childishly transparent tracts on miracles performed at shrines of the Virgin. Around the same time, two years before his death in 1606, appeared his two much more sophisticated expositions of Stoic philosophy, the *Manductio* and *Physiologia*.

---

[94] Lipsius (1939: 117); Oestreich (1982: 28–30, 35).

Always on guard for the ecclesiastical watchdogs, Lipsius was careful not to claim absolute validity for the Stoic system, but he tried to show that it was philosophy's best accommodation to Christianity.[95]

Taking this cautious approach, the *Manductio* concludes that the best philosophy must be eclectic, adhering to no single school; but in explicating the history, organization, and content of Stoicism, Lipsius worked hard to brighten its appeal to Christians. Aristotle prevails in natural philosophy. Plato outshines him in religion. But since one must use natural philosophy to find God's will working in creation, Stoicism will be the ideal choice because it was organized to discover God in nature. Although every schoolmaster has Aristotle's philosophy on his lips, the doctrine of the Stoics needs broader exposure. Still, the wise will choose eclectically, cutting and trimming as salvation and orthodoxy require; not all Stoic teachings are equally well suited to Christianity. The doctrine of ethically indifferent actions, for example, impairs moral integrity. Some of the Stoic ethical paradoxes serve the Christian well: it reinforces humility and poverty of spirit to hold that a kingdom should please the sage no more than slavery. But no circumstances can justify suicide, incest, or cannibalism. To tell the good advice from the bad, the wise aspire to universal knowledge, which obviously includes the world of nature; less obvious are the moral inferences that Seneca and Epictetus taught Lipsius to draw from man's natural condition. While Montaigne had denounced natural theology to honour a hidden God, Lipsius wanted to uncover nature's God through a philosophy that bases ethics and theology on physics. Ethically and theologically, the key premises are that God's laws are nature's laws and that the good life conforms to nature. Within nature the Stoics detected a *logos* or principle of order which they treated as an aspect of divinity; to Christians the *Logos* would be familiar as God's Word teaching mankind its place in the cosmos. Like other pagans, the Stoics talked as if the gods were many, though they really had in mind the various faces of providence.[96]

Lipsius recognized the importance of physics for Stoic philosophy in the *Manductio*, but he left the detailed analysis of natural philosophy as the foundation of ethics and theology for the *Physiologia*. The main burden of the work is to explain away conflicts between Stoic physics and Christianity or, failing that, to delete unresolved contradictions from a Christianized, Neo-Stoic natural philosophy. Stoic theology from a Christian point of view is uncomfortably materialist, pantheist, and determinist. When Lipsius found the Stoic God described in Diogenes Laertius as 'a craftsmanlike fire proceeding to create', he preserved the witness to creation by referring to Exodus, where a theophanic pillar of fire leads Israel through the wilderness. He maintained that the Stoics did not really equate God with air or *pneuma* or *spiritus*, but he accepted God as world-soul, interpreted as the All in which every living thing exists. When he read in Aulus Gellius that Chrysippus called fate 'a certain everlasting ordering of the whole', Lipsius identified fate with God's providential reason. God *is* fate, which thus poses no threat to divine might or freedom. Fate causes everything, but not every act is a *direct* effect of fate. Within the sphere of fate's *indirect* effects (*via* second causes), humans preserve their moral liberty and responsibility. Noble deeds and vile crimes are their own, rescued by the distinction between first and second causes. Matter is also primary and secondary. Like God, first matter is timeless and unchanging; second matter comes and goes. God does not make primary matter because he *is* primary matter; he creates only the secondary matter of natural objects. To fend off the charge of materialist blasphemy, Lipsius had to show that a corporeal God is theologically legitimate, so he pointed out how the Stoics described any real entity as active or passive and hence corporeal. As the first active being, God must be *corporeal* in this sense, though he is clearly not an ordinary *body* as Lipsius understood the term. To keep his faith with Christianity,

[96] Saunders (1955: 67–116).

Lipsius did some violence to Stoic conceptions of matter, body, and God in this analysis; and in defending the Stoic view of the soul as a vital *pneuma*, he did even less well by Christian standards, whether religious or philosophical.[97]

Politics and moral disorder: Erasmus, More, and Machiavelli

Versatile in his religious habits, Lipsius could also be morally pragmatic, influenced in this by the historian Tacitus. Both Lipsius and Guillaume du Vair, another theorist who sheltered in Stoicism from the religious storms of the late sixteenth century, were more receptive than many contemporaries to the view that reasons of state sometimes prevail over ordinary moral reasons — the Machiavellian doctrine of *ragione di stato*. 'Machiavellian' is the right word here: the actual phrase was not Machiavelli's, but Francesco Guicciardini, Innocent Gentillet, Jean Bodin, Giovanni Botero and others gave 'reason of state' a life of its own. In his *Six Books of Politics*, Lipsius openly defended Machiavelli in agreeing that public welfare sometimes requires the ruler to choose the useful lie over the inexpedient truth. Even Montaigne, another student of confessional strife, gave similar advice in writing 'Of the Useful and the Honorable' between 1585 and 1588. 'I will follow the good side right to the fire,' he declared, 'but not into it if I can help it.' By the end of this brief essay, Montaigne had gathered his own, honest choices safely under the cover of a private morality. He had also concluded that to 'argue the honour and beauty of an action from its utility' was only a 'pretext of reason'. But along the way he gave hostages to necessity. 'In every government', he conceded,

there are necessary offices which are not only abject but also vicious. Vices find their place in it and are employed for sewing our society together.... If they become excusable, inasmuch as we need them and the common necessity effaces their true quality, we still must let this part be played by the more vigorous ... who sacrifice their

[97] Ibid. 117–217, esp. 127–8, 140; Diogenes Laertius 7. 156; Aulus Gellius, *Attic Nights* 7. 2. 3; Long and Sedley (1987: i. 336); Exod. 13: 21.

honour and their conscience ... for the good of their country. ...
The public welfare requires that a man betray and lie and massacre;
let us resign this commission to more obedient and suppler people.[98]

At best, this is a personal evasion that confuses, if it does not
contradict, conclusions reached a few pages later. Thinking
out loud *and* on paper is the essayist's occupational hazard.
At worst, the passage takes many words to condone what
Machiavelli said succinctly in the *Discourses* about Romulus,
the patriarch of Rome who murdered his brother: 'If the deed
accuses him, the result excuses him.'[99] Montaigne suspected
and Machiavelli insisted that political ends justify means. Both
were engaged observers of contemporary politics as well as
readers of the ancient history newly illuminated by humanism.

Humanists since Petrarch had followed their moral curiosity
into the riskier paths of politics. They hoped that calm Stoics
and detached Platonists might tame Europe's warrior aristocracy and bring harmony to her swarming cities, goals that
eluded even the powers of Christian faith. Their aims were
peaceable and constructive, but their arguments were often
trite and formulaic. Most preferred virtue (*virtus*) to force
(*vis*), but they saw virtue as a means to glory, earthly or
heavenly, thus allowing the chivalry and their bourgeois mimics
a righteous way to fame, with all that this motive implies about
just wars and honourable peaces. In explicit terms, however,
humanists abandoned the scholastic doctrine of the just war
and repudiated the Aristotelian citizen-warrior, favouring the
Stoic opinion that all war is fratricide over the more bellicose
teachings of Augustine and Aquinas. Yet they assumed that
any ruler's *virtus* could be the same as Christian virtue, simply
adding conventional princely qualities (justice, clemency, trustworthiness) to moral attributes (wisdom, temperance, courage)
that belong to any good person. Outside Venice and Florence,
humanists of quattrocento Italy had to address the princes and
princelings who ruled everywhere, but the anomalous politics
of these two great cities gave rise to a special literature about

[98] Montaigne (1965: 600–1, 610); Meinecke (1965: 25–89); Skinner (1978:
i. 253–4).
[99] Machiavelli (1954: 116).

civic virtue—moral qualities that might belong to citizens or even the whole citizenry and thus transcend the personal traits (whether Christian or Stoic) of the individual ruler. Bruni's *Praise of the City of Florence* (1403–4) was the fountainhead of humanist republicanism, as distinct from the more aristocratic theories of mixed government that arose in the Venetian context, and the central issue in Florentine politics was the preservation of liberty by an effective polity and a strong army. Although Bruni and his successors thought of liberty mainly as the city's freedom from external constraint, they opted for republican rather than aristocratic government because all citizens have an incentive for virtuous conduct if the constitution protects individual as well as communal liberty.[100]

Civic obligation means that the virtuous citizen will choose the active over the contemplative life, *negotium* over *otium*. Moreover, while Aristotle had taught that only the aristocrat who inherits wealth and power has the time or means for full citizenship, a broader civic mandate subverts hereditary aristocracy, especially the rural feudalism of medieval Europe. If virtue is the true nobility, as Poggio, Platina, and other scholars contended, the genetic patent of feudal aristocracy may be false. At this point, when classicism had become a political threat, events and their own further researches saved the humanists from sedition. Bruni had many followers, but as the decades passed his message became less persuasive to scholars who served the *signori*. Other, less creative purveyors of political advice, like the two Decembrii who worked for the Visconti despots of Milan, developed a more saleable line of textbooks for tyrants, trying all the while to convince them that *virtus* is better than *vis*. Even in Florence the success of Cosimo de' Medici and his family reduced the appeal of republican theory, and the parallel growth of Platonic scholarship from Bruni to Ficino uncovered the ancient blueprint of the *Republic* to autocrats who might wish to be seen as philosopher-kings. Bartolomeo Scala's 1483 work *On Laws and Judgments* and Landino's treatise of 1485–7 *On True Nobility*

[100] Bruni (1987: 101–21); Adams (1962: 7–8, 88–111, 134–43); Skinner (1978: i. 68–112; 1988: 413–25).

were two leading products of this trend toward a humanist ideology of autocracy and civic quietism. If the best life was the life of the mind detached from worldly desire, then the *vita contemplativa* was no longer dereliction of civic duty.[101]

When humanists in northern Europe first turned to political theory, they did little but adapt earlier Italian versions of classical ideas to regional and historical circumstances. Some issues that gripped the Italians, such as the use of mercenaries, were less pressing north of the Alps, while others, above all the choice between republican and autocratic government, were not real options in England, France, or the Empire. But even before Luther, problems of social, cultural, and religious reform weighed on Erasmus, Thomas More, and other northern thinkers and caused them to frame the political debate in ways that departed from the Italian models. More wrote his long letter to Martin Dorp in 1515, but its fundamental claim that Peripatetic school philosophy is not the philosophy of Christ or a proper basis of Christian life was visible earlier, especially in two influential works by Erasmus, the *Handbook of the Christian Soldier* of 1503–4 and *The Praise of Folly* of 1511. Christ, who rules the hearts of the faithful, cannot be made to serve professors; neither lawyers nor logicians may dissect the living fabric of his Gospel. In political theory, the first major product of Erasmian Christianity was *The Education of a Christian Prince*, dedicated to the future Charles V in 1516, but it is a disappointing appendix to the robust *philosophia Christi*. The book requires the prince to be a good Erasmian Christian and a paragon of virtue, but, like other early modern theorists, Erasmus made honour the ruler's motive for virtue, thereby ratifying the old chivalric morality while trying to Christianize and classicize it. Erasmus was no ardent Platonist, but he saw government more as guarantor of order in the style of Plato's *Republic* than as guardian of liberty in the manner of Bruni's *Laudatio*. Anyone who thinks that humanism had to be democratic should read his repeated pleas to train the prince away from 'the great mass of people . . . swayed by

[101] Skinner (1978: i. 77–84, 105–9, 113–17; 1988: 419–29).

false opinions ... [like] those in Plato's cave'. His deepest conviction—that good education makes good politics—was common to the whole genre of 'mirror-for-princes' books. 'None is more worthy of ... honour', he maintained, 'than he who labors ... in the proper training of the prince. ... A country owes everything to a good prince: him it owes to the man who made him such by his moral principles.' Neither Luther nor More nor Machiavelli had as much confidence in the ruler's educability or the schoolteacher's powers. More credible, at least as representing his own belief, was what Erasmus said about the prince's obligations to justice and his proper attitude to war. On the latter point he had already declared himself in the well-known chapter of the 1515 *Adages*, 'War is Sweet to Those Who Know It Not', and later in the 1517 *Complaint of Peace*. In the *Institutio principis Christiani* he wrote that 'a good prince should never go to war at all unless ... he cannot possibly avoid it. If we were of this mind, there would hardly [ever] be a war.' Just as adamant was the advice that 'if you cannot defend your realm without violating justice ..., give up and yield to the importunities of the age! ... It is far better to be a just man than an unjust prince.' To imagine a moral distance greater than that between Erasmus and Machiavelli on this point is difficult.[102]

Unlike Machiavelli and More, Erasmus was never a minister of government. He became a celebrity, well-known to the mighty, but never bound to serve them politically. He never had to face the consequences of his advice to princes within a sphere of action for which he himself was accountable to the ruler and the ruled. The earlier humanist literature had subsumed this 'problem of counsel' within the old debate about action and contemplation, and its findings were as superficial

---

[102] Erasmus (1968: 141, 145, 148, 150, 155, 248 [Born trans.]); More (1963– : vol. xv, pp. xix–xxviii, 2–127); Adams (1962: 93–108, 164–8); Bainton (1969: 65–71, 90–7); Skinner (1978: i. 200–50; 1988: 443–8); Screech (1988: 1–11). On Erasmus see also Allen (1914); Smith (1923); Bataillon (1937); Mann Philipps (1959); Kohls (1966); Margolin (1967; 1972; 1986; 1987); Halkin (1969); Mesnard (1969); Tracy (1972); O'Rourke Boyle (1977; 1983); Chomarat (1981); Trinkaus (1983: 274–301); Rummel (1985; 1986); Schoeck (1988; 1990).

as the framework was conventional. The object of literary counsel might sometimes be the ruler's courtiers or even his subjects, but the audience for direct advice was usually the prince himself, and the humanists most often consulted the ruler's interest rather than their own when they agonized about giving advice. Most made the predictable choice and agreed to serve. From their own perspective as advisers, the main issues were personal dangers, physical and ethical, that might befall a scholar who puts himself within reach of princely passions, as well as the professional distractions that a busier life will bring. Deeper concerns about intellectual independence and moral responsibility seldom surfaced in the quattrocento literature, but they are at the forefront of More's *Utopia*, though it does not belong to the genre of advice books.[103]

Utopia, written in the third decade after the voyages of Columbus, was one of many early modern fictions set in the frame of a traveller's tale. Its full title says that it is about the *Best State of a Commonwealth [reipublicae statu] and the New Island of Utopia*; the author's purpose was to criticize the *status* of Christian Europe by comparing it to the imaginary Utopian *respublica*. Raphael Hythlodaeus, More's fictional informant who had sailed to the new world with Amerigo Vespucci, reported that the Utopians 'cling above all to mental pleasures. . . . Of these the principal part they hold to arise from the practice of the virtues and the consciousness of a good life.' Since the highest pleasures belong to the mind and the best mental pleasures involve thinking about virtue, virtue seems to be its own cognitive reward—a Stoicized and sublimated hedonism. Utopians cultivate virtue to root out the vices that infest Christendom, especially the chief vice of pride. Reason and natural virtue have made them better morally than Europeans who are Christian in name only, and Utopians are therefore quick to accept the Gospel as soon as they understand it. In some respects, the studious and regimented collectivism of Utopia recalls the medieval monastic ideal, but the sources of More's perfect society, the Stoic–Epicurean

[103] Skinner (1978: i. 213–20).

ethics and the Platonic politics, are squarely in the humanist tradition, and the purpose of his book was to advance the Erasmian project of social and moral change, using irony and polemic to shame Europeans into becoming better Christians. In matters of religion, Utopians are more open-minded than Christians, certainly more tolerant than More in the *Dialogue Concerning Heresies* of 1529, and they practise the relentless educational regimen that Erasmus preached, thus brightening More's darker view of the human condition corrupted by pride and other sins. Utopian society is a triumph of culture over nature, a continuing education programme without end, and Utopian man is perfectible within natural limits. All this makes sense as an extension of prior humanist political theory, but in one crucial case More broke with humanist precedent: he did not accept that the ruling class really possessed the virtues attributed to it or that its actual qualities were those that a Christian should be proud of.[104]

Class and property—social hierarchy and economic inequity —are the two main targets of the reforms implied in the account of Utopia given by Hythlodaeus in Book II of More's work. Self-interest or respect for Gospel teaching would long since have moved Europeans to adopt the Utopian system, he argues,

had not one single monster . . . striven against it—I mean, Pride. Pride measures prosperity not by her own advantages but by others' disadvantages. Pride would not consent to be made even a goddess if no poor wretches were left for her to domineer, . . . if the display of her riches did not . . . intensify their poverty.

Pride feeds the 'conspiracy of the rich' that passes for government in Christian nations, but in Utopia the antidote for pride is

[104] More (1963– : iv. 175 [Surtz trans.]); vi. 2. 439–72); Hexter (1965: 50–5, 59, 116–20); Skinner (1978: i. 255–7, 260–1; 1988: 448–51); Marius (1984: 123–51, 325–50, 386–406). For the Latin and English works in the Yale edn., see More (1963–); see also Chambers (1935); Surtz (1957*a*; 1957*b*); Marc'hadour (1963; 1969); McConica (1965); Skinner (1967); Schoeck (1976); White (1976; 1987); De Pina Martins (1979); Kristeller (1980*a*); Kinney (1981); Fox (1982); Kenny (1983); Logan (1983); Trinkaus (1983: 422–36); Martz (1990).

the principal foundation of their whole structure . . . , their common life and subsistence—without any exchange of money—[which] . . . overthrows all the nobility, magnificence, splendour, and majesty which are, in the estimation of the common people, the true glories and ornaments of the commonwealth.[105]

This appeal to vulgar esteem for pomp and riches is More's (intentionally) facile retort to Hythlodaeus at the end of Book II of *Utopia*, but at the end of Book I, before hearing the description of the island given in the second book, he offers more serious objections when Hythlodaeus claims that 'no happiness can be found in human affairs unless private property is utterly abolished'. More replies that sloth will suffocate industry if there is no 'motive of personal gain'; without laws to protect property, public disorder will destroy respect for government. The burden of the second book is to show in detail how the Utopians avoid the torpor and chaos that More predicts.[106]

Utopians keep nothing private, use no money domestically, trade houses every ten years, make chains and chamber-pots of gold, give their children jewels for toys, and go to extraordinary lengths to avoid war, regarding it as 'an activity fit only for beasts'. Hunting, the other great pastime of the nobility, they treat as 'the meanest part of the butcher's trade', but all men and women, except a few hundred scholars, work at crafts and at farming. Utopia expropriates the expropriators who in Europe waste the labour of those they oppress, leaving no place for 'the rich, especially the masters of estates, who are commonly termed gentlemen and noblemen . . . , [and] their retainers, . . . that whole rabble of good-for-nothing swashbucklers'.[107] Having levelled society, the Utopians build it up on the basis of the family, patriarchal and patrilocal. The eldest male 'rules the household. Wives wait on their husbands,

---

[105] More (1963– : iv. 241–5 [Surtz trans.]); Hexter (1965: 73–80); Skinner (1978: i. 260–1; 1988: 449–51).

[106] More (1963– : iv. 105–7 [Surtz trans.]); Hexter (1965: 34–47, 57, 64–71).

[107] More (1963– : iv. 61–5, 131, 139, 171, 199 [Surtz trans.]); Hexter (1973: 50–7, 193–7); Skinner (1978: i. 255–61).

children on their parents, and generally the younger on their elders.' Beyond the universal obligation to labour, women must cook the food and serve it, wear special dress, and marry at eighteen—four years before men. Women study, become priests, go to war with their husbands, end their marriages by mutual consent, and serve as special judges in other divorce cases. At least abstractly, More's sense of sexual equity may have been in advance of his time, but one feels its animal limits in the passage that justifies the Utopian custom of showing the bride and groom naked to each other before marriage. 'In buying a colt,' says Hythlodaeus, 'persons are so cautious that . . . they will not buy until they have taken off the saddle. . . . Yet in the choice of a wife, . . . they estimate the value of the whole woman from hardly a single handbreadth of her, only the face being visible.'[108]

The subtitle of *Utopia* gives More the title 'citizen and sheriff of . . . London', though he was actually deputy sheriff at the time and had been since 1510. When the book first appeared in Louvain in 1516, for all intents and purposes he was still a free public intellectual, like Erasmus, to whom he had sent a copy before publication. But a year later, when his role in quelling the xenophobic riots of Evil May Day enlarged his fame in London, More accepted Henry VIII's invitation to become a councillor, and by the summer of 1518 he was on the royal payroll. Having entered the king's service, wherein he had no great influence on policy for more than a decade, More sealed his practical response to the 'problem of counsel', whose theory he debates with Hythlodaeus in the first book of *Utopia*. Unlike Erasmus and other humanists, he found the question genuinely perplexing and treated it with seriousness and originality. The philosopher's role as adviser is to speak the truth and offer new ideas, says Hythlodaeus, which is why 'there is no room for philosophy with rulers'. More, conceding that school philosophy's 'new and strange ideas' will be out of place at court, recommends a tactful (*commodus*) and indirect (*obliquus*) line: 'What you cannot turn to good you must make as

---

[108] More (1963– : iv. 137, 187–9 [Surtz trans.]); Hexter (1973: 41–5).

little bad as you can.' Hythlodaeus objects that going mad is
no way to cure lunacy: 'To speak falsehoods ... may be the
part of a philosopher, but it is certainly not for me.' More's
tactic is a blunder as well as a crime. Evil companions will
corrupt the philosopher in politics, and the adviser who dis-
sembles will soon expose himself as a virus in the ruler's will:
'He would be counted a spy ... who gives only faint praise to
evil counsels.' What the prince wants is philosophical absolu-
tion, not advice.[109]

The philosopher may enter politics to ameliorate (with More)
or to annihilate. Or he may abstain from politics in order to
criticize freely (with Erasmus and Hythlodaeus). The first
course is closed to the critic who wants to give original advice
without accommodation. Because the second is dangerous,
few thinkers actually become revolutionaries. These dilemmas
of *theoretical* innovation are the heart of the dialogue of counsel in the first book of *Utopia*.[110] *Practical* innovation in politics
is the core of Machiavelli's counsel in *The Prince*, an advice
book written in 1513, three years before *Utopia*, but unknown
to More because it was published only in 1532. Abrupt political
change was on Machiavelli's mind because his professional
fortunes in Florence rose and fell in the decades around the
start of the sixteenth century when the Medici lost and regained
power several times, quickening the old debate about princely
or republican rule. Despite his long service to the Florentine
republic, and despite his republican sympathies in the *Discourses* of 1514–19, Machiavelli wrote *The Prince* when offering advice to the resurgent Medici seemed expedient to him,
as to other observers. His book, like others of its genre, aims
to show the prince how to win glory and keep it, and like the
others it makes something called 'virtue' (*virtù*) the great means
to that end. Christian moral theology, with its roots in Greek
and Latin terminology, had long since developed its own taxonomy of virtues and vices, an ethical vocabulary that was part
of the common lexicon of early modern Europe. Machiavelli

[109] More (1963– : iv. 1, 99–103 [Surtz trans.]); Hexter (1965: 103–38);
Marius (1984: 188–216).
[110] Hexter (1973: 85–93, 199–201).

debased that language, transforming it more profoundly than
More devalued such terms of praise as 'noble' or 'glorious'.
Machiavelli changed the sense of *virtù*, *stato*, and other words
in ways from which political and moral discourse in the West
has not recovered.[111]

Machiavelli believed that all governments rest on 'good laws
and good arms', but that the former result from the latter,
permitting him to 'leave aside talk of laws and speak about
arms', which he did at great length in *The Prince*, plainly
contradicting the humanist critique of warfare. The main objects of Machiavelli's counsel and the heroes of his book are
new princes, innovators (*innovatori*) in practical politics who
get what they want by 'depending on themselves and knowing
how to use force, . . . whence it happens that all armed prophets win, while the unarmed lose'. Political innovation in
Utopia is prophecy unarmed, the power of the word charged
by biblical example, refined by classical culture, but dampened
by the cynicism of Hythlodaeus and by More's hesitations.
Machiavelli, however, had the memory of Savonarola to convince him that the sword was sharper than the word, that even
Moses would have failed without weapons. Given the material
means of coercion, what allows the person who takes a *prin-
cipato* to 'keep it [*mantenerli*], with more or less difficulty, is
that the one who acquires it is more or less skilful [*virtuoso*]. . . .
This result, that a private person becomes a prince, presup-
poses either skill [*virtù*] or luck [*fortuna*].' No English renderings of *virtù* and *virtuoso* will do the job here, least of all
'virtue' and 'virtuous' with their overtones of Christian piety,
the furthest thing from Machiavelli's mind. In most cases, true
to its Latin roots, *virtù* in *The Prince* names qualities that bring
success in arms; it rarely carries any moral freight. *Virtù* is the
trait that permits innovation in politics, and since everyone
assumed that custom was the ground of legitimacy, what *virtù*
causes is illegitimate because it is unaccustomed. 'Avoid every
novel idea . . . for even if conditions are bettered thereby, the

---

[111] Ridolfi (1963: 145–54); Chabod (1965: 30–46); Hexter (1973: 189–97);
Skinner (1978: i. 117–18, 152–5; 1988: 430–6); above, Ch. 1, n. 44.

very innovation is a stumbling block': this was Erasmus' advice to the prince, and nothing out of the ordinary. Machiavelli understood that a *legitimate* secular order must be customary, but he encouraged the new prince to forget legitimacy and morality, as necessity demands. He devised a theory and a technique of *illegitimate* politics in which *virtù* is the quality that delegitimizes—quite unlike the task of virtue as a common moral category.[112]

One can scarcely exaggerate the violence done by Machiavelli's language and ideas to the discourse of virtues and vices that early modern Christians took for granted. Chapter 15 of *The Prince* dismisses the ruler's need for ordinary personal virtues—mercy, kindness, reverence, loyalty, generosity, and so on—and the next four chapters dispense with liberality, clemency, trustworthiness, and other special princely virtues. The lesson is a brutal one, beginning with the observation that

> the distance is so great between how one *lives* and how one *ought to live* that a person who neglects what *happens* for what *ought to happen* studies his destruction . . . , because, among the many who are not good, one who wants to do good everywhere must be destroyed. Hence, a prince who wants to keep what he has [*mantenere*] must learn how to be not good. . . . For a prince to have all the . . . qualities considered good would surely be most laudable, but, because this cannot be . . . , he must have enough sense to avoid the scandal of those vices that would cost him the state [*lo stato*]. . . .

What Machiavelli meant by *lo stato* was not the modern 'nation' or 'government' or 'people' or any values implied by such words. It was simply what the prince wants to get (*acquistare*) and to keep (*mantenere*), the crude object of political will along with the instruments that serve it. Professor Hexter's account of *lo stato* is classic: it is not 'a matrix of values' of any kind, nor even a moral scheme in which political success is right and failure is wrong. 'It is merely success to succeed, and failure to fail. Right is not might, might is not right; might is might, and that is what *Il Principe* is about.'[113]

---

[112] Machiavelli (1954: 18, 20, 39); Erasmus (1968: 211 [Born trans.]); Hexter (1973: 189–92); Pocock (1975: 156–7, 163–7).
[113] Machiavelli (1954: 50–1); Hexter (1973: 154–6, 167–71, 186–92).

The Prince is frightening to read—or should be—because it is so seductive. The argument is direct, the language clear, the examples apt and compelling. From the first chapters, what Machiavelli writes with such virtuosity is awful to contemplate, as only the text itself can show:

A new prince always needs to harm those he comes to rule.

People should either be pampered or extinguished.

One should never let things get disorderly in order to avoid a war.

There is no sure way to hold cities but to destroy them.

In [Cesare Borgia] . . . there was such ferocity and *virtù*, and he knew so well how people have to be gained or spent.

Cruel acts can be called good practices (if it is right to speak well of evil) when done all at once, out of the need to make oneself secure.

Because it is hard to mix the two together, it is much safer to be feared than loved.

A prudent ruler cannot keep his word, nor should he, when keeping it is not in his interest.

[A prince] must be a great fake and fraud; people are so simple. . . .

Luck is a lady: to keep her down, one must beat her and shove her around.[114]

These are epigrams of terror, theorems of a savage political calculus. Much of the power of Machiavelli's work comes from his mastery of form, but his talent did not stop with the gnomic sentence. He also told stories about ancient Rome and contemporary Europe, the latter often taken from his own professional experience. In Chapter 7, for example, where he recounts his admiration for Cesare Borgia, he tells how the duke used Remirro de Orco, 'a cruel and ready man', giving him total authority to subdue the Romagna and then making an end of him when 'excessive authority' was no longer expedient. Cesare hauled his efficient lieutenant before a kangaroo court, aiming

to show that, if any cruelty had occurred, it came not from him but from the harsh nature of his minister. One morning, when the time was right, he had him cut in two pieces and put in the town square in Cesena, with a piece of wood and a bloody knife beside him. The

[114] Machiavelli (1954: 6, 8, 13, 17, 26, 31, 54, 57, 82).

brutality of this spectacle satisfied the people and at the same time stunned them.

We remember the scene because it is hideous, so simple, so bloody in the morning sun. And we remember Cesare Borgia, the new prince in whom Machiavelli could find 'nothing to blame', making him a model 'for all those who rise to power by luck and with the arms of others'.[115] For a few years, at least, Cesare had followed where *virtù* led him in the eternal race with *fortuna*. His vices and virtues were beside the point, if one accepts Machiavelli's perverse verdict: 'In the actions of all people, especially princes . . . , look to the end. Let the prince prevail, then, and hold his *stato*: his means will always be judged honorable and praised by all.'[116]

The Prince is a quick masterpiece, faster with its grim advice than the longer and kinder *Discourses on the First Ten Books of Livy*, whose slower rhythms suit a loose reflection on an ancient text. If *The Prince* echoes the moral panic of Machiavelli's time and of later ages, the *Discourses* recall Bruni's more confident era and revive the case for civic virtue in a people vigilant for liberty. The *Discourses* lack the excitement and audacity of the earlier work, but novel and disquieting passages are not wanting. Machiavelli meant the stern lessons of *The Prince* for times when civic *virtù* has collapsed and *fortuna* reigns; if some lone soldier of innovation bullies *fortuna* and wins the day, his victory will inhibit civic life because those not frozen by fear of the new prince will scurry for favours and further degrade themselves. Machiavelli despised ordinary human nature because he rarely saw *virtù* in it, but his loathing was not complete. Because he believed it possible for his contemporaries to repeat the civic triumphs of republican Rome as recorded by Sallust and Livy, the *Discourses* propose a frame of political action open to the citizenry as a whole and therefore of a different moral order than the innovations of *The Prince*—but not entirely different.[117]

[115] Ibid. 24–5, 27.
[116] Ibid. 58; Pocock (1975: 156–7); Skinner (1988: 433–4).
[117] Pocock (1975: 156–7, 160–3); Skinner (1988: 435–7).

Machiavelli was sure that *virtù* could prosper only if the (adult, male, native) people had real liberty, so he was willing to sacrifice the ideals of order and harmony that often attracted earlier theorists to more aristocratic arrangements. If, to engender *virtù*, the commonwealth must breed unrest, so be it, and so much the worse for law and order. Laws are needed, to be sure, because people are evil and selfish; only the force of law makes them good. But in the special case of civic goodness —*virtù*—Christian precepts are ruinous: they corrupt and debilitate. Machiavelli did not reach this pertinacious conclusion by doubting the power of religion. On the contrary, so impressed was he by religion as a force in history that he wished to naturalize it as an instrument of politics. Behind the indictment of Christianity in the second book of the *Discourses* are the chapters of the first book that show how the Romans used religion to strengthen their republic. But religion has had the contrary effect on Christendom.

In those ancient times people loved liberty more . . . [because] they were stronger, . . . which, I believe, can be traced to the difference . . . between their religion and ours. Our religion shows us the . . . true way of life, . . . finding the greatest good in humility, lowliness and disdain for human things. . . . Hence, [Christian] bravery . . . [has to do] more with suffering than with doing brave things. Living this way seems to have made the world weak, . . . easy pickings for those bent on crime. . . . The world has turned effeminate, and Heaven has been disarmed . . . [through] the cowardice of people who have interpreted our religion according to laziness [*ozio*] rather than *virtù*.[118]

Perhaps Machiavelli really thought that a true reading of the Gospel would have stirred other Cesare Borgias to enlarge the power of other popes like Alexander VI. Or maybe, having called asceticism and humility 'the true way of life', he meant that the best morals cannot promote the best politics: Christian virtues will never equip the meek to inherit an earth ruled by *virtù*. If so, while early modern readers might have seen the *Discourses* as less vicious than *The Prince*, the gentler work should have given them small comfort in its basic moral dis-

---

[118] Machiavelli (1954: 36–7, 227); Headley (1988); Skinner (1988: 438–40).

position, which rests on the same relation of ends and means: 'never will a judicious intelligence blame anyone for any action out of the ordinary [*straordinaria*] if its purpose is to put a kingdom in order [*ordinare*] or set up a republic.' In this case, the frail Christian economy of virtues and vices can never sustain a politics that attains *virtù*, whether civic or autocratic. Europe's ordinary morality cannot guide the governance of her peoples or constrain the will of her princes. Humanism enabled Machiavelli to learn from antiquity and to find there a great part of what he needed to make himself a capable statesman, a prolific man of letters, and a brilliant political philosopher, but it also helped him open a fatal breach between ethics and politics that we have yet to fill.[119]

[119] Pocock (1975: 176–80).

5

Nature against Authority:
Breaking Away from the Classics

Books of learning and nature

Gabriel Naudé was a librarian, bibliophile, pamphleteer, and a contemporary of Descartes who moved in a circle of sceptical French intellectuals called 'learned libertines'. One target of Naudé's scepticism was superstitious magic. In 1625 he published his best-known book to show that famous people accused of magic were seldom guilty since there was really nothing unnatural to blame them for.[1] Naudé was no philosopher, but he was aware that beliefs about magic and other disputed phenomena were tied to the prevailing Peripatetic system, and he knew how the generations before him had weakened Aristotelianism by certifying such rival claims to philosophical sovereignty as Ficino's resurrected Platonism or the new access to ancient evidence on pre-Socratics, Stoics, and Epicureans. His crusade against magic interested him mainly in natural philosophy, so he noted how 'all those truths known to Aristotle are today rendered greatly suspect and dubious by a swarm of innovators . . . who truly have no other design than to shove aside the great edifice that Aristotle and his interpreters strove to build'. Naudé doubted everything, especially the prudence of originality, so he never let go of Aristotle. Yet he admired the *novatores* who dethroned the Stagirite—Patrizi, Telesio, Bruno, Bacon, Campanella—and he also sensed how the Peripatetics had poisoned their own system by pushing its naturalist implications past the bounds of Christian tolerance. As he witnessed the great intellectual changes of the day, when Descartes cut the cord that tied philosophy to humanism,

[1] Naudé (1625); Rice (1939); Pintard (1943); Spink (1960); Kristeller (1968a; 1979a); Popkin (1979: 87–109).

Naudé stayed loyal to his eclectic erudition.[2] He lived and died a humanist—and a sceptic.

Naudé was heir to a fully developed humanism and a reclassicized philosophy based on doctrines constructed in antiquity, decayed in the Middle Ages, revived in the Renaissance, and now familiar once again to all educated people. One cost of the triumphant humanism that shaped Naudé's education was the damage done to canons of judgement and action as a better-informed Europe witnessed the spectacle of authorities in conflict. A countervailing gain was that ancient ideas recovered and reworked by the humanists proved the case for cultural stability by cementing continuities between ancient and modern Stoicism, Platonism, Epicureanism, and Aristotelianism; in fact, in all cases except Scepticism, lines of tradition ran unbroken from the ancient era through the Middle Ages and into early modern times, even though sometimes they ran thin. In 1600, when Bruno died a martyr to free thought, Naudé was born into a century for which Ficino and Patrizi had already secured the teachings of Plotinus and Proclus, while ancient and medieval Peripatetic doctrine still survived in the writings of Case and Zabarella. None of these renovations, from a newly Platonized theology to a Neo-Stoic morality, could have thrived in early modern Europe without fundamental departures from their Graeco-Roman base—above all because pagan sages had new Christian masters to serve. True to its name, the Renaissance was an age of rebirth, but also a time for reconsideration of beliefs taken for granted in the ancient and medieval periods. Yet from the perspective of our own culture—one that finds meaning in the expression 'post-contemporary'—long tides of continuity seem to have run more strongly through the Renaissance than swift surges of change, all the more reason to admire the mavericks who moved more briskly than the sceptical Naudé to break with revered systems that could no longer contain them.

The Middle Ages, of course, had its own loners, dissidents, and solitary geniuses, many of whom, like Peter Abelard,

---

[2] Naudé (1625: 331); Gouhier (1958).

could not be good models for dissent in our period. At the same time, John Scotus Eriugena, Avicebron, David of Dinant, Roger Bacon, Ramon Lull, John Wyclif, and others found a hearing in the Renaissance for their quarrels with tradition. In at least one case—the nominalist critique of ontology that still ruled Parisian philosophy in the time of Vives and Lefèvre—a powerful medieval menace to authority cannot be separated at all from its early modern expression. The Mallorquin reformer Lull, a contemporary of Aquinas and Scotus, breached the usual intellectual categories but still interested Leibniz and later figures. Lull's mysticism, along with that of the German Meister Eckhart, had an impact on early modern thinkers that lies largely outside the scope of the classical traditions treated in this volume, but his views none the less mingled with the syncretisms of Ficino, Pico, and Steuco to re-emerge in Bruno's wanton speculations. Lull did not write the alchemical works attributed to him, but others provided an alternative, alchemical view of nature entailing sharp departures from the Peripatetic tetrads of elements, qualities, and causes. Alchemy began in late antiquity, developed in the Moslem world, and arrived in Latin Europe to spread alongside Aristotelian natural philosophy from the thirteenth century onward. Alchemical texts circulated abundantly, often attached to such familiar and authoritative names as Aristotle, Aquinas, Albert, or Lull, making it hard even today to tell the genuine from the counterfeit. Early modern thinkers were not as quick as later critics to assume that alchemy and other varieties of 'occultism' (like 'humanism', a nineteenth-century conception) could never be taken seriously by serious philosophers; so they used these alternative views along with traditional materials to construct some of the more venturesome conceptions that the Renaissance produced.

One Renaissance writer discussed above whose ideas overload the usual pigeonholes was Nicholas of Cusa, though he was not so radical as Bruno or Campanella. Cusanus was an unusual Christian, but still a more loyal one than these defectors from Dominican Thomism, who put more faith in a divinized nature than in any conventional God. A volatile blend of animist naturalism with religious temerity made the sometimes fatal difference for a number of thinkers of the late Renaissance, usually called 'philosophers of nature', though they were no more devoted to natural philosophy than Pomponazzi or Zabarella.[3] Unlike these Peripatetics, however, the new philosophers of nature felt that Aristotle's system could no longer regulate honest inquiry into nature. Therefore, they stopped trying to adjust the Aristotelian system and turned their backs on it altogether. Fracastoro, Paracelsus, Cardano, Telesio, Bruno, and the others (in some ways Patrizi belongs with them) get less credit as philosophical revolutionaries than Mersenne, Gassendi, and Descartes, but it is hard to imagine how these later French innovators could have cleared the ground for the scientific revolution without the subversive work of their Italian predecessors. Drastic differences in ontology, epistemology, ethics, and theology distinguish the new philosophy of nature from Peripatetic dogmas still taught in the schools of Naudé's time, while in other respects the philosophers of nature drew on Ficino's fifteenth-century Neoplatonism. Their strong and, in some cases, controlling fascination with occultism connected them with the Ficinian tradition, while their broader aversion to book learning prepared them for conceptions of nature relatively free of the usual Aristotelian strictures.

The universe of most of the philosophers of nature, like that of the Neoplatonists, was an enchanted world of ensouled objects linked together and joined to a higher realm of spirit and absolute being. A universal world-soul pervades all creation and makes all creatures, even rocks and stones, alive and sentient in some degree. Stars and planets are mighty living divinities, so astrological bonds and forces of sympathy unify all things in the lower world under the rule of the higher; microcosm reflects macrocosm as man's lesser world mirrors the greater world of universal nature. Hidden symmetries and illegible signatures of correspondence energize and symbolize

---

[3] Cassirer (1963: 140–52; 1974: i. 208–313); Kristeller (1964a: 91–144); Garin (1965a: 186–220); Ingegno (1988).

a world charged with organic sympathies and antipathies. The natural philosopher's job is to break these codes and uncover their secrets; his tools are experiential as well as magical. He watches nature closely to learn her arcana, and then he manipulates them for practical use. As he reads the book of nature, he foreshadows the Baconian scientist or engineer, but because his book is also a magician's manual he also recalls the magus of Ficino's *Three Books on Life*. Bruno wrote that '"magus" means a *wise* man who has the power to *act*'. Theory and praxis in these new natural philosophies seem progressive enough, but the next generations, who replaced *natural philosophy* with a newer *science*, so thoroughly discredited the idea of a philosophically based occultism that it may be tempting to write off Bruno, Campanella, and the others as woolly-brained enthusiasts.[4]

That it would be wrong to dismiss them so curtly becomes clearer, however, as one explores the physical and metaphysical arguments behind their occultism and their rejection of Peripatetic school philosophy. At times, all tradition and everything classical became the enemy, as they repudiated the humanist culture of erudition that often preferred learned citations to original ideas and seldom stooped to look at a natural object. Instead of learning from books, the philosophers of nature said that they went to school with experience; but the content and utility of their observations varied from the most exotic magical fantasies to more orderly empiricist programmes resembling the experimental science of the seventeenth century. The words 'experiment' and 'experience' were favourites of the philosophers of nature, who used these terms in contexts so wildly different that one scarcely knows where science begins and the seance ends.[5] No matter how misguided their observations, Paracelsus, Telesio, and others saw the book of

[4] Bruno (1962a: iii. 400); Walker (1958a); Védrine (1967: 354); Müller-Jahncke (1985); Copenhaver (1988c); above, n. 2.
[5] Zilsel (1945); Keller (1950); Cassirer (1963: 145–52); Garin (1965a: 187–93); Santillana and Zilsel (1970); Schmitt (1981: ch. 8); Ashworth (1990); Cook (1990: 409–17); Copenhaver (1990: 275–80); Eamon (1990); McMullin (1990: 54–6).

nature as displacing the artificial textual authority of Aristotle in philosophy and Galen in medicine. Having taunted these ancient giants, they armed themselves with a titanic arrogance that exaggerated their own detachment from tradition. They produced more bombast than results. Perhaps their most glaring failure was a view of mathematics that varied from merely ingenious curiosity to misunderstanding to loathing. True, most of the nature philosophers were more curious about mathematics than the typical Peripatetic, yet few of them— Cardano being the great exception—got much further than numerological speculation. Cardano stands with Cusanus and Patrizi as having at least recognized the fundamental value of mathematics. Perhaps their most important beneficiary in the early seventeenth century was Johann Kepler, who also appreciated the mystical aspects of numbers and shapes.

Giordano Bruno's philosophical passions

In 1584 the Cambridge Puritan and Ramist, William Perkins, published a tirade titled *Antidicsonus* against a book *On the Shadow of Reason* issued in the previous year by Alexander Dicson, a Scots disciple of Giordano Bruno, whose own treatise on *The Shadows of Ideas* had appeared in Paris in 1582. More Ramist battles were to come at Cambridge and conflicts much worse would face Bruno, but this particular scuffle started after Bruno had launched a small fad in England, a minor craze for his odd style of mnemonics. Because memory had long been one of the parts of rhetoric, ancient rhetoricians devised arts of memory, of which the most popular were those that used *places* and *images* to help the orator recall the parts of a speech. Consider an oration with an introduction in three sections, a main body of seven sections, and a two-part conclusion: such a speech might come more quickly to mind if pictured mentally as a temple with three steps for the introduction, seven pillars for the body, and two rooms inside for the conclusion. If seven pillars are too plain to jog the memory, one can imagine them not as bare locations but as places decorated with images, preferably images so bizarre as to be unforgettable. Artificial memory schemes of this type were common in medieval and Renaissance rhetoric, but Ramus discarded the art of memory because he had no need of it. His binary taxonomies displayed on the printed page worked better as mnemonic than as logical devices. Whether the schematic Ramist technique attracted Puritan ascetics as a kind of 'inner iconoclasm' is hard to say, but there is no doubt that Perkins preferred it as more natural and more efficient than the system that Dicson learned from Bruno, which Perkins denounced as evil and idolatrous.[6]

Why did Perkins react so harshly to an aid for memory? While he and Dicson exchanged their polemics, Bruno was making a small sensation in London and Oxford, two of many stops on the adventurous journeys that began with his flight from a Dominican convent in Naples in 1576, while not yet thirty years old.[7] Born in Nola near Naples in 1548, he became a friar while in his teens and a doctor of theology in 1575. What conflict of belief drove him from Catholic Italy is unclear, but he had no better luck with the Reformed ministers of Geneva, who jailed him in 1579, after which he spent nearly two years in Toulouse teaching astronomy and natural philosophy. His next stop was Paris in 1581, where the subjects of his public lectures included theology and memory. Bruno's memory system intrigued the French courtiers as a practical yet exotic tool; years earlier, in 1571, the papacy had brought

---

[6] Yates (1966: 2–18, 231–42, 266–86, esp. 235).

[7] The Latin works are in Bruno (1962a; 1957; 1964d; 1980); the Italian in Guzzo and Amerio (1956) and Bruno (1954; 1955; 1958; 1964c; 1973); see also the original documents in Spampanato (1933) and Mercati (1942). For translations of the Italian works by Singer, Greenberg, Michel, Lindsay, Hale, Imerti, Memmo, Jaki and Gosselin, and Lerner, see Greenberg (1950); Singer (1950); and Bruno (1954; 1962b; 1964a; 1964b; 1964e; 1975; 1977). The standard biography is Spampanato (1921), but in English see esp. Singer (1950) and Yates (1964). From the large secondary literature see, besides the introductory material in edns. and translations listed above, Tocco (1889; 1892); Gentile (1925); Corsano (1940); Firpo (1949); Badaloni (1955; 1988); Nelson (1958); Salvestrini (1958); Vasoli (1958a); Guzzo (1960); Kristeller (1964a: 127–44); Yates (1966; 1982–4: i); Védrine (1967); Ingegno (1968; 1978; 1985); Koyré (1968); Papi (1968); Aquilecchia (1971); Atanasijevic (1972); Michel (1973); Ciliberto (1979); Blum (1980); Rossi (1983); Gosselin (1987; 1988); Gatti (1989).

the young friar to Rome to develop powers of memory for which he was famous even then. The appeal of artificial memory to patrons mighty enough to protect him helps explain Bruno's continuing interest in the topic. The art of memory was his passport through a picaresque life that bounced him from one disappointed host to the next who might welcome him on reputation. But memory was more than a meal-ticket for Bruno, as one can see from his first surviving work, *De umbris idearum*, dedicated to Henri III of France.

The overriding and ineffable impulse in all of Bruno's thinking was an unrequited passion for infinite unity—metaphysical, moral, and epistemological. By treating substance as the divine rather than the particular, he did away with Aristotle's conception of the concrete individual substance which persists while its accidental features come and go, turning instead (like Spinoza) to a divine substantial unity as the enduring ground in which perishable particulars sustain their momentary being. Through physics and metaphysics he aimed at an elusive union with the infinite One. Through a cosmic moral reform he wished to overcome the discord and disunity that make mankind vicious. On the level of epistemology, he reached for an unreachable knowledge of the One that transcends phenomenal information about multiple physical objects; the paths toward unity through epistemic diversity are imagination and memory. 'In willing one observes [*speculor*] images [*phantasmata*], and thinking is either to become an image [*phantasia*] or to imagine [*phantasiare*] something', he claimed in his last work on memory, *On the Composition of Images*. 'Hence', he continued, 'we realize that we can complete no action of any kind befitting our nature without certain shapes and figures conceived from sensible objects through the external senses, then gathered and ordered internally.'[8] To understand why memory images seemed so important to Bruno, one must start with his use of the art of Ramon Lull, a medieval departure from the classical technique of places and images and a system

[8] Bruno (1962*a*: ii. 3. 103); Aristotle, *On the Soul* 431[a]1–19; Kristeller (1964*a*: 132–3); Yates (1964: 335; 1966: 298).

powerful enough to have stimulated many printed versions in the sixteenth century before attracting the interest of Descartes and Leibniz in the seventeenth.

Lull, who died in 1316, aimed at much more than memory.[9] He designed his *ars combinatoria* or art of combinations to represent reality directly and to give its user universal and simplified access to all the arts and sciences. By manipulating the letters and figures of the art, one could master nature, convert the heathen, and know God himself. In one sense, the Lullian art is a cosmic notation, a cipher for the structure of the universe and a set of rules for reading it. In the concise form most widespread in Bruno's day, the *Ars brevis*, the art starts with nine letters—*BCDEFGHIK*—and the missing *A* stands for the essence, unity, and perfection of the trinity. The nine letters are interpreted in six ways, as virtues, vices, questions, relations, levels of reality, and, in the absolute sense, as 'dignities' or divine names, causes, and attributes. Thus, God's *bonitas* or 'goodness' is the absolute meaning of *B*; *magnitudo* or 'greatness' of *C*; *duratio* or 'duration' of *D*; and so on. Lull arranged these letters in spatial and geometrical patterns, of which the most important were a table displaying groups of letters in columns and a set of concentric circles divided into nine segments, each containing one of the letters. By turning the circles, the artist could contemplate various combinations of letters, which could also be shown in tabular form. If *B* represents divine 'goodness' absolutely but 'difference' relatively and *E* refers to mankind in the scale of being, then the circular or tabular combination *BBE* points to the distinction between human goodness and divine. In a modest way, the art works as a kind of algorithm for defining questions and setting problems, roughly like the places of Agricola's dialectic; but greater ambitions emerge in other applications, as in the *New Treatise on Astronomy* that Lull wrote in 1297. Here, the letters *ABCD* stand for various zodiacal, planetary, elemen-

[9] Yates (1964: 173–98, 217–29, 237–41, 248–51, 306–7, 368–89; 1982–4: i. 3–125); Lohr (1988: 538–48). On Lull see also Carreras y Artau (1939–43: i. 231–640); Copleston (1960–6: ii. 456–9); Colomer (1961); Pring-Mill (1961); Platzeck (1962–4); Hillgarth (1971); Rossi (1983).

tary, and qualitative patterns, as follows, with variable Mercury combining all four letters and their attributes:

A	Air	Gemini, Libra, Aquarius	Jupiter	Wet and Hot
B	Fire	Aries, Leo, Sagittarius	Mars, Sun	Hot and Dry
C	Earth	Taurus, Virgo, Capricorn	Saturn	Dry and Cold
D	Water	Cancer, Scorpio, Pisces	Venus, Moon	Cold and Wet

If stellar and planetary powers above govern elementary terrestrial objects below, the permutations of *ABCD* signify important cosmological facts, which become even more meaningful when manipulated jointly with the nine letters and the figures of the general art. The relation between these two sets of signs has a basis in reality, because *B* to *K* are divine causes of which *A* to *D* are natural effects. Such patterns arise not only in astronomy but also in theology, medicine, law, and all the arts and sciences. Lull's art was a simple, abstract, compendious route to all learning and a pathway to the mystical contemplation that lay beyond. Since Lull claimed powers so stupendous for his method, one can see why Lullian memory need amount to no more than recalling the Lullian art.[10]

Lull was well known throughout Europe long before Bruno came to England; but even if Bruno had done no more than advocate the *ars combinatoria*, critics like Perkins might well have objected to its theological pretensions and unscriptural origins in the medieval mysticism of John Scotus Eriugena. As usual, however, Bruno went much further. Although Lull's art did not use the places and images of classical memory, Bruno combined images with Lull's letters and figures in a most provocative way in his *De umbris idearum*. As in several of his works, Bruno organized this book around the number thirty. After a short introductory dialogue, *De umbris* continues with thirty obscure paragraphs on 'intentions of shadows' and then thirty more on 'concepts of ideas'. The point seems to be to direct will and mind toward supercelestial ideas that cast shadows in the lower reaches of the cosmos, which is darkest of all here on earth. The person who lifts his mind higher in the

[10] Yates (1966: 173–98; 1982–4: i. 4–32, 46–59, 66–7, 78–83, 87, 98, 104, 110–21).

order of things can dispel the gloom and enlighten his understanding. Access to brighter and loftier realms comes through
thirty sets of five images representing various patterns of stellar
and planetary powers. Bruno made these one hundred and
fifty images deliberately weird, sure to stick in the imagination
like those of classical memory; but at the same time he used
them as talismans, signs of planets and stars like those that
Ficino described in his *Three Books on Life* as capable of
drawing down demonic forces from the skies. Moreover, Bruno
directed that the images be arranged on a memory-wheel
divided, unlike Lull's, into thirty segments marked with
Roman, Greek, and Hebrew letters. This wheel of star signs
or seals (*sigilla*) rests within other concentric circles whose
thirty letters signify groups of objects, qualities, and inventors.
Like Lull's system, Bruno's art of memory was supposed to
unlock the whole universe of knowledge to the artist, thus
disclosing the unity that embraces all diversity, but Bruno also
saw his memory as a source of magical power, a way of
tapping into the hidden circuits revealed by the art.[11] No
wonder that Perkins feared it and favoured the wispy abstractions of Ramist dialectic.

In 1583 Bruno published his most important work on memory, the *Ars reminiscendi*, whose first part briefly describes
thirty images or *sigilla* named 'field', 'sky', 'chain', 'tree',
'woods', and so forth. The eleventh seal is *vexillum* or 'banner',
so called because its users rally to it to 'understand that many
or few, more or fewer have the same reference, replacing
things needing a word or object. Neither Plato, Aristotle and
Diogenes alone will help you, nor the Pyrrhonian, Cynic and
Epicurean alone, but many who are related, alike and propor-
tional.' In place of all the most honoured philosophies Bruno
recommended his own heroic struggle for unity, expressed in
the next section of the *Art of Remembering* as a search for
links among all types of animate and inanimate object marshalled under a single banner. 'All things of nature and in
nature recognize commanders in all things assigned them as

[11] Bruno (1962a: ii. 1. 20, 41); Yates (1964: 192–203; 1966: 199–230).

soldiers,' he reasoned; 'Anaxagoras grasped this best, but Aristotle, father of the sophistic kind, could not manage it; from impossible, logical and fictive distinctions not befitting the truth of things, no wonder he could derive countless others unfit as well.'[12] Although Bruno was a supremely idiosyncratic thinker, this passage reveals his strongest likes and dislikes among ancient philosophers. He found much to admire in Anaxagoras and other pre-Socratics, much to despise in Aristotle, whom he held chiefly liable for the logic-chopping analysis that impedes a properly synthetic view of nature. In the dialogue *On Cause, Principle and One*, the pedant Poliinio is as silly a Peripatetic buffoon as any of Rabelais's characters, but in the same work Bruno also attacked Aristotle's critics, Patrizi and Ramus, because they only exchanged one vacuous verbalism for another. A contemporary whom Bruno praised in *De la causa* was Bernardino Telesio, author of a treatise *On the Nature of Things According to Their Own Principles*, and in the second dialogue of that work he showed why he approved of Telesio's naturalism:

It's easy enough to prepare a doctrine of proof, but proof itself is hard. . . . Our methodists and analysts do a poor job of implementing their organons, principles of methods and arts of arts. . . . But I say that a natural philosopher need not find all causes and principles, but only the physical. . . . Therefore, although [physical causes] can be said to have the first principle and cause as their own . . . , the relation is not always so necessary that knowledge of the one entails knowledge of the other, so one need not treat both in the same single discipline. . . . From knowledge of all dependent things we cannot infer other information about the first principle and cause except by the less effective means of the vestige.[13]

These lines are as good a summary as any of Bruno's dilemma. Like Telesio, he wanted an autonomous philosophy of nature, but he knew that such an inquiry must ultimately seek first principles beyond finite understanding. In the end, he opted

[12] Bruno (1962a: ii. 2. 79–82, 84, 132–3); Yates (1964: 205–9, 271–3; 1966: 243–65).
[13] Guzzo and Amerio (1956: 327–8, 354); Bruno (1962b: 77–8, 98–9; below, pp. 309–14.

for a monism that comprehends the finite and the infinite in a coincidence of opposites derived from Nicholas of Cusa. The writings in which he worked out his ontology and cosmology, never freed of ambiguities and contradictions, are naturally of greater scope than the memory treatises, which none the less form an important part of his ramshackle system. Bruno's arts of memory aimed to illuminate the vestiges of unity in diversity, to light up for the imagination traces of infinity darkly visible in the finite world of human apprehension.

Besides *De la causa*, Bruno wrote five other Italian dialogues in 1584–5; in two of them images are prominent. Fifty poetic emblems whose ancestry runs back to Petrarch's *Trionfi* give the *Heroic Frenzies* their literary structure, and forty-eight images of constellations provide the framework for the *Expulsion of the Triumphant Beast*. These works, along with the *Cabala of the Horse Pegasus*, are usually called Bruno's 'moral' dialogues. All were written and published in England in the same burst of creativity that produced *De la causa* and the two other 'metaphysical' dialogues, *On the Infinite Universe and Worlds* and the *Ash-Wednesday Supper*, both of 1584. Like most of Bruno's surviving works, all of them finished between 1582 and 1591, the six vernacular dialogues appeared in less than serene conditions, and some show the marks of haste more than others. None the less, schoolchildren and literary critics in Italy still read them as monuments of prose and poetry; they were the first major works of philosophy originally written in Italian. Bruno's use of comedy and satire to annihilate the hated pedants, and of myth and allegory to cover his ideological tracks, produced a richer and more unruly language than most philosophers have written. After Plato and Nietzsche, few philosophers in any age can have matched him in comic, poetic, or dramatic talent, which doubtless he would have expressed with less bluster and more elegance had his life been calmer. Besides the Italian dialogues, the memory treatises, and a play, *The Torchbearer*, his works fall into two other groups, both of philosophical interest. Most important are the three long Latin poems with prose accompaniment — actually a single composition — published in Frankfurt in 1591:

On the Triple Minimum; *On the Monad, Number and Figure*; and *On the Innumerables, the Immense and the Infigurable*. This 'Frankfurt trilogy' forms a coherent sequence, but Bruno's remaining Latin works are a miscellany, though several either attack Peripatetic philosophy or attempt a theory of magic.

Before Dicson's bout with Perkins, Bruno had already caused controversy in England, where he lived in London between 1583 and 1585 as a guest of the French ambassador and a member of the Italian *émigré* community. He also knew the friends of the Earl of Leicester and Sir Philip Sidney. It may have been one of that group—perhaps John Florio, an Italian born in England and Montaigne's translator—who brought Bruno to Oxford in the summer of 1583, where he seems to have astounded the dons by defending Copernicus in Italianate Latin and by leaning too heavily on Ficino's theory of astral magic. Referring in the *Cena de le ceneri* to one of his Oxford hosts, Bruno contrasted 'the incivility . . . [of] this swine . . . [to the] patience and humanity of the other, who showed indeed that he was a Neapolitan born, raised under a kinder sky. Let them tell you how they cancelled his public lectures . . . on the immortality of the soul and . . . the fivefold sphere.' Despite the fuss in Oxford, Bruno stayed in England and enjoyed a period of great productivity. After the *Art of Remembering*, the first fruit of these years was the *Cena*, in which Bruno proved less gracious to Fulke Greville and other Englishmen who befriended him than savage to the Oxford doctors, whom he found stupid and uncouth. The main burden of the *Cena* is Bruno's defence of the Copernican system and his account of an infinite universe populated by infinitely many worlds moving in an uncentred, relative space. He did far more than vulgarize the difficult astronomy of the *De revolutionibus*; he was the first to locate a heliocentric system in infinite space, though an infinite universe was by no means his invention. Besides Copernicus, his main inspirations in this regard were Lucretius and Nicholas of Cusa. He took a more refined approach to the same topics in the dialogue *On the Infinite Universe*, which blends Lucretian with Neoplatonic themes. Beginning with the assertion that limited and deceptive senses cannot report reliably on infinite space or countless worlds, he turned to the intellect to test the pros and cons, especially the principles of plenitude and sufficient reason that compel an infinite and omnipotent cause to produce effects of which it is capable. An infinity of particles moves through the universe in all directions to form innumerable suns and planets like our own, habitable by living beings like ourselves.[14]

Having adopted and transformed the astronomy of Copernicus, Bruno pictured the great Polish thinker not only as a revolutionary scientist but also as an intellectual liberator in the broader sense, to whom

we owe our emancipation from various false prejudices—not to say blindness—of the common and vulgar philosophy. Yet he himself did not see far beyond it because, as a student of mathematics rather than nature, he could not penetrate deeply enough to get at the roots of empty and improper principles or completely resolve all the difficulties in his path and so free himself and others from so much empty searching.

Trapped in the maze of mathematics and still caged in a false philosophy, Copernicus had started mankind on the true way, but he could make no more progress himself. Who better than Bruno to take the next steps?

Of the Nolan what shall I say? My place is not to praise him, perhaps, being as close to him as to myself. . . . If Columbus has been glorified in our day as one . . . long ago foretold, . . . what to make of this one who has rediscovered how to scale the sky. . . . He has loosed man's mind and knowledge. . . . He has forded the air, pierced the sky, coursed among the stars, passed the borders of the world and caused the great imaginary wall of spheres to vanish—the first, eighth, ninth, tenth and others added by the tales of useless mathematics or the blind sight of vulgar philosophy. In full view of every sense and reason, he has used the key of careful research to open the cloisters of truth which we have the power to open, and he has stripped nature of her veils and vestures.[15]

---

[14] Guzzo and Amerio (1956: 262–3); Bruno (1977: 186–7); Singer (1950: 26–71, 86–96, 102–15); Yates (1964: 205–11, 235–56); Koyré (1968: 28–57); Michel (1973: 154–268); Dick (1982: 61–9); cf. Westman and McGuire (1977).
[15] Guzzo and Amerio (1956: 196–200); Bruno (1977: 86–90).

From this lurid paean to himself, one can sense how high was Bruno's opinion of Bruno in comparison to such lesser lights as Copernicus and Columbus. No wonder he made so many enemies as he roamed from country to country, changing his outward religion as fast as his coat every time he slipped across another border.

Lucretius and Cusanus had talked about infinity in terms similar to Bruno's, but one was an Epicurean pagan who counted for little in Christian Europe, and the other covered his cosmology with the incense of mysticism. Bruno took method and matter from Cusanus, but not his pious motivations. His search for the undetectable One led not to mystical abnegation but to grandeur of moral effort. Having learned from Cusanus the cruel disproportion between man's finite perceptions and their infinite object, and recalling the Platonic puns on *erôs* and *hêrôs* that led Ficino, Leone Ebreo, and others to their notions of frenzied heroic love as divine malady, Bruno pictured his love-crazed hero in the *Heroic Frenzies* as driven toward a divine quarry that he can never capture. The madman's heroism consists in his persistence, even after realizing that the divine beloved remains cruelly distant from the human lover, who can never see God's light directly, only its dim reflections in nature and soul. It belongs not to theology but to natural philosophy to undertake the furious chase or *discursus* through sense, reason, and mind that will bring humanity as close to the One as it can come. Metaphors for the human condition are Icarus plunging down from the sun, a moth flying up into the flame, and, best of all, the hunter Actaeon: when Actaeon saw Artemis bathing naked, the goddess turned him into a deer, the hunter's prey, to be eaten by his own hounds.

Actaeon signifies the intellect bent on hunting divine wisdom. . . . Made the prey of his own dogs, chased by his own thoughts, he runs and takes a new path, renewed to go on . . . with greater ease . . . and a stronger wind into denser thickets, into the deserts, into the region of things beyond comprehension. Having been a common, ordinary man, he becomes rare and heroic. . . . Then his dogs kill him: for the mad, sensual, blind, and fantastic world his life ends, and he begins to live intellectually, to live the life of gods.

The philosophical hunter's learned ignorance is to stick to a quest that never succeeds; Bruno took this theme from Cusanus, who had written a tract *On Hunting for Wisdom* in 1463. Surveying the soul within and the material cosmos without, mankind sees God's shadows, but never the splendour itself. Even this partial light never comes to the idle, however; the blind must work and wander slowly and deliberately through the wilderness toward the sun. For those of strong mind and will, the hunt culminates when love for God annihilates bodily perception and discursive reason, opening the hunter's inner eyes to a beatific vision that effaces his torments in the peaceful glory of infinity. But, at least for mortals who can only see God's shadows in nature and the soul, beatitude itself is merely a vestige of infinity: vision of the divine is never direct or complete. Like Plotinus, whom he respected, Bruno protected the transcendence of the One, while pushing his naturalist monism past the limits of contradiction.[16]

The *Heroic Frenzies* give a morality to the individual searcher, derived in part from Ficino's views on will and intellect and fed by the larger tradition of Renaissance love treatises. The *Expulsion of the Triumphant Beast* turns to social ethics and religious reform, but in a cosmic setting. Jupiter, king of the gods, is the protagonist of the work, but he is a god grown old and weak with the decay of macrocosm and microcosm, reflected in Bruno's day by the political and religious disorder of Europe. In order to drive the beast of vice from the world, Jupiter begins in the skies with a plan for astrological reform. Heaven and the gods themselves must be purged if mortal lives are to be purified. Jupiter tells the Olympians that 'if we cleanse our dwelling, if we renew our heaven, there will be new constellations and influences, new impressions, new fortunes because the whole depends on this higher world'. From the skies Jupiter ejects forty-eight constellations representing vices—'the Twins of vile familiarity, the Bull that cares for base things, the Ram of thoughtlessness'—in order to replace them with contrary virtues and thus rout the vicious beast.

---

[16] Bruno (1954: 62–73, 204–9, with Michel's introd.); (1964e: 123–6); Guzzo and Amerio (1956: 605–7); Singer (1950: 125–32); Védrine (1967: 43–59, 111–15); Michel (1973: 57–73); Watts (1982: 207–9).

Precedents for cosmic renewal and celestial conflict between virtues and vices were available to Bruno in the Hermetic Corpus, and the *Spaccio* leaves no doubt of his high regard for the *Hermetica*, which he took to be the testament of an ancient Egyptian cult more to his liking than the anthropomorphic worship of Christians, Jews, or Greeks. From the Hermetic *Asclepius* he lifted a long passage that laments the abolition of Egypt's ancient gods and, by implication, the arrival of the new Christian deity who displaced them. Bruno did not approve every aspect of Egyptian idolatry, and he knew their custom of honouring 'live images of beasts', yet he had Jupiter defend this practice because 'animals and plants are living effects of Nature, . . . [which] is none other than God in things. . . . Diverse living things represent diverse divinities. . . . Whence all of God is in all things. . . . Those wise [Egyptians] . . . knew . . . Divinity to be latent in Nature.' Understanding how God lies hidden in things, the Egyptian sages also learned how to manipulate them magically in order to apply heavenly powers, including demonic powers, to earthly purposes.[17]

Magic, pantheism, idolatry, demonolatry, apostasy—just these few outrages from the long list in the *Spaccio* would have been enough to anger the authorities, but there were more besides: Bruno doubted immortality, taught metempsychosis, recommended free-thinking, deserted positive for natural religion, criticized the Bible, defamed the Jews, slandered the Protestants, betrayed the Catholics, and condemned civil governments besides. The strangest and most intense of Bruno's moral homilies is the *Cabala of the Horse Pegasus*, whose full punning title (*Cabala/Cavallo*) also mentions an *Asino*, an ass who sometimes doubles for the noble Pegasus, a winged horse like the soul-steeds in Plato's *Phaedrus*. Once again, themes of

[17] Guzzo and Amerio (1956: 499); Bruno, (1964*b*: 115–16, 235–6 [Imerti trans.]); Anaxagoras fragment B12 (Diels-Kranz); Singer (1950: 116–20); Guthrie (1962–81: ii. 271–88); Yates (1964: 211–34); Védrine (1967: 30–42). Yates's views on the Hermetic element in Bruno have been controversial, esp. among historians of science; see Westman and McGuire (1977); Vickers (1979); Copenhaver (1988*a*; 1990).

learned ignorance and coincident opposites point back to Cusanus in a dialogue that extends some of the motifs of the *Spaccio*. The real fools and asses are ministers who preach conventional religion and pedants who corrupt education, those too blind to see that asses, horses, and philosophers are all vitalized by the same force of divine mind. Souls migrate from one embodied form to another, expressing in one degree or another the spiritual power that enlivens all matter. When he flies up to Parnassus, the ass becomes Pegasus, but one of his earthly incarnations was Aristotle, who was too much an ass to understand the workings of nature.[18] Bruno's crusade against Aristotle was a lifelong affair, and one of its liveliest moments came with the dialogue *On Cause, Principle, and One*, where a critical issue is the central Aristotelian doctrine of matter and form—the hylemorphic theory of substance. Bruno's response to Aristotle on this and other points becomes more intelligible in the context of contemporary efforts to demolish or to abandon the intricate metaphysical architecture sustained over two millennia in the Peripatetic tradition. Before we examine Bruno's assault on Aristotelian physics and metaphysics, something more must be said of the ancient philosophy that he rejected and about other Renaissance philosophers who prepared the way for him.

New philosophies of nature

In Peripatetic natural philosophy, a physical substance is some particular composite of matter and form. Generation or coming-to-be occurs when matter (*hulê*) gains form (*morphê*), passing-away or corruption when form is lost. If a substance passes from one state to another, as from hot to cold, one term of the change may be seen as a form, the other as its negation or privation; what persists is the material substrate. Hence, matter, form, and privation account for the generation and corruption of substances. Matter without form is entirely indeterminate; it

[18] Guzzo and Amerio (1956: 539); Singer (1950: 120–5); Yates (1964: 257–62).

lacks quality and form but has the potency to acquire them. In order to have an identity as some one thing among others, a substance must actually possess distinguishing forms and qualities, said to be educed from the potency of its matter. Some features of a substance—a given colour or weight or shape in an apple, for instance—may not be essential; when they change or disappear, the apple remains the same substance, so they are called accidental forms or qualities. But suppose a human substance loses the feature of rationality. In Aristotelian terms, the person will no longer be human. The individual in question requires rationality in order to count as human; so the human has a substantial form as well as various accidental forms, and that substantial form is rational. Rationality is essential to humanity. But if the form of rationality gives the human substance its being as human, this will be true of all humans, who are members of the same species because they are *rational* animals. Evidently, the substantial or specific form cannot distinguish one human or one apple from others of their species. What makes this apple differ from that one is some definite batch of matter, but matter as a principle of individuation needs forms and qualities; unformed matter, prime matter, is utterly indistinct, so it has no real existence by itself. Only the composite substance, the real apple, actually exists on its own.

Aristotle himself complicated the problem of form when he gave it a leading role in sensation and intellection; these processes occur because disembodied sensible and intelligible forms of the object actually unite with the subject's faculties of mind and sense. How does the form of a substance as *known* differ from the form that *constitutes* the substance? Christian Peripatetics had less trouble with such questions when asked of natural objects—apples and other such things—than when they themselves were involved; the human substance gave more trouble because it had to be immortal. Having defined man's immortal soul as a substantial form and the mortal body as the matter informed by it, they faced such puzzles as the status of the soul after death, before rejoining the resurrected body. A temporarily bodiless form of the body or forms flitting from known to knower were by no means the only chinks in the armour of hylemorphism, but they gave Pomponazzi and others much to worry about. Pomponazzi's approach to the problem caused so much trouble because he took Aristotle's more materialist view of the soul so seriously. More expedient solutions tended to liberate a dematerialized substantial form from the body and to treat it as an autonomous entity. Indeed, by Bruno's time the doctrine of substantial or specific form had become a crux of debate and a focus of explanation in many areas of physics and metaphysics. Physicians, philosophers, theologians, and others depended on hylemorphism as much as we rely on evolution in biology or quantum mechanics in physics, but many of them sensed that the hylemorphic paradigm was crumbling.

Since the high Middle Ages, philosophers had often tried to adapt Peripatetic metaphysics to Christian purposes or to adjust it for various theoretical reasons, but Bruno did more than tinker. In *De la causa* and other works, he dismantled hylemorphism to replace it with a materialist naturalism that preserved certain elements of Aristotle's terminology—the words 'form' and 'matter', for example—but demolished his metaphysics.[19] Bruno's assault on Aristotle was fiercer and showier than other such attacks, but it was part of a larger wave of discontent with a system straining under its own excesses and elaborations after centuries of growth and inbreeding. In the sixteenth century and after, even professed Aristotelians from Pomponazzi to Cremonini undermined Peripatetic defenses by reading the Philosopher in rigorously naturalist terms. Others, armed with new information about Stoics, Epicureans, and pre-Socratics, proposed alternatives to part or all of Peripatetic natural philosophy. Many of these challengers were physicians, like Girolamo Fracastoro, who lived until 1553. Best remembered for the poem that gave syphilis its name, Fracastoro was also dedicated to an empirically based medicine. He studied the problem of contagion, often regarded in his time as an occult force, and treated it as one of a larger class of sympathies and antipathies, which he tried to extract from the

---

[19] Below, n. 28.

realm of magic. Referring to the atomism of Lucretius, he explained sympathy as a mechanical attraction resulting from a flow of particles between objects; the *seminaria* or seed-particles that carry contagion are especially fine and hence able to cover great distances and penetrate the bodies they strike. When he made 'spirit' a part of this same mechanism, Fracastoro had in mind a subtle material substance like the Stoic *pneuma*, not a magical ectoplasm.[20]

Less a philosopher in the modern sense than Fracastoro was Philippus Aureolus Theophrastus Bombastus von Hohenheim, known as Paracelsus. His name itself was a defiance. Born in Switzerland in 1493, he wandered all over Europe until his death in 1541, first apprenticed to his physician father, then studying medicine at Ferrara, and perhaps also learning magic from the monk Trithemius. He bloodied his hands as a military surgeon and earned respect for medical practice in Strasbourg and Basle, where two of his more eminent patients were Erasmus and his humanist publisher Johann Froben. Everywhere he went, Paracelsus shattered conventions and exasperated expectations. Early on, he declared his medical independence by burning the books of Galen and Avicenna. His own writings —a jumble of theology, chemistry, medicine, mysticism, folklore, and plain nonsense—resist brief description. Many of their sources are still hidden in the obscurities of Cabala, German folklore, and local traditions long since lost. He wrote mostly in a German dialect, and his Latin was idiosyncratic, to say the least. Some of the most influential and popular works published under his name are spurious. Later Paracelsian thought, which peaked in the seventeenth century, derived almost entirely from Latin texts and mixed the founder's doctrines with accretions and digests from his followers. The original works abhor all except biblical authority, though like other innovators Paracelsus owed more to tradition than he cared to admit.

He was primarily a medical reformer, but he derived his medical theory from a much more ambitious world-view that

[20] G. Rossi (1893); Pellegrini (1948); Di Leo (1953); P. Rossi (1954); Peruzzi (1980).

encompassed all philosophy. Like other philosophers of nature, he rejected the traditional quaternaries of elements, qualities, and humours, and he replaced them with a triad of first principles called mercury, salt, and sulphur. He described mercury as an active and spiritual force, converted chemically to smoke through combustion; physiologically it fixes the body's fluid content. Salt is passive and corporeal, left as ash after combustion and lending form and solidity to physiological change. Sulphur is an intermediate principle; its chemistry makes things combustible, and its role in physiology is to promote growth. When a piece of wood burns, combustion produces mercurial vapours, sulphurous flames, and salty ash. Like Aristotle's elements in relation to the fire, air, water, and earth of daily experience, the Paracelsian *tria prima* were not the same as ordinary mercury, salt, and sulphur. Their properties were much broader and more powerful. Paracelsian matter-theory was certainly novel in the context of normal natural philosophy, but it can be traced to Moslem alchemical theories of the eighth century. Chemistry was central to the Paracelsian world picture, and Paracelsian medicine was really 'iatrochemistry' or chemical medicine. Paracelsus did not invent iatrochemistry but he promoted it, popularized it, and started it on a vigorous career in the sixteenth and seventeenth centuries. Since health was supposed to depend on a balance of the three principles, Paracelsian medications were chemical combinations of mercury, sulphur, and salt. Besides the three material elements, Paracelsus posited a spiritual 'archeus' which acted as a unifying principle, roughly like the Peripatetic substantial form. Matter, spirit, and soul were fluid rather than discrete properties of reality in a universe where everything was more or less alive. Paracelsus believed in magic, astrology, and personal spiritual beings, but he derived these beliefs as much from personal observation as from the traditions that he wished to abandon.[21]

[21] Sudhoff (1894–9; 1936); Darmstaedter (1931); Sherlock (1948); Goldammer (1953; 1954); Pagel (1958; 1962; 1985; 1986); Debus (1965; 1977; 1978: 1–33, 101–5, 116–41); Dilg-Frank (1981); Webster (1982). The original texts are edited in Paracelsus (1922–33; 1923–73); (1951) groups English translations from the Sudhoff–Matthiessen edn. under various headings.

Another celebrated and rambunctious physician was Girolamo Cardano, who studied medicine at Pavia and Padua to prepare for his doctorate in 1526, after which he practised in Milan before winning his first fame for books on arithmetic and algebra, especially the *Ars Magna* of 1545. Five years later he published his most famous work, *On Subtlety*, a rambling miscellany of natural philosophy which eventually grew to twenty-one books and appeared in many reprints and revisions before and after Cardano's death in 1576. His book *On Variety* of 1557 was a sequel to the successful *De subtilitate*, and his treatises of 1560 *On the One* and *On Nature* extended the anti-Aristotelian implications of that work. About a fifth of Cardano's nearly fifty books deal with philosophical issues, though he is best known today for original work in algebra and probability. Seldom read now but widely cited in its own time and the century following was the *Fifteenth Book of Exoteric Exercises on Subtlety* by Julius Caesar Scaliger, a blast from an admirer of Aristotle bothered by Cardano's prose as well as his originality and sloppiness; Scaliger's title implied that there was enough wrong with *De subtilitate* to have filled fourteen other volumes. At one point, Scaliger thought that his attack had literally killed its victim, but it only helped enlarge his reputation, for better or for worse. *De natura* contains Cardano's strongest critiques of Aristotle, whom he continued to honour, but the first books of *De subtilitate*, which deal with physical principles, present the less pointed material that helped turn his contemporaries against Peripatetic natural philosophy.[22]

De natura confronts Aristotle straightforwardly on a number of topics: privation as an explanation of change, the nature of generation and corruption, the relation of corporeal to incorporeal substance, the existence of prime matter, the number of the elements, and so forth. These challenges are blunted in the

---

[22] Morley (1854); Margolin (1960; 1976a); Corsano (1961b); Ore (1965); Ongaro (1969); Ochman (1974; 1975); Trevisani (1975); Zanier (1975a); Céard (1977); Ingegno (1980); Fierz (1983); Maclean (1984); Bianchi (forthcoming); Kessler (forthcoming).

more expansive and maddeningly disorganized *De subtilitate*.[23] Although he spends the first paragraphs of the book defining 'subtlety', exactly what Cardano had in mind is hard to say. He seems to have meant that problems are subtle if they are extremely obscure and require the finest sense of discrimination to resolve. He certainly succeeded in demonstrating the first point. After an incredibly involved summary of the whole work, he begins with an orthodox account of matter as what persists when form expires, but then, with no bows to a divine creator, he goes on to describe matter as ungenerated and imperishable. Like Aristotle, he makes form a requirement for the actualization of matter, but he also claims that soul is everywhere because all bodies have a source of motion within them. But what he means by soul or *anima* turns out to be quite mechanical. He names three kinds of universal natural motion. One type of motion begins when nature acts to avoid a vacuum in a change which might otherwise leave *too little matter* for a given form; another starts in order to prevent interpenetration of bodies when change might yield *too much matter* for a particular form; the third occurs when heavy things fall and light things rise, but, having experienced the enormous power of the first two causes of motion in the explosive force of artillery, Cardano is ready almost to ignore the third, which was Aristotle's paradigm of all natural sublunar motion. He counts five natural principles—matter, form, soul, place, and motion—and he makes all of them eternal. No apologies to Aristotle. No worries about the creator. Except to suppose that it was largely unconscious, it is hard to account for Cardano's bravado. He was once detained by the Inquisition, but the charges are unknown.

Bernardino Telesio was just as daring but more deliberate and less prolific. Bacon, who criticized his empiricism as incomplete, honoured him as 'the first of the moderns'.[24] Telesio was born in 1509 in the far south of Italy, in the Calabrian

[23] Bk. I of *De subtilitate* is translated in Cardano (1934); Cardano (1962) is a translation of the autobiography. Otherwise, see Cardano (1967) for the collected Latin works.
[24] Bacon (1857–74: iii. 114).

town of Cosenza, to a family powerful in the region. At the age of nine he left for Milan, Rome, and finally Padua, where he began to study Aristotelian philosophy and Galenic medicine around 1530, when debate ran heavy on faults in the scholastic system explored by secular Aristotelians and empiricist physicians. The greatest of the former was Pomponazzi, of the latter Vesalius, who was anatomizing in Padua while Telesio studied there in the 1530s, when important humanist professors were also teaching in the university. Besides Paracelsus and Fracastoro, who published his *De sympathia* in 1546, others who anticipated Telesio in seeking a new basis for natural philosophy included the poet Marcello Palingenio Stellato, whose *Zodiac of Life* of 1535 combined Epicurean with Neoplatonic elements, and Simone Porzio, whose book *On Principles* of 1553 examined physical questions with notable independence of mind. After finishing his degree in 1535, Telesio may have contemplated these developments during a period of withdrawal in a monastery; he sought no university job, but by 1547 his ideas seem to have been in public circulation, and within a few years he was at work on the first version of his treatise *On the Nature of Things According to Their Own Principles*, one of the more incisive titles in Renaissance philosophy and a clear allusion to Lucretius. In 1553 he was back in Cosenza, where he gave much time to the Accademia Cosentina, while travelling frequently to Rome and Naples. Pressed by his followers, he published the original two book version of *De rerum natura* in 1563, having previously tested the soundness of his arguments in conversations with Vincenzo Maggi, a noted Paduan Peripatetic. Another edition followed in 1570; in 1575 Antonio Persio gave public lectures on the Telesian system in Venice, Padua, Bologna, and the south; and in 1586 appeared the definitive expansion to nine books. The author died two years later in Cosenza.[25]

[25] For reprints of the original Latin works see Telesio (1971a; 1971b), with introds. by Vasoli; Telesio (1910–23; 1965–77) are modern edns. and translations of *De rerum natura*. For brief biographies see Vasoli in Telesio (1971a: pp. v–xxi); and Gentile (1968a: 193–207); see also Fiorentino (1872–4); Gentile (1911); Troilo (1914); Van Deusen (1932); Abbagnano (1941: 47–79,

The proem to *De rerum natura* carries a subtitle for the work announcing it as a manifesto for natural philosophy emancipated from Peripatetic rationalism: 'the structure of the world and the nature and magnitude of bodies contained in it are not to be sought from reason, as the ancients did; they must be perceived from sensation and treated as being things themselves.'[26] True to this principle, Telesio laid out the ground-plan of his naturalism in the first two books of his treatise before taking on Aristotle in the third and devoting the rest of the volume to physical, biological, epistemological, and moral implications of his empirical premisses. If Aristotle studies being as such in his metaphysics, his physics deals with being in motion, but physical change (*metabolē*) or motion (*kinêsis*) includes transformations not only of quality, quantity, and place but also of substance; hence metaphysical issues became prominent in Peripatetic physics, as indeed they had been in the first two books of the Philosopher's *Physics*. After Galileo and Descartes, motion became a uniquely physical category, and a leading aim of post-Newtonian science has been to account for all change, even its own changes of mind, in terms of matter in motion. Telesio's pre-Galilean perspective was reversed. To make physics autonomous, he had to extricate it from a natural philosophy in which rational principles of form, matter, privation, and passage from potency to act covered change and motion of all kinds. He began with the crude evidence of his senses, all ultimately reducible to touch, and he asserted but never proved that sensation is nature's truest witness. Taken as a whole, the book is a frontal assault on the foundations of Peripatetic philosophy accompanied by a proposal for replacing Aristotelianism with a system more faithful to nature and experience.

First he noted that the sun is a light and bright body that emits heat, while cold comes from the dark, dense earth. Since heat and cold penetrate bodies, and body is impenetrable, these two active principles must be incorporeal, but to exist

175–290); Soleri (1945); Garin (1961a: 432–50; 1965a: 192–6); Kristeller (1964a: 91–109); Delcorno (1967); Franco (1969); Di Napoli (1973: 311–66).

[26] Telesio (1971a: 1).

they need to act upon bodily mass or passive matter, the third basic principle. In Aristotelian terms, they act like material and efficient causes; Telesio distrusted Aristotle's analysis of causation, and he shied away especially from unseen final and formal causes. Invisible, lifeless, and powerless in itself, matter dilates or contracts as heat or cold affect it; otherwise, it can do nothing but fall, which is not really action but absence of action. The heavens and the sun are the region of heat; cold belongs to earthy matter below. Earth and sun are changeless as such, but other bodies pass in and out of being as heat and cold struggle for possession of material mass. From this Heraclitian conflict arises the world's diversity, which Aristotle tried to explain with privation, matter, and form, but Aristotle's account fails at various key points. One failure was to make nature wasteful, a slumbering storehouse of idle forms waiting to be put to work. If all possible forms are really there waiting in matter's potency, what does it mean to say that any form is generated or corrupted? Rejecting metaphysical principles prior to the natural object because he considered them redundant, Telesio insisted that all the object's features are precisely coextensive and simultaneous with its organic development. One of these features is soul or *anima*, in the case of animals a material *spiritus* that grows from the seed and suffuses the whole body except for the bones. Unlike the Peripatetic soul, this *anima* is not the substantial form of the body. If it were, the body would vanish as soon as the soul leaves in death. The ensouled body is an organic or structural rather than a formal unity, like a ship made of many parts all sailing to the same port. One such part is the soul, which the body needs for movement and perception, but not for simple physical integrity.

Human animals like all others require a spiritual soul, but this material faculty cannot explain man's immortality or all his moral and religious instincts, so to account for these data of faith Telesio posited another, immaterial soul, infused by God and left outside the bounds of nature. This implanted soul needs its spiritual counterpart not only to perceive but also to reason. Spirit perceives objects by contact that alters it physically; in effect, perception occurs when spirit feels itself expanded or contracted by heat or cold. Aristotle had claimed that the soul becomes the forms that it perceives, but to avoid the absurdity of formal fire lit in the mind when one sees a flame, Telesio made perception a process of physical contact rather than ontological change; heat simply warms and enlarges the spirit. Yet this transaction is something more than a mechanical impression. The antipathy between cold and heat shows that even these simplest elements sense the hostility between them. When cold reacts against heat's movement toward some bit of matter, response to the aggressive motion requires a perceptive act which is not motion itself. Moreover, the physical apparatus of sensation includes not just discrete perceptions but also their comparison and organization into concepts and patterns of judgement and recollection, all within the ambit of the spiritual soul. Likewise, there is an appetite whose drives are entirely material, directed toward conserving the physical organism and maintaining the spirit in a pleasurably expansive state of warmth and motion. Parallel to sensation and appetite, an immaterial will seeks a divine end, and a rational soul contemplates its immortal destiny. Choices between the objects of these twin faculties give rise to free will. At the same time, however, Telesio proposes to naturalize even the moral basis of human action. Conservation of the spirit in a pleasant and secure state is itself a moral end, whose highest form consists in distinguishing ephemeral from durable pains and pleasures. The philosopher of nature provides a materially grounded ethics suited to the spiritual soul, leaving it to the theologian to deal with the higher immaterial purposes of the rational soul.[27] Telesio left an orderly, coherent system that fails on the crude side of simplicity; its epistemology is untested and its empiricism limited to gross and undisciplined observation. Despite his protestations, Telesio was actually less of an empiricist than the Aristotle of the zoological works, and he seems to have come no closer than such Peri-

---

[27] Abbagnano (1941: 47–79); Kristeller (1964a: 98–105); Gentile (1968a: 214–31); Vasoli in Telesio (1971a: pp. xiv–xx).

patetic contemporaries as Zabarella to a systematic experimental programme. Neither he nor Zabarella had any conception of the scientific power of mathematics. From a modern point of view, however, it stands to Telesio's credit that he was never charmed by occultism, unlike other philosophers of nature. His sense of empirical science, which included progressive ideas on space, vacuum, and other physical topics, grew out of a disenchanted world-view remarkable for its hard-headed clarity.

Bruno's natural philosophy had different virtues and defects: its extraordinary subtlety often destroys itself in the wildest inconsistency, in swings from monism to pluralism, from unitary substance to atomic discontinuity, from disdain for finite bodies to exaltation of material infinity. Bruno was in his early forties when prison closed his career in 1591. Even during the previous productive decade, his escapades in northern Europe ending in return to Venice and betrayal to the Inquisition can scarcely have enabled him to take a long view of his work, to eliminate contradictions and settle on a cleaner presentation of his thought. Recklessness was so much in Bruno's character that one hesitates to suggest that a 'mature' system was ever in the cards for him; if his achievement was immature, it was also precocious and rich, like that of Shelley or Nietzsche. If one can speak of a 'romantic temperament', Bruno surely had it. Had he mellowed his conduct and softened his tongue, he might not have gone to the stake in 1600, though before he died he attempted to conciliate his inquisitors, who would have been satisfied only with submission, while he kept debating. He recanted and then withdrew his recantation—of what we do not know because the most important records were destroyed. The clerics who jailed him for nine years and then murdered him were surely right to think Bruno a heretic; their worst fears seem to have focused on religious beliefs, to which he was indifferent (when indifference was not an option), rather than the liberty of philosophizing that was his grand and fatal passion. In fact, the final change of heart that led to his grisly execution may have occurred when philosophical issues came to the fore. One cannot say. What horrific credo had he transgressed to make his judges dispense with the usual grotesque mercy of garrotting before they lit the tinder? Bruno burned for philosophy; he was killed for moral, physical, and metaphysical views that terrified and angered the authorities. While pondering our irritations with his changes on such questions, it will be well to recall the price he paid to the hobgoblin of little minds and the demon of clear convictions.

Bruno was a great soul, though it may not have seemed so in 1584 when he first protested at length against Aristotelian physics and metaphysics in *De la causa*. In general, the position of this dialogue is monist, like that of other works that deal with the topic of being, while those on memory and knowledge often preserve the pluralist segregation of things from ideas. The words 'form' and 'matter' survive Bruno's savaging of hylemorphism, but not as independent principles of being. Unlike Aristotle, whose theory of substance was about concrete individuals, Bruno did not care about individual objects. He saw the particular forms that distinguish one thing from another as ripples in the calm sea of being, mere modes or accidents of universal matter. Nature thrives and breeds transitory forms out of living matter through her own internal force of soul. The single universal form is the world-soul that drives things from within as their principle. Causes that act externally are superficial; a deeper dynamism belongs to principles that move inside. Matter and form unite in the infinite substance that comprehends all. Infinite unitary substance is the opposite of diversity for Bruno and therefore an inversion of Peripatetic substantial form, whose job is to make the object the kind of thing it is. Individual souls in Bruno's system cannot be discrete specific forms because soul is really one; what enlivens a human and a fly are fragments of the same world-soul, which is like a light reflected in a shattered mirror whose splinters are the souls of particular beings. Ultimately, Bruno had little work for form to do, but he gave matter a more dignified role than Christian Peripatetics usually allowed it. Forms come and go as matter endures, ensouled, alive, and divine. Matter is both corporeal and incorporeal, but its bodily manifestations are no more than contractions of a primal matter unlimited by corporeal division. What harm to call such matter divine? God is in things; divinity and the infinite living cosmos are the same, except to timorous theologians who think that abasing nature glorifies God. Albertus, Aquinas, and other eminent scholastics called Avicebron (Ibn Gabirol) and David of Dinant pantheists and materialists because their matter theory infringed the divine prerogative of incorporeality; but Bruno found these thinkers good company.[28]

Like Plotinus, Bruno made matter absolutely indeterminate, but he took this non-feature of matter as proof of its richness. The One is infinite, and so is its material substrate, which is also stable, unitary, eternal, and uncreated; God and the world are the same, so they must be coeval. The unity and stability of being are guaranteed at both extremes of quantity by the coincidence of maximum and minimum. The atomic minimum is a real concrete thing, not a mathematical abstraction. In fact, one of Bruno's flaws was his attitude toward mathematics, which ranged from apathy to animosity with occasional pauses in which he devised a dilettante numerology. Despite his wish to destroy Aristotle's authority in natural philosophy, Bruno kept to a physics at least as qualitative as the Stagirite's. None the less, the minimum yields no experience of quality, so its features must be inferred rationally, by reasons opposed to Peripatetic dogma. In his closed world Aristotle allowed matter to be potentially divisible without limit, but the atoms in Bruno's infinite universe are well-defined minima because they have a least size; they are tiny spheres, indivisible, impenetrable, and homogeneous. Only their arrangement in various structures produces material variety. Some minima—the smallest possible cat, for example—may be organic or structural rather than atomic wholes, and hence corruptible. But an atom is immutable because it is a simple unity, while larger objects made of atoms are transitory aggregates. The atomism of Bruno's earlier works calls on an ordering mind to regulate the shifting swarms of particles, but in the later Latin poem

[28] Singer (1950: 96–101); Guzzo (1960: 69–93); Védrine (1967: 139–46, 269–97); Michel (1973: 126–32); Blum (1980: 57–75).

On the Triple Minimum, the atom itself becomes a soul, defined either 'privatively' as the smallest part of the continuum (like a letter of the alphabet in an infinite library) or 'negatively' as escaping all limit and definition. The continuum of ordinary matter disaggregates into privative atoms, but infinite soul has no breaks or boundaries; minimal and maximal souls must coincide. Without the world-soul to vitalize it, matter and its atoms would be nothing. Even the negative minimum or monad differs from the Leibnizian entity of the same name, which is created, perceptive, and radically alone—'windowless', in fact —while Bruno's uncreated and insentient monads need the splendour of soul to activate them. Soul's light shines from within, however; no external cause forms the atoms into the shapes that make up the visible world. 'In everything is a share of everything', said Anaxagoras, and Bruno added that everything is God.[29]

Bruno's statue stands in Rome in the Field of Flowers, on the spot where he was burned. Eventually, he became a hero to those who saw him as a martyr for free science and philosophy in their fight against ideological repression; but another view of Bruno hails him chiefly as a progressive in morals and religion, a magical reformer who wanted to save Europe from a decadent Christianity by reviving the Hermetic cult of ancient Egypt. Fortunately, there was enough in Bruno's great soul to please all his friends and annoy all his enemies: the pantheist, the materialist, the libertine free-thinker, and philosophical rogue; the magus, the Lullist, the memory wizard; the atomist, the Copernican, the proponent of infinite worlds, and the advocate of spacious liberty in philosophy. Tommaso Campanella was his immediate heir, another renegade Dominican whom the church imprisoned two years before Bruno died and kept confined for twenty-six more. Born in 1568 in Calabria, Telesio's region, Campanella considered himself a good Catholic, but he was probably a worse danger to the establishment than Bruno, for he had messianic fantasies that incited

[29] Singer (1950: 71–9, 86–92); Guzzo (1960: 95–109); Védrine (1967: 61–7, 127–57, 261–5, 288–97, 323–44); Michel (1973: 132–49, 242–5); above, n. 17.

zany insurrectionist plots which might have done material damage.[30] Having recouped some of its losses after the Reformation, the post-Tridentine church was not amused when the author of the *Monarchy of the Messiah* planned to make the papacy the centre of secular as well as spiritual world government. Today, Campanella's best-remembered book is the *City of the Sun*, a saner utopian design for social reform that gained an immense readership in frequent translations into many languages.

Campanella's first surviving work, *Philosophy Demonstrated by the Senses*, is an immense anti-Peripatetic polemic in defence of Telesio, published in 1591 against a Peripatetic who had attacked the great Calabrian's treatise *On the Nature of Things*. Campanella tried unsuccessfully to meet Telesio before he died, and he chose to build a new philosophy on his countryman's naïve empiricism rather than devise yet another variation on the airy constructs of the Aristotelians. For his independent thinking he was accused of heresy and confined to his convent, the first of many long spells of detention. From the tone and content of his book, one can see why the Thomist Dominicans feared that they had hatched a monster:

> The top Peripatetics, what empty-headed nitwits . . . ! Prime matter is supposed to be nothing really and privation nothing, and yet form gets drawn from the potency of prime matter, which is nothing and does not exist. . . . How great is the ignorance of these people: they want to act like gods, not baulking at producing beings from non-beings, making things out of illusions to trick people.

Campanella denied hylemorphism and replaced it with his own

---

[30] There is no comprehensive edn. of Campanella's works, and few have been translated into English; see Campanella (1638; 1854; 1925; 1927; 1939; 1949– ; 1957; 1960; 1962; 1974; 1975). The standard biography is Amabile (1882; 1887); from the large secondary literature see esp. Blanchet (1920); Firpo (1940; 1947); Di Napoli (1947; 1973: 427–968); Walker (1958a: 203–36); Corsano (1961a); Badaloni (1965); Femiano (1965; 1968; 1969; 1973); Franco (1969); *Tommaso Campanella nel IV centenario* (1969); *Tommaso Campanella . . . Miscellanea* (1969); Amerio (1972); Bock (1974); Gadol (1976); Headley (1988; 1990a; 1990b). Part of what follows is a modified version of the section on Campanella in my chapter on occultism in the forthcoming *Cambridge History of Seventeenth-Century Philosophy*.

doctrine, sometimes obscured by the old terminology in which he expressed it. The ideas that he rejected were the core of Peripatetic philosophy: that substantial form is a principle of being superior to matter; that form is educed from the potency of matter; that soul is the form of the body; and that the mind knows by abstracting forms from objects. Above all, Campanella insisted that form was known directly through the senses. The Peripatetics had pried form away from sensation, so Campanella anchored it to body. Matter is simply bodily mass, the body or matter of common experience needing no abstract forms to make it real. 'It would be wrong', he argued, 'to say that matter is bodily because of form. . . . Body is body in its own right and . . . the same . . . as matter, quantity, substrate and bodily mass.' We draw our first distinctions among objects from their shape, which we also call 'form', and this leads us by analogy to the concept of internal form. But internal form is a mode or quality of the object, not a being in its own right. Having dispensed with substantial form, Campanella replaced it with Telesio's heat and cold, which cause the particles in a body to take on different arrangements or 'temperaments'. He equated form with temperament and described temperament as the structure of matter heated or cooled. This novel approach first appears in book two of *Philosophia sensibus demonstrata*, where Campanella writes that

each thing has by nature a consimilar constitutive heat . . . consimilar, I mean, to the heat of a particular star . . . [so that] each thing in the universe can have its own star . . . corresponding to its constitutive heat and leading to procreation and growth, as Hermes, Enoch and Mercurius said . . . , [who] saw such effects and, not knowing how to investigate their causes, attributed them to occult influences and the souls of the stars.

In other words, although the young Campanella believed in astrological causation, he did not believe that celestial causes were *occult*. In effect, he proposed a physical theory of *manifest* forces, heat and cold, to replace the traditional doctrine of occult powers which had long been tied to the hylemorphic metaphysics that he also rejected.[31]

Unlike Telesio, however, who did his best to liberate physics from metaphysics, Campanella was not unfriendly to metaphysics as such. He wanted to change metaphysics, not destroy it. Although his *Eighteen Books of Metaphysics* appeared only in 1638, the year before he died, Campanella had shown interest in writing a metaphysics by 1590 and had produced a version of it by 1602–3. In the published work, he criticized Telesio for attributing too much to the purely natural agency of heat and cold in forming natural bodies, suggesting that these physical powers could act only as instruments of a diviner cause whose various levels he identified as God, the 'primalities', their 'influences', and the world-soul. The distinctive ingredients of Campanella's new metaphysics began to get broad public exposure in the brief *Compendium of Nature* of 1617 and in the 1620 edition of his book *On the Sense in Things and on Magic*. The subtitle of this ebullient volume proclaims its subject as 'occult philosophy, showing the cosmos to be a living, conscious statue of god' and describes the world's 'parts and particles [as] having sensation ... enough for their conservation'. Most of Campanella's arguments for pansensism remain within the limits of Telesio's physical programme. Since all natural action results from the contrariety of heat and cold, a hot object must somehow be aware that cold is its enemy, otherwise the natural impulse of each active force to inform matter would go uncontested; hostilities would cease, and generation and corruption would end. When Campanella claims that the spirits diffused through nature laugh and weep, however, one may read him simply as expressing a physical antinomy—the common fact of dilation and constriction—poetically. He crossed the line between physics and metaphysics only when he began to describe his complex scheme for God as creator and sustainer of nature:

God is more within things than the forms themselves, ... impressing

---

[31] Campanella (1638: 134–9; 1925: 94; 1939: 232; 1974: 63–8, 227–8, 234, 311, 447).

in them the power not only to reach an end but to know how to reach it. . . . All sense is participant in the first wisdom, . . . [and] every form is participant in God. And because god is most powerful, wise, and loving, . . . all beings are composed of Power, Wisdom, and Love, and every being exists because it *can* be, *knows how* to be, and *loves* to be, and when it lacks the power or knowledge or love of being, it dies or changes.

By placing the trinitarian God of power, wisdom, and love — the 'divine Monotriad' of the three primalities — within all things as the ground of their being, Campanella added a metaphysical dimension, an immaterial, god-begotten wisdom, to the physical sense that Telesio had found in nature. Thus, although he admitted in *De sensu* that magic is an 'occult wisdom' and called certain forces and phenomena in nature 'occult', Campanella had not reverted to the hylemorphic occultism rejected in his earlier work, though by this time he had worked out an alternative metaphysics of magic.[32]

The doctrine of primalities and influences runs throughout Campanella's mature work but appears most clearly in the *Metaphysics*, which also describes the role of these Neoplatonic triads in occult causation. Having decided that Telesio's heat and cold needed divine assistance, Campanella described God as directing natural events not by external impulse, as an archer shoots an arrow, but by an internal sense; otherwise things would be *impelled towards* their ends when God intends that they should *seek* them.

In all things God sowed great influences — Necessity, Fate, and Harmony — as participants in the primalities — Power, Sense, and Love. . . . God uses their actions regulated by the assistance of angels in forming [things] so that they correspond to the divine ideas, no differently than a blacksmith, using fire, iron, anvil, hammer . . . and assistants to hammer and carry, adjusts [the material] to his idea and then forms it into swords, mattocks, stoves, and clocks.

Necessity, Fate and Harmony act metaphysically in physical nature. Taken abstractly, these three great 'influences' seem to correspond to the distinct properties of objects; to the concur-

[32] Campanella (1638: 141; 1925: pp. xxxi, 9, 19–20, 131–3, 221, 254).

rent relations of those properties; and to their functional consequences. They proceed from the primalities, which reflect the triune God, whose ideas they transmit to objects with the aid of angels. God, primalities, influences, ideas, and angels are all metaphysical agents in a process that terminates in a natural object whose form—the product of heat and cold acting as physical instruments of those metaphysical agents—is no less a material structure in Campanella's *Metaphysics* than it was in his youthful Telesian manifesto. However, Campanella's analysis of causation in the *Metaphysics* seems, at first glance, to admit occult activity excluded in the *Philosophia sensibus demonstrata*, where an occult quality is merely a mistake made by astrologers who misunderstand the physical power of heat.[33]

Writing in 1607 to a correspondent who compared his philosophical accomplishments to Giovanni Pico's, Campanella replied that Pico was 'too lofty' a rival for him. 'His philosophy went more above the words of others than into nature', he wrote, 'from which he learned almost nothing, and he condemned the astrologers because he did not look at their experiences. When I was nineteen I condemned them too, but later I saw that within great foolishness they harboured a very lofty wisdom.' In fact, even Campanella's youthful critique of astrology in *Philosophia sensibus demonstrata* concedes much to the stars and planets within the limits of physical action, and his later work makes astral causation compatible with the metaphysics of the primalities. At least two motives lay behind Campanella's growing passion for astrology: first, he found evidence in solar astrology for his messianic and prophetic politics; second, as he once told Galileo, his methodological commitment to an observational natural philosophy constantly convinced him of the truth of astrology. If it seems that even a little empiricism ought to have led Campanella away from astrology and magic, then one should recall his early association with Giambattista Della Porta, around the time when the latter's *Natural Magic* was republished in 1589. Cassirer once described Della Porta's catalogue of unkempt observations as

---

[33] Campanella (1638: 138–41, 176–7).

leading 'not to the refutation but to codification of magic'. Because three decades in prison gave him little chance to see the world at first hand, Campanella was in Della Porta's debt for vicarious experience. But he criticized Della Porta's empiricism because it worked 'only to collect facts without finding their causes'. Actually, it was Della Porta's failure to find a 'reason for the sympathy and antipathy in things' that decided Campanella to write *De sensu*. In this work and elsewhere, he felt he had achieved both empirical proof and theoretical understanding of magic and astrology, devoting to the latter not only a separate treatise, *Seven Books on Astrology*, but also considerable attention in his other major works. His confidence in astrological power was so firm that, after many years in prison, he risked reputation and safety by helping Pope Urban VIII to work astrological spells against the doom forecast for him in 1626, and later he tried to forestall his own death in the same way.[34]

Campanella's philosophy is not easy to digest. His work is forbidding in its size alone, not to mention its complexity and its uneven development in a career that kept his books out of circulation for long periods. During part of his imprisonment he enjoyed some freedoms, including access to books, visitors, even students, but at other times his jailers were brutally repressive. The *Philosophia sensibus demonstrata* was never reprinted in his lifetime after the first edition of 1591. The *Metaphysics* appeared only a year before his death. The *Theology* and the *Great Epilogue* were first published in this century. The *Astrology* saw several editions, pirated and authorized, after 1629, and the best-known of his works on magic, the *De sensu*, came out in Frankfurt in 1620, then appeared later in Paris in 1636 and again in 1637. In effect, Campanella became an active citizen of the republic of letters during two periods of frequent publication. Between 1617 and 1623 his books appeared in Frankfurt, where followers saw him as a prophet of religious reform. But from 1629 to 1638 it

[34] Campanella (1925: 221–2; 1927: 134, 177); Blanchet (1920: 201–6); Walker (1958a: 205–12); Cassirer (1963: 152).

was French 'Campanellists' who championed his cause. Who were his backers among French intellectuals in the age of Descartes, Gassendi, and Mersenne; what did they really think of him; why did they think about him at all? For one thing, Campanella had shown good taste and good fortune in his choice of enemies: he disliked the right ancients, and the right moderns disliked him. Gabriel Naudé put him among 'the swarm of innovators' who besieged the Peripatetic fortress.[35] Campanella's assault on Peripatetic dogma won him the enmity of the same ecclesiastical establishment that harassed Galileo, thereby gaining him the sympathy that the bolder French *savants* lavished on the great scientist. If some of them saw the flames that consumed Bruno casting a morbid light on Campanella, for others it was the healing shadow of Galileo's tragedy that saved his reputation, especially when his audacious *Apology for Galileo* became known after 1622. The victim and the critic—each was an effective persona for Campanella.

Campanella's *De sensu* was a fashionable book, enough on the lips of the learned to have interested the young Descartes around 1623, but to some of the Christian faithful it was also dangerous. When Father Marin Mersenne sent his first major work to press in 1623—the *Questions on Genesis*—the priest felt such horror at the pansensist *De sensu* that he wanted it burned, more than an academic discourtesy after Giulio Cesare Vanini's execution in Toulouse only four years earlier. But before publication was complete, Mersenne learned of the *Apology for Galileo*, which gave him cause to make kinder if still cautious mention of Campanella's ideas on the plurality of worlds in later additions to his Genesis commentary. He also opened a correspondence with Campanella and offered in 1624 to arrange for publication of the *Metaphysics*. Even so, the kindly Mersenne's attitude toward the irreverent Dominican remained on the whole quite hostile in his early works, where Mersenne linked Campanella with Bruno, Vanini, and other heretics. Mersenne had not yet worked out a philosophical position to replace the Aristotelianism that he saw collapsing

[35] Above, n. 2.

around him. He distrusted Campanella and other anti-Peripatetics not only because their ideas—especially the world soul so prominent in *De sensu*—threatened his faith but also because he found them credulous. They broke Montaigne's rule that one must establish the fact of an alleged wonder before worrying about its cause. Perhaps Mersenne feared that someone like Campanella would stabilize occultism just when he and his friends were ending its long career as a serious subject of learned discourse.[36]

Jacques Gaffarel, a peripheral member of the circle of learned libertines who corresponded with Mersenne and investigated the elder Pico's Cabala, began to see Campanella in 1628, around the time when he was working astrological magic with the Pope. His visits helped make Campanella (like Galileo) an obligatory stop on the Italian tours of ambitious young Frenchmen. Gaffarel quizzed him about the magical powers that foiled the tortures of his inquisitors. He also let him know about Father Mersenne's unkind suggestion that his book deserved burning. Before Gaffarel's visit, Campanella had probably not seen the Genesis commentary, but from then on he was edgy about Mersenne, who in the mean time had tempered his opposition to Campanella and often asked about him. By 1632, Gassendi and other French intellectuals were in touch with Campanella, and he received visits from Naudé, whom he sent on important publishing errands. These people who became Campanella's cheering section in France were instigators of the scientific revolution and sceptical critics of superstition and dogmatism. It was probably Naudé, scourge of the Rosicrucians and author of the *Apology for All the Great Persons Who Have Been Falsely Suspected of Magic*, whose liking for Campanella gave him this new access to Mersenne's prestigious circle. Jailed again in 1633, released, then cornered again by the Spanish in 1634, Campanella found asylum with the French ambassador in Rome and, on the pope's advice, fled to France in the autumn of that year. In December he arrived in Paris

---

[36] Mersenne (1623: 130, 937–46, 1164); Montaigne (1965: 785); on Mersenne see Lenoble (1971); Dear (1988).

disguised in the habit of Mersenne's own order. Mersenne learned that Campanella was still angry with him, but he hoped for reconciliation and looked forward to a meeting. All went well until some time in the new year, when Campanella was overheard making negative comments on Gassendi's Epicureanism. Finally, he and Mersenne met several times, but their encounters ended Campanella's moment in the sun of the French mind. Mersenne blanched at Campanella's arrogant dismissal of French intellectual achievement, noting that he 'treated him for what he was worth' when Campanella recommended the astrology that Mersenne despised. Granting Campanella 'a good memory and a fertile imagination', he concluded that 'he will teach us nothing in the sciences' even if he was one of Italy's 'two great men'.[37]

Although Louis XIII had received Campanella at court in February, 1635, within little more than a year he was complaining to his new friends about their slowness to comment on the 1636 edition of *De sensu*. Fervent Campanellists of two years before were not answering Campanella's letters. None the less, the 1637 edition of *De sensu*, augmented by a *Defence*, bore a dedication to Cardinal Richelieu, who arranged for Campanella to cast the horoscope of the Dauphin born on 5 September 1638. As prelude to the reign of the Sun King, the *Horoscopus serenissimi Delphini* made an odd coda to the career of the author of *The City of the Sun*. Campanella's warm reception by king and cardinal did nothing to thaw the hearts of the *savants* who had written him off. His death in 1639 (fated, so he thought, by an eclipse that came a few days later) passed unnoticed in Mersenne's correspondence, but on the last day of that year Mersenne issued another verdict: 'he made no observations, contenting himself with speculation and often fooling himself for want of experience.' A true if incomplete judgement, and certainly less categorical than what Descartes had said to Mersenne in the previous year, breaking his silence on Campanella for the second time. Descartes had admitted to Huygens in 1638 that he remembered reading *De*

[37] Mersenne (1933–88: v. 201, 209, 214).

sensu and other works by Campanella fifteen years earlier, adding that he saw 'so little solidity' in them that he could not recall them and (curiously for such a pioneer) that he found intellectual loners like Campanella more culpable in their mistakes 'than those who fail only in company by following the tracks of many others'. Eight months later, when Mersenne mentioned the newly published *Metaphysics* to Descartes, the great philosopher's reply was even chillier: 'What I have seen previously of Campanella allows me to hope for nothing good from his book. . . . I have no wish to see it.'[38]

Thus was Campanella banished from the history of modern philosophy by its greatest founder. For his own purposes, Descartes may have been right to ignore Campanella, as he dropped almost all the baggage of Renaissance erudition. But the historian can take a longer view. In the larger sense, Campanella's challenge to Aristotle and his promotion of an empiricist naturalism were part of a movement in Renaissance natural philosophy that began with Achillini, Nifo, and Pomponazzi, continued with Cardano, Telesio, and Bruno and bore its richest fruits in the work of Galileo, Mersenne, Gassendi, and Descartes himself. In a narrower sense, Campanella was especially effective in removing the traditional philosophical underpinnings from the branch of pre-Cartesian natural philosophy that interested him most of all—natural magic. More than any of the other *novatores*, including even Bruno, Campanella offered a systematic critique of hylemorphic metaphysics in the special case of natural magic; but, although he tried to substitute a new metaphysics of magic for the old one that he destroyed, the anti-Peripatetic innovators who listened attentively to his polemic against occult qualities and substantial forms would not pay equal respect to the metaphysics of the primalities. Campanella failed where Mersenne had most cause to fear him—in his attempt to tie natural magic to a complete and systematic philosophy. But, despite himself, he succeeded where Mersenne also succeeded. He brought natural

---

[38] Ibid. viii. 722; Descartes (1964–76: i. 31; ii. 436, 659–60; iii. 522; iv. 718; v. 547).

magic very near its end as a serious department of natural philosophy. Campanella's pansensism or animism, grounded in an elaborate metaphysics, finally and strongly distinguishes his organic world-view from the victorious mechanical philosophy created by Mersenne, Gassendi, and others who made Campanella an intellectual fashion in the early 1630s. Campanella's place in the history of philosophy stands as much on his metaphysical differences with these *libertins érudits* as on the materialist habits of mind that he shared with them. Although he lived through the fourth decade of the seventeenth century, the Renaissance shaped his philosophical programme, and his remarkable career, in and out of jail, shows how thinkers of the new Cartesian age discarded the heritage of the generations before them.

6

Renaissance Philosophy and Modern Memory

In 1499 an Italian humanist named Polidoro Vergilio—better known as Polydore Vergil because he lived most of his life in England—published a reference book titled *De inventoribus rerum* on the topic of discoveries or inventions in the arts and sciences and various areas of human and material culture. Later expansions of *De inventoribus* added material on church institutions, and the work became enormously successful. Thirty Latin editions had appeared by the time Polydore died in 1555, and by the early eighteenth century more than a hundred versions had accumulated in eight languages, including Russian. The sixteenth chapter of the first book is 'On the Origin of Philosophy and Its Two Beginnings; Who First Invented Ethics and Dialectic and Introduced Dialogues'. Fifteen previous chapters cover religion, cosmogony, language, marriage, literature, grammar, poetry, drama, history, rhetoric, music, and other subjects before taking up philosophy. Because it requires only a few paragraphs and because no contemporary English version exists, I have given the whole chapter on philosophy below, as an example of a humanist's conception of the origins of the discipline, composed at the close of the fifteenth century but still influential in Leibniz's lifetime.[1]

Cicero *On Duties* calls philosophy 'devotion to wisdom' and 'expeller of vices and explorer of virtue' in the *Tusculans*. Philosophy is generally thought to have come to the Greeks from the barbarians. For they say that the Magi were the first famous wise men among the Persians; among the Babylonians and Assyrians it was the Chaldaeans; among the Indians the Gymnosophists, the founder of whose school was named Buddha, according to Jerome's *Against Jovinian*; among

[1] Vergilio (1554: 58–60), emended in a few places; Copenhaver (1978b).

the Britons and Celts or Gauls it was the Druids; among the Phoenicians Mochus; Zamolxis and Orpheus among the Thracians; Atlas among the Libyans; and all these, according to Laertius, were considered wise men. The Egyptians, however, say that Vulcan was the son of the Nile and that he revealed the elements of philosophy. But Laertius also declares that philosophy came from the Greeks since they say that their Musaeus and Linus were the first wise men.

In fact, according to Eusebius, philosophy originated with the Hebrews, as did almost all the other disciplines. Citing Porphyry, who says that the philosophers of the Greeks came more than a thousand years after Moses, Eusebius demonstrates most abundantly in book eleven of the *Preparation for the Gospel* that they took their philosophy from the Jews, since at first they did not even have a name for philosophy, only afterward. For according to Lactantius in Book III, Pythagoras was the first to use the term 'philosophy' or 'love of wisdom' and call himself 'philosopher' or 'lover of wisdom', saying that God alone is wise; formerly, in fact, what is now called 'philosophy' was called *sophia* or 'wisdom', and those who professed it were called *sophi* or 'wise men'.

Philosophy had two beginnings, however. Anaximander called one 'Ionian' because Thales of Miletus was from Ionia, and Thales was Anaximander's teacher. The other was called 'Italian' after Pythagoras, who founded it and did a great deal of work on philosophy in Italy. In Book X of the *Preparation for the Gospel*, Eusebius adds a third, the 'Eleatic', calling Xenophanes of Colophon its founder.

In addition, they divide philosophy into three parts, according to Cicero *On the Orator*: the obscurity of nature, the subtlety of discourse, and then life and morals; the Greeks call the first physics, the second dialectic, and the third ethics. Plato took this division along with all the precepts of his philosophy from the Hebrews, so Eusebius says. Physics deals with the world and what it contains; Archelaus first brought it to Athens from Ionia. But ethics, which Socrates revealed, deals with life and morals. Cicero in the fifth book of the *Tusculans* writes that Socrates first called philosophy down from heaven, established it in cities, even introduced it into homes, and he compelled it to inquire about life and morals, good and evil. Dialectic, which contributes to the methods of both the other parts, originated with Zeno of Elea. Others divide philosophy into five parts, however: physics, metaphysics, ethics, mathematics and logic.

But we have overstepped our limits, for it is not our business to define and clarify every topic, only to give information about origins;

so let us return to our appointed task. We learn from Diogenes Laertius that Plato first of all introduced dialogues, or rather wrote better dialogues than anyone else, for Aristotle in the first book *On Poets* teaches that Alexamenus of Styra or Teos invented the dialogue.

From the repeated invocations of Cicero through the parade of other named and unnamed sources—Jerome, Eusebius, Lactantius, Porphyry, Diogenes Laertius, Niccolò Perotti, Giovanni Tortelli—Polydore's story is typically humanist in style and content. The very topic of ancient origins, mythical as well as historical, was an obsession of his trade, and Polydore's dependence on Cicero, Diogenes, and the Fathers conformed to a Christianized expression of humanism eventually crystallized by Erasmus. Diogenes told Polydore that philosophy grew out of primeval barbarian wisdom; so, in order to rescue philosophy from the pagans, Polydore simply narrowed this claim about a non-Greek origin and lodged it among the Jews of Mosaic times, thus opening a clear path to Christian posterity with a few detours for heathen advances. The Greeks get credit for naming philosophy, organizing its parts, and adding such improvements as the philosophical dialogue. Cicero, whom Polydore names five times in this brief chapter, has a privileged place among the pagan sages; his mastery of language lifts him above the others. Plato appears only twice, Aristotle but once, when Polydore cites a lost work *On Poets* mentioned by Diogenes rather than the familiar *Poetics*. The real fountainhead of philosophy was Moses, a conclusion that made humanist historicism safer in an age of fierce religious jealousies. Polydore wrote his book on discoveries after Bruni and other quattrocento humanists had laid the foundations for more mature and comprehensive investigations of the history of philosophy, but his quick summary served a wide readership after earlier humanist accounts had been forgotten.

The first books titled 'history of philosophy' and resembling later examples of the genre appeared in the middle of the seventeenth century in England and the Low Countries; Thomas Stanley issued his *History of Philosophy* in London in 1655, and Georg Horn's *Historia philosophica* appeared in

Leiden in the same year, thus inaugurating a tradition of historical writing that continues to our own day. The present Oxford *History of Western Philosophy* belongs to a line that reaches back to Stanley and Horn through Jakob Brucker and other scholars who shaped the genre in later periods.[2] Stanley's *History* is a post-Baconian formulation that owes much of its structure and ideology to seventeenth-century developments outside the present inquiry, but it is also a work of erudition and hence very much a product of early modern humanist scholarship. Ironically, it was the Renaissance, so seldom remembered by modern philosophers, that first gave their discipline a continuous and purposeful sense of history. Aristotle himself and Plato also had tried to overcome their predecessors by describing and then rebutting them; in this sense, philosophy had its historical motivations from the first. Cicero, Sextus, Philoponus, and other ancient thinkers recorded their rivals in order to criticize them, while other writers, like Diogenes Laertius and the author of the *Opinions of Philosophers* attributed to Plutarch, set out to write history as such—or doxography, to be more precise. In one way or another, ancient philosophers left the evidence that remains to describe them, but until the Renaissance the surviving materials lay scattered and unexamined among the larger body of texts that now constitute the corpus of classical literature. Not just in philosophy but in all other respects, modern historical thought began in the Renaissance. Except in certain biblical and theological contexts, medieval philosophers worried less about past ideas; few of them shared the curiosity that may have stirred Walter Burley to consult a rare text of Diogenes. In so far as Aquinas understood Greek philosophy as a product of historical change, he took his bearings uncritically from Aristotle's remarks in the *Physics*, *Metaphysics*, and elsewhere.

Sharper readings of philosophy's distant past emerged in the late fourteenth and early fifteenth centuries, after Petrarch had developed a more complete view of Latin textual remains and

[2] Santinello (1981) is the 1st vol. of a *Storia delle storie generali della filosofia*; the chs. by Malusa, pp. 3–62, and Tolomio, pp. 63–163, are most relevant to the Renaissance.

Italian students of Chrysoloras had gained access to Greek sources. In 1416 Bruni finished a *Life of Cicero* that improved on earlier recapitulations of Plutarch; his *Life of Aristotle* appeared in 1429 while Traversari was translating Diogenes. Manetti's *Life of Socrates* applied Bruni's technique in another important case, and Bruni's *Isagoge* also inspired such works as Bartolomeo Scala's 1458 letter *On the Nobler Sects of Philosophers*. Abandoning or perhaps never grasping historical actualities, Scala took an abstract scheme from Varro by way of Augustine that counted nearly three hundred possible sectarian divisions on the question of the greatest good; he failed to sustain Bruni's concrete historicism in other respects as well. None the less, Scala, Ficino, Landino, and other quattrocento scholars helped to historicize philosophy by holding philosophers responsible to higher and higher standards of documentation and technique, even if individual products of the new history fell short of the ideal. Giovanni Antonio Flaminio's school tract of 1524 *On the Origin of Philosophy* purveyed moral maxims in a framework of philosophical celebrities linked by easy patterns of discipleship. In 1518 Johann Reusch published a *Declamation on True Philosophy* whose title betrays its rhetorical intentions. Vives, who was not a professional philosopher, published his *Origins, Sects, and Praises of Philosophy* in the same year. He wanted to blend philosophy with wisdom in a learned Christian pedagogy, so he treated philosophy as an umbrella for the liberal arts rather than as a distinct discipline. Still, the *De initiis* brought the first phase of humanist history of philosophy to its apex; its author's aims were not far from Polydore Vergil's, but the product was better informed and better expressed.[3]

The effect of humanist historiography on philosophy was ideological as well as technical; humanist veneration of the classics was itself a broad political posture. The new classicism had its most lasting success in Europe's classrooms, at first in the schools, then in the universities. In later centuries it took industrial, commercial, and technological revolutions, exten-

---

[3] Malusa (1981: 3–13); Grafton (1988*b*: 772–6); above, Ch. 4, n. 7.

sions of political and social rights, and several global wars to erode the conviction that all education must start with the Greek and Latin classics. Like other traditional class privileges, classical education has not fared well in a time when fame dies every fifteen minutes and money buys power much faster than learning. But among the few people well enough educated to take philosophy seriously, the old humanist historicism still reinforces a more generalized need to consult thinkers of any period, past or present, who might bring philosophical insight. Professional urgency has joined with a senescent humanism to keep philosophy aware of ancient wisdom. Books and articles on Plato and Aristotle pour from the presses, and even the Hellenistic schools attract their share of attention. For the time being, ancient philosophy retains a contemporary audience.

Another modern partnership of ideology and professionalism keeps a readership for medieval philosophy. After the Turks and the plague, few things had a worse press in early modern Europe than scholasticism, which Renaissance authors seldom mentioned except to attack it. Scholastic thought entered the history of philosophy as a discrete period either in broad humanist invective against post-classical decadence or in more pointed confessional propaganda that depicted medieval thinkers as having betrayed the Gospels and the Fathers. In either case, the schoolmen became traitors to true philosophy, and outside the seminaries and other church schools they remained so through the Enlightenment until 1879, when Pope Leo XIII's bull *Aeterni Patris* consolidated a renewed interest in Thomism and launched the Neo-Scholastic movement.[4] Especially in the United States, growing demand for secondary and university education prompted Jesuits and other Roman Catholic orders to restore the Thomist curriculum, which naturally called for new editions of scholastic texts and fresh research in medieval philosophy. Jesuit professors eventually found strange allies in logicians who followed up the initiatives of Frege and Russell. Philosophers who noticed that modern

---

[4] Garin (1961*a*: 466–79); Malusa (1981: 51–4); Tolomio (1981: 66–7); Fitzpatrick (1982).

logic has less in common with Aristotle than with Peter of
Spain legitimized medieval thought for their colleagues, some
of whom went on to uncover other connections with the Middle
Ages. Medieval and ancient philosophies live in the contemporary curriculum as objects of professional interest bolstered
by ideology. Renaissance philosophy developed its own ideological leanings, but they have been less effective in the modern
world.

Humanism was a product of the Renaissance but it was not
about the Renaissance; humanists wrote about antiquity and
propagandized for the classics with great effect, but they promoted the philosophical views of their own period less convincingly. Humanism also supported Christian reform through
such figures as Vives, Lefèvre, and Erasmus, whose well-
intended criticisms of the medieval church alienated the
Catholic establishment, while Protestants either dismissed them
as half-hearted or shouted down their protests with louder
complaints that drowned humanist pleas for religious reform.
To address the modern world, neither classicism nor Christianity needed to preserve the memory of their Renaissance
champions, whose other ideological drives were weaker deter-
minants of historiography. One of these was the urge to discover cultural unity beneath the manifest diversity of the
ancient textual record. Cusanus pictured the philosopher as a
hunter intent on a single distant goal that keeps vanishing over
the horizon of variety. From his earliest works *On the Four
Sects of Philosophers* and other topics, Ficino worked up a
research programme that not only *collected* the facts of history
in order to reconstruct philosophy but also *co-ordinated* them
toward a clearer Platonic and providential unity than Aristotle
had revealed to the schools. By Steuco's time Ficino's conception had become a 'perennial' philosophy derived in stages
from superficial doctrinal differences originally planted by God
as seeds of a deeper unitary truth. Agreement on fundamentals
was Steuco's peaceable aim, where Patrizi's polemic purpose
was to show how Platonic concord eclipses the discord of the
Peripatetics. Even when unity is invisible, the learned philosopher can detect it; Patrizi thought he had done so when he

highlighted ten of Plato's dialogues as more meaningful than the others and as constituting a disguised order of thought wherein Plato had imitated Hermes and other ancient theologians. By scattering his ideas, by leaving them inconclusive, by veiling them in myth and allegory, Plato had buried the Hermetic secrets, leaving them for the sage to unearth and use for the foundations of a philosophy fit to last perennially.[5]

Ficino's conception of an ancient Hermetic-Platonic philosophy, later amplified by Steuco and Patrizi, differs somewhat from Pico's concordist historiography. Ficino turned away from Aristotle to keep his eyes fixed on Plato's harmony with Christianity, but Pico's broader vision looked for accord between the two mightiest ancients. For Pico, diversity seemed less a cloud of mistakes darkening some static truth than the gradual uncovering of unity through inquiry that error can stimulate as well as impede. Plato and Aristotle may seem to be at odds, but their rifts are merely verbal; the new Cabalist hermeneutic can crack the hardest textual surface to find the unity beneath. Pico, Bessarion, and other quattrocento thinkers made philosophical symphonies and concords a habit of high fashion in the next century, when Symphorien Champier, Francesco de' Vieri, Jacopo Mazzoni, and others continued the tradition. Even the Aristotelians—Crisostomo Javelli, Giulio Castellani, Giovanni Battista Bernardi—developed their own versions of concordism. Bernardi's approach was particularly fruitful. After Pico's *Conclusions* and other works had transformed scholastic theses meant for disputation into testimonials of deeper harmony among philosophers, Bernardi took the next step of assembling a concordist catalogue of philosophical ideas, thus anticipating the philosophical dictionaries and encyclopedias of the next century. For us, an encyclopedia is instrumental, a tool for quick and sporadic reference. But Alsted and others constructed systems, systems of systems, and encyclopedias for seventeenth-century readers who still believed somehow in the unity of truth.[6] Throughout the early

---

[5] Malusa (1981: 14–25); above, 132–7, 141–9, 156–60, 184–5, 190–1.
[6] Malusa (1981: 25–37); below, n. 19.

modern period, from Ficino and Pico to Newton and Leibniz, such convictions supported a pattern of historiography—*prisca theologia, philosophia perennis, pax philosophiae*—that could never have emerged without the humanists, even though it did not preserve their fame for modern times. Other myths of classicism and Christianity outlived the fable of ancient theology because they conflicted less flagrantly with the findings of history.

The purpose of the ancient theology was to sanctify pagan learning by connecting it with a still more ancient source of gentile wisdom that reinforces sacred revelation. Rather than baptize the heathens as Ficino or the elder Pico wished, some early modern critics damned them, and one of the most aggressive thinkers of this school was the younger Pico. He saw an impassable gulf between Christian and pagan belief where his uncle had tried to build bridges. In broader literary contexts Leon Battista Alberti, Filippo Beroaldo the elder, and others had already ridiculed the quarrelsome pagan schools, but Gianfrancesco went after them with the full philosophical armament of scepticism. From Sextus he acquired not only techniques of critical doubt but also concrete cases of intellectual error among the reverend ancients. Armed with this new data, Gianfrancesco turned the history of philosophy into a chronicle of dogmatic mistakes made when people attempted a purely human philosophy without divine guidance. Secular philosophy as such is not only mistaken; it is an occasion of sin. In his book *On the Pagan Philosophers* of 1594, G. B. Crispo re-issued Pico's warning about the pagans to Catholics of the Counter-Reformation, but he aimed his guns at Plato, while for their own different reasons Pico and Patrizi had concentrated their fire on Aristotle. Given the example of the younger Pico, Crispo in some sense profited from his fideist scepticism, but the rigors of post-Tridentine orthodoxy stifled any real critical instincts in his work. When Montaigne wished in the 'Apology' that some scholar as talented as Lipsius might compile a history of ancient moral philosophy, he doubtless saw better than Crispo how Sextus provided material, model, and motive for a genuinely critical history, something to surpass Pico's polemic in scholarly substance and credibility.[7] No discovery of the Renaissance remains livelier in modern philosophy than scepticism, yet again this gift of the humanists has not made them household names. How many contemporary philosophers can manage two sentences about Sextus himself, much less Gianfrancesco Pico?

For various reasons, not least of all religious, we remember Erasmus, Vives, Reuchlin, and perhaps Valla better than the younger Pico, who was more a philosopher than any of them except Valla, the least famous of the other four. All five helped make humanism a weapon of religious reform by teaching the new history and philology to those who preferred the designs of providence to decrees from Rome and who wished to revive patristic and apostolic literature as antidotes to scholasticism. For such critics the history of Christianity was no longer a continuous pageant leading from the birth of Christ to the last judgement. Within Christian history they located a period of scholastic decadence that had reverted to pagan deceptions and divided the age of the Fathers from the present days of renewal. Just as the younger Pico had declared secular philosophy sinful as such, so reborn Christians found all of scholastic thought morally unfit, a philosophy destined providentially to perplex the unsaved. Kaspar Peucer was a follower of Melanchthon and a moderate in religion. His *Chronicon Carionis* none the less treated the history of scholasticism as a warning to the unregenerate. He charged that the church of Rome had used Aristotelian rationalism to shore up its own defenses of canon law against Roman lawyers who spoke for the just claims of Empire. Peucer saw the evils of the Gothic age not so much as a slow decline from the Fathers and the Gospels as deliberate ecclesiastical treason. He thought that things first fell apart in the late sixth century, but he put the beginnings of scholasticism in the early eleventh century and traced its three phases over the subsequent five hundred years to the beginnings of reform in his own era. Peucer's motives were clearly confessional, but he established a plausible his-

---

[7] Malusa (1981: 7–51); above, Ch. 4, n. 87.

torical outline for scholastic thought, while humanists were busy sorting the various schools and successions of ancient philosophy.[8]

Thus, before the end of the sixteenth century two major elements in the currently canonical scheme of past philosophy were well in place. Early modern thinkers had identified and described an *ancient* period and a *medieval* period in the history of Western philosophy. Naturally, they were less clear about their own place in the order of things, and until recently modern critics showed little interest in them. By contrast, the continuity of modern philosophy with the accomplishments of Bacon, Descartes, Locke, Leibniz, and other seventeenth-century figures makes it possible to speak meaningfully of the whole period since Descartes as 'post-Cartesian', though finer discriminations are obviously possible and useful. The point is that contemporary philosophers still address selected figures of the post-Cartesian era, along with Plato, Aristotle, and other older thinkers, as people like themselves asking similar questions. Continuities with the ancient and medieval periods are not so many or so lively, but for reasons mentioned above, professional as well as ideological, they are strong enough. Not so with Renaissance philosophy, as a few examples will show.

Bertrand Russell's *History of Western Philosophy*, published in 1945 and frequently reprinted, is doubtless the most familiar general account of the subject by a leading philosopher of the twentieth century. It is a belletristic book written in a mood of affable aristocratic omniscience, an engaging amateur's history of the type that used to earn an author praise as 'a Renaissance man'. Because Russell was a great mind and a gifted writer more tuned to past philosophy than most of his contemporaries or successors, bits of his history deserve attention as the *aperçus* of a first-rate thinker, but few would now regard the story he tells as fair or reliable. Yet his enormous philosophical authority and worldwide political celebrity gave the work immense influence, especially on readers with no professional

---

[8] Malusa (1981: 51–8); Tolomio (1981: 66–7, 102–4).

interest in philosophy. Dividing the history of philosophy into 'ancient', 'Catholic', and 'modern' parts, Russell recognized the cultural and political importance of the Renaissance and introduced the modern era with a chapter running from 'the Renaissance to Hume'. He ended the previous section with Ockham and Wyclif. Early modern material occupies less than six per cent of Russell's long text, whose verdict is that the Renaissance 'produced no important theoretical philosopher' and 'was not a period of great achievement in philosophy'. That Russell thought poorly of early modern philosophy is natural enough, since he knew little about it. Only three Renaissance figures, one philosophically eminent, rate more than a few lines: Machiavelli, Erasmus, and More. Ficino, Pico, Ramus, and Bruno never appear; Montaigne was an essayist who wrote about cannibals and resembled Shakespeare in being 'content with confusion'; Valla was an anti-clerical Epicurean. Valla at least was on the right side of an evolving modernity whose two major features were 'the diminishing authority of the Church, and the increasing authority of science'.[9]

Russell's Renaissance reads like Burckhardt and Victor Hugo digested by Macaulay. Cardinals serve each other poison while liberal princes patronize free-thinking scholars. But the 'humanists . . . were too busy acquiring knowledge of antiquity to . . . produce anything original in philosophy'. Philosophically, the main work of the Renaissance was to destroy 'the rigid scholastic system' and substitute 'Plato for the scholastic Aristotle'. Russell acknowledged humanism as 'a step towards emancipation, since the ancients disagreed . . . , and individual judgement was required to decide which of them to follow'.[10] But he drew a crude and poorly informed sketch of the Renaissance. Facile whig history may seem out of place in someone whose German governess and French cook brought him languages with his breakfast; who found it natural as a teenager to encrypt a journal in Greek characters; who recalled reading Dante and Machiavelli in Italian along with Gibbon and Mill

9 Russell (1945: pp. v–viii, 391–2, 491, 498, 500, 504–22, 872).
10 Ibid. 495, 500–3; Ferguson (1948: 131–2, 198–213).

(his 'godfather') before he went to Cambridge in 1890. But Russell also had a 'grandmother, . . . the most important person to me throughout my childhood, . . . a Scotch Presbyterian, Liberal in politics and religion' who wrote anti-metaphysical doggerel and dreamed of her grandson as a Unitarian minister. Russell grew apart from her in early adolescence but observed that her 'animus against metaphysics continued to the end of her life'. 'When she discovered that I was interested in metaphysics,' he wrote in his *Autobiography*, 'she told me that the whole subject could be summed up in the saying: "What is mind? No matter. What is matter? Never mind." At the fifteenth or sixteenth repetition of this remark, it ceased to amuse me.'[11] No doubt he did grow tired of her, but her 'animus' remained with him in more ways than one. Lady Russell's ghost still stirs in modern philosophy's official memory. The tutelary wraith of Whig history has done her work, for example, in D. J. O'Connor's *Critical History of Western Philosophy*, published in 1964, reprinted seven times by 1985, and serving here (arbitrarily) as an example of a successful contemporary textbook that pays even less attention to the Renaissance than Russell did, with none of Russell's literary pretensions. It is a collection of readings on past figures and periods written mainly by 'outstanding contemporary philosophers representing a wide range of philosophical views'. Not wide enough, apparently, to show any interest in Renaissance thought among more than two dozen current practitioners. O'Connor's authors move immediately from Augustine, Aquinas, and Ockham to Bacon, Hobbes, and Descartes. D. W. Hamlyn's recent *History of Western Philosophy* allots three pages to the period between Ockham and Bacon, giving most of its eleven-page chapter on 'The Renaissance' to Bacon and Hobbes and introducing it with this puzzled yet summary verdict: 'It may seem a paradox that a period that saw the flowering of much else—of science, of art and of literature—was a period in which philosophy was at a low ebb. It is nevertheless a fact.'[12]

---

[11] Russell (1967–9: i. 15–18, 53).
[12] O'Connor (1985), from the back cover of the paperback edn.; Hamlyn (1987: 123–33).

Histories of special subjects leave the same gaps as general histories. The widely and rightly admired history of logic by the Kneales devotes nearly three hundred pages to the time between the pre-Socratics and Ockham, followed by over four hundred more on developments between Leibniz and the twentieth century. In between, part of a chapter discusses 'humanism and the rise of natural science', but half of these twenty pages go to Bacon, Descartes, Hobbes, the *Port Royal Logic*, and later contributions. The only Renaissance figures treated at any length are Ramus and Zabarella. Valla earns a single mention as one of 'two writers who started the corruption' when 'genuine logic was neglected for rhetoric and books which purported to be on logic quoted Cicero as often as Aristotle'. The other corrupter was Agricola, who turns up twice disguised as 'Rudolphus Agrippa'. Trapezuntius, Lefèvre, Mair, and Vives are nowhere to be found.[13] The same pattern shapes the article on the 'History of Metaphysics' in the *Encyclopedia of Philosophy*, which runs from the Milesians to Ockham and then from Descartes to logical positivism, phenomenology, and existentialism. The article credits Descartes with 'the revival of metaphysics in the seventeenth century' but omits any mention of the circumstances that required such a revival during the two-and-a-half centuries between Ockham's death and Descartes's birth. Ficino, Suárez, Bruno, and Campanella fade from the metaphysical scene.[14] The same *Encyclopedia* carries no articles on a third of roughly three dozen Renaissance philosophers who figure in this volume: Petrarch rates a few columns, but not Bruni; Mair gets half a page, but not Lefèvre; Plethon appears, but not Trapezuntius; Ramus, but not Talon; the elder Pico, but not the younger; and so on.

Introducing his influential *Eight Philosophers of the Italian Renaissance* in 1964, three years before the *Encyclopedia* was published, Professor Kristeller called his topic 'comparatively neglected', noting that 'the large amount of work ... by Fiorentino and Dilthey, Cassirer and Gentile, Garin, Nardi

---

[13] Kneale and Kneale (1962: 298–320, esp. 298, 300, 303).
[14] *EP*, v. 289–300, esp. 295.

and many other scholars has not yet been sufficiently absorbed by the average textbook or course'.[15] Now, almost three decades after these contributions by Kristeller, the Kneales, and the editors of the *Encyclopedia*, the situation has improved, at least at the level of specialist scholarship. The secondary source bibliography in the *Cambridge History of Renaissance Philosophy* published in 1988 runs to more than sixty pages and over two thousand entries. The editors of the *Cambridge History* comment that

an increasingly scholarly and sophisticated approach to ... Renaissance philosophy has gradually developed over the last fifty years. For the most part, however, the fruits of these researches have yet to find their proper place within the broad outlines of the history of the subject. This applies above all to English-language histories.[16]

The *Cambridge History* has doubtless begun to repair this neglect, but the failure of memory is a large one and worth overcoming. A final example will show that the problem remains to be solved. The 'Editorial Statement' in the first issue (1984) of the *History of Philosophy Quarterly* addresses itself to

the new, substantively engagé mode of history-of-philosophy writing that has become popular of late. The *HPQ* plans to focus on papers that cultivate philosophical history in the spirit of *philosophia perennis*. . . , those manifesting a strong interaction between contemporary and historical concerns.

After twenty-six issues, as of April 1990, the journal's coverage of Western historical periods was as follows, measured by articles devoted to each era: twentieth century, 14 per cent; nineteenth century, 8 per cent; eighteenth century, 28 per cent; seventeenth century, 15 per cent; Renaissance, 2 per cent; Middle Ages, 5 per cent; antiquity, 29 per cent.

It seems odd that a journal launched in 'the spirit of *philo-*

---

[15] Kristeller (1964a: 2); for other writings relevant to the historiography of philosophy, see Kristeller (1968b; 1981; 1982; 1985d; 1985e: 3–23, 111–27; 1990b).

[16] *CHRP*, 2, 869–930.

sophia perennis' should find so little to say about the age that
invented the concept of perennial philosophy. To locate a
philosophical tradition which has long taken the Renaissance
more seriously, of course, one need look no further than the
names mentioned by Kristeller just above. Cassirer's *Erkenntnisproblem*, first published in 1906, already contains in its
first volume a full account of the early modern thinkers by-
passed by Russell and other Anglo-American critics as they
distanced themselves from Hegelian, Neo-Kantian, and other
Continental traditions. Whether through opposition or emula-
tion, Burckhardt's earlier essay owed a great deal to Hegel, as
did Warburg's later explorations of art history, by way of Karl
Lamprecht. In our own time, Kristeller's researches are those
of a thinker who has described himself as guided by a Kantian
notion of reason and as formed by such teachers as Jaspers,
Husserl, and Heidegger. Perhaps as Anglo-American philosophers learn more about Continental thought, they will also
become curious about its deeper sense of the past.[17]

In any case, Renaissance philosophy, like any past enterprise of comparable scope and import, must first be taken on
its own terms. Valla, Ficino, Pomponazzi, Bruno, Montaigne,
and other, lesser figures will reward anyone's curiosity. The
period as a whole is a rich one that obviously deserves more
scholarly and philosophical attention than it has received. For
many modern readers, however, even an author as fluent as
Montaigne may seem forbidding because he wrote in a foreign
language and an alien style. Valla, Ficino, Bruno, and others
will seem even less friendly because their works are only partly
translated and their manner even stranger. Yet the same is
true of most medieval philosophers and, as far as expression
goes, of many ancients too. Differences from our predecessors
should motivate historical inquiry, not suppress it. Provided
that we respect their integrity, we might also note the family
resemblances and tribal debts that connect us with our distant
philosophical cousins of the centuries before Descartes. His-

---

[17] Gombrich (1969; 1986); Kerrigan and Braden (1989: 3–54, 73–81);
Kristeller (1990*b*); above, Ch. 3, n. 63, on perennial philosophy.

torians who recognize such similarities and obligations have given us a clearer picture of the discipline's past. But our links with the early modern period have philosophical as well as historical value, analytical as well as descriptive uses. In any of the usual divisions of philosophy we can find connections with the Renaissance that remain as vital for contemporary thought as our ties with ancient or medieval or post-Cartesian times. Consider just three cases in moral philosophy, metaphysics, and language, chosen as exemplary but not comprehensive or even representative instances.

Reviewing a recent book on *Three Rival Versions of Moral Enquiry* by Alasdair MacIntyre, a British philosopher now teaching in the United States, Jenny Teichman, a Cambridge philosopher, has this to say about the work of a person whom she introduces as having been named 'the philosophers' philosopher' by a British newspaper:

Mr. MacIntyre's project, here as elsewhere, is to put up a fight against philosophical relativism. Like many philosophers, he is bewitched by his enemy, a Gorgon that keeps reappearing in . . . ever more terrible forms. The current form is the 'incommensurability' . . . of differing . . . conceptual schemes. . . . He labels and discusses three significantly different standpoints: the encyclopedic, the genealogical and the traditional. . . . The third or traditional approach is represented by St. Thomas Aquinas, . . . ultimately harking back to Socrates and Aristotle. Mr. MacIntyre tends to exaggerate the difficulty of reconciling conflicting conceptual schemes. . . . He simply ignores those bits of philosophy in which real and universally acknowledged progress has occurred: the logic of the last 150 years, for example, and the philosophy of science of today. . . . It seems to me that Mr. MacIntyre is not fair to the analytical school . . . [which] in my view . . . resembles Aquinas's own technique of answering questions by drawing distinctions. This is not surprising, because there is a shared ancestry in the philosophy of ancient Greece. . . . Whether or not Mr. MacIntyre deserves the title of philosophers' philosopher, . . . he must be the past, present, future and all-time philosophical historians' historian of philosophy.[18]

Even quoted at length, this review says more than excerpts can

[18] Teichman (1990).

fairly represent. Answers to the following questions at least are required or implied: who is a philosopher? who is a leading philosopher? who is a historian instead of a philosopher? which philosophical pedigree is best? who can claim the best pedigree? Although MacIntyre's announced topic is *Versions of Moral Enquiry*, and although Teichman identifies moral relativism as his Gorgon, these are questions of jurisdiction and genealogy (one of the 'versions' discussed by MacIntyre), not questions of moral philosophy. But they are normal questions, whether from Teichman's point of view or MacIntyre's, and they suggest that at some point all ambitious philosophers must reckon with their ancestors. The review, addressed to the audience of an American Sunday newspaper, never doubts that moral relativism is a Gorgon worth waking; but while challenging MacIntyre's account of his relation to Aquinas, Scotus, Augustine, Aristotle, and Socrates—heroes all in canonical memory—Teichman never mentions Montaigne or any other Renaissance figure who made relativism a *modern* problem in a *Christian* culture no longer worried about Gorgias or Protagoras. When Christians vanquished pagans, the force of ancient philosophy withered among the ruins of classical culture, but moral conviction took root in Europe's new unitary faith. Later, when Christianity shattered in the sixteenth century, rival claims to religious hegemony shook the moral order again. Nietzsche reported the death of God, but he came too late to kill him. Machiavelli, Luther, Pomponazzi, Montaigne, and their contemporaries were first at the scene of the crime, which dragged on for centuries. Meanwhile, the driest academic researches of the humanists nourished fatal doubts as they revealed more and more about the ancients—conflicts, contradictions, hesitations, uncertainties, and other scandals. The revived scepticism of Sextus Empiricus was the strongest single agent of disbelief, but by Naudé's time humanism itself subverted conviction. Anyone who wonders why moral relativism should still seem monstrous to a modern philosopher would do well to examine its early modern origins. In more general terms, the common assumption that moral philosophy *ought* to examine *choices* among ethical claims or systems—the notion that there can be genuinely competing versions even of moral *inquiry*—had to be re-established in the Renaissance.

Just because they could make a bêtter case for one *or* another of the ethical systems of different ancient schools, philosophers reared on the new philology became agents of moral confusion, which was not at all what they wanted. Lipsius offered an alternative to the usual Peripatetic ethics and Bruno flouted the most cherished Christian conventions, but neither lacked moral confidence or the will to preach. One can see a different disproportion between intention and result in the Peripatetic textbooks of metaphysics and natural philosophy that became as popular as original Aristotelian works by the late sixteenth century and soon began to crowd them out of Europe's classrooms. As compared to the state of metaphysics in modern times, the *Metaphysical Disputations* that Suárez published in 1597 seem robustly confident. Having sorted reality into three kinds—the infinite uncreated, the immaterial created, and the material created—Suárez assigned three large tasks to metaphysics based on his theologically conditioned belief that an infinite and uncreated reality is prior to and responsible for the other two types. Metaphysics is first of all a kind of theology or divine science which studies the necessary entity that causes the other orders of reality to exist. Metaphysics is also a science of being *as* being which examines the broadest features of all types of reality, created and uncreated, immaterial and material, actual and possible. Finally, metaphysics is first philosophy, the originator and organizer of axioms used by philosophers and theologians as premises of more specific arguments. First philosophy and ontology (a seventeenth-century coinage) are thus secondary to metaphysical theology. By underwriting all other rational inquiry, metaphysics supports a Christian philosophy whose structure is deductive and whose major divisions are natural theology, natural philosophy, and rational psychology. This self-assured system is a far cry from the timid, shrunken metaphysics of our century, well-described by the opening sentence of the relevant article in the *Encyclopedia of Philosophy*: 'Almost everything in metaphysics is controversial, and . . . there is little agreement among those who call themselves metaphysicians about what precisely it is that they are attempting.' Suárez had no such qualms. He wanted his philosophy grand in its symmetries, bold in its aspirations. Still, one should note that the *Disputationes metaphysicae* were the work of a priest who needed to arm a proselytizing religion against the incursions of philosophical naturalism, rationalism, and scepticism.[19]

As far as original philosophy is concerned, Suárez, Pereira, and other Jesuits were the last major voices of an old system about to expire. But as teachers they left textbooks that set the pattern of school philosophy for decades to come, and their work was enormously influential in Protestant as well as Catholic lands. Seventeenth-century writers packaged similar material in a new genre called the *cursus philosophicus* or 'philosophy course', typically the product of a single author. One such work that caught Descartes's eye was the *Summary of Philosophy in Four Parts* of 1609 by Eustache de St Paul. The bulk of this *Summa* covers natural philosophy, leaving the remainder for metaphysics, ethics, and logic, but, as the new science continued its rise through the seventeenth century, Peripatetic natural philosophy competed poorly, so it sank into a state of subordination to metaphysics. That school philosophy would appeal to Protestant professors was clear from the success of the Basle edition of Zabarella's *Opera logica* in 1594 and the Mainz edition of Suárez's *Disputations* in 1605. The last major series of Peripatetic commentaries, those prepared by the Coimbra Jesuits in the 1590s, were also read in Protestant schools. By the late sixteenth century Calvinists were using patterns of analytical and synthetic method like those outlined by Zabarella to make theological inferences from revelation and philosophical deductions from observed or introspected information. Keckermann, Alsted, and others began to talk of 'systems' as structures of knowledge made coherent by some one principle of organization. They thought of learning not so much as a process driven by inquiry as a body of information controlled by rules. They treated the traditional

[19] Copleston (1960–6: iii. 335–405); *EP*, v. 300; Lohr (1988: 609–20).

liberal arts and sciences and the newer disciplines as lesser,
rule-bound systems located within a greater universal or encyclopedic system, of which Alsted published two notable examples in 1620 and 1630. Metaphysics, still more or less in its
Peripatetic guise, was a large piece of the new encyclopedia,
but it was no longer the heart of a living philosophy.[20]

Key terms of pre-Cartesian physics and metaphysics, words
that we have not yet learned to do without, labelled the com-
partments of the late scholastic encyclopedia. But when we
talk about 'form', 'matter', 'substance', 'quality', and other
items of this old lexicon, we seldom understand them in the
Peripatetic manner. Having thrived for two millennia, metaphysical and natural philosophy in the old style wasted away in
the seventeenth century when Bacon, Galileo, Descartes,
Gassendi, Hobbes, Boyle, Locke, Newton, and others either
refuted or abandoned or simply ignored it. These were thinkers of independent genius, but, as Newton recognized in his
remark to Hooke about 'standing on the shoulders of giants',
they were not exempt from history.[21] Before Descartes could
turn his back on the past, the past had to be made safe for
repudiation, and in metaphysics the Renaissance had accom-
plished this taming of a great philosophical force, in large
measure unintentionally. As with moral philosophy, the worst
threat to metaphysical certainty was not a frontal assault on
dogma from the sceptics, though their doubts were destructive
enough in their own right; the more invincible and insidious
enemy was multiple authority. The prospect of *choosing* among
metaphysical claims or among attitudes toward metaphysics as
diverse as those put forward by Valla, Ficino, Suárez, and
Campanella was a terrible freedom for a culture so well-inte-
grated in its beliefs. Metaphysics was no distant philosophical
preoccupation in the Renaissance. People died for metaphysics
because several centuries of vigorous scholastic debate had
secured its role as the basis of cosmology, ethics, and theology.
Doctrines as sacred as belief in the trinity, rites as holy as the

---

[20] Copleston (1960–6: iii. 344–6); Lohr (1988: 617–38); Schmitt (1988:
798–804).
[21] Newton (1959–77: i. 416).

eucharist, and assumptions as basic as human lordship of a planet set at the centre of the universe had acquired firm metaphysical underpinnings; the danger in dislodging them for new foundations or for none at all was a fearful risk indeed. Nothing less than cosmic anxiety could justify John Donne's lines in 'The First Anniversary', written in 1611, a year after Bacon finished his *New Atlantis* and Galileo first saw the moons of Jupiter:

> And new philosophy calls all in doubt,
> The element of fire is quite put out;
> The sun is lost, and the earth, and no man's wit
> Can well direct him where to look for it.
> And freely men confess that this world's spent,
> When in the planets and the firmament
> They seek so many new; they see that this
> Is crumbled out again to his atomies.
> 'Tis all in pieces, all coherence gone;
> All just supply, and all relation:
> Prince, subject, father, son, are things forgot,
> For every man alone thinks he hath got
> To be a phoenix. . . .[22]

Things seemed to fall apart physically, morally, and even politically in a system tied together by metaphysical bonds that no longer held. After the Renaissance, no metaphysics would ever again achieve the supremacy enjoyed by the Peripatetic system for most of twenty centuries. Whether one sees this transformation as a liberation or a catastrophe, the immensity of the change must surely be clear. Perhaps it helps explain our own metaphysical reserve.

Closer to our time, metaphysics of the kind taught by T. H. Green and F. H. Bradley had all but expired when A. J. Ayer issued his proclamation on *Language, Truth and Logic* in the mid-1930s. Titling his first chapter the 'Elimination of Metaphysics', Ayer named his moribund victim at the start, declaring metaphysical claims to be nonsense and urging that 'if

[22] Ll. 205–17.

philosophy is to be accounted a genuine branch of knowledge it must be defined in such a way as to distinguish it from metaphysics'. In one sense, this annihilation of one of philosophy's historic parts was another echo of the demolition of tradition that was well under way by the end of the sixteenth century, and between Telesio's time and Ayer's many prominent philosophers had joined the troop that eventually exploded all of metaphysics. In fact, in order to justify himself historically, Ayer argued that 'the majority of those . . . commonly supposed to have been great philosophers were primarily not metaphysicians but analysts'; he then appointed Locke, Berkeley, Hume, Hobbes, Bentham, and Mill to this saving remnant. That the shape of Ayer's 'majority' is distinctly circular and its character solidly British is less interesting for present purposes than his views about the linguistic nature of the philosophical analysis behind his arguments. 'As an analyst', he wrote, the philosopher 'is not directly concerned with the physical properties of things, . . . only with the way in which we speak about them.' At the same time, the philosopher examines language only as a residue of 'logical activity, . . . [not for] empirical study of the linguistic habits of any group of people'.[23] Unconsciously or not, the first of these two statements represents the most important specific connection between central philosophical concerns of the Renaissance and those of recent Anglo-American philosophy. Along with many other British and North American philosophers after Bradley, Ayer turned to language as the main or only object of analysis and so retraced steps taken long before by Bruni, Valla, Agricola, and Ramus. There is no reason to think he was aware of Renaissance philosophers of language, however, or that he would have respected their oratorical motivations. Yet the 'linguistic habits' of particular Latin and Greek authors were major interests of important Renaissance philosophers.

In moral philosophy Ayer's main finding was another claim about language, 'that sentences which simply express moral

---

[23] Ayer (1952: 33, 44, 52, 70). For the history of modern Anglo-American philosophy, see Warnock (1958); Warnock (1960); Urmson (1967); Passmore (1968).

judgments do not say anything. They are pure expressions of feeling' that communicate one's ethical impulses and urge them on others without making any true or false assertions.[24] In the long run, Ayer's emotivism was an extreme result of the relativizing of moral inquiry that the Renaissance learned from antiquity; but, as in metaphysics, many other battles had to be fought between Montaigne's time and Ayer's to make moral philosophy ripe for the kill. By 1903 G. E. Moore had already turned against what he called 'metaphysical ethics' and thereby pointed moral philosophy in a linguistic direction. He took the epigram for his *Principia ethica* from Joseph Butler, a philosophical bishop of the eighteenth century who wrote that 'everything is what it is and not another thing'.[25] Whether to count this as an insight, a platitude, or a rule of method will depend on one's view of Moore's philosophy of common sense, which sought to make things clearer by minute and unflinchingly literal *analysis* of the odd things that philosophers say. Analysis meant taking sentences and words apart, reducing and dissolving language to make it plainer and reveal its logical structure. Applied to moral philosophy, the goal of Moore's analysis was not to tally different uses of the word 'good' but to learn which things might be good in themselves. In the end, 'good' turns out to be an atom of moral meaning, lacking parts and therefore impervious to analysis. But in the mean time, there was a good deal to say about moral claims, and Moore went at them with a childlike but tenacious simplicity that mesmerized some of the best talents of the century. Lord Keynes, who knew Moore well and admired 'the beauty of the literalness of [his] . . . mind,' wrote that 'he could not distinguish love and beauty and truth from the furniture'. Ernest Gellner, who was less entranced by Moore, wondered if he was 'a philosopher or a pedant of such outstanding ability as to push pedantry and literal-mindedness to a point where it became a philosophy'.[26] In any case—even though Moore's most important test of analysis ended with an unanalyzed result and even though he

---

[24] Ayer (1952: 108).
[25] Moore (1956: title-page, 139–41).
[26] Keynes quoted in Warnock (1960: 54–5); Gellner (1968: 98).

was not primarily interested in language—it was largely his example that made linguistic analysis a leading habit of Anglo-American philosophy, which also copied Moore in making philosophy accountable for its conflicts with common sense. In both respects, the pragmatic and the linguistic, Moore had enough in common with Valla and Vives that his apostles of present and future generations ought to take note of their shared interests.

Russell, Moore's colleague at Cambridge, championed a logical atomism that distrusted ordinary language as the imperfect mask of a perfect language whose syntax ought to be expressible in logical notation. Actual language was the vile body, logic the clean bones beneath: the philosopher anatomizes. This was the surgical protocol that Ludwig Wittgenstein followed in the *Tractatus* of 1921; so thorough was he that the patient was either cured for good or dead and gone, freeing Wittgenstein to quit philosophy and take up schoolteaching. He had probed the tissue of ordinary language for logical form, and he looked for a symbolism to represent the logical skeleton from which all actual language must hang. Later, around the time when Ayer published his manifesto for logical positivism, Wittgenstein repudiated the logical atomism of the *Tractatus* as philosophical whimsy and began to formulate the aphorisms that would appear posthumously in 1953 as *Philosophical Investigations*. Perhaps the most famous line from this poetic book, which opens with a passage in Latin from Augustine, is the one that says 'the meaning of a word is its use in language'. Valla could have written the same sentence, though he would have meant something different by it, but *that* difference deserves philosophical scrutiny informed by history. Whether Wittgenstein ever heard of Valla is an interesting point but not a crucial one. Tracking influence is only one job for the history of philosophical ideas; another is to find patterns of conceptual similarity and difference that may have analytical use quite apart from any considerations of narrative or personality.[27] In all likelihood Wittgenstein would have disagreed.

[27] Wittgenstein (1967: 20 [43]); on Wittgenstein's context see Pears (1970) and Kenny (1975), in addition to the works mentioned above in n. 23. On

The power of his mind, the force of his will, his exploits in engineering, architecture, music, even warfare left peers and students in awe of him. He seemed 'like . . . some figure of the Renaissance,' but they were ready to believe that his later work lay 'outside any philosophical tradition and without literary sources of influence. . . . The author of the *Tractatus* had learned from Frege and Russell. . . . The author of the *Philosophical Investigations* has no ancestors in philosophy.' Eyes less dazed have seen conscious connections with Kant, Schopenhauer, even Freud, not to speak of well-documented relations with the Vienna Circle. Others have pointed out the impersonal kinship that links Wittgenstein with Renaissance philosophers of language like Valla.[28] Unlike Wittgenstein, Valla would have been happy just to know all he could about one *particular language*, Latin, as expressed in one set of *texts*, those left by the classical authors, and in this respect his philosophical vision was surely narrower than Wittgenstein's. Whether the examples of usage that Wittgenstein dissected were introspected or empirically discovered, they were certainly not *texts* embedded in the matrix of authorial language that Valla recognized. But both philosophers were natural historians of language disenchanted with metaphysics and despising the academic philosophies of their times.

Gilbert Ryle, a superb classicist as well as a fine philosopher who admitted curiosity about his forerunners, described visits to Cambridge in the early 1930s when 'veneration for Witt-

resemblances between Valla and Wittgenstein, see Waswo (1987: 5–6, 63, 98–9, 103–4), who claims that 'we may find explicit theories of semantically constitutive language in Valla or Luther without regarding them as seeds that were inevitably to blossom in Wittgenstein'. For reactions to Waswo, see above, Ch. 4, n. 35.

[28] Malcolm (1958: 15); Pears (1970: 114); above, n. 27; on contemporary approaches to the history of philosophy, see Taylor (1984); MacIntyre (1984); Rorty (1984) and other chs. in Rorty, Schneewind, and Skinner (1984). See MacIntyre (1984: 39–40) for the following: 'Quine has joked that there are two sorts of people interested in philosophy, those interested in philosophy and those interested in the history of philosophy. . . . The counter-joke is: the people interested in philosophy now are doomed to become those whom only those interested in the history of philosophy are going to be interested in in a hundred years' time.'

genstein was so incontinent that ... my mentions of other philosophers were greeted with jeers'. He also recalled how Wittgenstein suggested 'that he himself was proud not to have studied other philosophers ... and that people who did ... were ... unauthentic philosophers, which was often but not always true'.[29] As a student and teacher at Oxford, Ryle had been held to a historical curriculum, and much of his experience was that of a classical scholar who as an original philosopher never cut his ties to the ancients. That Ryle, J. L. Austin, and others who encouraged ordinary language philosophy at Oxford were excellent classicists seems more than accidental. Russell certainly thought so. Around 1959, he ridiculed the Oxford philosophers for reviving an error

which has recurred at intervals through the history of philosophy and theology. Its most logical and complete form was ... the Abecedarian heresy [which] ... maintained that all human knowledge is evil, and, since it is based upon the alphabet, it is a mistake to learn even the ABC. ... An ally of Luther, after adopting this heresy, 'forsook all study of Holy Scripture and looked for Divine truth at the mouths of those who ... were accounted the most ignorant.'

Later and milder proponents of the same view were Pascal, Rousseau, Tolstoy, and finally the 'Oxford Abecedarians [who] do not reject *all* human learning, but only such as is not required for a First in Greats—i.e., such as has been discovered since the time of Erasmus'.[30] In pinning his opponents to a particular historical neighbourhood, Russell got the address right, even if he underestimated the philosophical weight of Ryle's Renaissance antecedents and mistakenly took Erasmus as their most important spokesman. When Ryle claimed that the doctrine of universals arises from a grammatical mistake, his real ally in heresy was not Erasmus but the Ciceronian Nizolio, for whom synecdoche was the most misleading of all expressions.[31] But Lord Russell's scorn for ordinary language philosophy was as much cultural and political as philosophical. One of its bitterest formulations came from Gellner, whose

[29] Quoted in Lyons (1980: 4).
[30] Russell's introd. to Gellner (1968: 14–15).
[31] Above, pp. 207–9.

polemic Russell prefaced with the remarks above on the Abecedarians.

Linguistic Philosophy . . . not merely does not teach anyone how to make shoes, but it also claims to abstain from telling anyone how to live, how to find his soul, how to choose his pictures, how to vote, how or where or whether to worship, whether or which authority to obey, and even how to think or talk! Not only does it claim not to do these things, or very seldom . . . , it is extremely proud of this fact. . . . Linguistic philosophy, at long last, provided a philosophic form eminently suitable for gentlemen. Nothing is justified.[32]

Although his later work confirmed the programme of the Oxford philosophers, Wittgenstein preached a more practical gospel to his Cambridge disciples. In 1944 he asked an American follower why he studied 'philosophy if all that it does for you is to enable you to talk . . . about some abstruse questions of logic, etc., and if it does not improve your thinking about the important questions of everyday life'.[33] Moore's way of philosophizing, as extended and refined by Ryle, Austin, Strawson, and others, left itself open to such questions: the study of ordinary language was no ticket to ordinary life, despite Wittgenstein's wishes. Like some Renaissance humanists who spoke from studious security for an active life in the world of here and now, the Oxford philosophers gave their critics the impression of preciosity campaigning hypocritically for plain speech and good sense. Listing the ways in which Moore paved the way for linguistic philosophy, Gellner mentions 'the notion that philosophy makes no difference, . . . that old philosophic doctrines are all erroneous and that their error is best shown up by careful, protracted investigation of the terms occurring in them, . . . an alienation from the modern world, . . . artificiality, pedantry, an ivory-towerism, procrastination'.[34] The point about older philosophies, at least, is unfair to Ryle and his colleagues, especially Austin, who came closer than Ryle to a philologized philosophy in the Renais-

---

[32] Gellner (1968: 264).
[33] Malcolm (1958: 39); Kenny (1975: 13).
[34] Gellner (1968: 102).

sance style. Austin told his friends that he ought to have been an engineer instead of a classicist, but he filled his articles with acute grammatical distinctions. He gave his William James lectures of 1955 a conspicuously monosyllabic title, *How To Do Things with Words*, but when in the first lecture he needed just the right example to clarify his notion of performative utterance for the Harvard students and faculty, the ancient muse descended. He wanted to illustrate how we may 'assume without realizing that the outward utterance [of a promise] is a description, *true or false*, of the occurrence of the inward performance', and, knowing the Greek of Euripides to be on the lips of all who heard him, he could do no better than to find 'the classic expression . . . in the *Hippolytus* (l. 612), where Hippolytus says

ἡ γλῶσσ᾽ ὀμώμοχ᾽, ἡ δὲ φρὴν ἀνώμοτος

i.e., "my tongue swore to, but my heart (or mind or other backstage artiste) did not"'[35] Maybe Russell was right. What had been classic in the time of Erasmus still did the trick for Austin. But formal logic was still formal logic, as it had been when Mair and Lefèvre taught in Paris. While Austin and Ryle developed ordinary language philosophy in the 1930s in reaction to the technical abstractions that followed Russell and Whitehead's *Principia Mathematica*, Tarski and then Carnap devised new programmes of formalized metalogic and metalanguage to satisfy the contrary impulse. Logic and language were still locked in struggles rehearsed earlier in the Renaissance, which had also devised a pattern of memory for Western philosophy while deconstructing its metaphysics and disestablishing its ethics. Perhaps Heraclitus should have the last words, as Plato recorded them:

πάντα χωρεῖ καὶ οὐδὲν μένει, καὶ . . . δὶς ἐς τὸν αὐτὸν ποταμὸν οὐκ ἂν ἐμβαίης.

Everything goes on, nothing stays, and . . . twice into the same river you would not walk.[36]

[35] Austin (1962: 9–10); Berlin (1973).
[36] Plato, *Cratylus* 402A.

Bibliography

Both primary and secondary sources are given in the same list below; most books and articles listed are those cited in the notes, though some are given for general bibliographical purposes. Abbreviations for journals and reference works are given below. Colloquia, symposia, proceedings papers, and other collections are listed by editor or author when possible; otherwise, they appear alphabetically by the first word of the title.

Abbreviations for Journals and Reference Works

AF	*Archivio di Filosofia*
AGP	*Archiv für Geschichte der Philosophie*
AHDLMA	*Archives d'histoire doctrinale et littéraire du moyen âge*
AHR	*American Historical Review*
AK	*Archiv für Kulturgeschichte*
AP	*Archives de philosophie*
AR	*Archiv für Reformationsgeschichte*
AS	*Annals of Science*
ASNSP	*Annali della Scuola Normale Superiore di Pisa, Classe di lettere e filosofia*
BHR	*Bibliothèque d'humanisme et renaissance*
CH	*Church History*
CHLGEMP	*The Cambridge History of Later Greek and Early Medieval Philosophy*, ed. A. H. Armstrong, Cambridge (1970).
CHLMP	*The Cambridge History Of Later Medieval Philosophy*, ed. N. Kretzmann, A. Kenny, J. Pinborg and E. Stump, Cambridge (1982).
CHRP	*The Cambridge History of Renaissance Philosophy*, ed. C. B. Schmitt with Q. Skinner, E. Kessler and J. Kraye, Cambridge (1988).
CP	*Classical Philology*
DSB	*Dictionary of Scientific Biography*, New York (1970–80).

EHR	*English Historical Review*
EP	*The Encyclopedia of Philosophy*, ed. P. Edwards, New York (1967).
FS	*Franciscan Studies*
GCFI	*Giornale critico della filosofia italiana*
GRBS	*Greek, Roman and Byzantine Studies*
HL	*Humanistica Lovaniensia*
HPQ	*History of Philosophy Quarterly*
HTCWP	*A History of Twelfth-Century Western Philosophy*, ed. P. Dronke, Cambridge (1988)
IMU	*Italia medioevale e umanistica*
JHI	*Journal of the History of Ideas*
JHP	*Journal of the History of Philosophy*
JMH	*Journal of Modern History*
JMRS	*Journal of Medieval and Renaissance Studies*
JWCI	*Journal of the Warburg and Courtauld Institutes*
MH	*Medievalia et Humanistica*
MRS	*Medieval and Renaissance Studies*
PJ	*Philosophisches Jahrbuch*
RCSF	*Rivista critica di storia della filosofia*
RLI	*Rivista di letteratura italiana*
RQ	*Renaissance Quarterly*
RP	*Revue philosophique*
SCJ	*Sixteenth Century Journal*
SMRH	*Studies in Medieval and Renaissance History*
SP	*Studies in Philology*
SR	*Studies in the Renaissance*

Primary and Secondary Sources

Abbagnano, N. (ed.) (1941), *Bernardino Telesio e la filosofia del Rinascimento*, Milan.

Abel, G. (1978), *Stoizismus und frühe Neuzeit: Zur Entstehungsgeschichte modernen Denkens im Felde von Ethik und Politik*, Berlin.

Abrusci, V. M. *et al.* (eds.) (1983), *Atti del Convegno internazionale di storia della logica*, Bologna.

Adams, R. P. (1962), *The Better Part of Valor: More, Erasmus, Colet and Vives on Humanism, War and Peace, 1496–1535*, Seattle.

Agricola, R. (1703), *Opera*, Leiden.

—— (1967), *Rodolphi Agricolae Phrisii de inventione dialectica libri omnes et integri et recogniti . . . cum aliis non parum multis eodem pertinentibus . . .*, repr., Frankfurt/Main.

Agrippa, H. C. (1970), *Opera*, ed. R. Popkin, repr., New York.

Aiton, E. J. (1985), *Leibniz: A Biography*, Boston.

Akkerman, F., and Vanderjagt, A. J. (eds.) (1988), *Rodolphus Agricola Phrisius, 1444–1485: Proceedings of the International Conference at the University of Groningen*, Leiden.

Alberti, L. B. (1890), *Opera inedita et pauca separatim impressa*, ed. G. Mancini, Florence.

—— (1960–73), *Opere volgari*, ed. C. Grayson, Bari.

Allen, D. C. (1944), 'The Rehabilitation of Epicurus and his Theory of Pleasure in the Early Renaissance', *SP* 41: 1–15.

Allen, J. W. (1960), *A History of Political Thought in the Sixteenth Century*, London.

Allen, M. J. B. (1975), 'The Absent Angel in Ficino's Philosophy', *JHI* 36: 219–40.

—— (1977), 'Ficino's Lecture on the Good?', *RQ* 30: 160–71.

—— (1980a), 'Cosmogony and Love: The Role of *Phaedrus* in Ficino's *Symposium* Commentary', *JMRS* 10: 131–53.

—— (1980b), 'Two Commentaries on the *Phaedrus*: Ficino's Indebtedness to Hermias', *JWCI* 43: 110–29.

—— (1980c), 'The Sibyl in Ficino's Oaktree', *Modern Language Notes*, 95: 205–10.

—— (1981), *Marsilio Ficino and the Phaedran Charioteer*, Berkeley, Calif.

—— (1982a), 'Ficino's Theory of the Five Substances and the Neoplatonists' *Parmenides*', *JMRS* 12: 19–44.

—— (1982b), 'Marsilio Ficino on Plato's Pythagorean Eye', *Modern Language Notes*, 97: 171–82.

—— (1984a), 'Marsilio Ficino on Plato, the Neoplatonists and the Christian Doctrine of the Trinity', *RQ* 37: 555–84.

—— (1984b), *The Platonism of Marsilio Ficino: A Study of His* Phaedrus *Commentary, its Sources and Genesis*, Berkeley, Calif.

—— (1986), 'The Second Ficino–Pico Controversy: Parmenidean Poetry, Eristic and the One', in Garfagnini (1986: i. 417–55).

—— (1987), 'Marsilio Ficino's Interpretation of Plato's *Timaeus* and its Myth of the Demiurge', in Hankins, Monfasani, and Purnell (1987: 399–439).

—— (1988), 'Marsile Ficin, Hermès et le Corpus Hermeticum', in Faivre (1988: 110–19).

—— (1989), *Icastes: Marsilio Ficino's Interpretation of Plato's Sophist*

(Five Studies and a Critical Edition with Translation), Berkeley, Calif.

—— (forthcoming), 'Homo ad zodiacum: Marsilio Ficino and the Boethian Hercules.'

—— and White, R. A. (1981), 'Ficino's Hermias Translation and a New Apologue', *Scriptorium*, 35: 39–47.

Allen, P. S. (1906), 'The Letters of Rudolph Agricola', *EHR* 21: 302–17.

—— (1914), *The Age of Erasmus*, Oxford.

Amabile, L. (1882), *Fra Tommaso Campanella, la sua congiuria, i suoi processi, la su pazzia*, Naples.

—— (1887), *Fra Tommaso Campanella ne' castelli di Napoli, in Roma, in Parigi*, Naples.

Amerio, R. (1972), *Il sistema teologico di Tommaso Campanella*, Milan.

Anagnine, E. (1937), *Pico della Mirandola: sincretismo religioso-filosofico*, Bari.

Anastos, M. (1948), 'Pletho's Calendar and Liturgy', *Dumbarton Oaks Papers*, 4: 183–305.

Andrés, M. (1976–7), *La teologia española en el siglo XVI*, Madrid.

Andrés Marcos, T. (1947), *Los imperialismos de Juan Ginés de Sepúlveda en su Democrates alter*, Madrid.

Anglo, S. (ed.) (1977), *The Damned Art: Essays in the Literature of Witchcraft*, London.

Anton, J. P. (ed.) (1967), *Naturalism and Historical Understanding*, Buffalo.

Antonaci, A. (1971–8), *Marcantonio Zimara: Ricerche sull'aristotelismo del rinascimento*, Lecce.

—— (1984–), *Ricerche sul neoplatonismo del Rinascimento: Francesco Patrizi da Cherso*, Bari.

Antonazzi, G. (1985), *Lorenzo Valla e la polemica sulla donazione di Costantino*, Rome.

Aquilecchia, G. (1968), 'Appunti su G. B. Della Porta e l'Inquisizione', *Studi Secenteschi*, 9: 3–31.

—— (1971), *Giordano Bruno*, Rome.

—— (1976), 'Giambattista Della Porta e l'Inquisizione', in *Schede di Italianistica*, Turin: 219–54.

Arcari, P. M. (1935), *Il pensiero politico di Francesco Patrizi da Cherso*, Rome.

Aristotelismo padovano e filosofia aristotelica (1960), *Atti del XII convegno internazionale di filosofia*, ix, Florence.

Aristotle (1984), *The Complete Works of Aristotle*, ed. J. Barnes, Princeton, NJ.

Aristotle and Averroes (1962), *Omnia opera*, repr., Frankfurt.

Arts libéraux et philosophie au moyen âge: Actes du quatrième congrès international de philosophie médiévale, Université de Montréal, 27 août–2 septembre 1967 (1969), Montreal.

Ashworth, E. J. (1974), *Language and Logic in the Post-Medieval Period*, Dordrecht/Boston.

—— (1982), 'The Eclipse of Medieval Logic', *CHLMP*: 787–96.

—— (1985), *Studies in Post-Medieval Semantics*, London.

—— (1986), 'Renaissance Man as Logician: Josse Clichtove (1472–1543) on Disputations', *History and Philosophy of Logic*, 7: 15–29.

—— (1988), 'Traditional Logic', *CHRP*: 143–72.

Ashworth, W. (1990), 'Natural History and the Emblematic World View', in Lindberg and Westman (1990: 303–32).

Atanasijevic, K. (1972), *The Metaphysical and Geometrical Doctrine of Bruno as Given in his Work* De triplici minimo, trans. G. Tomashevich, St Louis, Mo.

Atti del convegno internazionale di studio, Giovan Battista Benedetti e il suo tempo (1987), Venice.

Atti del Symposium internazionale di storia, metodologia, logica e filosofia della scienza: Galileo nella storia e nella filosofia della scienza (1967), Vinci.

Austin, J. L. (1962), *How To Do Things with Words*, Cambridge, Mass.

Ayer, A. J. (1952), *Language, Truth and Logic*, New York.

Backus, I. (1983), 'Agrippa on "Human Knowledge of God" and "Human Knowledge of the External World"', *AGP* 65: 147–59.

Bacon, F. (1857–74), *Works*, ed. J. Spedding, London.

Badaloni, N. (1955), *La filosofia di Giordano Bruno*, Florence.

—— (1959–60), 'I fratelli Della Porta e la cultura magica e astrologica a Napoli nel' 500', *Studi storici*, 1: 677–715.

—— (1965), *Tommaso Campanella*, Milan.

—— (1988), *Giordano Bruno: tra cosmologia e etica*, Bari.

Bainton, R. (1969), *Erasmus of Christendom*, New York.

Banfi, A. (ed.) (1953), *La crisi dell'uso dogmatico della ragione*, Milan.

Baron, H. (1927), 'Willensfreiheit und Astrologie bei Marsilio Ficino und Pico della Mirandola', *Kultur- und Universalgeschichte*: 145–70.

—— (1938), 'Cicero and Roman Civic Spirit in the Middle Ages and

Early Renaissance', *Bulletin of the John Rylands Library*, 22: 72–97.

—— (1961), 'Machiavelli: The Republican Citizen and Author of the *Prince*', *EHR* 76: 217–53.

—— (1966), *The Crisis of the Early Italian Renaissance: Civic Humanism and Republican Liberty in an Age of Classicism and Tyranny*, Princeton, NJ.

—— (1968*a*), *Humanistic and Political Literature in Florence and Venice at the Beginning of the Quattrocento: Studies in Criticism and Chronology*, New York.

—— (1968*b*), *From Petrarch to Leonardo Bruni: Studies in Humanistic and Political Literature*, Chicago.

—— (1968*c*), 'The *Querelle* of the Ancients and Moderns as a Problem for Renaissance Scholarship', in Kristeller and Wiener (1968: 95–114).

—— (1985), *Petrarch's 'Secretum': Its Making and Meaning*, Cambridge, Mass.

Barozzi, L. and Sabbadini, R. (1891), *Studi sul Panormita e sul Valla*, Florence.

Bataillon, M. (1937), *Erasme et l'Espagne*, Paris.

Baxandall (1971), *Giotto and the Orators: Humanist Observers of Painting in Italy and the Discovery of Pictorial Composition, 1350–1450*, Oxford.

Bédarida, H. (ed.) (1950), *Pensée humaniste et tradition chrétienne aux XVᵉ et XVIᵉ siècles*, Paris.

Bedouelle, G. (1976), *Lefèvre d'Étaples et l'intelligence des Écritures*, Geneva.

Beltrán de Heredia, V. (1939), *Francisco de Vitoria*, Barcelona.

Bentley, J. H. (1983), *Humanists and Holy Writ: New Testament Scholarship in the Renaissance*, Princeton, NJ.

—— (1987), *Politics and Culture in Renaissance Naples*, Princeton, NJ.

Berlin, I. (1973), 'Austin and the Early Beginnings of Oxford Philosophy', in G. Warnock (1973: 1–16).

—— (1982), *Against the Current: Essays in the History of Ideas*, ed. H. Hardy and R. Hausheer, London.

Bertalot, L. (1975), *Studien zum italienischen und deutschen Humanismus*, ed. P. O. Kristeller, Rome.

Bertelli, S. *et al.* (eds.) (1980), *Florence and Venice: Comparisons and Relations*, Florence.

—— *et al.* (eds.) (1989), *Florence and Milan, Comparisons and*

Relations: Acts of Two Conferences at Villa I Tatti in 1982–1984, Florence.

Bérubé, C. (ed.) (1978), *Regnum hominis et regnum dei: Acta quarti Congressus Scotistici internationalis Patavii, 24–29 septembris 1976*, Rome.

Bett, H. (1932), *Nicholas of Cusa*, London.

Bianca, C. (1980), 'La formazione della biblioteca latina del Bessarione', in *Scrittura, biblioteche e stampa a Roma nel Quattrocento*, Vatican City: 103–65.

Bianchi, M. L. (forthcoming), 'Scholastische Motive im ersten und zweiten Buch des *De subtilitate* Girolamo Cardans'.

Biblioteca degli Ardenti della Città di Viterbo: Studi e ricerche nel 150° della fondazione (1960), Viterbo.

Biechler, J. E. (1975), *The Religious Language of Nicholas of Cusa*, Missoula, Mont.

Bigi, E. (1967), *La cultura del Poliziano e altri studi umanistici*, Pisa.

Billanovich, G. (1947), *Petraca letterato*, Rome.

—— (1951), 'Petrarch and the Textual Criticism of Livy', *JWCI* 14: 137–208.

—— (1953), *I primi umanisti e le tradizioni dei classici latini*, Fribourg.

—— (1981), *La tradizione del testo di Livio e le origini dell'umanesimo*, Padua.

Birkenmajer, A. (1970), 'Le Rôle joué par les médecins et les naturalistes dans la réception d'Aristote au XIIe et XIIIe siècles,' in *Études d'histoire des sciences et de la philosophie du moyen âge*, Wrocław.

Blanchet, L. (1920), *Campanella*, Paris.

Blau, J. L. (1944), *The Christian Interpretation of the Cabala in the Renaissance*, New York.

Bluhm, H. (ed.) (1965), *Essays in History and Literature Presented to Stanley Pargellis*, Chicago.

Blum, P. R. (1980), *Aristoteles bei Giordano Bruno: Studien zur philosophischen Rezeption*, Munich.

Boase, A. M. (1970), *The Fortunes of Montaigne: A History of the Essays in France, 1580–1669*, New York.

Bochenski, I. M. (1970), *A History of Formal Logic*, trans. I. Thomas, 2nd edn., New York.

Bock, G. (1974), *Tommaso Campanella*, Tübingen.

Boggess, W. F. (1970), 'Aristotle's *Poetics* in the Fourteenth Century', *SP* 67: 278–94.

Bolgar, R. R. (1954), *The Classical Heritage and Its Beneficiaries*,

Cambridge.

—— (ed.) (1971), *Classical Influences on European Culture, A.D. 500–1500*, Cambridge.

—— (ed.) (1976), *Classical Influences on European Culture, A.D. 1500–1700*, Cambridge.

Bolzoni, L. (1980), *L'universo dei poemi possibili: Studi su Francesco Patrizi da Cherso*, Rome.

Bonilla y San Martin, A. (1929), *Luis Vives y la filosofia del Renacimiento*, Madrid.

Bosco, U. (1968), *Francisco Petrarca*, 4th edn., Bari.

Bottin, F. (1972), 'La teoria del *regressus* in Giacomo Zabarella', in Giacon (1972: 48–70).

Bouwsma, W. J. (1973), *The Culture of Renaissance Humanism*, Washington, DC.

Bowen, B. C. (1972), 'Cornelius Agrippa's *De vanitate*: Polemic or Paradox?', *BHR* 34: 249–65.

Bracciolini, P. (1964–9), *Opera omnia*, ed. R. Fubini, repr., Turin.

Branca, V. (ed.) (1964), *Umanesimo europeo e umanesimo veneziano*, Florence.

—— (ed.) (1967), *Rinascimento europeo e rinascimento veneziano*, Florence.

—— (1973), 'Ermolao Barbaro and late Quattrocento Venetian Humanism', in Hale (1973: 218–43).

—— (1980), 'L'umanesimo veneziano alla fine del Quattrocento: Ermolao Barbaro e il suo circolo', in *Storia della cultura veneta*, iii.1, Vicenza: 123–75.

—— (1983), *Poliziano e l'umanesimo della parola*, Turin.

—— (1986), 'Tra Ficino "Orfeo ispirato" e Poliziano "Ercole ironico"', in Garfagnini (1986: ii. 459–75).

Breen, Q. (1952), 'Giovanni Pico della Mirandola on the Conflict of Philosophy and Rhetoric', *JHI* 13: 384–426.

—— (1954), 'The *Observationes in M.T. Ciceronem* of Marius Nizolius', *SR* 1: 49–58.

—— (1955a), 'Mario Nizolio's *Contradisquisitio*', *Rinascimento* 6: 195–208.

—— (1955b), 'Marius Nizolius (1488–1567): Ciceronian Lexicographer and Philosopher', *AR* 46: 62–87.

—— (1958), 'The *Antiparadoxicon* of Marcantonius Majoragius or, A Humanist Becomes a Critic of Cicero as a Philosopher', *SR* 5: 37–48.

Brezzi, P., and Lorch, M. (eds.) (1984), *Umanesimo a Roma nel*

Quattrocento: Atti del Convegno ... New York, 1–4 dicembre 1981, Rome.

Brickman, B. (1941), *An Introduction to Francesco Patrizi's* Nova de universis philosophia, New York.

Broadie, A. (1985), *The Circle of John Mair: Logic and Logicians in Pre-Reformation Scotland*, Oxford.

—— (1987), *Introduction to Medieval Logic*, Oxford.

Brown, A. (1979), *Bartolomeo Scala, 1430–1497, Chancellor of Florence: The Humanist as Bureaucrat*, Princeton, NJ.

—— (1986), 'Platonism in Fifteenth-Century Florence and its Contribution to Early Modern Political Thought', *JMH* 58: 383–413.

Brown, F. S. (1963), *Religious and Political Conservativism in the Essais of Montaigne*, Geneva.

Brown, J. E. (1978), 'The Science of Weights,' in Lindberg (1978a: 179–205).

Bruni, L. (1741), *Epistolarum libri VIII*, ed. L. Mehus, Florence.

—— (1969), *Humanistisch-philosophische Schriften*, ed. H. Baron, repr., Wiesbaden.

—— (1987), *The Humanism of Leonardo Bruni: Selected Texts*, ed. and trans. G. Griffiths, J. Hankins, and D. Thompson, Binghamton, NY.

Bruno, G. (1954), *Des Fureurs Héroïques (De gl'heroici furori)*, ed. and trans. P.-H. Michel, Paris.

—— (1955), *La cena de le ceneri*, ed. G. Aquilecchia, Turin.

—— (1957), *Due dialoghi sconosciuti e due dialoghi noti*, ed. G. Aquilecchia, Turin.

—— (1958), *Dialoghi italiani*, ed. G. Gentile and G. Aquilecchia, Florence.

—— (1962a), *Jordani Bruni Nolani opera latine conscripta*, repr., Stuttgart/Bad Cannstatt.

—— (1962b), *Five Dialogues by Giordano Bruno: Cause, Principle and Unity*, trans. J. Lindsay, New York.

—— (1964a), *Giordano Bruno's* The Heroic Frenzies: *A Translation with Introduction and Notes*, Chapel Hill, NC.

—— (1964b), *The Expulsion of the Triumphant Beast*, trans. A. D. Imerti, New Brunswick, NJ.

—— (1964c), *Il Candelaio*, ed. G. Barberi Squarotti, Turin.

—— (1964d), 'Praelectiones geometricae' e 'Ars deformationum', ed. G. Aquilecchia, Rome.

—— (1964e), *The Heroic Frenzies: A Translation with Introduction and Notes*, trans. P. E. Memmo, Chapel Hill, NC.

—— (1973), *De la causa, principio et uno*, ed. G. Aquilecchia, Turin.

—— (1975), *The Ash Wednesday Supper: La cena de le ceneri*, trans. S. L. Jaki, The Hague.

—— (1977), *The Ash Wednesday Supper: La cena de le ceneri*, ed. and trans. E. Gosselin and L. Lerner, Hamden, Conn.

—— (1980), *Opere latine*, ed. C. Monti, Turin.

Brush, C. B. (1966), *Montaigne and Bayle: Variations on the Theme of Scepticism*, The Hague.

Bruton, O. G. (1953), 'The Debate between Bartolomé de Las Casas and Juan Ginés de Sepúlveda over the Justice of the Spanish Conquest of America: Spain, 1550', Princeton University dissertation.

Bruyère, N. (1984), *Méthode et dialectique dans l'œuvre de La Ramée: Renaissance et âge classique*, Paris.

Buck, A. (1957), *Das Geschichtsdenken der Renaissance*, Krefeld.

—— (1976), *Die Rezeption der Antike in den romanischen Literaturen der Renaissance*, Berlin.

—— (ed.) (1981*a*), *Juan Luis Vives: Wolfenbütteler Arbeitsgespräch*, Hamburg.

—— (ed.) (1981*b*), *Die Rezeption der Antike: zum Problem der Kontinuität zwischen Mittelalter und Renaissance: Vortrage gehalten anlasslich des ersten Kongresses des Wolfenbütteler Arbeitskreises für Renaissanceforschung*, Hamburg.

—— (ed.) (1987), *Das Ende der Renaissance: Europäische Kultur um 1600*, Wiesbaden.

—— and Heitmann, K. (1983), *Die Antike-Rezeption in den Wissenschaften während der Renaissance*, Weinheim.

—— and Herding, O. (eds.) (1975), *Der Kommentar in der Renaissance*, Boppard.

Bühler, C. (1960), *The Fifteenth-Century Book: The Scribes, the Printers, the Decorators*, Philadelphia.

—— (1973), *Early Books and Manuscripts*, New York.

Buhler, S. M. (1990), 'Marsilio Ficino's *De stella magorum* and Renaissance Views of the Magi', *RQ* 43: 348–71.

Bullard, M. (1990), 'Marsilio Ficino and the Medici', in Verdon and Henderson (1990: 467–92).

Burckhardt, J. (1990), *The Civilization of the Renaissance in Italy*, trans. S. Middlemore, ed. P. Burke and P. Murray, London.

Burdach, K. (1963), *Reformation, Renaissance, Humanismus*, 3rd edn., Darmstadt.

Burke, P. (1970), *The Renaissance Sense of the Past*, New York.

—— (1974), *Tradition and Innovation in Renaissance Italy, 1420–1540*,

London.

Burke, P. (1977), 'Witchcraft and Magic in Renaissance Italy: Gian-francesco Pico and his *Strix*', in Anglo (1977: 32–52).

—— (1981), *Montaigne*, Oxford.

Burns, J. H. (1954), 'New Light on John Major', *Innes Review*, 5: 83–100.

Burnyeat, M. F. (ed.) (1983), *The Skeptical Tradition*, Berkeley, Calif.

Bush, D. (1939), *The Renaissance and English Humanism*, Toronto.

—— (1952), *Classical Influences in Renaissance Literature*, Cambridge, Mass.

Butler, P. (1940), *The Origin of Printing in Europe*, Chicago.

Cammelli, G. (1941–54), *I dotti bizantini e le origini dell'umanesimo*, Florence.

Campana, A. (1946), 'The Origin of the Word "Humanist"', *JWCI* 9: 60–73.

Campanella, T. (1638), *Universalis philosophiae seu metaphysicarum rerum iuxta propria dogmata, partes tres, libri 18*, Paris.

—— (1854), *Opere*, ed. A. d'Ancona, Turin.

—— (1925), *Del senso delle cose e della magia*, ed. A Bruers, Bari.

—— (1927), *Lettere*, ed. V. Spampanato, Bari.

—— (1939), *Epilogo magno (Fisiologia Italiana)*, ed. C. Ottaviano, Rome.

—— (1949–), *Theologicorum libri*, ed. R. Amerio, Florence.

—— (1957), *Magia e grazia*, ed. R. Amerio, Rome.

—— (1960), *Monarchia messiae*, ed. L. Firpo, Turin.

—— (1962), *La Città del Sole*, ed. A. Seroni, Milan.

—— (1974), *La filosofia che i sensi ci additano (Philosophia sensibus demonstrata)*, ed. L. de Franco, Naples.

—— (1975), *Opera latina Francofurti impressa annis 1617–1630*, ed. L. Firpo, Turin.

Camporeale, S. (1972), *Lorenzo Valla: Umanesimo e teologia*, Florence.

—— (1976), 'Lorenzo Valla tra medioevo e rinascimento: *Encomion S. Thomae*, 1457', *Memorie domenicane*, NS 7: 3–190.

—— (1988), 'Lorenzo Valla e il *De falso credita donatione*: Retorica, libertà ed ecclesiologia nel '400', *Memorie domenicane*, NS 19: 191–293.

Cantimori, D. (1937), 'Rhetoric and Politics in Italian Humanism', *JWCI* 1: 83–162.

—— (1975), *Umanesimo e religione nel Rinascimento*, Turin.

Cardano, G. (1934), *The First Book of Jerome Cardan's* De subtilitate, *Translated from the Original Latin with Text, Introduction and Commentary*, ed. and trans. M. M. Cass, Williamsport, Penn.

—— (1962), *The Book of My Life (De vita propria liber)*, trans. J. Stoner, New York.

—— (1967), *Opera omnia*, ed. C. Spon, repr., New York.

Il Cardinale Bessarione nel V centenario della morte (1472–1972) (1974), Rome.

Carreras y Artau, T. and Carreras y Artau, J. (1939–43), *Historia de la filosofía española: Filosofía cristiana de los siglos XIII al XV*, Madrid.

Carvalho, J. de (1952), *Francisco Sanches, filósofo*, Braga.

Casacci, A. (1926), 'Gli *Elegantiarum libri* di Lorenzo Valla', *Atene e Roma*, NS 3: 187–203.

Case, J. (1599), *Lapis philosophicus seu commentarius in 8° libros physicorum Aristotelis. . .* , Oxford.

Caspari, F. (1968), *Humanism and the Social Order in Tudor England*, New York.

Cassirer, E. (1945), 'Ficino's Place in Intellectual History', *JHI* 6: 483–501.

—— (1946), *The Myth of the State*, ed. C. W. Hendel, New Haven, Conn.

—— (1963), *The Individual and the Cosmos in Renaissance Philosophy*, trans. M. Domandi, New York.

—— (1968), 'Giovanni Pico della Mirandola: A Study in the History of Renaissance Ideas', in Kristeller and Wiener (1968: 11–60).

—— (1974), *Das Erkenntnisproblem in der Philosophie und Wissenschaft der neueren Zeit*, Darmstadt.

—— , Kristeller, P. O., and Randall, J. H., Jr. (eds.) (1948), *The Renaissance Philosophy of Man: Selections in Translation*, Chicago.

Cassuto, U. (1965), *Gli ebrei a Firenze nell'età del Rinascimento*, repr., Florence.

Castelli, E. (ed.) (1951), *Umanesimo e scienza politica: Atti del Congresso internazionale di studi umanistici, Roma–Firenze, 1949*, Milan.

—— (ed.) (1960), *Umanesimo e esoterismo*, Padua.

Castelli, P. (ed.) (1980), *Un toscano del '400: Poggio Bracciolini, 1380–1459: Catalogo della mostra*, Terranuova Bracciolini.

—— et al. (1984), *Il Lume del Sole: Marsilio Ficino, Medico dell'Anima: Figline Valdarno, Vecchio Palazzo Comunale, 18 maggio–19 agosto 1984*, Florence.

Castellio, S. (1981), *De arte dubitandi et confidendi, ignorandi et sciendi*, ed. E. Feist Hirsch, Leiden.

Cavazza, S. (1982), 'Platonismo e riforma religiosa: la *Theologia vivificans* di Jacques Lefèvre d'Étaples', *Rinascimento*, ser. 2, 22: 99–149.

Cavini, W. (1977), 'Appunti sulla prima diffusione in occidente delle opere di Sesto Empirico', *Medioevo*, 3: 1–20.

Céard, J. (1977), *La Nature et les prodiges : L'Insolite au 16ᵉ siècle en France*, Geneva.

Centenario del Cardinale Bessarione (1973), *Miscellanea francescana*, 73: 249–386.

Chabod, F. (1965), *Machiavelli and the Renaissance*, trans. D. Moore, London.

Chadwick, H. (1990), *Boethius: The Consolations of Music, Logic, Theology and Philosophy*, Oxford.

Chambers, R. W. (1935), *Thomas More*, London.

Charbonnel, R. (1919), *La Pensée italienne au XVIᵉ siècle et le courant libertin*, Paris.

Chartier, R. (1987), *The Cultural Uses of Print in Early Modern France*, trans. L. Cochrane, Princeton, NJ.

Chastel, A. (1954), *Marsile Ficin et l'art*, Geneva.

—— (1961), *Art et humanisme à Florence au temps de Laurent le Magnifique: Études sur la renaissance et l'humanisme platonicien*, Paris.

Chinard, G. (1970), *L'Exotisme américain dans la littérature française au XVIᵉ siècle d'après Rabelais, Ronsard, Montaigne*, repr., Geneva.

Chomarat, J. (1981), *Grammaire et rhétorique chez Érasme*, Paris.

Ciliberto, M. (1979), *Lessico di Giordano Bruno*, Rome.

Clark, A. C. (1909), *Inventa italorum*, Oxford.

Clubb, L. G. (1965), *Giambattista Della Porta: Dramatist*, Princeton, NJ.

Clulee, N. H. (1988), *John Dee's Natural Philosophy: Between Science and Religion*, London.

Coccia, A. (1974), 'Vita e opere del Bessarione', in *Il Cardinale Bessarione*: 24–51.

Cochrane, E. (ed.) (1970), *The Late Italian Renaissance, 1425–1630*, London.

—— (1981), *Historians and Historiography in the Italian Renaissance*, Chicago.

Cogan, M. (1984), 'Rodolphus Agricola and the Semantic Revolutions of the History of Invention', *Rhetorica*, 2: 163–94.

Colish, M. L. (1962), 'The Mime of God: Vives on the Nature of Man', *JHI* 23: 3–20.

—— (1985), *The Stoic Tradition from Antiquity to the Early Middle Ages*, Leiden.

Collins, A. B. (1974), *The Secular is Sacred: Platonism and Thomism in Marsilio Ficino's* Platonic Theology, The Hague.

Colomer, E. (1961), *Nikolaus von Kues und Ramon Llull aus Handscriften der Kueser Bibliothek*, Berlin.

Convegno internazionale: L'Averroismo in Italia (Roma, 18–20 aprile 1977) (1979), Rome.

Cook, H. J. (1990), 'The New Philosophy and Medicine in Seventeenth-Century England', in Lindberg and Westman (1990: 397–436).

Copenhaver, B. P. (1977), 'Lefèvre d'Étaples, Symphorien Champier and the Secret Names of God', *JWCI* 40: 189–211.

—— (1978a), *Symphorien Champier and the Reception of the Occultist Tradition in Renaissance France*, The Hague.

—— (1978b), 'The Historiography of Discovery in the Renaissance: The Sources and Composition of Polydore Vergil's *De inventoribus rerum*, I–III', *JWCI* 41: 192–214.

—— (1984), 'Scholastic Philosophy and Renaissance Magic in the *De vita* of Marsilio Ficino', *RQ* 37: 523–54.

—— (1986), 'Renaissance Magic and Neoplatonic Philosophy: *Ennead* 4. 3. 5 in Ficino's *De vita coelitus comparanda*', in Garfagnini (1986: ii. 351–69).

—— (1987a), 'Iamblichus, Synesius and the *Chaldaean Oracles* in Marsilio Ficino's *De vita libri tres*: Hermetic Magic or Neoplatonic Magic?', in Hankins, Monfasani, and Purnell (1987: 441–55).

—— (1987b), 'Science and Philosophy in Early Modern Europe: The Historiographical Significance of the Work of Charles B. Schmitt', *AS* 44: 507–17.

—— (1988a), 'Hermes Trismegistus, Proclus, and the Question of a Philosophy of Magic in the Renaissance', in Merkel and Debus (1988: 79–110).

—— (1988b), 'Translation, Terminology and Style in Philosophical Discourse', *CHRP*: 77–110.

—— (1988c), 'Astrology and Magic', *CHRP*: 264–300.

—— (1990), 'Natural Magic, Hermetism, and Occultism in Early Modern Science', in Lindberg and Westman (1990: 261–301).

—— (1992), *Hermetica: The Greek* Corpus Hermeticum *and the Latin* Asclepius *in English Translation, with Notes and Introduction*,

Cambridge.

Copleston, F. (1960–66), *A History of Philosophy*, Westminster, Md.

Corsano, A. (1940), *Il pensiero di Giordano Bruno nel suo svolgimento storico*, Florence.

—— (1961*a*), *Tommaso Campanella*, Bari.

—— (1961*b*), 'Il *Liber de ludo aleae* di Girolamo Cardano: ragione e fortuna', *GCFI* 40: 87–91.

Cosenza, M. E. (1962–7), *Biographical and Bibliographical Dictionary of Italian Humanists and of the World of Classical Scholarship in Italy, 1300–1800*, Boston.

Couliano, I. P. (1987), *Eros and Magic in the Renaissance*, trans. M. Cook, Chicago.

Coulter, J. A. (1976), *The Literary Microcosm: Theories of Interpretation of the Later Neoplatonists*, Leiden.

Crahay, R. (1980), 'Un manifeste religieux d'anticulture: Le *De incertitudine et vanitate scientiarum et artium* de Corneille Agrippa', in Margolin (1980: 889–924).

Cranefield, P. (1970), 'On the Origin of the Phrase *Nihil est in intellectu quod non prius fuerit in sensu*', *JHM* 25: 77–80.

Cranz, F. E. (1953), 'Saint Augustine and Nicholas of Cusa in the Tradition of Western Thought', *Speculum*, 28: 297–316.

—— (1958), 'The Prefaces to the Greek Editions and Latin Translations of Alexander of Aphrodisias, 1450 to 1575', *Proceedings of the American Philosophical Society*, 102: 510–46.

—— (1974), 'Cusanus, Luther and the Mystical Tradition', in Trinkaus and Oberman (1974: 93–103).

—— (1978), 'The Publishing History of the Aristotle Commentaries of Thomas Aquinas', *Traditio*, 34: 157–92.

—— (1987), 'Editions of the Latin Aristotle Accompanied by the Commentaries of Averroes', in Mahoney (1976*a*: 116–28).

—— and Schmitt, C. B. (1984), *A Bibliography of Aristotle Editions, 1501–1600*, 2nd edn., Baden-Baden.

Craven, W. G. (1981), *Giovanni Pico della Mirandola, Symbol of his Age: Modern Interpretations of a Renaissance Philosopher*, Geneva.

Crescini, A. (1965), *Le origini del metodo analitico: il Cinquecento*, Udine.

—— (1972), *Il problema metodologico alle origini della scienza moderna*, Rome.

Crociata, M. (1987), *Umanesimo e teologia in Agostino Steuco: Neoplatonismo e teologia della creazione nel 'De perenni philosophia'*, Rome.

Crombie, A. C. (1953), *Robert Grosseteste and the Origins of Experimental Science, 1100–1700*, Oxford.

—— (1959), *Medieval and Early Modern Science*, New York.

—— (1977), 'Mathematics and Platonism in Sixteenth-Century Italian Universities and in Jesuit Educational Policy', in Maeyama and Saltzer (1977: 63–94).

Crouzel, H. (1977), *Une controverse sur Origène à la renaissance: Jean Pic de la Mirandole et Pierre Garcia*, Paris.

Cruz Costa, J. (1942), *Ensaio sôbre a vida e a obra do filósofo Francisco Sanches*, São Paulo.

Cusanus, N. (1954), *Of Learned Ignorance*, trans. G. Heron, London.

—— (1962), *Unity and Reform: Selected Writings of Nicholas de Cusa*, trans. J. P. Dolan, Chicago.

—— (1967), *Werke (Neuausgabe des Strassburger Drucks von 1488)*, ed. P. Wilpert, Berlin.

—— (1986), *De ludo globi: The Game of Spheres*, trans. P. M. Watts, New York.

—— (1989), *The Layman: On Wisdom and the Mind*, trans. M. L. Fuhrer, Ottawa.

Dal Pra, M. (1966), 'Una *oratio* programmatica di G. Zabarella', *RCSF* 21: 286–90.

D'Amico, J. F. (1983), *Renaissance Humanism in Papal Rome: Humanists and Churchmen on the Eve of the Reformation*, Baltimore.

—— (1988*a*), 'Humanism and Pre-Reformation Theology', in Rabil (1988: iii. 349–73).

—— (1988*b*), 'Humanism in Rome', in Rabil (1988: i. 264–88).

Darmstaedter, E. (1931), *Arznei und Alchemie: Paracelsus-Studien*, Leipzig.

De Bellis, D. (1975), 'Niccolò Leonico Tomeo, interprete di Aristotele naturalista', *Physis*, 17: 71–93.

—— (1980), 'La vita e l'ambiente di Niccolò Leonico Tomeo', *Quaderni per la storia dell'università di Padova*, 13: 37–75.

Dear, P. (1988), *Mersenne and the Learning of the Schools*, Ithaca, NY.

De Pina Martins, J. V. (1979), *L'Utopie de Thomas More et l'humanisme*, Paris.

De Rosa, D. (1980), *Coluccio Salutati: il cancelliere e il pensatore politico*, Florence.

Debus, A. G. (1965), *The English Paracelsians*, London.

—— (1977), *The Chemical Philosophy: Paracelsian Science and Medicine in the Sixteenth and Seventeenth Centuries*, New York.

Debus, A. G. (1978), *Man and Nature in the Renaissance*, Cambridge.

Del Torre, M. A. (1968), *Studi su Cesare Cremonini: Cosmologia e logica nel tardo Aristotelismo padovano*, Padua.

Delcorno, C. (1967), 'Il Commentario *De fulmine* di Bernardino Telesio', *Aevum*, 41: 474–506.

Della Porta, G. (1589), *Magiae naturalis libri XX*, Naples.

—— (1957), *Natural Magick*, repr., New York.

Della Torre, A. (1902), *Storia dell'Accademia platonica di Firenze*, Florence.

Dell'Acqua, G., and Münster, L. (1965), 'I rapporti di Giovanni Pico della Mirandola con alcuni filosofi ebrei', *L'Opera*: 2, 149–68.

Descartes, R. (1964–76), *Œuvres de Descartes*, ed. C. Adam and P. Tannery, Paris.

—— (1985), *The Philosophical Writings of Descartes*, trans. J. Cottingham, R. Stoothoff, and D. Murdoch, Cambridge.

Devereux, J. A. (1969), 'The Object of Love in Ficino's Philosophy', *JHI* 30: 161–70.

—— (1975), 'The Textual History of Ficino's *De amore*', *RQ* 28: 173–82.

Di Leo, E. (1953), *Scienza e umanesimo in Girolamo Fracastoro*, 2nd edn., Salerno.

Di Napoli, G. (1947), *Tommaso Campanella, filosofo della restaurazione cattolica*, Padua.

—— (1963), *L'immortalità dell'anima nel rinascimento*, Turin.

—— (1965), *Giovanni Pico della Mirandola e la problematica dottrinale del suo tempo*, Rome.

—— (1971), *Lorenzo Valla: filosofia e religione nell'umanesimo italiano*, Rome.

—— (1973), *Studi sul rinascimento*, Naples.

Dibon, P. (1954–), *La Philosophie néerlandaise au siècle d'or*, Paris.

Dick, S. J. (1982), *Plurality of Worlds: The Origins of the Extraterrestrial Life Debate from Democritus to Kant*, Cambridge.

Dickens, A. G. (1976), *The German Nation and Martin Luther*, London.

—— and Tonkin, J. (1985), *The Reformation in Historical Thought*, Oxford.

Diels, H. (ed.) (1981), *Commentaria in Aristotelem graeca*, Berlin.

Dilg-Frank, R. (ed.) (1981), *Kreatur und Kosmos: Internationale Beitrage zur Paracelsusforschung*, Stuttgart.

Dillon, J. (1977), *The Middle Platonists: A Study of Platonism, 80 B.C. to A.D. 220*, London.

Dionisotti, A. C., Grafton, A., and Kraye, J. (eds.) (1988), *The Uses of Greek and Latin: Historical Essays*, London.

Dod, B. G. (1982), 'Aristoteles Latinus', *CHLMP*: 46–79.

Donazzolo, P. (1912), 'Francesco Patrizio di Cherso erudito del secolo XVI', *Atti e memorie della società Istriana di archeologia e storia patria*, 28: 1–147.

Dorez, L., and Thuasne, L. (1897), *Pic de la Mirandole en France (1485–1488)*, Paris.

Drake, S. (1976), *Galileo Against the Philosophers*, Los Angeles.

—— (1981), *Galileo at Work: His Scientific Biography*, Chicago.

Dréano, M. (1969), *La Pensée religieuse de Montaigne*, rev. edn., Paris.

Du Vair, G. (1945), *De la sainte philosophie: Philosophie morale des Stoïques*, ed. G. Michaut, Paris.

Duhem, P. (1906–13), *Études sur Léonard de Vinci*, Paris.

—— (1913–59), *Le Système du monde*, Paris.

—— (1985), *To Save the Phenomena: An Essay on the Idea of Physical Theory from Plato to Galileo*, trans. E. Dolan and C. Maschler, Chicago.

Dumutriu, A. (1977), *History of Logic*, Tunbridge Wells.

Düring, I. (1968), 'The Impact of Aristotle's Scientific Ideas in the Middle Ages and at the Beginning of the Scientific Revolution', *AGP* 50: 115–33.

Eamon, W. (1990), 'From the Secrets of Nature to Public Knowledge', in Lindberg and Westman (1990: 333–65).

Ebbesen, S. (1982), 'Ancient Scholastic Logic as the Source of Medieval Scholastic Logic', *CHLMP*: 101–27.

Ebert, H. (1929–30), 'Augustinus Steuchus und seine *Philosophia perennis*: Ein kritischer Beitrag zur Geschichte der Philosophie', *PJ* 42: 342–56, 510–26; 43: 92–100.

Edwards, W. F. (1960), 'The Logic of Jacopo Zabarella (1533–1589)', dissertation, Columbia Univ.

—— (1967), 'Randall on the Development of Scientific Method in the School of Padua: A Continuing Reappraisal', in Anton (1967: 53–68).

—— (1969), 'Jacopo Zabarella: A Renaissance Aristotelian's View of Rhetoric and Poetry and Their Relation to Philosophy', *Arts liberaux*: 843–54.

—— (1976), 'Niccolò Leoniceno and the Origins of Humanist Discussion of Method', in Mahoney (1976a: 283–305).

Eisenbichler, K., and Pugliese, O. Z. (eds.) (1986), *Ficino and*

Renaissance Neoplatonism, Toronto.

Eisenstein, E. (1980), *The Printing Press as an Agent of Change: Communications and Cultural Transformations in Early Modern Europe*, Cambridge.

Elford, D. (1988), 'William of Conches', *HTCWP*: 308–27.

Élie, H. (1950–1), 'Quelques maîtres de l'université de Paris vers l'an 1500', *AHDLMA* 18: 193–243.

Epicurisme au XVIᵉ siècle (1969), *Actes du VIIIᵉ congrès de l'Association Guillaume Budé*, Paris: 639–727.

Erasmus, D. (1906–58), *Opus epistolarum Desiderii Erasmi Roterdami*, ed. P. S. Allen, Oxford.

—— (1908), *Ciceronianus or A Dialogue on the Best Style of Speaking*, trans. I. Scott, New York.

—— (1941), *The Praise of Folly*, trans. H. H. Hudson, New York.

—— (1961–2), *Opera omnia, emendatiora et auctiora . . . studio et opera Joannis Clerici*, repr., Hildesheim.

—— (1964), *The 'Adages' of Erasmus: A Study with Translations*, trans. M. M. Phillips, Cambridge.

—— (1965*a*), *The Colloquies of Erasmus*, trans. C. R. Thompson, Chicago.

—— (1965*b*), *Il Ciceroniano o dello stile migliore*, ed. A. Gambaro, Brescia.

—— (1968), *The Education of a Christian Prince*, trans. L. K. Born, New York.

—— (1974–), *Collected Works*, Toronto.

—— (1978), *Literary and Educational Writings*, ii: *De Copia; De ratione studii*, ed. and trans. C. R. Thompson, in *Collected Works*, xxiv, Toronto.

—— (1979), *The Praise of Folly*, trans. C. H. Miller, New Haven, Conn.

—— (1990), *Erasmus' Annotations on the New Testament: Acts, Romans, I and II Corinthians*, ed. A. Reeve and M. Screech, Leiden.

Ettinghausen, H. (1972), *Francisco de Quevedo and the Neostoic Movement*, Oxford.

Eymard d'Angers, J. (1976), *Recherches sur le stoïcisme aux XVIᵉ et XVIIᵉ siècles*, ed. L. Antoine, Hildesheim.

Faider, P. (1922), *Juste Lipse*, Mons.

Faivre, A. (ed.) (1988), *Présence d'Hermès Trismégiste*, Paris.

Faust, A. (1922), 'Die Dialektik Rudolph Agricolas: Ein Beitrag zur Charakteristik des deutschen Humanismus', *AGP* 34: 118–35.

Febvre, L. (1962), *Le Problème de l'incroyance au XVIe siècle*, Paris.

—— and Martin, H.-J. (1971), *L'Apparition du livre*, 2nd edn., Paris.

Femiano, S. (1965), *Lo spiritualismo di Tommaso Campanella*, Naples.

—— (1968), *La metafisica di Tommaso Campanella*, Milan.

—— (1969), 'L'Antiaristotelismo essenziale di Tommaso Campanella', in *Tommaso Campanella . . . (1568–1968)*: 137–59.

—— (1973), *Studi sul pensiero di Tommaso Campanella*, Bari.

Ferguson, W. K. (1948), *The Renaissance in Historical Thought: Five Centuries of Interpretation*, Boston.

Ferm, V. (ed.) (1950), *A History of Philosophical Systems*, New York.

Fernández-Santamaria, J. A. (1977), *The State, War and Peace: Spanish Political Thought in the Renaissance, 1516–1559*, Cambridge.

Festugière, A.-J. (1941), *La Philosophie de l'amour de Marsile Ficin et son influence sur la littérature française au XVIe siècle*, 2nd edn., Paris.

Ficino, M. (1956), *Commentaire sur le Banquet de Platon*, ed. and trans. R. Marcel, 1956.

—— (1959), *Opera omnia*, repr., Turin.

—— (1964–70), *Théologie platonicienne de l'immortalité des âmes*, ed. and trans. R. Marcel, Paris.

—— (1975), *Marsilio Ficino: The Philebus Commentary*, ed. and trans. M. J. B. Allen, Berkeley, Calif.

—— (1975–), *The Letters of Marsilio Ficino: Translated from the Latin by Members of the Language Department of the School of Economic Science, London*, London.

—— (1981), *Marsilio Ficino and the Phaedran Charioteer: Introductions, Texts, Translations*, ed. and trans. M. J. B. Allen, Berkeley, Calif.

—— (1989), *Three Books on Life: A Critical Edition and Translation with Introduction and Notes*, ed. and trans. C. V. Kaske and J. R. Clarke, Binghamton, NY.

—— (1990), *Lettere I: Epistolarum familiarium liber I*, ed. S. Gentile, Florence.

Field, A. (1988), *The Origins of the Platonic Academy of Florence*, Princeton, NJ.

Fierz, M. (1983), *Girolamo Cardano, 1501–1576: Physician, Natural Philosopher, Mathematician, Astrologer and Interpreter of Dreams*, trans. H. Niman, Boston.

Figgis, J. N. (1960), *Political Thought from Gerson to Grotius:*

1414–1625, New York.

Figgis, J. N. (1965), *The Divine Right of Kings*, New York.

Fioravanti, G. (1983), 'L'apologetica anti-giudaica di Giannozzo Manetti', *Rinascimento*, ser. 2, 23: 3–32.

Fiorentino, F. (1868), *Pietro Pomponazzi: studi storici su l'idea di natura nel risorgimento italiano*, Florence.

—— (1872–4), *Bernardino Telesio ossia studi storici su la scuola bolognese e padovana del secolo XVI*, Florence.

—— (1911), *Studi e ritratti della Rinascenza*, Bari.

Firenze e la Toscana dei Medici nell'Europa del'500 (1983), Florence.

Firpo, L. (1940), *Bibliografia degli scritti di Tommaso Campanella*, Turin.

—— (1947), *Ricerche campanelliane*, Florence.

—— (1949), *Il processo di Giordano Bruno*, Naples.

Fitzpatrick, P. J. (1982), 'Neoscholasticism', *CHLMP*: 838–52.

Flasch, K. (1973), *Die Metaphysik des Einen bei Nikolaus von Kues*, Leiden.

Fletcher, G., and Schuete, M. B. (eds.) (1976), *Paradosis: Studies in Memory of Edwin A. Quain*, New York.

Flodr, M. (1973), *Incunabula classicorum: Wiegendrucke der griechischen und römischen Literatur*, Amsterdam.

Flores, E. (1980), *Le scoperte di Poggio e il testo di Lucrezio*, Naples.

Florilegium Historiale: Essays Presented to Wallace K. Ferguson (1971), Toronto.

Fois, M. (1969), *Il pensiero cristiano di Lorenzo Valla nel quadro storico-culturale del suo ambiente*, Rome.

Foster, K. (1984), *Petrarch: Poet and Humanist*, Edinburgh.

Fox, A. (1982), *Thomas More: History and Providence*, Oxford.

Fracastoro, G. (1555), *Opera omnia*, Venice.

Frame, D. M. (1955), *Montaigne's Discovery of Man: The Humanization of a Humanist*, New York.

—— (1965), *Montaigne: A Biography*, New York.

—— (1969), *Montaigne's Essais: A Study*, Englewood Cliffs, NJ.

—— (1977), *François Rabelais: A Study*, New York.

Franco, L. de (1969), 'La *Philosophia sensibus demonstrata* di Tommaso Campanella e la dottrina di Bernardino Telesio', *Tommaso Campanella (1569–1638)*: 115–39.

Freudenberger, T. (1935), *Augustinus Steuchus aus Gubbio*, Münster.

Friedman, J. (1978), *Michael Servetus: A Case Study in Total Heresy*, Geneva.

—— (1983), *The Most Ancient Testimony: Sixteenth Century Christian-*

Hebraica in the Age of Renaissance Nostalgia, Athens, Oh.

Friedrich, H. (1984), *Montaigne*, Paris.

Fryde, E. B. (1983), *Humanism and Renaissance Historiography*, London.

Fubini, R. (1975), 'Note su Valla e la composizione del *De voluptate*', in *I classici nel medioevo e nell'umanesimo*, Genoa: 11–57.

—— (1984), 'Ficino e i Medici all'avvento di Lorenzo il Magnifico', *Rinascimento*, ser. 2, 24: 3–52.

—— (1987), 'Ancora su Ficino e i Medici', *Rinascimento*, ser. 2, 27: 275–91.

Fubini, R., and Caroti, S. (eds.) (1980), *Poggio Bracciolini: Mostra di codici e documenti fiorentini*, Florence.

Funkenstein, A. (1986), *Theology and the Scientific Imagination from the Middle Ages to the Seventeenth Century*, Princeton, NJ.

Gabotto, F. (1889), 'L'epicureismo di Lorenzo Valla', *Rivista di filosofia scientifica*, ser. 2, 8: 651–72.

Gadol, J. (1969), *Leon Battista Alberti: Universal Man of the Early Renaissance*, Chicago.

—— (1976), 'Tommaso Campanella: The Agony of Political Theory in the Counter-Reformation', in Mahoney (1976a: 164–89).

Gaeta, F. (1955), *Lorenzo Valla: Filologia e storia nell'umanesimo italiano*, Naples.

Galilei, G. (1965), *Le opere*, ed. A. Favaro and I. Del Lungo, repr., Florence.

Gandillac, M. de (1942), *La Philosophie de Nicolas de Cuse*, Paris.

—— (1982), 'Neoplatonism and Christian Thought in the Fifteenth Century (Nicholas of Cusa and Marsilio Ficino)', in O'Meara (1982: 143–68).

García Villoslada, R. (1938), *La universidad de París durante los estudios de Francisco de Vitoria O.P. (1507–1522)*, Rome.

Garfagnini, G. (ed.) (1983), *Scienze, credenze occulte, livelli di cultura: Convegno internazionale di studi (Firenze, 26–30 giugno 1980)*, Florence.

—— (ed.) (1986), *Marsilio Ficino e il ritorno di Platone: Studi e documenti*, Florence.

Garin, E. (1937a), *Giovanni Pico della Mirandola: Vita e dottrina*, Florence.

—— (1937b), 'Ἐνδελέχεια e ἐντελέχεια nelle discussioni umanistiche', *Atene e Roma*, ser. 2, 5: 177–87.

—— (1938), 'La *dignitas hominis* e la letteratura patristica', *La Rinascita*, 4: 102–46.

380 Bibliography

Garin, E. (1939), 'Aristotelismo e platonismo del rinascimento', *La Rinascita*, 2: 641–71.

—— (1942), 'Marsilio Ficino, Girolamo Benivieni e Giovanni Pico', *GCFI* 23: 93–9.

—— (1947–50), 'Le traduzioni umanistiche di Aristotele nel secolo XV', *Atti e memorie dell'Accademia Fiorentina di scienze morali, 'La Colombaria'*, NS 2: 55–104.

—— (1950), 'Lo spirito cristiano di Pico della Mirandola', in Bédarida (1950: 169–84).

—— (1951), 'Ritratto di Marsilio Ficino', *Belfagor*, 6: 289–301.

—— (ed.) (1952), *Prosatori latini del Quattrocento*, Milan.

—— (1954), *Medioevo e rinascimento*, Bari.

—— (1957a), *L'educazione in Europa, 1400–1600*, Bari.

—— (1957b), 'Noterella Telesiana', *GCFI* 3rd ser., 11: 56–62.

—— (1958), *Studi sul platonismo medievale*, Florence.

—— (1959), 'Ricerche sull'epicureismo del Quattrocento', *Epicurea in memoriam Hectoris Bignone*, Genoa: 217–37.

—— (1960), 'Le "elezioni" e il problema dell'astrologia', in Castelli (1960: 17–37).

—— (1961a), *La cultura filosofica del rinascimento italiano*, Florence.

—— (1961b), 'Cusano e i platonici italiani del Quattrocento', in *Nicolò Cusano* (1961).

—— (1965a), *Italian Humanism: Philosophy and Civic Life in the Renaissance*, Oxford.

—— (1965b), 'Le interpretazioni del pensiero di Giovanni Pico', *L'Opera*: 1, 3–33.

—— (1966a), *Storia della filosofia italiana*, 2nd edn., Turin.

—— (1966b), *Educazione umanistica in Italia*, Bari.

—— (1967a), *Ritratti di umanisti*, Florence.

—— (1967b), *La cultura del rinascimento: Profilo storico*, 1967.

—— (1969a), *L'età nuova: Ricerche di storia della cultura dal XII al XVI secolo*, Naples.

—— (1969b), *Science and Civic Life in the Italian Renaissance*, trans. P. Munz, New York.

—— (1972), *Portraits from the Quattrocento*, trans. V. Velen and E. Velen, New York.

—— (1976), *Rinascite e rivoluzioni: movimenti culturali dal XIV al XVIII secolo*, 2nd edn., Bari.

—— (1983a), *Astrology in the Renaissance: The Zodiac of Life*, trans. C. Jackson, J. Allen, and C. Robertson, London.

—— (1983b), *Il ritorno dei filosofi antichi*, Naples.

—— (1985), '*Phantasia e Imaginatio* fra Marsilio Ficino e Pietro Pomponazzi', *GCFI* 5th ser., 5: 349–61.

—— (1986), 'Marsilio Ficino e il ritorno di Platone', in Garfagnini (1986: i. 3–13).

—— (1988), *Ermetismo del rinascimento*, Rome.

Gatti, H. (1989), *The Renaissance Drama of Knowledge: Giordano Bruno in England*, London.

Gaza, T. (1866), *Opera*, in *Patrologia graeca*, clxi, ed. J.-P. Migne, Paris.

—— (1975), *Epistole*, trans. and ed. E. Pinto, Naples.

Geanakoplos, D.J. (1962), *Greek Scholars in Venice: Studies in the Dissemination of Greek Learning from Byzantium to Western Europe*, Cambridge, Mass.

—— (1966), *Byzantine East and Latin West: Two Worlds of Christendom in Middle Ages and Renaissance*, New York.

—— (1974), 'The Discourse of Demetrius Chalcondyles on the Inauguration of Greek Studies at the University of Padua in 1463', *SR* 21: 118–44.

—— (1976), *Interaction of the 'Sibling' Byzantine and Western Cultures in the Middle Ages and Italian Renaissance (330–1600)*, New Haven, Conn.

—— (1988), 'Italian Humanism and the Byzantine Émigré Scholars', in Rabil (1988: i. 350–71).

—— (1989), *Constantinople and the West: Essays in the Late Byzantine (Palaeologan) and Italian Renaissances and the Byzantine and Roman Churches*, Madison, Wis.

Gellner, E. (1968), *Words and Things*, Harmondsworth.

Gentile, G. (1911), *Bernardino Telesio*, Bari.

—— (1925), *Giordano Bruno e il pensiero del Rinascimento*, 2nd edn., Florence.

—— (1968a), *Il pensiero italiano del Rinascimento*, 4th edn., Florence.

—— (1968b), *Studi sul Rinascimento*, 3rd edn., Florence.

Gentile, S. (1981), 'Per la storia del testo del *Commentarium in Convivium* di Marsilio Ficino', *Rinascimento*, ser. 2, 21: 3–27.

—— (1983), 'In margine all'epistola *De divino furore* di Marsilio Ficino', *Rinascimento*, NS 23: 33–77.

—— (1986), 'L'epistolario Ficiniano: Criteri e problemi di edizione', in Garfagnini (1986: i. 229–38).

—— (1987), 'Note sullo "Scrittoio" di Marsilio Ficino', in Hankins, Monfasani, and Purnell (1987: 339–97).

Gentile, S., Niccoli, S., and Viti, P. (1984), *Marsilio Ficino e il ritorno di Platone: Mostra di manoscritti, stampe e documenti, 17 maggio–16 giugno 1984*, Florence.

Gerl, H. B. (1974), *Rhetorik als Philosophie: Lorenzo Valla*, Munich.

—— (1981), *Philosophie und Philologie: Leonardo Brunis Übertragung der Nikomachischen Ethik in ihren philosophischen Prämissen*, Munich.

Gersh, S. E. (1978), *From Iamblichus to Eriugena: An Investigation of the Prehistory and Evolution of the Pseudo-Dionysian Tradition*, Leiden.

—— (1986), *Middle Platonism and Neoplatonism: The Latin Tradition*, Notre Dame, Ind.

Gerulaitis, L. V. (1976), *Printing and Publishing in Fifteenth-Century Venice*, Chicago.

Getino, L. G. A. (1930), *El maestro Francisco de Vitoria: su vida, su doctrina e influencia*, Madrid.

Giacon, C. (ed.) (1972), *Saggi e ricerche su Aristotele, S. Bernardo, Zabarella . . .* , Padua.

Giannantonio, P. (1971), *Cristoforo Landino e l'umanesimo volgare*, Naples.

—— (1972), *Lorenzo Valla, filologo e storiografo dell'umanesimo*, Naples.

Giard, L. (1985), 'La production logique de l'Angleterre au XVIe siècle', *Études philosophiques*, 3: 303–24.

Gilbert, A. H. (1938), *Machiavelli's 'Prince' and its Forerunners*, Durham, NC.

Gilbert, F. (1965), *Machiavelli and Guicciardini: Politics and History in Sixteenth Century Florence*, Princeton, NJ.

Gilbert, N. W. (1960), *Renaissance Concepts of Method*, New York.

—— (1963), 'Galileo and the School of Padua', *JHP* 1: 223–31.

Gill, J. (1959), *The Council of Florence*, Cambridge.

Gillispie, C. C. (ed.) (1970–80), *Dictionary of Scientific Biography*, New York.

Gilson, E. (1986), *Humanisme et renaissance*, ed. J.-F. Courtine, Paris.

Giménez Fernández, M. (1962), *Tratado de Indias y el doctor Sepúlveda*, Caracas.

Ginés de Sepúlveda, J. (1780), *Opera*, Madrid.

Glaesener, H. (1938), 'Juste Lipse et Guillaume du Vair', *Revue belge de philologie et d'histoire*, 17: 27–42.

Gleason, J. B. (1989), *John Colet*, Berkeley, Calif.

Goldammer, K. (1953), *Paracelsus: Natur und Offenbarung*, Hanover.

—— (1954), *Paracelsus-Studien*, Klagenfurt.

Goldbrunner, H. (1968), 'Durandus de Alvernia, Nicolaus von Oresme und Leonardo Bruni: Zu den Übersetzungen der pseudo-aristotelischen *Ökonomik*', *AK* 50: 200–39.

Goldschmidt, E. P. (1943), *Medieval Texts and their First Appearance in Print*, London.

Gombrich, E. H. (1969), *In Search of Cultural History*, Oxford.

—— (1971), *Norm and Form: Studies in the Art of the Renaissance*, 2nd edn., London.

—— (1972), *Symbolic Images: Studies in the Art of the Renaissance*, London.

—— (1986), *Aby Warburg: An Intellectual Biography, with a Memoir on the History of the Library by F. Saxl*, 2nd edn., Chicago.

González, R. C. (1946), *Francisco de Vitoria, estudio bibliografico*, Buenos Aires.

Gordon, P. W. G. (trans.) (1974), *Two Renaissance Book Hunters: The Letters of Poggius Bracciolini to Nicolaus de Niccolis*, New York.

Gordon-Bournique, G. (1987), 'A. O. Lovejoy and the "History of Ideas"', *JHI* 48: 207–10.

Gosselin, E. (1976), *The King's Progress to Jerusalem: Some Interpretations of David during the Reformation Period and their Patristic and Medieval Background*, Malibu, Calif.

—— (1987), 'Fra Giordano Bruno's Catholic Passion', in Hankins, Monfasani, and Purnell (1987: 537–61).

—— (1988), 'Bruno's "French Connection": A Historiographical Debate', in Merkel and Debus (1988: 166–81).

—— and Lerner, L. S. (1975), 'Galileo and the Long Shadow of Bruno', *Archives internationales d'histoire des sciences*, 25: 223–46.

Gouhier, H. (1958), *Les Premières Pensées de Descartes: Contribution à l'histoire de l'anti-renaissance*, 1958.

Grafton, A. (1983–), *Joseph Scaliger: A Study in the History of Classical Scholarship*, i: *Textual Criticism and Exegesis*, Oxford.

—— (1988a), 'Quattrocento Humanism and Classical Scholarship', in Rabil (1988: iii. 23–55).

—— (1988b), 'The Availability of Ancient Works', *CHRP*: 767–91.

—— (1990), *Forgers and Critics: Creativity and Duplicity in Western Scholarship*, Princeton, NJ.

—— (1991), *Defenders of the Text: The Traditions of Scholarship in* an *Age of Science, 1450–1800*, Cambridge, Mass.

Grafton, A. and Blair, A. (eds.) (1990), *The Transmission of Culture in Early Modern Europe*, Philadelphia.

—— and Jardine, L. (1986), *From Humanism to the Humanities: Education and the Liberal Arts in Fifteenth- and Sixteenth-Century Europe*, Cambridge, Mass.

Graiff, F. (1976), 'I prodigi e l'astrologia nei commenti di Pietro Pomponazzi al *De caelo*, alla *Meteora* e al *De generatione*', *Medioevo*, 2: 331–61.

—— (1979), 'Aspetti del pensiero di Pietro Pomponazzi nelle opere e nei corsi del periodo bolognese', *Annali dell'Istituto di filosofia, Università di Firenze*, 1: 69–130.

Grant, E. (1971), *Physical Science in the Middle Ages*, New York.

—— (1978), 'Aristotelianism and the Longevity of the Medieval World View', *History of Science*, 16: 93–106.

—— (1981), *Much Ado about Nothing: Theories of Space and Vacuum from the Middle Ages to the Scientific Revolution*, Cambridge.

—— (1982), 'The Effect of the Condemnation of 1277', *CHLMP*: 537–9.

—— (1984), 'Were there Significant Differences between Medieval and Early Modern Scholastic Natural Philosophy? The Case for Cosmology', *Noûs*, 18: 4–16.

Grassi, E. (1980), *Rhetoric as Philosophy: The Humanist Tradition*, University Park, Penn.

Gravelle, S. S. (1981), 'Humanist Attitudes to Convention and Innovation in the Fifteenth Century', *JMRS* 2: 193–209.

—— (1982), 'Lorenzo Valla's Comparison of Latin and Greek and the Humanist Background', *BHR* 44: 269–89.

—— (1988), 'The Latin-Vernacular Question and Humanist Theory of Language and Culture', *JHI* 49: 367–87.

—— (1989), 'A New Theory of Truth', *JHI* 50: 333–6.

Gray, H. H. (1965), 'Valla's *Encomium of St. Thomas Aquinas* and the Humanist Conception of Christian Antiquity', in Bluhm (1965: 37–51).

—— (1968), 'Renaissance Humanism: the Pursuit of Eloquence', in Kristeller and Wiener (1968: 199–216).

Grayson, C. (1960), *A Renaissance Controversy: Latin or Italian?* Oxford.

Grazia, S. de (1989), *Machiavelli in Hell*, Princeton, NJ.

Greenberg, S. (1950), *The Infinite in Giordano Bruno, with a Translation of his Dialogue* Concerning the Cause, Principle and One,

New York.

Gregory, T. (1988), 'The Platonic Inheritance', *HTCWP*: 54–80.

Grendler, P. F. (1969), *Critics of the Italian World, 1530–1560: Antonfrancesco Doni, Nicolò Franco and Ortensio Lando*, Princeton, NJ.

—— (1977), *The Roman Inquisition and the Venetian Press, 1540–1605*, Princeton, NJ.

—— (1981), *Culture and Censorship in Late Renaissance Italy and France*, London.

—— (1984), *Aldus Manutius: Humanist, Teacher and Printer*, Providence, RI.

—— (1988), 'Printing and Censorship', *CHRP*: 25–53.

—— (1989), *Schooling in Renaissance Italy: Literacy and Learning, 1300–1600*, Baltimore.

Gundersheimer, W. (ed.) (1969), *French Humanism: 1470–1600*, London.

Guthrie, W. K. C. (1962–81), *A History of Greek Philosophy*, Cambridge.

Guzzo, A. (1960), *Giordano Bruno*, Turin.

—— and Amerio, R. (eds.) (1956), *Opere di Giordano Bruno e di Tommaso Campanella*, Milan.

Hackforth, R. (1972), *Plato's Phaedrus, Translated with an Introduction and Commentary*, Cambridge.

Hale, J. R. (1963), *Machiavelli and Renaissance Italy*, New York.

—— (ed.) (1973), *Renaissance Venice*, London.

Halkin, L. E. (1969), *Érasme et l'humanisme chrétien*, Paris.

Hall, R. A. (1942), *The Italian 'Questione della lingua'*, Chapel Hill, NC.

Hall, V. (1950), 'The Life of Julius Caesar Scaliger (1484–1558)', *Transactions of the American Philosophical Society*, 40/2: 85–170.

Hamilton, A. (1981), *The Family of Love*, Cambridge.

Hamilton, B. (1963), *Political Thought in Sixteenth-Century Spain: A Study of the Political Ideas of Vitoria, De Soto, Suárez and Molina*, Oxford.

Hamlyn, D. W. (1987), *A History of Western Philosophy*, New York.

Hanke, L. (1959), *Aristotle and the American Indians*, Bloomington, Ind.

—— (1974), *All Mankind is One: A Study of the Disputation between Bartolomé de Las Casas and Juan Ginés de Sepúlveda in 1550 on the Religious and Intellectual Capacity of the American Indians*, De Kalb, Ill.

Hankins, J. (1986), 'Some Remarks on the History and Character of Ficino's Translation of Plato', in Garfagnini (1986: i. 287–304).

—— (1987a), 'A Manuscript of Plato's *Republic* in the Translation of Chrysoloras and Uberto Decembrio with Annotations of Guarino Veronese (Reg. Lat. 1131)', in Hankins, Monfasani, and Purnell (1987: 149–88).

—— (1987b), 'Plato in the Middle Ages', in Strayer (1982–9: ix. 694–704).

—— (1990a), *Plato in the Italian Renaissance*, Leiden.

—— (1990b), 'Cosimo de' Medici and the "Platonic Academy"', *JWCI* 53: 144–62.

—— (1991), 'The Myth of the Platonic Academy of Florence', *RQ* 44: 429–75.

—— , Monfasani, J., and Purnell, F., Jr. (eds.) (1987), *Supplementum Festivum: Studies in Honor of Paul Oskar Kristeller*, Binghamton, NY.

Hannaway, O. (1975), *The Chemists and the Word: The Didactic Origins of Chemistry*, Baltimore.

Harry Austryn Wolfson Jubilee Volume on the Occasion of His Seventy-Fifth Birthday, English Section (1965), Jerusalem.

Harth, H. (1968), 'Leonardo Brunis Selbstverständnis als Übersetzer', *AK* 50: 41–63.

Haskins, C. H. (1957), *The Renaissance of the Twelfth Century*, Cleveland.

Hay, D. (1977), *Annalists and Historians: Western Historiography from the Eighth to the Eighteenth Century*, London.

Headley, J. M. (1963), *Luther's View of Church History*, New Haven, Conn.

—— (ed.) (1968), *Medieval and Renaissance Studies: Proceedings of the Southeastern Institute of Medieval and Renaissance Studies, Summer 1967* (1968), Chapel Hill, NC.

—— (1987), 'The Reformation in Historical Thought', *JHI* 48: 521–32.

—— (1988), 'On the Rearming of Heaven: the Machiavellism of Tommaso Campanella', *JHI* 49: 387–404.

—— (1990a), 'Tommaso Campanella and Jean de Launoy: The Controversy over Aristotle and his Reception in the West', *RQ* 43: 529–49.

—— (1990b), 'Tommaso Campanella and the End of the Renaissance', *JMRS* 20: 157–74.

Heath, T. (1971), 'Logical Grammar, Grammatical Logic and

Humanism in Three German Universities', *SR* 18: 9–64.

Heller, H. (1972), 'The Evangelicism of Lefèvre d'Étaples: 1525', *SR* 19: 42–77.

Helton, T. (ed.) (1961), *The Renaissance: A Reconsideration of the Theories and Interpretations of the Age*, Madison, Wis.

Hempfer, K. W., and Straub, E. (eds.) (1983), *Italien und die Romania in Humanismus und Renaissance: Festschrift für Erich Loos*, Wiesbaden.

Heninger, S. K. (1974), *Touches of Sweet Harmony: Pythagorean Cosmology and Renaissance Poetics*, San Marino, Calif.

Henry, J. (1979), 'Francesco Patrizi da Cherso's Concept of Space and its Later Influence', *AS* 36: 549–75.

—— and Hutton, S. (eds.) (1990), *New Perspectives on Renaissance Thought: Essays in the History of Science, Education and Philosophy in Memory of Charles B. Schmitt*, London.

Hexter, J. H. (1965), *More's Utopia: The Biography of an Idea*, New York.

—— (1973), *The Vision of Politics on the Eve of the Reformation: More, Machiavelli, and Seyssel*, New York.

Hillgarth, J. N. (1971), *Ramon Lull and Lullism in Fourteenth-Century France*, Oxford.

Hirsch, R. (1955), 'Pre-Reformation Censorship of Printed Books', *Library Chronicle*, 21: 100–5.

—— (1974), *Printing, Selling and Reading, 1450–1550*, 2nd edn., Wiesbaden.

—— (1978), *The Printed Word: Its Impact and Diffusion*, London.

—— (1980), *The Emergence of Printing and Publishing as a Trade, 1450–1550*, Ann Arbor, Mich.

Holmes, G. (1969), *The Florentine Enlightenment, 1400–50*, New York.

Hooykaas, R. (1958), *Humanisme, science et reforme: Pierre de la Ramée (1515–1572)*, Leiden.

Hopkins, J. (1979), *Nicholas of Cusa on God as Not-Other: A Translation and Appraisal of De li non aliud*, Minneapolis.

—— (1980), *A Concise Introduction to the Philosophy of Nicholas of Cusa*, 2nd edn., Minneapolis.

—— (1981a), *Nicholas of Cusa on Learned Ignorance: A Translation and Appraisal of De docta ignorantia*, Minneapolis.

—— (1981b), *Nicholas of Cusa's Debate with John Wenck: A Translation and Appraisal of De ignota litteratura and Apologia doctae ignorantiae*, Minneapolis.

Hopkins, J. (1983a), *Nicholas of Cusa's Metaphysics of Contraction*, Minneapolis.

—— (1983b), *Nicholas of Cusa's Dialectical Mysticism: Text, Translation and Interpretive Study of* De visione dei, Minneapolis.

Horowitz, M. C. (1971), 'Pierre Charron's View of the Source of Wisdom', *JHP* 9: 443–57.

—— (1974), 'Natural Law as the Foundation for an Autonomous Ethics: Pierre Charron's *De la sagesse*', *SR* 21: 204–27.

Howell, W. S. (1956), *Logic and Rhetoric in England, 1500–1700*, Princeton, NJ.

Hughes, P. E. (1984), *Lefèvre: Pioneer of Ecclesiastical Renewal in France*, Grand Rapids, Mich.

L'Humanisme allemand (1480–1540): 18ᵉ Colloque international de Tours, Munich/Paris (1979).

Huppert, G. (1970), *The Idea of Perfect History: Historical Erudition and Historical Philosophy in Renaissance France*, Urbana, Ill.

Iannizzotto, M. (1959), *Saggio sulla filosofia di Coluccio Salutati*, Padua.

Idel, M. (1988), *Kabbalah: New Perspectives*, New Haven, Conn.

IJsewijn, J. (ed.) (1985), *Roma humanistica: Studia in honorem . . . Iosaei Ruysschaert* (*HL* 34A).

—— and Paquet, J. (eds.) (1978), *Les Universités à la fin du moyen âge: Actes du Congrès international de Louvain, 26–30 mai 1975*, Louvain.

Ingegno, A. (1968), 'Il primo Bruno e l'influenza di Marsilio Ficino', *RCSF* 23: 149–70.

—— (1978), *Cosmologia e filosofia nel pensiero di Giordano Bruno*, Florence.

—— (1980), *Saggio sulla filosofia di Cardano*, Florence.

—— (1985), *La sommersa nave della religione: Studio sulla polemica anticristiana del Bruno*, Naples.

—— (1988), 'The New Philosophy of Nature', *CHRP*: 236–63.

Iriarte, J. (1935), *Kartesischer oder Sanchezischer Zweifel?* Bottrop.

—— (1940), 'Francisco Sánchez el Escéptico disfrazado de Carneades en discusión epistolar con Cristóbal Clavio', *Gregorianum*, 21: 413–51.

Jacquart, D. (1988), 'Aristotelian Thought in Salerno', *HTCWP*: 407–28.

Jardine, L. (1974a), *Francis Bacon: Discovery and the Art of Discourse*, Cambridge.

—— (1974b), 'The Place of Dialectic Teaching in Sixteenth Century

Cambridge', *SR* 21: 31–62.

—— (1975), 'Humanism and the Sixteenth Century Cambridge Arts Course', *History of Education*, 4: 16–31.

—— (1977), 'Lorenzo Valla and the Intellectual Origins of Humanist Dialectic', *JHP* 15: 143–64.

—— (1981), 'Dialectic or Dialectical Rhetoric? Agostino Nifo's Criticism of Lorenzo Valla', *RCSF* 36: 253–70.

—— (1982), 'Humanism and the Teaching of Logic', *CHLMP*: 797–807.

—— (1983), 'Lorenzo Valla: Academic Scepticism and the New Humanist Dialectic', in Burnyeat (1983: 253–86).

—— (1988), 'Humanistic Logic', *CHRP*: 173–98.

—— (1990), 'Inventing Rudolph Agricola: Cultural Transmission, Renaissance Dialectic, and the Emerging Humanities', in Grafton and Blair (1990: 39–86).

Jardine, N. (1976), 'Galileo's Road to Truth and the Demonstrative Regress', *Studies in the History and Philosophy of Science*, 7: 277–318.

—— (1988), 'Epistemology of the Sciences', *CHRP*: 685–711.

Jolivet, J. (1988), 'The Arabic Inheritance', *HTCWP*: 113–48.

Jones, R. M. (1959), *Spiritual Reformers in the 16th and 17th Centuries*, Boston.

Jungkuntz, R. P. (1962), 'Christian Approval of Epicureanism', *CH* 31: 279–93.

Kahn, V. (1983), 'The Rhetoric of Faith and the Use of Usage in Lorenzo Valla's *De libero arbitrio*', *JMRS* 13: 91–109.

—— (1985), *Rhetoric, Prudence and Skepticism in the Renaissance*, Ithaca, NY.

Kalish, D., Montague, R., and Mar, G. (1980), *Logic: Techniques of Formal Reasoning*, 2nd edn., New York.

Kaske, C. (1982), 'Marsilio Ficino and the Twelve Gods of the Zodiac', *JWCI* 45: 195–202.

—— (1986), 'Ficino's Shifting Attitude towards Astrology in the *De vita coelitus comparanda*, the Letter to Poliziano, and the *Apologia* to the Cardinals', in Garfagnini (1986: ii. 371–81).

Kater, T. (1908), *Johann Ludwig Vives und seine Stellung zu Aristoteles*, Erlangen.

Keefer, M. H. (1988), 'Agrippa's Dilemma: Hermetic "Rebirth" and the Ambivalences of *De vanitate* and *De occulta philosophia*', *RQ* 41: 614–53.

Keller, A. C. (1950), 'Zilsel, the Artisans, and the Idea of Scientific

Progress in the Renaissance', *JHI* 11: 235–40.

Keller, A. C. (1957), 'Montaigne on the Dignity of Man', *PMLA* 72: 43–54.

Kelley, D. R. (1970a), *The Foundations of Modern Historical Scholarship: Language, Law and History in the French Renaissance*, New York.

—— (1970b), 'Philology and the Mirror of History', *Journal of Interdisciplinary History*, 1: 125–36.

—— (1973), *François Hotman: A Revolutionary's Ordeal*, Princeton, NJ.

—— (1981), *The Beginning of Ideology: Consciousness and Society in the French Reformation*, Cambridge.

—— (1984), *History, Law and the Human Sciences: Medieval and Renaissance Perspectives*, London.

—— (1988), 'The Theory of History', *CHRP*: 746–61.

—— (1990a), 'What is Happening to the History of Ideas?' *JHI* 51: 3–25.

—— (1990b), *The Human Measure: Social Thought in the Western Legal Tradition*, Cambridge.

Kennedy, G. A. (1969), *Quintilian*, New York.

—— (1980), *Classical Rhetoric and its Christian and Secular Tradition from Ancient to Modern Times*, Chapel Hill, NC.

Kennedy, L. A. (1979), 'The Philosophical Manuscripts of Cesare Cremonini', *Manuscripta*, 23: 79–87.

—— (1980), 'Cesare Cremonini and the Immortality of the Human Soul', *Vivarium*, 18: 143–58.

Kenney, E. J. (1974), *The Classical Text: Aspects of Editing in the Age of the Printed Book*, Berkeley, Calif.

Kenny, A. (1975), *Wittgenstein*, Harmondsworth.

—— (1983), *Thomas More*, Oxford.

—— (1985), *Wyclif*, Oxford.

—— and Pinborg, J. (1982), 'Medieval Philosophical Literature', *CHLMP*: 11–42.

Kent, D. (1978), *The Rise of the Medici: Faction in Florence, 1426–1434*, Oxford.

Ker, W. P. (1958), *The Dark Ages*, New York.

Kerner, G. C. (1966), *The Revolution in Ethical Theory*, Oxford.

Kerrigan, W., and Braden, G. (1989), *The Idea of the Renaissance*, Baltimore.

Kessler, E. (1968), *Das Problem des frühen Humanismus: Seine philosophische Bedeutung bei Coluccio Salutati*, Munich.

—— (1978), *Petrarca und die Geschichte: Geschichtschreibung,*

Rhetorik, Philosophie im Übergang vom Mittelalter zur Neuzeit, Munich.

—— (1979), 'Humanismus und Naturwissenschaft bei Rudolf Agricola', in *L'Humanisme allemand*: 141–57.

—— (1980), 'Freiheit des Willens in Vallas *De libero arbitrio*', in Margolin (1980: 637–47).

—— (1988), 'The Intellective Soul', *CHRP*: 485–534.

—— (forthcoming), 'Alles ist eines wie der Mensch und das Pferd: zu Cardanos Naturbegriff'.

—— Lohr, C. and Sparn, W. (eds.) (1988), *Aristotelismus und Renaissance: In memoriam Charles Schmitt*, Wiesbaden.

Kibre, P. (1936), *The Library of Pico della Mirandola*, New York.

—— (1978), 'Arts and Medicine in the Universities of the Later Middle Ages', in IJsewijn and Paquet (1978: 213–27).

—— and Siraisi, N. (1978), 'The Institutional Setting: The Universities', in Lindberg (1978*a*: 121–44).

Kieszkowski, B. (1936), *Studi sul platonismo del Rinascimento in Italia*, Florence.

Kinney, D. R. (1981), 'More's *Letter to Dorp*: Remapping the Trivium', *RQ* 34: 179–210.

Kirkwood, G. M. (ed.) (1975), *Poetry and Poetics from Ancient Greece to the Renaissance: Studies in honour of James Hutton*, Ithaca, NY.

Kisch, G. (1955), *Humanismus und Jurisprudenz: Der Kampf zwischen mos italicus und mos gallicus an der Universität Basel*, Basle.

—— (1972), *Studien zur humanistischen Jurisprudenz*, Berlin.

Klein, R. (1956), 'L'Imagination comme vêtement de l'âme chez Marsile Ficin et Giordano Bruno', *Revue de métaphysique et de morale*, 61: 18–39.

—— (1960), 'L'Enfer de Marsile Ficin', in Castelli (1960: 47–84).

—— (1970), *La Forme et l'intelligible: Écrits sur la renaissance et l'art moderne*, Paris.

Klibansky, R. (1981), *The Continuity of the Platonic Tradition during the Middle Ages: Plato's* Parmenides *in the Middle Ages and the Renaissance*, Munich.

——, Panofsky, E., and Saxl, F. (1964), *Saturn and Melancholy: Studies in the History of Natural Philosophy, Religion and Art*, London.

—— and Paton, H. J. (eds.) (1936), *Philosophy and History: Essays Presented to Ernst Cassirer*, Oxford.

Klutstein, I. (1986), 'Marsile Ficin et les Oracles Chaldaïques', in Garfagnini (1986: i. 331–8).

Klutstein, I. (1987), *Marsilio Ficino et la théologie ancienne: Oracles chaldaïques, hymnes orphiques, hymnes de Proclus*, Florence.

Kneale, W., and Kneale, M. (1962), *The Development of Logic*, Oxford.

Knös, B. (1950), 'Gémiste Pléthon et son souvenir', *Lettres d'humanité*, 9: 97–184.

Kohls, E. W. (1966), *Die Theologie des Erasmus*, Basle.

Korkowski, E. (1976), 'Agrippa as Ironist', *Neophilologus*, 60: 594–607.

Koyré, A. (1961), *Études d'histoire de la pensée philosophique*, Paris.

—— (1966a), *Études galiléennes*, 2nd edn., Paris.

—— (1966b), *Études d'histoire de la pensée scientifique*, Paris.

—— (1968), *From the Closed World to the Infinite Universe*, Baltimore.

—— (1971), *Mystiques, spirituels, alchimistes du XVIe siècle allemand*, Paris.

Kraye, J. (1979), 'Francesco Filelfo's Lost Letter *De ideis*', *JWCI* 42: 236–49.

—— (1981), 'Francesco Filelfo on Emotions, Virtues and Vices: A Re-examination of His Sources', *BHR* 43: 129–40.

—— (1983), 'Cicero, Stoicism and Textual Criticism: Poliziano on κατόρθωμα', *Rinascimento*, ser. 2, 23: 79–110.

—— (1986), 'The pseudo-Aristotelian *Theology* in Sixteenth- and Seventeenth-Century Europe', in Kraye, Ryan, and Schmitt (1986: 265–86).

—— (1988), 'Moral Philosophy', *CHRP*: 303–86.

—— Ryan, W. F., and Schmitt, C. B. (eds.) (1986), *Pseudo-Aristotle in the Middle Ages: The Theology and Other Texts*, London.

Kretzmann, N. (1982), 'Syncategoremata, exponibilia, sophismata', *CHLMP*: 211–45.

Kristeller, P. O. (1937), *Supplementum Ficinianum: Marsilii Ficini Florentini philosophi Platonici opuscula inedita et dispersa*, Florence.

—— (1939), 'Florentine Platonism and its Relations with Humanism and Scholasticism', *CH* 8: 201–11.

—— (1950), 'Renaissance Philosophies', in Ferm (1950: 227–39).

—— (1951a), 'A New Manuscript Source for Pomponazzi's Theory of the Soul from his Paduan Period', *Revue internationale de philosophie*, 5: 144–57.

—— (1951b), 'Umanesimo e filosofia nel rinascimento italiano', in Castelli (1951: 507–16).

—— (1953), *Die italienischen Universitäten der Renaissance*, Krefeld.

—— (1955a), 'Ficino and Renaissance Platonism', *Personalist*, 36: 238–49.

—— (1955b), 'Il Petrarca, l'umanesimo e la scolastica', *Lettere italiane*, 7: 367–88.

—— (1955–6), 'Two Unpublished Questions on the Soul by Pietro Pomponazzi', *MH* 9: 76–101; 10: 151.

—— (1956), *Studies in Renaissance Thought and Letters*, Rome.

—— (1957), 'Nuove fonti per la medicina salernitana del secolo XII', *Rassegna storica salernitana*, 18: 61–75.

—— (1959), 'Renaissance Platonism', in Werkmeister (1959: 87–107).

—— (1960), 'Ludovico Lazzarelli e Giovanni da Correggio, due ermetici del Quattrocento, e il manoscritto II.D.I.4 della Biblioteca Comunale degli Ardenti di Viterbo', in *Biblioteca degli Ardenti*: 13–37.

—— (1961a), *Renaissance Thought: The Classic, Scholastic and Humanist Strains*, New York.

—— (1961b), 'Sebastiano Salvini: A Florentine Humanist and Theologian, and a Member of Marsilio Ficino's Platonic Academy', in Prete (1961: 205–43).

—— (1964a), *Eight Philosophers of the Italian Renaissance*, Stanford, Calif.

—— (1964b), 'Some Original Letters and Autograph Manuscripts of Marsilio Ficino', in *Studi . . . in onore di T. De Marinis*: 5–33.

—— (1964c), *The Philosophy of Marsilio Ficino*, trans. V. Conant, Gloucester, Mass. (See Kristeller, 1988a.)

—— (1965a), 'Giovanni Pico della Mirandola and His Sources', in *L'Opera . . . di Giovanni Pico*: 35–142.

—— (1965b), 'A Thomist Critique of Marsilio Ficino's Theory of the Will and Intellect: Fra Vicenzo Bandello da Castelnuovo O.P. and His Unpublished Treatise Addressed to Lorenzo de' Medici', in *Harry Austryn Wolfson Jubilee Volume . . .* : 463–94.

—— (1965c), 'Renaissance Aristotelianism', *GRBS* 6: 157–74.

—— (1966), 'Marsilio Ficino as a Beginning Student of Plato', *Scriptorium*, 20: 41–54.

—— (1968a), 'The Myth of Renaissance Atheism and the French Tradition of Free Thought', *JHP* 6: 233–43.

—— (1968b), 'The European Significance of Florentine Platonism', in Headley (1968: 206–29).

—— (1972a), 'The Impact of Early Humanism on Thought and Learning', in Levy (1972: 120–57).

—— (1972b), *Renaissance Concepts of Man and Other Essays*, New

York.

Kristeller, P. O. (1974), *Medieval Aspects of Renaissance Learning: Three Essays*, ed. and trans. E. P. Mahoney, Durham, NC.

—— (1975), 'The Latin Poems of Giovanni Pico della Mirandola', in Kirkwood (1975: 185–206).

—— (1976a), 'L'État présent des études sur Marsile Ficin', in *Platon et Aristote à la Renaissance*: 59–77.

—— (1976b), 'Bartholomaeus, Musandinus and Maurus of Salerno and Other Early Commentators of the 'Articella', With a Tentative List of Texts and Manuscripts', *IMU* 19: 57–87.

—— (1977), 'Philosophy and Medicine in Medieval and Renaissance Italy', in Spicker (1978: 29–40).

—— (1978), 'The First Printed Edition of Plato's Works and the Date of its Publication', in *Science and History* . . . : 25–35.

—— (1979a), 'Between the Renaissance and the French Enlightenment: Gabriel Naudé as an Editor', *RQ* 32: 41–72.

—— (1979b), *Renaissance Thought and its Sources*, ed. M. Mooney, New York.

—— (1979c), 'Die Stellung der Ethik in Denken der Renaissance', *Quellen und Forschungen aus italienischen Archiven und Bibliotheken*, 59: 273–95.

—— (1980a), 'Thomas More as a Renaissance Humanist', *Moreana*, 17: 5–22.

—— (1980b), *La Scuola Medica di Salerno secondo ricerche e scoperte recenti* (Quaderni del Centro di Studi e documentazione della Scuola Medica Salernitana, 5), Salerno.

—— (1981), 'Historical Scholarship and Philosophical Thought', *Minerva*, 18: 313–23.

—— (1982), 'The Renaissance in the History of Philosophical Thought', in *The Renaissance: Essays in Interpretation*: 127–52.

—— (1983a), *Aristotelismo e sincretismo nel pensiero di Pietro Pomponazzi*, Padua.

—— (1983b), 'Marsilio Ficino as a Man of Letters and the Glosses Attributed to Him in the Caetani Codex of Dante', *RQ* 36: 1–47.

—— (1983c), 'Petrarcas Stellung in der Geschichte der Gelehrsamkeit', in Hempfer and Straub (1983: 102–21).

—— (1983d), 'Marsilio Ficino e Venezia', in *Miscellanea . . . in onore di Vittore Branca*: 475–92.

—— (1983e), 'Il pensiero del rinascimento: Problemi e ricerche', *ASNSP* ser. 3, 13.4: 1007–23.

—— (1984), 'La cultura umanistica a Roma nel Quattrocento', in

Brezzi and Lorch (1984: 323–32).

—— (1985*a*), 'Latin and Vernacular in Fourteenth- and Fifteenth-Century Italy', *Journal of the Rocky Mountain Medieval and Renaissance Association*, 6: 105–26.

—— (1985*b*), 'Jewish Contributions to Italian Renaissance Culture', *Italia*, 4: 7–20.

—— (1985*c*), 'Marsilio Ficino and the Roman Curia', in IJsewijn (1985: 83–98).

—— (1985*d*), 'Philosophy and its Historiography', *Journal of Philosophy*, 82: 618–25.

—— (1985*e*), *Studies in Renaissance Thought and Letters*, ii, Rome.

—— (1986*a*), 'Marsilio Ficino and his Work after Five Hundred Years', in Garfagnini (1986: i. 15–196).

—— (1986*b*), *Studi sulla scuola medica salernitana*, Naples.

—— (1987), 'Proclus as a Reader of Plato and Plotinus and his Influence in the Middle Ages and in the Renaissance', in *Proclus, Lecteur*: 191–211.

—— (1988*a*), *Il pensiero filosofico di Marsilio Ficino*, Florence. (See Kristeller, 1964*c*.)

—— (1988*b*), 'Humanism and Moral Philosophy', in Rabil (1988: iii. 271–309).

—— (1988*c*), 'Humanism', *CHRP*: 113–37.

—— (1990*a*), *Renaissance Thought and the Arts: Collected Essays*, Princeton, NJ.

—— (1990*b*), *A Life of Learning* (Charles Homer Haskins Lecture), New York.

—— and Cranz, F. E. (eds.) (1960–), *Catalogus translationum et commentariorum: Medieval and Renaissance Latin Translations and Commentaries*, Washington, DC.

—— and Randall, J. H., Jr. (1941), 'The Study of the Philosophies of the Renaissance', *JHI* 2: 449–96.

—— and Wiener, P. P. (eds.) (1968), *Renaissance Essays from the Journal of the History of Ideas*, New York.

Kuksewicz, Z. (1982*a*), 'The Potential and the Agent Intellect', *CHLMP*: 595–601.

—— (1982*b*), 'Criticisms of Aristotelian Psychology and the Augustinian-Aristotelian Synthesis', *CHLMP*: 623–8.

Kultur- und Universalgeschichte: Walter Goetz zu seinem 60. Geburtstage dargebracht von Fachgenossen, Freunden und Schulern, Leipzig (1927).

Kuntz, M. L. (1981), *Guillaume Postel, Prophet of the Restitution of*

All Things: His Life and Thought, The Hague.

Labalme, P. H. (ed.) (1980), *Beyond Their Sex: Learned Women of the European Past*, New York.

Labowsky, L. (1961–8), 'Bessarion Studies, 1–5', *MRS* 5: 108–62; 6: 173–205.

—— (1968), 'An Unknown Treatise by Theodore Gaza', *MRS* 4: 173–205.

—— (1979), *Bessarion's Library and the Biblioteca Marciana: Six Early Inventories*, Rome.

Laistner, M. L. W. (1966), *Thought and Letters in Western Europe: A.D. 500 to 900*, Ithaca, NY.

Lamberton, R. (1986), *Homer the Theologian: Neoplatonist Allegorical Reading and the Growth of the Epic Tradition*, Berkeley, Calif.

Lampros, S. P. (1910), 'Αργυροπούλεια, Athens.

Lapidge, M. (1988), 'The Stoic Inheritance', *HTCWP*: 81–112.

Leclerc, J. (1955), *Histoire de la tolérance au siècle de la réforme*, Paris.

Lefèvre d'Étaples, J. (1972), *The Prefatory Epistles of Jacques Lefèvre d'Étaples and Related Texts*, ed. E. F. Rice, Jr., New York.

Leibniz, G. W. (1969), *Philosophical Papers and Letters: A Selection*, ed. and trans. L. E. Loemker, 2nd edn., Dordrecht.

Lenoble, R. (1971), *Mersenne, ou la naissance du mécanisme*, Paris.

Levi, A. H. T., (ed.) (1970), *Humanism in France at the End of the Middle Ages and in the Early Renaissance*, New York.

Levine, J. M. (1973), 'Reginald Pecock and Lorenzo Valla on the Donation of Constantine', *SR* 20: 118–43.

Levy, B. S. (ed.) (1972), *Developments in the Early Renaissance*, Albany, NY.

Liebeschütz, H. (1970), 'Western Christian Thought from Boethius to Anselm', *CHLGEMP*: 534–639.

Limbrick, E. (1977), 'Was Montaigne Really a Pyrrhonian?' *BHR* 39: 67–80.

Lindberg, D. (ed.) (1978*a*), *Science in the Middle Ages*, Chicago.

—— (1978*b*), 'The Transmission of Greek and Arabic Learning to the West', in Lindberg (1978*a*: 52–90).

—— and Westman, R. (eds.) (1990), *Reappraisals of the Scientific Revolution*, Cambridge.

Lipsius, J. (1675), *Opera omnia*, Basle.

—— (1939), *Two Bookes of Constancie*, trans. J. Stradling, ed. R. Kirk and C. M. Hall, New Brunswick, NJ.

—— (1978–), *Epistolae*, ed. A. Gerlo *et al.* Brussels.

Lloyd, A. C. (1970), 'The Later Neoplatonists', *CHLGEMP*: 269–325.

—— (1990), *The Anatomy of Neoplatonism*, Oxford.

Lloyd, G. E. R. (1968), *Aristotle: The Growth and Structure of his Thought*, Cambridge.

Logan, George M. (1983), *The Meaning of More's Utopia*, Princeton, NJ.

Lohr, C. H. (1967–74), 'Medieval Latin Aristotle Commentaries', *Traditio*, 23–4, 26–30.

—— (1972), 'Addenda et corrigenda', *Bulletin de philosophie médiévale*, 14: 116–26.

—— (1974), 'Renaissance Latin Aristotle Commentaries', *SR* 21: 228–89.

—— (1975–80), 'Renaissance Latin Aristotle Commentaries', *RQ* 28–33, 35.

—— (1976), 'Jesuit Aristotelianism and Sixteenth Century Metaphysics', in Fletcher and Schuete (1976: 203–20).

—— (1982), 'The Medieval Interpretation of Aristotle', *CHLMP*: 80–98.

—— (1988), 'Metaphysics', *CHRP*: 537–638.

Lojacono, E. (1985), 'Giorgio de Trebizonda: La tradizione retorica bizantina e l'idea di metodo', in Schoeck (1985: 80–100).

Long, A. A. (1986), *Hellenistic Philosophy: Stoics, Epicureans, Sceptics*, 2nd edn., Berkeley, Calif.

—— and Sedley, D. N. (eds.) (1987), *The Hellenistic Philosophers*, Cambridge.

Lorch, M. (1976), '*Voluptas, molle quoddam et non invidiosum nomen:* Lorenzo Valla's defence of *Voluptas* in the Preface to his *De voluptate*', in Mahoney (1976a: 214–28).

—— (1985), *A Defense of Life: Lorenzo Valla's Theory of Pleasure*, Munich.

—— (1988), 'Italy's Leading Humanist: Lorenzo Valla', in Rabil (1988: i. 332–49).

Losada, A. (1948–9), *Juan Ginés de Sepúlveda a través de su 'epistolario' y nuevos documentos*, Madrid.

Lovejoy, A. O. (1936), *The Great Chain of Being: A Study of the History of an Idea*, Cambridge, Mass.

Lowry, M. (1979), *The World of Aldus Manutius: Business and Scholarship in Renaissance Venice*, Oxford.

Lubac, H. de (1974), *Pic de la Mirandole: Études et discussions*,

Paris.

Lübke, A. (1968), *Nikolaus von Kues: Kirchenfürst zwischen Mittelalter und Neuzeit*, Munich.

Luther, M. (1958–), *Luther's Works*, ed. J. Pelikan and H. T.
Lehmann, St Louis, Miss.

—— (1961), *Martin Luther: Selections from his Writings*, ed. J.
Dillenberger, New York.

—— (1966), *Werke*, repr., Weimar/Graz.

Lyons, W. (1980), *Gilbert Ryle: An Introduction to his Philosophy*,
Brighton.

Mabilleau, L. (1881), *Étude historique sur la philosophie de la renaissance en Italie: Cesare Cremonini*, Paris.

Maccagnolo, E. (1988), 'David of Dinant and the Beginnings of
Aristotelianism in Paris', *HTCWP*: 429–42.

McConica, J. K. (1965), *English Humanists and Reformation Politics
under Henry VIII and Edward VI*, Oxford.

McFarlane, I. D., and Maclean, I. (eds.) (1982), *Montaigne: Essays
in Memory of Richard Sayce*, Oxford.

McGowan, M. (1974), *Montaigne's Deceits: The Art of Persuasion in
the Essais*, Philadelphia.

McGrath, A. (1987), *The Intellectual Origins of the European Reformation*, Oxford.

—— (1990), *A Life of John Calvin: A Study in the Shaping of Western
Culture*, Oxford.

Machiavelli, N. (1954), *Opere*, ed. M. Bonfantini, Milan.

—— (1977), *The Prince: A New Translation, Backgrounds, Interpretations*, ed. and trans. R. M. Adams, New York.

MacIntyre, A. (1984), 'The Relationship of Philosophy to its Past', in
Rorty, Schneewind and Skinner (1984: 31–48).

Mack, P. (1983), 'Rudolph Agricola and Renaissance Dialectic', dissertation, Univ. of London.

—— (1985), 'Rudolph Agricola's Reading of Literature', *JWCI* 48:
23–41.

Maclean, I. (1984), 'The Interpretation of Natural Signs: Cardano's
De subtilitate versus Scaliger's *Exercitationes*', in Vickers (1984:
231–45).

McMullin, E. (1990), 'Conceptions of Science in the Scientific Revolution', in Lindberg and Westman (1990: 27–92).

McTighe, T. P. (1958), 'The Meaning of the Couple *complicatio-
explicatio* in the Philosophy of Nicholas of Cusa', *Proceedings of
the American Catholic Philosophical Association*, 32: 206–14.

—— (1970), 'Nicholas of Cusa's Theory of Science and its Metaphysical Background', in *Nicolò Cusano agli inizi del mondo moderno*: 317–39.

Maddison, F., Pelling, M., and Webster, C. (eds.) (1977), *Essays on the Life and Work of Thomas Linacre, c. 1460–1524*, Oxford.

Maechling, E. E. (1977), 'Light Metaphysics in the Natural Philosophy of Francesco Patrizi da Cherso', dissertation, Univ. of London.

Maeyama, Y., and Saltzer, W. G. (eds.) (1977), *Prismata: Naturwissenschaftsgeschichtliche Studien: Festschrift für Willy Hartner*, Wiesbaden.

Magia, astrologia e religione nel rinascimento: Convegno polacco-italiano (Varsavia: 25–27 settembre 1972) (1974), Wrocław.

Mahoney, E. P. (1968), 'Nicoletto Vernia and Agostino Nifo on Alexander of Aphrodisias: An Unnoticed Dispute', *RCSF* 23: 268–96.

—— (1970*a*), 'Agostino Nifo's Early Views on Immortality', *JHP* 8: 451–60.

—— (1970*b*), 'Pier Nicola Castellani and Agostino Nifo on Averroes' Doctrine of the Agent Intellect', *RCSF* 25: 387–409.

—— (1971*a*), 'Agostino Nifo's *De sensu agente*', *AGP* 53: 119–42.

—— (1971*b*), 'A Note on Agostino Nifo', *Philological Quarterly*, 50: 125–32.

—— (1974), 'St. Thomas and the School of Padua at the End of the Fifteenth Century', *Proceedings of the American Catholic Philosophical Association*, 48: 277–85.

—— (ed.) (1976*a*), *Philosophy and Humanism: Renaissance Essays in Honor of Paul Oskar Kristeller*, New York.

—— (1976*b*), 'Nicoletto Vernia on the Soul and Immortality', in Mahoney (1976*a*: 144–63).

—— (1976*c*), 'Agostino Nifo and St. Thomas Aquinas', *Memorie Dominicane*, NS 7: 195–226.

—— (1978*a*), 'Nicoletto Vernia's Question on Seminal Reasons', *FS* 16: 303–9.

—— (1978*b*), 'Duns Scotus and the School of Padua around 1500', in Bérubé (1978: ii. 215–27).

—— (1980), 'Albert the Great and the *Studio Patavino* in the Late Fifteenth and Early Sixteenth Centuries', in Weisheipl (1980: 537–63).

—— (1982*a*), 'Metaphysical Foundations of the Hierarchy of Being according to Some Late-Medieval and Renaissance Philosophers', in Morewedge (1982: 165–257).

400 Bibliography

Mahoney, E. P. (1982b), 'Neoplatonism, the Greek Commentators, and Renaissance Aristotelianism', in O'Meara (1982: 169–177).

—— (1982c), 'Sense, Intellect and Imagination in Albert, Thomas and Siger', *CHLMP*: 602–22.

—— (1983), 'Philosophy and Science in Nicoletto Vernia and Agostino Nifo', in Poppi (1983: 135–202).

—— (1986), 'Marsilio Ficino's Influence on Nicoletto Vernia, Agostino Nifo and Marcantonio Zimara', in Garfagnini (1986: ii. 509–31).

—— (1987), 'Lovejoy and the Hierarchy of Being', *JHI* 48: 211–30.

Mahoney, M. S. (1978), 'Mathematics', in Lindberg (1978a: 145–78).

Maier, I. (1965), *Les Manuscrits d'Ange Politien*, Geneva.

—— (1966), *Ange Politien: La Formation d'un poète humaniste (1469–80)*, Geneva.

Maillard, J. F. (1971), 'Le *De harmonia mundi* de Georges de Venise', *Revue de l'histoire des religions* 179: 181–203.

Mair, J. (1892), *A History of Great Britain as well England and Scotland Compiled from the Ancient Authorities by John Major* . . . , trans. A. Constable, ed. A. MacKay, Edinburgh.

Malcolm, N. (1958), *Ludwig Wittgenstein: A Memoir*, London.

Malusa, L. (1981), 'Le premesse rinascimentali all'attività storiografica in filosofia', in Santinello (1981– : i. 3–62).

Mancini, G. (1891), *Vita di Lorenzo Valla*, Florence.

Manetti, G. (1974), *Vita Socratis*, ed. M. Montuori, Florence.

—— (1975), *De dignitate et excellentia hominis*, ed. E. R. Leonard, Padua.

—— (1979), *Vita Socratis et Senecae*, ed. A. De Petris, Rome.

Mann, N. (1984), *Petrarch*, Oxford.

Mann Phillips, M. (1959), *Erasmus and the Northern Renaissance*, London.

Marcel, R. (1958), *Marsile Ficin (1433–1499)*, Paris.

—— (1965), 'Pic de la Mirandole et la France: De l'Université de Paris au Donjon de Vincennes', *L'Opera*: i. 205–30.

Marc'hadour, G. (1963), *L'Univers de Thomas More: Chronologie critique de More, Érasme et leur époque, 1477–1536*, Paris.

—— (1969), *Thomas More et la Bible*, Paris.

Margolin, J.-C. (1960), 'Rationalisme et irrationalisme dans la pensée de Jerôme Cardan', *Revue de l'université de Bruxelles*, 13. 1–40.

—— (1967), *L'Idée de nature dans la pensée d'Erasme*, Basle.

—— (ed.) (1972), *Colloquia Erasmiana Turonensia: Douzième stage international d'études humanistes*, Toronto.

—— (1974), 'Platon et Aristote à la renaissance', *BHR* 36: 157–73.

—— (1976*a*), 'Cardan, interprète d'Aristote', *Platon et Aristote à la Renaissance*: 307–33.

—— (1976*b*), 'L'enseignement des mathématiques en France', in Sharratt (1976: 109–55).

—— (ed.) (1980), *Acta Conventus Neo-Latini Turonensis; IIIᵉ Congrès international d'études néo-latines*, Paris.

—— (1986), *Érasme: Le prix des mots et de l'homme*, London.

—— (1987), *Érasme dans son miroir et dans son sillage*, London.

Marius, R. (1984), *Thomas More: A Biography*, New York.

Marrou, H. I. (1956), *A History of Education in Antiquity*, trans. G. Lamb, London.

Marsilio of Padua (1967), *The Defender of the Peace: the* Defensor Pacis, trans. A. Gewirth, New York.

Martines, L. (1963), *The Social World of the Florentine Humanists, 1390–1460*, Princeton, NJ.

—— (1968), *Lawyers and Statecraft in Renaissance Florence*, Princeton, NJ.

Martz, L. L. (1990), *Thomas More: The Search for the Inner Man*, New Haven, Conn.

Masai, F. (1956), *Pléthon et le platonisme de Mistra*, Paris.

Matsen, H. S. (1968), 'Alessandro Achillini (1463–1512) as a Professor of Philosophy in the "Studio" of Padua', *Quaderni per la storia dell'Università di Padova*, 1: 91–109.

—— (1974), *Alessandro Achillini (1463–1512) and his Doctrine of 'Universals' and 'Transcendentals'*, Lewisburg, Pa.

—— (1975), 'Alessandro Achillini (1463–1512) and "Ockhamism" at Bologna (1490–1500)', *JHP* 13: 437–51.

Mattioli, E. (1980), *Luciano e l'umanesimo*, Naples.

Mechoulan, H. (1974), *L'Antihumanisme de J. G. de Sepúlveda: Étude critique du 'Democrates primus'*, Paris.

Medioevo e rinascimento: Studi in onore di Bruno Nardi (1955), Florence.

Meerhoff, K. (1968), *Rhétorique et poétique au 16ᵉ siècle en France: Du Bellay, Ramus et les autres*, Leiden.

Meinecke, F. (1965), *Machiavellism: The Doctrine of Raison d'État and its Place in Modern History*, trans. D. Scott, New York.

Menapace Brisca, L. (1952), 'La retorica di Francesco Patrizi o del platonico antiaristotelismo', *Aevum*, 26: 434–61.

Mercati, A. (1942), *Il sommario del processo di Giordano Bruno*, Vatican City.

Merkel, I., and Debus, A. (eds.) (1988), *Hermeticism and the Renaissance: Intellectual History and the Occult in Early Modern Europe*, Washington, DC.

Merlan, P. (1970), 'Greek Philosophy from Plato to Plotinus', *CHLGEMP*: 11–132.

Mersenne, M. (1623), *Quaestiones in Genesim . . .* , Paris.

—— (1933–88), *Correspondance du P. Marin Mersenne, religieux minime*, ed. C. de Waard and R. Pintard, Paris.

Mesnard, P. (1969), *Érasme ou le christianisme critique*, Paris.

Miccolis, S. (1965), *Francisco Sánchez*, Bari.

Michaud-Quantin, P. (1969), 'L'Emploi des termes *logica* et *dialectica* au moyen âge', *Arts libéraux*: 855–62.

Michel, P. H. (1973), *The Cosmology of Giordano Bruno*, trans. R. Maddison, London.

Micheli, P. (1917), *La vita e le opere di Angelo Poliziano*, Livorno.

Minio-Paluello, L. (1970), 'Boethius', *DSB*: 2, 228–36.

—— (1972), *Opuscula: The Latin Aristotle*, Amsterdam.

Miscellanea Augusto Campana (*Medioevo e Umanesimo*, 44), (1981), Padua.

Miscellanea di studi in onore di Vittore Branca (1983), Florence.

Miscellanea marciana di studi bessarionei (1976), Padua.

Mohler, L. (1923–42), *Kardinal Bessarion als Theologe, Humanist und Staatsmann*, Paderborn.

—— (1943–9), 'Theodoros Gazes, seine bisher ungedruckten Schriften und Briefe', *Byzantinische Zeitschrift*, 42: 50–75.

Mommsen, T. E. (1942), 'Petrarch's Conception of the "Dark Ages"', *Speculum*, 17: 226–42.

—— (1959), *Medieval and Renaissance Studies*, ed. E. F. Rice, Ithaca, NY.

Monfasani, J. (1976), *George of Trebizond: A Biography and a Study of his Rhetoric and Logic*, Leiden.

—— (1981a), 'Bessarion Latinus', *Rinascimento*, ser. 2, 21: 165–209.

—— (1981b), 'Il Perotti e la controversia tra platonici ed aristotelici', *Respublica litterarum*, 4: 195–231.

—— (1983a), 'Still More on "Bessarion Latinus"', *Rinascimento*, ser. 2, 23: 217–35.

—— (1983b), 'The Byzantine Rhetorical Tradition and the Renaissance', in Murphy (1983: 174–87).

—— (1984), Review of *Laurentii Valle repastinatio*, ed. G. Zippel, in *RLI* 2: 177–94.

—— (1987a), 'Three Notes on Rhetoric', *Rhetorica*, 5: 107–18.

—— (1987*b*), 'For the History of Marsilio Ficino's Translation of Plato', *Rinascimento*, 27: 293–9.

—— (1987*c*), 'Pseudo-Dionysius the Areopagite in Mid-Quattrocento Rome', in Hankins, Monfasani, and Purnell (1987: 189–219).

—— (1987*d*), Review of *Laurentii Valle de professione religiosorum*, *RLI* 5: 351–65.

—— (1988), 'Humanism and Rhetoric', in Rabil (1988: iii. 171–211).

—— (1989), 'Was Lorenzo Valla an Ordinary Language Philosopher?' *JHI* 50: 309–23.

—— (1990), 'Lorenzo Valla and Rudolph Agricola', *JHP* 28: 181–200.

Monnerjahn, E. (1960), *Giovanni Pico della Mirandola*, Wiesbaden.

Montaigne, M. de (1962), *Œuvres*, Paris.

—— (1965), *The Complete Essays of Montaigne*, trans. D. M. Frame, Stanford, Calif.

—— (1987), *An Apology for Raymond Sebond*, ed. and trans. M. Screech, London.

Moore, G. E. (1956), *Principia Ethica*, Cambridge.

More, T. (1963–), *The Complete Works of St. Thomas More*, New Haven, Conn.

—— (1989), *Utopia*, ed. and trans. G. Logan and R. Adams, Cambridge.

Moreau, J. (1960), 'Doute et savoir chez Francisco Sanches', *Portugiesische Forschungen des Görresgesellschaft*, 1st ser., *Aufsätze zur Portugiesischen Kulturgeschichte*, 1: 24–50.

—— (1966), 'Sanchez précartésien', *RP* 2: 264–70.

Moreira de Sá, A. (1947), *Francisco Sanchez, filósofo e matemático*, Lisbon.

Morewedge, P. (ed.) (1982), *Philosophies of Existence, Ancient and Medieval*, New York.

Morley, H. (1854), *Jerome Cardan: The Life of Girolamo Cardano of Milan, Physician*, London.

Muccillo, M. (1975), 'La storia della filosofia presocratica nelle *Discussiones peripateticae* di Francesco Patrizi da Cherso', *La cultura*, 13: 48–105.

—— (1981), 'La vita e le opere di Aristotele nelle *Discussiones peripateticae* di Francesco Patrizi da Cherso', *Rinascimento*, ser. 2, 21: 53–119.

—— (1986), 'Marsilio Ficino e Francesco Patrizi da Cherso', in Garfagnini (1986: ii. 615–79).

Müller-Jahncke, W.-D. (1973), 'Magie als Wissenschaft im frühen

16. Jahrhundert: Die Beziehungen zwischen Magie, Medizin und Pharmazie im Werk des Agrippa von Nettesheim (1486–1535)', dissertation, Philipps Universität, Marburg.

Müller-Jahncke, W.-D. (1985), *Astrologisch-magische Theorie und Praxis in der Heilkunde der frühen Neuzeit*, Stuttgart.

Münster, L. (1953), 'Alessandro Achillini, anatomico e filosofo, professore dello Studio di Bologna (1463–1512)', *Rivista di storia delle scienze mediche e naturali*, 15: 7–22, 54–77.

Muller, R. A. (1984), '*Vera philosophia cum sacra theologia nusquam pugnat*: Keckermann on Philosophy, Theology and the Problem of Double Truth', *SCJ* 15: 341–65.

Muraro, L. (1978), *Giambattista Della Porta mago e scienzato*, Milan.

Murdoch, J. E. (1982), 'Infinity and Continuity', *CHLMP*: 564–91.

—— and Sylla, E. (eds.) (1975), *The Cultural Context of Medieval Learning*, Dordrecht.

—— —— (1978), 'The Science of Motion', in Lindberg (1978a: 206–64).

Murphy, J. J. (1974), *Rhetoric in the Middle Ages: A History of Rhetorical Theory from Saint Augustine to the Renaissance*, Berkeley, Calif.

—— (ed.) (1978), *Medieval Eloquence*, Berkeley, Calif.

—— (ed.) (1983), *Renaissance Eloquence: Studies in the Theory and Practice of Renaissance Rhetoric*, Berkeley, Calif.

Nardi, B. (1945), *Sigieri di Brabante nel pensiero del rinascimento italiano*, Rome.

—— (1958), *Saggi sull'aristotelismo padovano dal secolo XIV al XVI*, Florence.

—— (1965), *Studi su Pietro Pomponazzi*, Florence.

—— (1971), *Saggi sulla cultura veneta del Quattro e Cinquecento*, Padua.

Naudé, G. de (1625), *Apologie pour tous les grands personnages qui ont esté faussement soupçonnez de magie*, Paris.

Nauert, C. G. (1965), *Agrippa and the Crisis of Renaissance Thought*, Urbana, Ill.

—— (1979), 'Humanists, Scientists and Pliny: Changing Approaches to a Classical Author', *AHR* 84: 72–85.

Nauwelaerts, M. A. (1963), *Rodolphus Agricola*, The Hague.

Nelson, J. C. (1958), *Renaissance Theory of Love: The Context of Giordano Bruno's 'Eroici furori'*, New York.

Neuhausen, K. A., and Trapp, E. (1979), 'Lateinische Humanistenbriefe zu Bessarions Schrift *In calumniatorem Platonis*', *Jahrbuch de österreichischen Byzantinistik*, 28: 141–65.

Newton, I. (1959–77), *The Correspondence of Isaac Newton*, ed. H. W. Turnbull, A. R. Hall *et al*. Cambridge.

Nicolò Cusano: Relazioni presentate al Convegno interuniversitario di Bressanone (1961), Florence.

Nicolò Cusano agli inizi del mondo moderno: Atti del Congresso internazionale in occasione del V centenario della morte di Nicolò Cusano, Bressanone, 6–10 settembre 1964 (1970), Florence.

Nizolio, M. (1956), *De veris principiis et vera ratione philosophandi contra pseudophilosophos libri IV*, ed. Q. Breen, Rome.

Nizzoli, A. (1970), *Mario Nizolio e il rinnovamento scientifico moderno (1488–1566)*, Como.

Nolhac, P. de (1907), *Pétrarque et l'humanisme*, 2nd edn., Paris.

Nordman, V. A. (1932), *Justus Lipsius als Geschichtsforscher und Geschichtslehrer*, Helsinki.

Noreña, C. G. (1970), *Juan Luis Vives*, The Hague.

—— (1975), *Studies in Spanish Renaissance Thought*, The Hague.

—— (1989), *Juan Luis Vives and the Emotions*, Carbondale, Ill.

North, J. D. (1986), *Horoscopes and History*, London.

Nuchelmans, G. (1980), *Late Scholastic and Humanist Theories of the Proposition*, Amsterdam.

Oakley, F. (1962), 'On the Road from Constance to 1688: The Political Thought of John Major and George Buchanan', *Journal of British Studies*, 2: 1–31.

—— (1964), *The Political Thought of Pierre d'Ailly: The Voluntarist Tradition*, New Haven, Conn.

—— (1965), 'Almain and Major: Conciliar Theory on the Eve of the Reformation', *AHR* 70: 673–90.

—— (1979), *The Western Church in the Later Middle Ages*, Ithaca, NY.

—— (1984), *Omnipotence, Covenant and Order: An Excursion in the History of Ideas from Abelard to Leibniz*, Ithaca, NY.

—— (1987), 'Lovejoy's Unexplored Option', *JHI* 48: 231–45.

Oberman, H. A. (1981), *Masters of the Reformation: The Emergence of a New Intellectual Climate*, trans. D. Martin, Cambridge.

—— (1983), *The Harvest of Medieval Theology: Gabriel Biel and Late Medieval Nominalism*, 3rd edn., Durham, NC.

—— (1987), '*Via Antiqua* and *Via Moderna*: Late Medieval Prolegomena to Early Reformation Thought', *JHI* 48: 23–40.

—— (1989), *Luther: Man between God and the Devil*, New Haven, Conn.

Ochman, J. (1974), 'Il determinismo astrologico di Girolamo Cardan', *Magia, astrologia e religione*: 123–9.

—— (1975), 'Les Horoscopes des religions établis par J. Cardano 1501–76', *Revue de synthèse*, 96: 35–51.

O'Connor, D. J. (ed.) (1985), *A Critical History of Western Philosophy*, New York.

Oestreich, G. (1975), 'Justus Lipsius als Universalgelehrter zwischen Renaissance und Barock', in Scheurleer and Posthumus Meyjes (1975: 177–201).

—— (1982), *Neostoicism and the Early Modern State*, ed. B. Oestreich and H. G. Koenigsberger, trans. D. McLintock, Cambridge.

O'Kelly, B. (ed.) (1966), *The Renaissance Image of Man and the World*, Columbus, Oh.

Olivieri, L. (ed.) (1983), *Aristotelismo veneto e scienza moderna*, Padua.

O'Malley, J. W. (1968), *Giles of Viterbo on Church and Reform*, Leiden.

—— (1974), 'Some Renaissance Panegyrics of Aquinas', *RQ* 27: 174–92.

—— (1979), *Praise and Blame in Renaissance Rome: Rhetoric, Doctrine and Reform in the Sacred Orators of the Papal Court*, Durham, NC.

—— (1981), *Rome and the Renaissance: Studies in Culture and Religion*, London.

O'Meara, D. J. (ed.) (1981), *Studies in Aristotle*, Washington, DC.

—— (ed.) (1982), *Neoplatonism and Christian Thought*, Norfolk, Va.

Ong, W. J. (1958), *Ramus and Talon Inventory*, Cambridge, Mass.

—— (1983), *Ramus, Method and the Decay of Dialogue*, Cambridge, Mass.

Ongaro, G. (1969), 'Girolamo Cardano e Andrea Vesalio', *Rivista di storia della medicina*, 13: 51–61.

Onoranze a Francesco Patrizi da Cherso: Catalogo della mostra bibliografica (1957), Trieste.

L'Opera e il pensiero di Giovanni Pico della Mirandola nella storia dell'umanesimo: Convegno internazionale (Mirandola: 15–18 settembre 1963) (1965), Florence.

Ore, O. (1965), *Cardano: The Gambling Scholar*, New York.

O'Rourke Boyle, M. (1977), *Erasmus on Language and Method in Theology*, Toronto.

—— (1983), *Rhetoric and Reform: Erasmus' Civil Dispute with Luther*, Cambridge, Mass.

Overfield, J. H. (1976), 'Scholastic Opposition to Humanism in Pre-Reformation Germany', *Viator*, 7: 371–420.

—— (1984), *Humanism and Scholasticism in Late Medieval Germany*, Princeton, NJ.

Ozment, S. (1980), *The Age of Reform, 1250–1550: An Intellectual and Religious History of Late Medieval and Reformation Europe*, New Haven, Conn.

Padley, G. A. (1976), *Grammatical Theory in Western Europe, 1500–1700: The Latin Tradition*, Cambridge.

—— (1985–8), *Grammatical Theory in Western Europe, 1500–1700*, Cambridge.

Pagden, A. R. D. (1975), 'The Diffusion of Aristotle's Moral Philosophy in Spain', *Traditio*, 31: 287–313.

—— (1982), *The Fall of Natural Man: The American Indian and the Origins of Comparative Ethnology*, Cambridge.

—— (ed.) (1987), *The Languages of Political Theory in Early Modern Europe*, Cambridge.

—— (1990), *Spanish Imperialism and the Political Imagination: Studies in European and Spanish-American Social and Political Theory, 1513–1830*, New Haven, Conn.

Pagel, W. (1958), *Paracelsus: An Introduction to Philosophical Medicine in the Era of the Renaissance*, Basle.

—— (1962), *Das medizinische Weltbild des Paracelsus: Seine Zusammenhänge mit Neuplatonismus und Gnosis*, Wiesbaden.

—— (1985), *Religion and Neoplatonism in Renaissance Medicine*, London.

—— (1986), *From Paracelsus to Van Helmont: Studies in Renaissance Medicine and Science*, London.

Pagnoni, M. R. (1974), 'Prime note sulla tradizione medievale ed umanistica di Epicuro', *ASNSP* ser. 3, 4: 1443–77.

Panizza, L. (1978), 'Lorenzo Valla's *De vero falsoque bono*, Lactantius and Oratorical Scepticism', *JWCI* 41: 76–107.

Panofsky, E. (1955), *Meaning in the Visual Arts*, Garden City, NY.

—— (1962), *Studies in Iconology: Humanistic Themes in the Art of the Renaissance*, New York.

—— (1968), *Idea*, New York.

—— (1969), *Renaissance and Renascences in Western Art*, New York.

Pantin, I. (1988), 'Les "Commentaires" de Lefèvre d'Étaples au Corpus Hermeticum', in Faivre (1988: 167–83).

Paparelli, G. (1955), 'La Taumatologia di Giambattista Della Porta', *Filologia romanza*, 2: 418–29.

Papi, F. (1968), *Antropologia e civiltà nel pensiero di Giordano Bruno*, Florence.

Paracelsus, P. (1922–33), *Sämtliche Werke*, ed. K. Sudhoff and W. Matthiessen, Munich.

—— (1923–73), *Die theologischen und religionswissenschaftlichen Schriften*, ed. K. Sudhoff *et al.* Munich/Wiesbaden.

—— (1951), *Selected Writings*, ed. and trans. J. Jacobi and N. Guterman, Princeton, NJ.

Park, K. (1980), 'Albert's Influence on Late Medieval Psychology', in Weisheipl (1980: 501–35).

—— (1988), 'The Organic Soul', *CHRP*: 464–84.

Parry, J. H. (1966), *The Spanish Seaborne Empire*, London.

Passmore, J. (1968), *A Hundred Years of Philosophy*, Harmondsworth.

Pater, W. (1910), *The Renaissance: Studies in Art and Poetry*, London.

Patrizi, F. (1581), *Discussionum peripateticarum tomi quattuor*, Basle.

—— (1591), *Nova de universis philosophia*, Ferrara.

Patterson, A. M. (1970), *Hermogenes and the Renaissance: Seven Ideas of Style*, Princeton, NJ.

Pears, D. (1970), *Ludwig Wittgenstein*, New York.

Pellegrini, F. (1948), *Fracastoro*, Trieste.

Percival, W. K. (1975), 'The Grammatical Tradition and the Rise of the Vernaculars', *Current Trends in Linguistics*, 13/1: 231–75.

—— (1982), 'Changes in the Approach to Language', *CHLMP*: 808–17.

—— (1983), 'Grammar and Rhetoric in the Renaissance', in Murphy (1983: 303–30).

—— (1988), 'Renaissance Grammar', in Rabil (1988: iii. 67–79).

Perreiah, A. R. (1967), 'A Biographical Introduction to Paul of Venice', *Augustiniana*, 17: 450–61.

—— (1982), 'Humanist Critiques of Scholastic Dialectic', *SCJ* 13: 3–22.

—— (1986), *Paul of Venice: A Bibliographical Guide*, Bowling Green, Oh.

Perrone Compagni, V. (1975), '*Picatrix Latinus*: Concezioni filosofico-religiose e prassi magica', *Medioevo*, 1: 237–337.

—— (1978), 'La magia cerimoniale del Picatrix nel rinascimento', *Atti dell'Accademia di scienze morali e politiche di Napoli*, 88: 279–330.

—— (1982), 'Una fonte di Cornelio Agrippa: il *De harmonia mundi* di Francesco Zorzi', *Annali dell'Istituto di filosofia, Università di Firenze*, 4: 45–74.

Peruzzi, E. (1980), 'Antioccultismo e filosofia naturale nel *De sympathia et antipathia rerum* di Girolamo Fracastoro', *Atti e memorie dell'Accademia toscana di scienze morali 'La Colombaria'*, 45: 41–131.

Peter of Spain (1972), *Tractatus* Called Afterwards *Summule logicales*, ed. L. M. De Rijk, Assen.

Petersen, P. (1921), *Geschichte der aristotelischen Philosophie im protestantischen Deutschland*, Leipzig.

Petrarch, F. (1965), *Francisci Petrarchae . . . opera quae extant omnia*, repr., Ridgewood, NJ.

—— (1971), *A Humanist among Princes: An Anthology of Petrarch's Letters and of Selections from his Other Works*, trans. D. Thompson *et al.*, New York.

—— (1975), *Opere Latine*, ed. A. Bufano, Turin.

Pfeiffer, R. (1968), *History of Classical Scholarship from the Beginnings to the End of the Hellenistic Age*, Oxford.

—— (1976), *History of Classical Scholarship from 1300 to 1850*, Oxford.

Philoponus, J. (1987), *Against Aristotle on the Eternity of the World*, trans. C. Wildberg, ed. R. Sorabji, Ithaca, NY.

Piano Mortari, V. (1978), *Diritto, logica, metodo nel secolo XVI*, Naples.

Pico, G. (1572), *Opera*, Basle.

—— (1942), *De hominis dignitate; Heptaplus; De ente et uno*, ed. E. Garin, Florence.

—— (1946–52), *Disputationes adversus astrologiam divinatricem*, ed. E. Garin, Florence.

—— (1965), *On the Dignity of Man; On Being and the One; Heptaplus*, trans. C. G. Wallia, P. J. W. Miller, and D. Carmichael, Indianapolis.

—— (1973), *Conclusiones sive theses DCCCC Romae anno 1486, publice disputandae, sed non admissae: Texte établi . . . avec l'introduction et les annotations critiques*, ed. B. Kieskowski, Geneva.

—— (1984), *Commentary on a Canzone of Benivieni*, trans. S. Jayne, New York.

Pico, G. F. (1601), *Opera quae extant omnia*, Basle.

—— (1969), *Opera omnia*, repr., Hildesheim.

—— (1984), *Über die Vorstellung; De imaginatione: Lateinisch-deutsche Ausgabe*, ed. C. B. Schmitt, K. Park, and E. Kessler, Munich.

Pierre de la Ramée (Ramus); Revue des sciences philosophiques et théologiques (1986), 70: 2–100.

Pine, M. (1986), *Pietro Pomponazzi: Radical Philosopher of the Renaissance*, Padua.

Pintard, R. (1943), *Le Libertinage érudit dans la première moitié du XVIIe siècle*, Paris.

Pintaudi, R. (1977), *Lessico Graeco-latino Laur. Ashb. 1439*, Rome.

Platon et Aristote à la Renaissance: XVIe Colloque de Tours (De Pétrarque à Descartes, 32) (1976), Paris.

Platzeck, E.-W. (1962–4), *Raimund Lull*, Düsseldorf.

Pocock, J. G. A. (1975), *The Machiavellian Moment: Florentine Political Thought and the Atlantic Republican Tradition*, Princeton, NJ.

Poggio Bracciolini, 1380–1980: Nel 6° centenario della nascita (1982), Florence.

Poliziano, A. (1971), *Opera*, repr., Basle.

Il Poliziano e il suo tempo (1957), Florence.

Pomponazzi, P. (1567), *Opera*, Basle.

—— (1954), *Tractatus de immortalitate animae*, ed. G. Morra, Bologna.

—— (1957), *Libri quinque de fato, de libero arbitrio et de praedestinatione*, Lugano.

—— (1966–70), *Corsi inediti dell'insegnamento padovano*, ed. A. Poppi.

—— (1970), *De naturalium effectuum causis sive de incantationibus*, Hildesheim.

Ponte, G. (1981), *Leon Battista Alberti, umanista e scrittore*, Genoa.

Popkin, R. H. (1979), *The History of Scepticism from Erasmus to Spinoza*, rev. edn., Berkeley, Calif.

—— (1988), 'Theories of Knowledge', *CHRP*: 668–84.

—— and Schmitt, C. B. (1987), *Scepticism from the Renaissance to the Enlightenment*, Hanover.

Poppi, A. (1964), 'L'antiaverroismo della scolastica padovana alla fine del secolo XV', *Studia patavina*, 11: 102–24.

—— (1966), *Causalità e infinità nella scuola padovana dal 1480 al 1513*, Padua.

—— (1970a), *Introduzione all'aristotelismo padavano*, Padua.

—— (1970b), *Saggi sul pensiero inedito di Pietro Pomponazzi*, Padua.

—— (1972), *La dottrina della scienza in Giacomo Zabarella*, Padua.

—— (ed.) (1983), *Scienza e filosofia all'Università di Padova nel Quattrocento*, Padua.

—— (1988), 'Fate, Fortune, Providence and Human Freedom',

CHRP: 641–67.

Prantl, C. (1855–70), *Geschichte der Logik im Abendlande*, Leipzig.

Prelog, J. (1983), 'Die Handschriften und Drucke von Walter Burleys *Liber de vita et moribus philosophorum*', *Codices manuscripti*, 9: 1–18.

Prete, S. (ed.) (1961), *Didascaliae: Studies in Honor of Anselm M. Albareda, Prefect of the Vatican Library, Presented by a Group of American Scholars*, New York.

Pring-Mill, R. D. F. (1961), *El microcosmos lul-lia*, Palma de Mallorca.

Procacci, G. (1965), *Studi sulla fortuna del Machiavelli*, Rome.

Proclus, lecteur et interprète des anciens (Colloques internationaux du CNRS), (1987), Paris.

Prost, A. (1881–2), *Corneille Agrippa: Sa vie et ses œuvres*, Paris.

Purnell, F. (1971), 'Jacopo Mazzoni and his Comparison of Plato and Aristotle', dissertation, Columbia Univ.

—— (1972), 'Jacopo Mazzoni and Galileo', *Physis*, 14: 273–94.

—— (1976), 'Francesco Patrizi and the Critics of Hermes Trismegistus', *JMRS* 6: 155–78.

—— (1977), 'Hermes and the Sibyl: A Note on Ficino's *Pimander*', *RQ* 30: 305–10.

—— (1986), 'The Theme of Philosophic Concord and the Sources of Ficino's Platonism', in Garfagnini (1986: ii. 397–415).

—— (1987), 'The Hermetist as Heretic: An Unpublished Censure of Foix de Candale's *Pimandre*', in Hankins, Monfasani, and Purnell (1987: 525–35).

Rabb, T. K., and Seigel, J. E. (eds.) (1969), *Action and Conviction in Early Modern Europe: Essays in Memory of E. H. Harbison*, Princeton, NJ.

Rabelais, F. (1973), *Œuvres complètes*, ed. G. Demerson, Paris.

Rabil, A. (ed.) (1988), *Renaissance Humanism: Foundations, Forms and Legacy*, Philadelphia.

Radetti, G. (1889), 'L'Épicurismo italiano negli ultimi secoli del medioevo', *Rivista di filosofia scientifica*, 8: 552–63.

Raimondi, E. (1974), 'Il primo commento umanistico a Lucrezio', *Tra Latino e Volgare*: 641–74.

Raith, W. (1967), *Die Macht des Bildes: Ein humanistisches Problem bei Gianfrancesco Pico della Mirandola*, Munich.

Ramus, P. (1964*a*), *Dialecticae institutiones; Aristotelicae animadversiones*, ed. W. Risse, repr., Stuttgart/Bad Canstatt.

—— (1964*b*), *Dialectique (1555)*, ed. M. Dassonville, Geneva.

412　　　　　　　　　　*Bibliography*

Ramus, P. (1970), *Scholae in liberales artes*, ed. W. J. Ong, repr., Hildesheim.

—— (1986), *Arguments in Rhetoric against Quintilian: Translation and Text of Peter Ramus's Rhetoricae distinctiones in Quintilianum (1549)*, trans. C. Newlands, ed. J. Murphy, DeKalb, Ill.

—— and Talon, O. (1971), *Œuvres diverses*, ed. N. Bergeron, Geneva.

Randall, J. H. (1961), *The School of Padua and the Emergence of Modern Science*, Padua.

—— (1968), 'The Development of Scientific Method in the School of Padua', in Kristeller and Wiener (1968: 217–51).

—— (1976), 'Paduan Aristotelianism Reconsidered', in Mahoney (1976a: 275–82).

Reeve, M. D. (1980), 'The Italian Tradition of Lucretius', *IMU* 23: 27–48.

Reif, P. (1969), 'The Textbook Tradition in Natural Philosophy, 1600–1650', *JHI* 20: 17–32.

The Renaissance: Essays in Interpretation (1982), London.

Renan, E. (1882), *Averroès et l'averroïsme: Essai historique*, 4th edn., Paris.

Renaudet, A. (1953), *Préréforme et humanisme à Paris pendant les premières guerres d'Italie (1494–1517)*, 2nd edn., Paris.

—— (1954), *Érasme et l'Italie*, Geneva.

—— (1969), 'Paris from 1494 to 1517: Church and University, Religious Reforms; Culture and the Humanists' Critiques', in Gundersheimer (1969: 65–89).

Reynolds, L. D. (ed.) (1986), *Texts and Transmission: A Survey of the Latin Classics*, Oxford.

—— and Wilson, N. G. (1991), *Scribes and Scholars: A Guide to the Transmission of Greek and Latin Literature*, 3rd edn., Oxford.

Rice, E. F. (1958), *The Renaissance Idea of Wisdom*, Cambridge, Mass.

—— (1969), 'The Humanist Idea of Christian Antiquity: Lefèvre d'Étaples and his Circle', in Gundersheimer (1969: 163–80).

—— (1970), 'Humanist Aristotelianism in France: Jacques Lefèvre d'Étaples and His Circle', in Levi (1970: 132–49).

—— (1971), 'Jacques Lefèvre d'Étaples and the Medieval Christian Mystics', *Florilegium Historiale*: 89–124.

—— (1976), 'The *De magia naturali* of Jacques Lefèvre d'Étaples', in Mahoney (1976a: 19–29).

—— (1985), *St. Jerome in the Renaissance*, Baltimore.

Rice, J. V. (1939), *Gabriel Naudé, 1600-1653*, Baltimore.

Ridolfi, R. (1963), *The Life of Niccolò Machiavelli*, trans. C. Grayson, Chicago.

Risse, W. (1964), *Die Logik der Neuzeit*, Stuttgart.

Ritter, G. (1921-2), *Studien zur Spätscholastik*, Heidelberg.

Rizzo, S. (1973), *Il lessico filologico degli umanisti*, Rome.

Rokita, G. (1971), 'Aristoteles, Aristotelicus, Aristotelicotatus, Aristoteleskunst', *Archiv für Begriffsgeschichte*, 15: 51-93.

Rorty, R. (1984), 'The Historiography of Philosophy: Four Genres', in Rorty, Schneewind, and Skinner (1984: 49-75).

——, Schneewind, J. B., and Skinner, Q. (eds.) (1984), *Philosophy in History: Essays on the Historiography of Philosophy*, Cambridge.

Rose, P. L. (1975), *The Italian Renaissance of Mathematics: Studies on Humanists and Mathematicians from Petrarch to Galileo*, Geneva.

—— (1980), *Bodin and the Great God of Nature: The Moral and Religious Universe of a Judaizer*, Geneva.

—— and Drake, S. (1971), 'The Pseudo-Aristotelian "Questions of Mechanics" in Renaissance Culture', *SR* 18: 65-104.

Rossi, G. (1893), *Girolamo Fracastoro in relazione all'aristotelismo e alle scienze del rinascimento*, Pisa.

Rossi, P. (1953*a*), 'Il *De principiis* di Mario Nizolio', *AF XX*: 57-92.

—— (1953*b*), 'La celebrazione della retorica e la polemica antimetafisica del *De principiis* di Mario Nizolio', in Banfi (1953: 99-221).

—— (1953*c*), 'Ramismo, logica, retorica nei secoli XVI e XVII', *RCSF* 12: 357-65.

—— (1954), 'Il metodo induttivo e la polemica antioccultista in Girolamo Fracastoro', *RCSF* 9: 485-99.

—— (1974), *Francesco Bacone: della magia alla scienza*, rev. edn., Turin.

—— (1982), 'The Aristotelians and the "Moderns": Hypothesis and Nature', *Annali dell'Istituto e Museo di storia della scienza di Firenze*, 8: 3-17.

—— (1983), *Clavis universalis: Arti della memoria e logica combinatoria da Lullo a Leibniz*, 2nd edn., Bologna.

Rotondo, A. (1958), 'Niccolò Tignosi da Foligno (Polemiche aristoteliche di un maestro del Ficino)', *Rinascimento*, 9: 217-55.

Rubinstein, N. (1958-64), 'Poggio Bracciolini: cancelliere e storico di Firenze', *Atti e memorie dell'Accademia Petrarca di lettere, arti e scienze di Arezzo*, 37: 215-39.

—— (1966), *The Government of Florence under the Medici (1434 to*

1494), Oxford.

Ruderman, D. B. (1988), 'The Italian Renaissance and Jewish Thought', in Rabil (1988: i. 382–433).

Rummel, E. (1985), *Erasmus as a Translator of the Classics*, Toronto.

—— (1986), *Erasmus' Annotations on the New Testament: From Philologist to Theologian*, Toronto.

Rupp, G. (1964), *Luther's Progress to the Diet of Worms*, New York.

Russell, B. (1945), *A History of Western Philosophy and Its Connection with Political and Social Circumstances from the Earliest Times to the Present Day*, New York.

—— (1967–9), *The Autobiography of Bertrand Russell*, Boston.

Ruysschaert, J. (1949), *Juste Lipse et les Annales de Tacite: Une méthode de critique textuelle au XVIᵉ siècle*, Louvain.

Ryle, G. (1971), *Collected Papers*, London.

Sabbadini, R. (1885), *Storia del ciceronianismo*, Turin.

—— (1922), *Il metodo degli umanisti*, Florence.

—— (1967), *Le scoperte dei codici latini e greci ne' secoli XIV e XV*, ed. E. Garin, Florence.

Saitta, G. (1928), *Filosofia italiana e umanesimo*, Venice.

—— (1954), *Marsilio Ficino e la filosofia dell'umanesimo*, 3rd edn., Bologna.

—— (1961), *Il pensiero italiano nell'umanesimo e nel Rinascimento*, 2nd edn., Florence.

Salutati, C. (1891–1911), *Epistolario*, ed. F. Novati, Rome.

—— (1913), *De tyranno*, ed. A. von Martin, Berlin.

—— (1947), *De nobilitate legum et medicinae; De verecundia*, ed. E. Garin, Florence.

—— (1951), *De laboribus Herculis*, ed. B. L. Ullman, Zurich.

—— (1957), *De seculo et religione*, ed. B. L. Ullman, Florence.

—— (1985), *De fato et fortuna*, ed. C. Bianca, Florence.

Salvestrini, V. (1958), *Bibliografia di Giordano Bruno, 1582–1950*, ed. L. Firpo, 2nd edn., Florence.

Sanches, F. (1988), *That Nothing is Known (Quod nihil scitur)*, ed. and trans. E. Limbrick and D. F. S. Thomson, Cambridge.

Sancipriano, M. (1957), *Il pensiero psicologico e morale di Giovanni Ludovico Vives*, Florence.

Sandys, J. E. (1908), *A History of Classical Scholarship*, Cambridge.

Santillana, G. de, and Zilsel, E. (1970), *The Development of Rationalism and Empiricism*, Chicago.

Santinello, G. (1962), *Leon Battista Alberti: una visione estetica del mondo e della vita*, Florence.

—— (ed.) (1970), *Nicolò Cusano agli inizi del mondo moderno*, Florence.

—— (ed.) (1981–), *Storia delle storie generali della filosofia*, Brescia.

Sarton, G. (1948), *Introduction to the History of Science*, Baltimore.

Sasso, G. (1958), *Niccolò Machiavelli: Storia del pensiero politico*, Naples.

Saunders, J. L. (1955), *Justus Lipsius: The Philosophy of Renaissance Stoicism*, New York.

Saxl, F. (1936), '*Veritas filia temporis*', in Klibansky and Paton (1936: 197–222).

—— (1957), *Lectures*, London.

Sayce, R. A. (1972), *The Essays of Montaigne: A Critical Exploration*, London.

Scaglione, A. (1961), 'The Humanist as Scholar and Politian's Conception of the *Grammaticus*', *SR* 8: 49–70.

Scheurleer, T. H. L., and Posthumus Meyjes, G. H. M. (eds.) (1975), *Leiden University in the 17th Century*, Leiden.

Schevill, F. (1949), *The Medici*, New York.

Schiavone, M. (1957), *Problemi filosofici in Marsilio Ficino*, Milan.

Schiffman, Z. S. (1984), 'Montaigne and the Rise of Scepticism in Early Modern Europe: A Reappraisal', *JHI* 45: 499–516.

Schmitt, C. B. (1967), *Gianfrancesco Pico della Mirandola (1469– 1533) and his Critique of Aristotle*, The Hague.

—— (1970), 'Gianfrancesco Pico della Mirandola and the Fifth Lateran Council', *AR* 61: 161–78.

—— (1972a), *Cicero Scepticus: A Study of the Influence of the Academica in the Renaissance*, The Hague.

—— (1972b), 'The Recovery and Assimilation of Ancient Scepticism in the Renaissance', *RCSF* 27: 363–84.

—— (1975), 'Philosophy and Science in Sixteenth-Century Universities: Some Preliminary Comments', in Murdoch and Sylla (1975: 485–537).

—— (1981), *Studies in Renaissance Philosophy and Science*, London.

—— (1982), 'Andreas Camutius on the Concord of Plato and Aristotle with Scripture', in O'Meara (1982: 178–84).

—— (1983a), *Aristotle and the Renaissance*, Cambridge, Mass.

—— (1983b), *John Case and Aristotelianism in Renaissance England*, Kingston/Montreal.

—— (1984), *The Aristotelian Tradition and Renaissance Universities*, London.

—— (1987), 'Giambattista Benedetti and the Aristotelian Tradition',

416 *Bibliography*

Atti . . . Benedetti: 127–37.

Schmitt, C. B. (1988), 'The Rise of the Philosophical Textbook', *CHRP*: 792–804.

—— (1989), *Reappraisals in Renaissance Thought*, ed. C. Webster, London.

—— and Knox, D. (1985), *Pseudo-Aristoteles Latinus: A Guide to Latin Works Falsely Attributed to Aristotle before 1500*, London.

—— and Ryan, W. F. (eds.) (1983), *Pseudo-Aristotle, the* Secret of Secrets: *Sources and Influences*, London.

Schmidt-Biggemann, W. (1983), *Topica universalis*, Hamburg.

Schnauer, H. (1972), *Modi essendi: Interpretationen zu den Schriften 'De docta ignorantia', 'De coniecturis', und 'De venatione sapientiae' von Nikolaus von Kues*, Aschendorff.

Schoeck, R. J. (1976), *The Achievement of Thomas More: Aspects of his Life and Works*, Victoria, BC.

—— (ed.) (1985), *Acta Conventus Neo-Latini Bononiensis: Proceedings of the Fourth International Congress of Neo-Latin Studies*, Binghamton, NY.

—— (1988), *Erasmus grandescens: The Growth of a Humanist's Mind and Spirituality*, Nieuwkoop.

—— (1990), *Erasmus of Europe: The Making of a Humanist*, Edinburgh.

Scholem, G. (1954), *Major Trends in Jewish Mysticism*, New York.

—— (1974), *Kabbalah*, Jerusalem.

—— (1987), *Origins of the Kabbalah*, ed. and trans. R. Werblowsky and A. Arkush, Princeton, NJ.

Schüling, H. (1969), *Die Geschichte der axiomatischen Methode im 16. und beginnenden 17. Jahrhundert*, Hildesheim.

Schultze, F. (1874), *Georgios Gemisthos Plethon und seine reformatorischen Bestrebungen*, Jena.

Science and History: Studies in Honor of Edward Rosen (Studia Copernica, 16) (1978), Wrocław.

Sciences de la Renaissance (1973), Paris.

Scott, I. (1910), *Controversies over the Imitation of Cicero as a Model of Style*, New York.

Screech, M. A. (1956), 'Some Stoic Elements in Rabelais's Religious Thought', *Études rabelaisiennes*, 1: 73–97.

—— (1979), *Rabelais*, Ithaca, NY.

—— (1983), *Montaigne and Melancholy: The Wisdom of the Essays*, London.

—— (1988), *Erasmus: Ecstasy and the Praise of Folly*, London.

Secret, F. (1958), *Le Zohar dans les kabbalistes chrétiens de la renaissance*, Paris.

—— (1964), *Les kabbalistes chrétiens de la renaissance*, Paris.

—— (1965), 'Nouvelles précisions sur Flavius Mithridates, maître de Pic de la Mirandole et traducteur de commentaires de Kabbale', *L'Opera*: 2, 169–87.

—— (1976), 'Gianfrancesco Pico della Mirandola, Lilio Gregorio Giraldi et l'alchimie', *BHR* 38: 93–108.

Seigel, J. E. (1968), *Rhetoric and Philosophy in Renaissance Humanism: The Union of Eloquence and Wisdom, Petrarch to Valla*, Princeton, NJ.

—— (1969), 'The Teaching of Argyropoulos and the Rhetoric of the First Humanists', in Rabb and Seigel (1969: 237–60).

Seigfried, H. (1967), *Wahrheit und Metaphysik bei Suarez*, Bonn.

Senger, H. G. (1971), *Die Philosophie des Nikolaus von Kues vor dem Jahr 1440*, Münster.

Sensi, M. (1971–2), 'Niccolò Tignosi da Foligno: L'opera e il pensiero', *Annali della facoltà di lettere e filosofia, Università degli studi di Perugia*, 9: 359–495.

Setz, W. (1975), *Lorenzo Vallas Schrift gegen die Konstantinische Schenkung*, Tübingen.

Seznec, J. (1961), *The Survival of the Pagan Gods: The Mythological Tradition and its Place in Renaissance Humanism and Art*, trans. B. F. Sessions, New York.

Sharratt, P. (1975), 'Nicolaus Nancelius, *Petri Rami vita*', *HL* 24: 161–277.

—— (ed.) (1976), *French Renaissance Studies, 1540–70: Humanism and the Encyclopedia*, Edinburgh.

—— (1982), 'Ramus, philosophe indigne', *Bulletin de l'Association Guillaume Budé*: 187–206.

—— (1987), 'Recent Work on Peter Ramus', *Rhetorica*, 5: 7–58.

Shaw, P. (1978), 'La versione ficiniana della *Monarchia*', *Studi danteschi*, 51: 298–408.

Sheldon-Williams, I. P. (1970), 'The Greek Platonist Tradition from the Cappadocians to Maximus and Eriugena', *CHLGEMP*: 421–533.

Shepherd, W. (1837), *The Life of Poggio Bracciolini*, Liverpool.

Sherlock, T. P. (1948), 'The Chemical Work of Paracelsus', *Ambix*, 3: 33–63.

Sibiuda, R. (1966), *Theologia naturalis seu liber creaturarum*, ed. F. Stegmüller, Stuttgart/Bad Canstatt.

418 *Bibliography*

Sicherl, M. (1957), *Die Handschriften, Ausgaben und Übersetzungen von Iamblichus* De mysteriis, Berlin.

—— (1962), 'Neuentdeckte Handschriften von Marsilio Ficino und Johannes Reuchlin', *Scriptorium*, 16: 50–61.

Sigmund, P. E. (1963), *Nicholas of Cusa and Medieval Political Thought*, Cambridge, Mass.

Simone, F. (1949), *La coscienza della rinascita negli umanisti francesi*, Rome.

—— (1969), *The French Renaissance: Medieval Tradition and Italian Influence in Shaping the Renaissance in France*, trans. H. G. Hall, London.

Simposio Francesco Suárez; Cuadernos salmantinos de filosofia (1980), 7: 3–394.

Singer, D. W. (1950), *Giordano Bruno: His Life and Thought: With Annotated Translation of his Work On the Infinite Universe and Worlds*, New York.

Siraisi, N. G. (1973), *Arts and Sciences at Padua*, Toronto.

—— (1981), *Taddeo Alderotti and his Pupils: Two Generations of Italian Medical Learning*, Princeton, NJ.

—— (1987), *Avicenna in Renaissance Italy: The Canon and Medical Teaching in Italian Universities after 1500*, Princeton, NJ.

—— (1990), *Medieval and Early Renaissance Medicine: An Introduction to Knowledge and Practice*, Chicago.

Sirat, C. (1985), *A History of Jewish Philosophy in the Middle Ages*, Cambridge.

Skinner, Q. (1967), 'More's *Utopia*', *Past and Present*, 38: 153–68.

—— (1978), *The Foundations of Modern Political Thought*, Cambridge.

—— (1981), *Machiavelli*, Oxford.

—— (1988), 'Political Philosophy', *CHRP*: 389–452.

Skulsky, H. (1968), 'Paduan Epistemology and the Doctrine of the One Mind', *JHP* 6: 341–61.

Smith, P. (1923), *Erasmus*, New York.

Soleri, G. (1945), *Telesio*, Brescia.

Sonnino, L. A. (1968), *A Handbook to Sixteenth-Century Rhetoric*, London.

Sorabji, R. (ed.) (1987), *Philoponus and the Rejection of Aristotelian Science*, London.

—— (ed.) (1990), *Aristotle Transformed: The Ancient Commentators and their Influence*, London.

Soudek, J. (1958), 'The Genesis and Tradition of Leonardo Bruni's

Annotated Latin Version of the (pseudo-)Aristotelian *Economics*', *Scriptorium*, 12: 260–8.

—— (1968), 'Leonardo Bruni and his Public: A Statistical and Interpretative Study of his Annotated Latin Version of the (pseudo-) Aristotelian *Economics*', *SMRH* 5: 51–136.

—— (1976), 'A Fifteenth Century Humanistic Bestseller: The Manuscript Diffusion of Leonardo Bruni's Annotated Latin Version of the (pseudo-)Aristotelian *Economics*', in Mahoney (1976*a*: 129–43).

Southern, R. W. (1970), *Western Society and the Church in the Middle Ages*, Harmondsworth.

Sozzi, L. (1982), *La 'Dignité de l'homme' à la renaissance*, Turin.

Spade, P. (1982), 'The Semantics of Terms', *CHLMP*: 188–96.

Spampanato, V. (1921), *Vita di Giordano Bruno*, Messina.

—— (1933), *Documenti della vita di Giordano Bruno*, Florence.

Spanneut, M. (1973), *Permanence du Stoicisme: De Zénon à Malraux*, Gembloux.

Spicker, S. F. (ed.) (1978), *Organism, Medicine and Metaphysics: Essays in honour of Hans Jonas*, Dordrecht.

Spingarn, J. (1908), *A History of Literary Criticism in the Renaissance*, 2nd edn., New York.

Spink, J. S. (1960), *French Free-Thought from Gassendi to Voltaire*, London.

Spitz, L. W. (1963), *The Religious Renaissance of the German Humanists*, Cambridge, Mass.

Stadler, M. (1983), *Rekonstruktion einer Philosophie der Ungegenständlichkeit: Zur Struktur des cusanischen Denkens*, Munich.

Stein, L. (1889), 'Der Humanist Theodor Gaza als philosoph', *AGP* 2: 426–58.

Steuco, A. (1972), *De perenni philosophia*, ed. C. B. Schmitt, repr., New York.

Stinger, C. L. (1977), *Humanism and the Church Fathers: Ambrogio Traversari (1386–1439) and Christian Antiquity in the Italian Renaissance*, Albany, NY.

—— (1985), *The Renaissance in Rome*, Bloomington, Ind.

La storia della filosofia come sapere critico: Studi offerti a Mario Dal Pra (1980), Milan.

Stormon, E. J. (1980), 'Bessarion before the Council of Florence: A Survey of his Early Writings (1423–1437)', *Byzantina Australiensia*, 1: 128–56.

Strayer, J. R. (1982–9), *Dictionary of the Middle Ages*, New York.

Strowski, F. (1931), *Montaigne*, 2nd edn., Paris.
—— (1938), *Montaigne: Sa vie publique et privée*, Paris.
Struever, N. S. (1970), *The Language of History in the Renaissance: Rhetoric and Historical Consciousness in Florentine Humanism*, Princeton, NJ.
—— (1983), 'Lorenzo Valla: Humanist Rhetoric and the Critique of the Classical Languages of Morality', in Murphy (1983: 191–206).
Studi di bibliografia e di storia in onore di Tammaro De Marinis (1964), Verona.
Studia humanitatis: Ernesto Grassi zum 70. Geburtstag (1973), Munich.
Stump, E. (1989), *Dialectic and its Place in the Development of Medieval Logic*, Ithaca, NY.
Suárez, F. (1856–78), *Opera omnia*, ed. M. André and C. Berton, Paris.
Sudhoff, K. (1894–9), *Versuch einer Kritik der Echtheit der Paracelsischen Schriften*, Berlin.
—— (1936), *Paracelsus: Ein deutsches Lebensbild aus den Tagen der Renaissance*, Leipzig.
Surtz, E. L. (1957a), *The Praise of Pleasure: Philosophy, Education and Communism in More's Utopia*, Cambridge, Mass.
—— (1957b), *The Praise of Wisdom: A Commentary on the Religious and Moral Problems and Background of St. Thomas More's Utopia*, Chicago.
Tarabochia Canavero, A. (1971–2), *La presenza di S. Agostino nella 'Theologia platonica' di Marsilio Ficino*, Milan.
Tateo, F. (1960), *Astrologia e moralità in Giovanni Pontano*, Bari.
—— (1961), 'Poggio Bracciolini e la dialogistica del Quattrocento', *Annali della Facoltà di lettere e filosofia, Università di Bari*, 165–204.
—— (1972), *Lorenzo de' Medici e Angelo Poliziano*, Bari.
—— (1976), *L'umanesimo meridionale*, 2nd edn., Bari.
Tavardon, P. (1977), 'Le Conflict de Georges Gémiste Pléthon et de Georges Scholarios au sujet de l'expression d'Aristote τὸ ὂν λέγεται πολλαχῶς', *Byzantion*, 47: 268–78.
Taylor, C. (1984), 'Philosophy and its History', in Rorty, Schneewind, and Skinner (1984: 17–30).
Taylor, J. W. (1921), 'Georgius Gemistus Pletho's Criticism of Plato and Aristotle', dissertation, Univ. of Chicago.
—— (1925a), *Theodore Gaza's De fato*, Toronto.
—— (1925b), 'More Light on Theodore Gaza's *De fato*', *CP* 21:

233–40.

Teichman, J. (1990), 'Three Rival Versions of Moral Inquiry', *New York Times Book Review*, 12 Aug.: 14.

Telesio, B. (1910–23), *De rerum natura*, ed. V. Spampanato, Modena/Genoa/Rome.

—— (1965–77), *De rerum natura*, ed. and trans. L. de Franco, Cosenza/Florence.

—— (1971*a*), *De rerum natura iuxta propria principia libri IX*, ed. C. Vasoli, repr., Hildesheim.

—— (1971*b*), *Varii de naturalibus rebus*, ed. C. Vasoli, repr., Hildesheim.

Thibaudet, A. (1963), *Montaigne*, Paris.

Thomson, I. (1966), 'Manuel Chrysoloras and the Early Italian Renaissance', *GRBS* 7: 63–82.

Tierney, B. (1955), *Foundations of the Conciliar Theory: The Contributions of the Medieval Canonists from Gratian to the Great Schism*, Cambridge.

—— (1982), *Religion, Law and the Growth of Constitutional Thought, 1150–1650*, Cambridge.

Tigerstedt, E. N. (1968), 'Observations on the Reception of the Aristotelian *Poetics* in the Latin West', *SR* 15: 7–24.

—— (1969), *Plato's Idea of Poetical Inspiration*, Helsinki.

—— (1974), *The Decline and Fall of the Neoplatonic Interpretation of Plato: An Outline and Some Observations*, Helsinki.

—— (1977), *Interpreting Plato*, Stockholm.

Timmermans, B. (1938), 'Valla et Érasme, défenseurs d'Épicure', *Neophilologus*, 23: 174–9.

Tiraboschi, G. (1805–12), *Storia della letteratura italiana*, new edn., Venice.

Tocco, F. (1889), *Le opere latine di Giordano Bruno*, Florence.

—— (1892), *Le fonti più recenti della filosofia del Bruno*, Rome.

Toffanin, G. (1929), *Che cosa fu l'umanesimo*, Florence.

—— (1964), *Storia dell'umanesimo*, 2nd edn., Bologna.

Tolomio, I. (1981), 'Il genere "*Historia philosophica*" tra Cinquecento e Seicento', in Santinello (1981– : 63–163).

Tommaso Campanella (1569–1638): Miscellanea di studi nel 4° centenario della sua nascita (1969), Naples.

Tommaso Campanella nel IV centenario della nascita (1568–1968) (1969), Naples.

Torrance, T. F. (1969–70), '1469–1969: La Philosophie et la théologie de Jean Mair ou Major, de Haddington (1469–1550)', *AP*

32: 531–47; 33: 261–93.

Tracy, J. D. (1972), *Erasmus: The Growth of a Mind*, Geneva.

Tra Latino e Volgare: Per Carlo Dionisotti (1974), Padua.

Trapezuntius, G. (1984), *Collectanea Trapezuntiana: Texts, Documents and Bibliographies of George of Trebizond*, ed. J. Monfasani, Binghamton, NY.

Trentman, J. A. (1968), 'Extraordinary Language and Medieval Logic', *Dialogue*, 7: 286–91.

—— (1976), 'The Study of Logic and Language in England in the Early 17th Century', *Historiographia linguistica*, 3: 179–201.

—— (1982), 'Scholasticism in the Seventeenth Century', *CHLMP*: 818–37.

Trevisani, F. (1975), 'Symbolisme et interpretation chez Descartes et Cardan', *RCSF* 30: 27–47.

Trinkaus, C. (1940), *Adversity's Noblemen: The Italian Humanists on Happiness*, New York.

—— (1968), 'The Problem of Free Will in the Renaissance and the Reformation', in Kristeller and Wiener (1968: 187–98).

—— (1970), *In Our Image and Likeness: Humanity and Divinity in Italian Humanist Thought*, London.

—— (1979), *The Poet as Philosopher: Petrarch and the Formation of Renaissance Consciousness*, New Haven, Conn.

—— (1983), *The Scope of Renaissance Humanism*, Ann Arbor, Mich.

—— (1986), 'Marsilio Ficino and the Ideal of Human Autonomy', in Garfagnini (1986: i. 197–210).

—— (1987), '*Antiquitas versus modernitas*: An Italian Humanist Polemic and its Resonance', *JHI* 48: 11–21.

—— (1988a), 'Italian Humanism and Scholastic Theology', in Rabil (1988: iii. 327–48).

—— (1988b), 'Renaissance Semantics and Metamorphoses', *MH* NS 16: 177–87.

—— (1989a), 'Colluccio Salutati's Critique of Astrology in the Context of his Natural Philosophy', *Speculum*, 64: 46–68.

—— (1989b), 'Humanistic Dissidence: Florence versus Milan, or Poggio versus Valla', in Bertelli (1989: 1, 17–40).

—— (1990), 'Renaissance Ideas and the Idea of the Renaissance', *JHI* 51: 667–84.

—— and Oberman, H. (eds.) (1974), *The Pursuit of Holiness in Late Medieval and Renaissance Religion: Papers from the University of Michigan Conference*, Leiden.

Trinquet, R. (1972), *La Jeunesse de Montaigne: ses origines familiales, son enfance et ses études*, Paris.

Troilo, E. (ed.) (1914), *La filosofia di Bernardino Telesio ristretta in brevità e scritta in lingua toscana*, Bari.

Troilo, S. (1931–2), 'Due traduttori dell' *Etica Nicomachea*: Roberto di Lincoln e Leonardo Bruni', *Atti del R. Istituto veneto di scienze, lettere ed arti*, 91/2: 275–305.

Troje, H. E. (1971), *Graeca leguntur: Die Aneignung des byzantinischen Rechts und die Entstehung eines humanistischen Corpus iuris civilis in der Jurisprudenz des 16. Jahrhunderts*, Cologne.

Turner, C. J. G. (1969), 'The Career of George-Gennadius Scholarius', *Byzantion*, 39: 420–55.

Ullman, B. L. (1960), *The Origin and Development of Humanist Script*, Rome.

—— (1963), *The Humanism of Coluccio Salutati*, Padua.

—— (1973), *Studies in the Italian Renaissance*, 2nd edn., Rome.

—— and Stadter, P. A. (1972), *The Public Library of Renaissance Florence: Niccolò Niccoli, Cosimo de' Medici and the Library of San Marco*, Padua.

Ullmann, W. (1977), *Medieval Foundations of Renaissance Humanism*, London.

Umanesimo e rinascimento: Studi offerti a Paul Oskar Kristeller (1980), Florence.

Umanesimo e simbolismo (1958), Padua.

Urmson, J. O. (1967), *Philosophical Analysis: Its Development between the Two World Wars*, Oxford.

Valla, L. (1922), *The Treatise of Lorenzo Valla on the Donation of Constantine: Text and Translation into English*, ed. and trans. C. B. Coleman, New Haven, Conn.

—— (1934), *De libero arbitrio*, ed. M. Anfossi, Florence.

—— (1953), *Scritti filosofici e religiosi*, ed. G. Rasdetti, Florence.

—— (1962), *Opera omnia*, repr., Turin.

—— (1970*a*), *De vero falsoque bono*, ed. M. Lorch, Bari.

—— (1970*b*), *Collatio novi testamenti*, ed. A. Perosa, Florence.

—— (1977), *On Pleasure; De voluptate*, trans. A. K. Hieatt and M. Lorch, New York.

—— (1982), *Laurentii Valle respastinatio dialecticae et philosophiae*, ed. G. Zippel, Padua.

—— (1984), *Epistole*, ed. O. Besomi and M. Regoliosi, Padua.

—— (1985), *The Profession of the Religious and the Principal Arguments from the Falsely Believed and Forged Donation of Constan-*

tine, Toronto.

Valla, L. (1986), *De professione religiosorum*, ed. M. Cortesi, Padua.

Van Deusen, N. C. (1932), *Telesio: The First of the Moderns*, New York.

Van Dorsten, J. A. (1973), *The Radical Arts: First Decade of an Elizabethan Renaissance*, London.

Van Melsen, A. G. (1960), *From Atomos to Atom: The History of the Concept Atom*, New York.

Van Zuylen, W. H. (1934), *Bartholomaeus Keckermann: Sein Leben und Wirken*, Leipzig.

Vansteenberghe, E. (1920), *Le Cardinal Nicolas de Cues (1401–1464)*, Paris.

Vasoli, C. (1958*a*), 'Umanesimo e simbolismo nei primi scritti lulliani e mnemotecnici del Bruno', *Umanesimo e simbolismo*: 251–304.

—— (1958*b*), 'Dialettica e retorica in Rodolfo Agrippa', *Atti dell'Accademia toscana di scienze e lettere, 'La Colombaria'*, 22: 307–55.

—— (1959), 'Su una Dialectica attribuita all'Argiropulo', *Rinascimento*, 10: 157–64.

—— (1968*a*), *La dialettica e la retorica dell'umanesimo: 'Invenzione' e 'metodo' nella cultura del XV e XVI secolo*, Milan.

—— (1968*b*), *Studi sulla cultura del rinascimento*, Manduria.

—— (1969), *Umanesimo e rinascimento*, Palermo.

—— (1974), *Profezia e ragione: Studi sulla cultura del Cinquecento e del Seicento*, Naples.

—— (1978), *L'enciclopedismo del Seicento*, Naples.

—— (1980), 'Francesco Patrizi e la tradizione ermetica', *Nuova rivista storica*, 64: 25–40.

—— (1983*a*), 'Logica ed "enciclopedia" nella cultura tedesca del tardo Cinquecento e del primo Seicento: Bartholomaeus Keckermann', in Abrusci *et al.* (1983: 97–116).

—— (1983*b*), *Immagini umanistiche*, Naples.

—— (1984*a*), 'Bartholomaeus Keckermann e la storia della logica', *La storia . . . Studi offerti a Mario Dal Pra*: 240–59.

—— (1984*b*), 'La retorica e la cultura del rinascimento', *Rhetorica*, 2: 121–37.

—— (1986), 'Marsilio Ficino e Francesco Giorgio Veneto', in Garfagnini (1986: ii. 533–54).

—— (1988*a*), 'L'Hermétisme à Venise, de Giorgi à Patrizi', in Faivre (1988: 120–51).

—— (1988*b*), 'The Renaissance Concept of Philosophy', *CHRP*:

57–74.
—— (1988c), *Filosofia e religione nella cultura del rinascimento*, Naples.

Védrine, H. (1967), *La Conception de la nature chez Giordano Bruno*, Paris.

Velden, H. E. J. M. van der (1911), *Rodolphus Agricola, Roelof Huusman: Een nederlandsch Humanist der vijftiende eeuw*, Leiden.

Verbeke, G. (1953), 'Guillaume Moerbeke, traducteur de Proclus', *Revue philosophique de Louvain*, 51: 358–73.

—— (1983), *The Presence of Stoicism in Medieval Thought*, Washington, DC.

Verde, A. (1973–86), *Lo Studio fiorentino, 1473–1503*, Florence and Pistoia.

—— (1974), 'Giovanni Argiropoulo e Lorenzo Buonincontri: professori nello Studio fiorentino', *Rinascimento*, 2nd ser., 14: 279–87.

Verdon, T., and Henderson, J. (eds.) (1990), *Christianity and the Renaissance*, Syracuse, NY.

Vergilio, P. (1554), *Polydori Vergilii Urbinatis de rerum inventoribus libri octo*, Basle.

Vespasiano da Bisticci (1963), *Renaissance Princes, Popes and Prelates: The Vespasiano Memoirs, Lives of Illustrious Men of the XVth Century*, trans. W. George and E. Waters, New York.

Vicentini, U. (1954), 'Francesco Zorzi O.F.M., teologo cabalista', *Le Venezie francescane*, 21: 121–59.

Vickers, B. (1968), *Francis Bacon and Renaissance Prose*, Cambridge.

—— (1970), *Classical Rhetoric in English Poetry*, London.

—— (1979), 'Frances Yates and the Writing of History', *JMH* 51: 287–316.

—— (ed.) (1984), *Occult and Scientific Mentalities in the Renaissance*, Cambridge.

—— (ed.) (1985), *Arbeit, Musse, Meditation: Betrachtungen zur 'Vita activa' und 'Vita contemplativa'*, Zürich.

—— (1986), 'Valla's Ambivalent Praise of Pleasure: Rhetoric in the Service of Christianity', *Viator*, 17: 271–319.

—— (1988a), *In Defence of Rhetoric*, Oxford.

—— (1988b), 'Rhetoric and Poetics', *CHRP*: 715–45.

Victor, J. M. (1978), *Charles de Bovelles, 1479–1553: An Intellectual Biography*, Geneva.

Villey, P. (1933), *Les Sources et l'évolution des Essais de Montaigne*, 2nd edn., Paris.

—— (1935), *Montaigne devant la posterité*, Paris.

426 Bibliography

Vitale, M. (1984), *La questione della lingua*, Palermo.

Vitoria, F. de (1932–52), *Commentarios a la* Secunda secundae *de Santo Tomás*, ed. V. Beltrán de Heredia, Salamanca.

—— (1933–6), *Relecciones teológicas*, ed. L. Getino, Madrid.

—— (1960), *Obras*, ed. T. Urdánoz, Madrid.

—— (1967), *Relectio de Indis o libertad de los Indios*, ed. L. Pereña and J. M. Pérez Prendes, Madrid.

Vives, J. L. (1782–5), *Joannis Ludovici Vivis Valentini opera omnia, distributa et ordinata . . . a Gregorio Majansio . . .*, Valencia.

—— (1968), *Vives'* Introduction to Wisdom: *A Renaissance Textbook*, trans. M. L. Tobriner, NewYork.

—— (1974), *De anima et vita*, ed. and trans. M. Sancipriano, Padua.

—— (1979a), *Against the Pseudodialecticians: A Humanist Attack on Medieval Logic: The Attack on the Pseudodialectians and On Dialectic, Book III, v, vi, vii from The Causes of the Corruption of the Arts*, ed. and trans. R. Guerlac, Dordrecht.

—— (1979b), *In pseudodialecticos*, ed. C. Fantazzi, Leiden.

—— (1987), *Early Writings I: De initiis sectis et laudibus philosophiae; Veritas fucata; Anima senis; Pompeius fugiens*, ed. and trans. C. Matheeussen, C. Fantazzi, and E. George, Leiden.

—— (1989), *De conscribendis epistolis*, ed. and trans. C. Fantazzi, Leiden.

—— (1991), *Early Writings*, ii, ed. J. IJsewijn and A. Fritsen, Leiden.

Voigt, G. (1893), *Die Wiederbelebung des classischen Alterthums*, ed. M. Lehnerdt, 3rd edn., Berlin.

Waddington, C. (1855), *Ramus (Pierre de la Ramée): Sa vie, ses écrits et ses opinions*, Paris.

Waddington, R. (1973), 'The Sun at the Center: Structure as Meaning in Pico della Mirandola's *Heptaplus*', *JMRS* 3: 69–86.

Walker, D. P. (1958a), *Spiritual and Demonic Magic from Ficino to Campanella*, London.

—— (1958b), 'The Astral Body in Renaissance Medicine', *JWCI* 21: 119–33.

—— (1972), *The Ancient Theology: Studies in Christian Platonism from the Fifteenth to the Eighteenth Century*, London.

—— (1978), *Studies in Musical Science in the Late Renaissance*, London.

—— (1985), *Music, Spirit and Language in the Renaissance*, ed. P. Gouk, London.

—— (1986), 'Ficino and Astrology', in Garfagnini (1986: ii. 341–9).

Wallace, W. A. (1972–4), *Causality and Scientific Explanation*, Ann

Arbor, Mich.

—— (1978), 'The Philosophical Setting of Medieval Science', in Lindberg (1978a: 91–119).

—— (1981a), *Prelude to Galileo: Essays on Medieval and Sixteenth-Century Sources of Galileo's Thought*, Dordrecht/Boston.

—— (1981b), 'Aristotle and Galileo: The Uses of 'ΥΠΟΘΕΣΙΣ (*Suppositio*) in Scientific Reasoning', in O'Meara (1981: 47–77).

—— (1984), *Galileo and his Sources: The Heritage of the Collegio Romano in Galileo's Science*, Princeton, NJ.

—— (1986), 'The Certitude of Science in Late Medieval and Renaissance Thought', *HPQ* 3: 281–91.

—— (1988), 'Traditional Natural Philosophy', *CHRP*: 201–35.

Wallach, L. (ed.) (1966), *The Classical Tradition: Literary and Historical Studies in Honor of Harry Caplan*, Ithaca, NY.

Wallis, R. T. (1972), *Neo-Platonism*, London.

Walser, E. (1914), *Poggius Florentinus: Leben und Werke*, Leipzig.

Walton, C. (1970), 'Ramus and Socrates', *Proceedings of the American Philosophical Society*, 114: 119–39.

—— (1971), 'Ramus and Bacon on Method', *JHP* 9: 289–302.

Warburg, A. (1932), *Gesammelte Schriften*, ed. F. Rougemont and G. Bing, Leipzig/Berlin.

Warnock, G. J. (1958), *English Philosophy since 1900*, London.

—— (ed.) (1973), *Essays on J. L. Austin*, Oxford.

Warnock, M. (1960), *Ethics since 1900*, Oxford.

Waswo, R. (1987), *Language and Meaning in the Renaissance*, Princeton, NJ.

—— (1989), 'Motives of Misreading', *JHI* 50: 324–32.

Watanabe, M. (1963), *The Political Ideas of Nicholas of Cusa*, Geneva.

Watts, P. M. (1982), *Nicolaus Cusanus: A Fifteenth Century Vision of Man*, Leiden.

—— (1987), 'Pseudo-Dionysius the Areopagite and Three Renaissance Neoplatonists: Cusanus, Ficino and Pico on Mind and Cosmos', in Hankins, Monfasani, and Purnell (1987: 149–88).

Wear, A. *et al.* (eds.) (1985), *The Medical Renaissance of the Sixteenth Century*, Cambridge.

Webster, C. (1982), *From Paracelsus to Newton: Magic and the Making of Modern Science*, Cambridge.

Weinberg, B. (1942), 'Scaliger versus Aristotle on Poetics', *Modern Philology*, 39: 337–60.

—— (1961), *A History of Literary Criticism in the Italian Renaissance*,

428   Bibliography

Chicago.

Weinberg, J. R. (1948), *Nicolaus of Autrecourt*, Princeton, NJ.

—— (1967), *A Short History of Medieval Philosophy*, Princeton, NJ.

Weinstein, D. (1970), *Savonarola and Florence: Prophecy and Patriotism in the Renaissance*, Princeton, NJ.

Weisheipl, J. A. (1971), *The Development of Physical Theory in the Middle Ages*, Ann Arbor, Mich.

—— (ed.) (1980), *Albertus Magnus and the Sciences: Commemorative Essays, 1980*, Toronto.

Weiss, J. M. (1981), 'The Six Lives of Rudolph Agricola: Forms and Functions of the Humanist Biography', *HL* 30: 19–39.

Weiss, R. (1947), *The Dawn of Humanism in Italy*, London.

—— (1949), *Il primo secolo dell'umanesimo*, Rome.

—— (1964), *The Spread of Italian Humanism*, London.

—— (1967), *Humanism in England during the Fifteenth Century*, 3rd edn., Oxford.

—— (1969), *The Renaissance Discovery of Classical Antiquity*, Oxford.

—— (1977), *Medieval and Humanist Greek*, Padua.

Werkmeister, W. H. (ed.) (1959), *Facets of the Renaissance: Essays by W. K. Ferguson*, Los Angeles.

Werner, K. (1889), *Franz Suarez und die Scholastik der letzten Jahrhunderte*, Regensburg.

Wesseler, M. (1974), *Die Einheit von Wort und Sache: Der Entwurf einer rhetorischen Philosophie bei Marius Nizolius*, Munich.

Westman, R. S., and McGuire, J. E. (1977), *Hermeticism and the Scientific Revolution*, Los Angeles.

Wetherbee, W. (1988), 'Philosophy, Cosmology, and the Twelfth-Century Renaissance', *HTCWP*: 21–53.

White, T. I. (1976), 'Aristotle and *Utopia*', *RQ* 29: 635–75.

—— (1987), 'Legend and Reality: The Friendship between More and Erasmus', in Hankins, Monfasani, and Purnell (1987: 489–504).

Wightman, W. P. D. (1964), '*Quid sit methodus?* "Method" in Sixteenth Century Medical Teaching and Discovery', *JHM* 19: 360–76.

—— (1973), 'Les Problèmes de méthode dans l'enseignement médical à Padoue et à Ferrare', *Sciences de la Renaissance*: 187–95.

Wilamowitz-Moellendorf, U. von (1982), *History of Classical Scholarship*, trans. A. Harris, ed. H. Lloyd-Jones, London.

Wilkins, E. H. (1955), *Studies in the Life and Work of Petrarch*, Cambridge, Mass.

—— (1958), *Petrarch's Eight Years in Milan*, Cambridge, Mass.

—— (1959), *Petrarch's Later Years*, Cambridge, Mass.

—— (1960), *Petrarch's Correspondence*, Padua.

—— (1961), *Life of Petrarch*, Chicago.

—— (1978), *Studies on Petrarch and Boccaccio*, ed. A Bernardo, 1978.

Wilmott, M. J. (1984), 'Francesco Patrizi da Cherso's Humanist Critique of Aristotle', dissertation, Univ. of London.

—— (1985), '*Aristoteles exotericus, acroamaticus, mysticus*: Two Interpretations of the Typological Classification of the *Corpus Aristotelicum* by Francesco Patrizi da Cherso', *Nouvelles de la république des lettres*, 2: 67–95.

Wilson, D. J. (1987), 'Lovejoy's *The Great Chain of Being* after Fifty Years', *JHI* 48: 187–206.

Wilson, N. G. (1983), *Scholars of Byzantium*, London.

Wind, E. (1967), *Pagan Mysteries in the Renaissance*, rev. edn., Harmondsworth.

Wirszubski, C. (1989), *Pico della Mirandola's Encounter with Jewish Mysticism*, Cambridge, Mass.

Witt, R. G. (1976), *Coluccio Salutati and his Public Letters*, Geneva.

—— (1977), 'Coluccio Salutati and the Concept of the *poeta theologus* in the Fourteenth Century', *RQ* 30: 538–46.

—— (1982), 'Medieval *Ars dictaminis* and the Beginnings of Humanism: A New Construction of the Problem', *RQ* 35: 1–35.

—— (1983), *Hercules at the Crossroads: The Life and Thought of Coluccio Salutati*, Durham, NC.

—— (1988), 'Medieval Italian Culture and the Origins of Humanism as a Stylistic Ideal', in Rabil (1988: i. 29–55).

Wittgenstein, L. (1967), *Philosophical Investigations*, trans. G. E. M. Anscombe, Oxford.

Wittschier, H. W. (1968), *Giannozzo Manetti: Das Corpus der Orationes*, Cologne/Graz.

Wolters, A. (1986), 'The First Draft of Ficino's Translation of Plotinus', in Garfagnini (1986: i. 305–29).

—— (1987), 'Poliziano as a Translator of Plotinus', *RQ* 40: 421–64.

Woodhouse, C. M. (1986), *Gemistos Plethon: The Last of the Hellenes*, Oxford.

Woodward, W. H. (1906), *Studies in Education during the Age of the Renaissance*, Cambridge.

—— (1963), *Vittorino da Feltre and other Humanist Educators*, New York.

Wundt, M. (1939), *Die deutsche Schulmetaphysik des 17. Jahrhunderts*, Tübingen.

Yates, F. A. (1947), *The French Academies of the Sixteenth Century*, London.

—— (1959), *The Valois Tapestries*, London.

—— (1964), *Giordano Bruno and the Hermetic Tradition*, London.

—— (1965), 'Giovanni Pico della Mirandola and Magic', in *L'Opera ... di Giovanni Pico*: 159–203.

—— (1966), *The Art of Memory*, Chicago.

—— (1969), *Theatre of the World*, Chicago.

—— (1975), *Astraea: The Imperial Theme in the Sixteenth Century*, London.

—— (1979), *The Occult Philosophy in the Elizabethan Age*, London.

—— (1982–4), *Collected Essays*, London.

Zabarella, J. (1966a), *Opera logica*, repr., Hildesheim.

—— (1966b), *Commentaria in tres libros de anima* ... , repr., Frankfurt.

—— (1966c), *De rebus naturalibus libri XXX* ... , repr., Frankfurt.

Zambelli, P. (1960), 'A proposito del *De vanitate scientiarum et artium* di Cornelio Agrippa', *RCSF* 15: 166–80.

—— (1965), *Di un'opera sconosciuta di Cornelio Agrippa: Il 'Dialogus de vanitate scientiarum et ruina cristianae religionis'*, Castrocaro Terme.

—— (1966), '*Humanae literae, verbum divinum, docta ignorantia* negli ultimi scritti di Enrico Cornelio Agrippa', *GCFI* 45: 101–31.

—— (1969), 'Agrippa von Nettesheim in den neueren kritischen Studien und in den Handschriften', *AK* 51: 264–95.

—— (1970), 'Cornelio Agrippa, Erasmo e la teologia umanistica', *Rinascimento*, ser. 2, 10: 29–88.

—— (1973a), 'Platone, Ficino e la magia', in *Studia humanitatis*: 121–42.

—— (1973b), 'Il problema della magia naturale nel Rinascimento', *RCSF* 28: 271–96.

—— (1975), 'I problemi metodologici del necromante Agostino Nifo', *Medioevo*, 1: 129–71.

—— (1976), 'Magic and Radical Reformation in Agrippa of Nettesheim', *JWCI* 39: 69–103.

—— (1977), *Une réincarnation de Jean Pic à l'époque de Pomponazzi: Les thèses magiques et hérétiques d'un aristotélicien oublié, Tiberio Russiliano Sesto Calabrese (1519)*, Mainz.

—— (1978), 'Aut diabolus aut Achillinus: Fisionomia, astrologia e demonologia nel metodo di un aristotelico', *Rinascimento*, ser. 2, 18: 59–86.

—— (1980), 'Scienza, filosofia, religione nella Toscana di Cosimo I', in Bertelli *et al.* (1980: 2, 3–52).

—— (1983), 'Fine del mondo o inizio della propaganda?' in Garfagnini (1983: 291–368).

—— (ed.) (1986), *'Astrologi hallucinati': Stars and the End of the World in Luther's Time*, Berlin.

—— (1988), 'Scholastic and Humanist Views of Hermeticism and Witchcraft', in Merkel and Debus (1988: 125–53).

Zanier, G. (1975a), 'Cardano e la critica delle religioni', *GCFI* 54: 89–98.

—— (1975b), *Ricerche sulla diffusione e fortuna del 'De incantationibus' di Pomponazzi*, Florence.

—— (1977), *La medicina astrologica e la sua teoria: Marsilio Ficino e i suoi critici contemporanei*, Rome.

—— (1981), 'Struttura e significato delle *Disputationes* pichiane', *GCFI* 40: 54–86.

—— (1983a), 'Ricerche sull'occultismo a Padova nel secolo XV', in Poppi (1983: 345–72).

—— (1983b), *Medicina e filosofia tra '500 e '600*, Milan.

Zanta, L. (1975), *La Renaissance du stoïcisme au XVIe siècle*, Geneva.

Zika, C. (1976), 'Reuchlin's *De verbo mirifico* and the Magic Debate of the Late Fifteenth Century', *JWCI* 39: 104–38.

Zilsel, E. (1945), 'The Genesis of the Concept of Scientific Progress', *JHI* 6: 325–49.

Index